The Cambridge Companion to Spenser provides an introduction to Spenser that is at once accessible and rigorous. Fourteen specially commissioned essays by leading scholars bring together the best recent writing on the work of the most important non-dramatic English Renaissance poet. The contributions provide all the essential information required to appreciate and understand Spenser's rewarding and challenging work. The *Companion* guides the reader through Spenser's poetry and prose, and provides extensive commentary on his life, the historical and religious context in which he wrote, his wide reading in classical, European and English poetry, his sexual politics and use of language. Emphasis is placed on Spenser's relationship to his native England, and to Ireland – where he lived for most of his adult life – as well as the myriad of intellectual contexts which inform his writing. A chronology and further reading lists make this volume indispensable for any student of Spenser.

CAMBRIDGE COMPANIONS TO LITERATURE

CAMBRIDGE COMPANIONS TO CULTURE

THE CAMBRIDGE
COMPANION TO
SPENSER

EDITED BY

ANDREW HADFIELD

University of Wales, Aberystwyth

PUBLISHED BY THE PRESS SYNDICATE OF THE UNIVERSITY OF CAMBRIDGE
The Pitt Building, Trumpington Street, Cambridge CB2 1RP, United Kingdom

CAMBRIDGE UNIVERSITY PRESS
The Edinburgh Building, Cambridge CB2 2RU, UK
40 West 20th Street, New York, NY 10011–4211, USA
10 Stamford Road, Oakleigh, Melbourne 3166, Australia
Ruiz de Alarcón 13, 28014 Madrid, Spain
Dock House, The Waterfront, Cape Town 8001, South Afgrica

http://www.cambridge.org

First published 2001

Printed in the United Kingdom at the University Press, Cambridge

Typeset in Sabon 10/13pt.   System 3b2   [CE]

A catalogue record for this book is available from the British Library

Library of Congress cataloguing in publication data

The Cambridge companion to Spenser / edited by Andrew Hadfield
p.   cm. – (Cambridge companions to literature)
Includes bibliographical references and index.
ISBN 0 521 64199 3 – ISBN 0 521 64570 0 (pb.)
1. Spenser, Edmund, 1552?–1599 – Criticism and interpretation.
2. Spenser, Edmund, 1552?–1599 – Handbooks, manuals, etc.
I. Title: Companion to Spenser. II. Hadfield, Andrew. III. Series.
PR2364.C36 2001
821'.3–dc21   00-065084

ISBN 0 521 64199 3 hardback
ISBN 0 521 64570 0 paperback

For Anne, Robert and Olivia Rossell

CONTENTS

ILLUSTRATIONS

CONTRIBUTORS

Paul Alpers, *University of California, Berkeley*
David Baker, *University of Hawaii at Manoa*
Colin Burrow, *Gonville and Caius College, Cambridge*
Patrick Cheney, *Pennsylvania State University*
Roland Greene, *Stanford University*
Linda Gregerson, *University of Michigan, Ann Arbour*
Andrew Hadfield, *University of Wales, Aberystwyth*
John N. King, *The Ohio State University*
Richard A. McCabe, *Merton College, Oxford*
Willy Maley, *University of Glasgow*
Anne Lake Prescott, *Barnard College, University of Columbia*
Richard Rambuss, *Emory University*
Susanne Wofford, *University of Wisconsin-Madison*

ACKNOWLEDGEMENTS

It has been a great pleasure to work on this volume. I shall always be grateful to Josie Dixon for asking me to edit it. I have enjoyed working with both her and Ray Ryan at Cambridge University Press. I have also enjoyed working with the distinguished list of contributors I have been fortunate enough to assemble, and from whom I have learnt so much about Spenser, editing and writing. My thanks to various colleagues who have read and commented helpfully on material when asked; Claire Jowitt, Willy Maley, Ray Ryan, and the anonymous readers employed by Cambridge University Press. Without the prompt help of Norman K. Farmer, Jr., the cover picture might have been very different. I owe longer-term debts to numerous teachers and scholars who have helped develop my interest in and ideas on Spenser over the years, but especially Patricia Coughlan, Anne Fogarty, Brian Gibbons, Thomas Healey, David Lindley and Robert Welch. My family, as ever, have been patient and helpful while I have been completing this book: love and thanks to Alison, Lucy, Patrick and Maud.

ABBREVIATIONS

CI	*Critical Inquiry*
CL	*Comparative Literature*
Colin Clout	*Colin Clouts Come Home Againe*
Cummings	R. M. Cummings, ed., *Spenser: The Critical Heritage* (New York: Barnes and Noble, 1971)
ELH	*English Literary History*
ELR	*English Literary Renaissance*
ESC	*English Studies in Canada*
FQ	*The Faerie Queene*
Hamilton	Edmund Spenser, *The Faerie Queene*, ed. A. C. Hamilton (London: Longman, 1977)
IUR	*Irish University Review*
JEGP	*Journal of English and Germanic Philology*
JMRS	*Journal of Medieval and Renaissance Studies*
Met.	Ovid, *Metamorphoses*
MLA	*The Modern Language Association of America*
MLN	*Modern Language Notes*
MLQ	*Modern Language Quarterly*
MLR	*The Modern Language Review*
MP	*Modern Philology*
MRTS	*Medieval and Renaissance Texts and Studies*
MS	Manuscript
N&Q	*Notes and Queries*
P&P	*Past and Present*
PBA	*Proceedings of the British Academy*
PL	John Milton, *Paradise Lost*
PMLA	*Publications of the Modern Language Society of America*
Poetical Works	*The Poetical Works of Edmund Spenser*, ed. J. C.

	Smith and E. De Selincourt (Oxford: Oxford University Press, 1912).
PQ	*Philological Quarterly*
RES	*Review of English Studies*
RP	*Renaissance Papers*
RQ	*Renaissance Quarterly*
SC	*The Shepheardes Calender*
Sidney, *Apology*	Sir Philip Sidney, *An Apology for Poetry*, ed. Geoffrey Shepherd (Manchester: Manchester University Press, 1973)
SEL	*Studies in English Literature, 1500–1900*
Selected Shorter Poems	Douglas Brooks-Davies, ed., *Spenser's Selected Shorter Poems* (London: Longman, 1995)
SP	*Studies in Philology*
Spenser Encyclopedia	A. C. Hamilton, ed., *The Spenser Encyclopedia* (London, Toronto and Buffalo: Routledge and Toronto University Press, 1990)
Sp. St.	*Spenser Studies*
State	*A View of the State of Ireland, from the first printed edition (1633)*, ed. Andrew Hadfield and Willy Maley (Oxford: Blackwell, 1997)
TLS	*The Times Literary Supplement*
TSLL	*Texas Studies in Language and Literature*
TUSE	*Tulane University Studies in English*
UTQ	*University of Toronto Quarterly*
Variorum	*The Works of Edmund Spenser*, ed. Edwin Greenlaw et al., Variorum Edition, 11 vols. (Baltimore: The Johns Hopkins Press, 1932–58)
View	Edmund Spenser, *A View of the Present State of Ireland*, ed. W. L. Renwick (Oxford: Clarendon Press, 1970)
Yale	*The Yale Edition of the Shorter Poems of Edmund Spenser*, ed. William A. Oram et al. (New Haven: Yale University Press, 1989)
YES	*Yearbook of English Studies*

CHRONOLOGY

c 1552–4	Spenser born in London.
1553	Death of Edward VI and accession of Mary.
1554	Mary marries Philip II of Spain. Execution of Lady Jane Grey. English Church reconciled to Rome.
1555	Persecution of Protestants; Bishops Ridley and Latimer burnt at the stake.
1558	Death of Mary and accession of Elizabeth.
1559	Acts of Uniformity and Supremacy passed, renouncing papal authority in England.
1561	Enrols in Merchant Taylor's School under the headship of Richard Mulcaster as a 'poor scholar'.
1567	Accession of James VI of Scotland. Revolt in Netherlands against Spanish rule.
1569	*Feb.* Publishes anonymous translations of 'Visions by Petrarch' and 'Visions of Du Bellay' in Jan van der Noot's *A Theatre wherein be represented as wel the miseries and calamities that follow the voluptuous Worldlings, As also the greate joyes and plesures which the faithfull do enjoy.* *May* Enters Pembroke Hall, Cambridge, as a sizar (i.e., servant's duties are required in return for a grant of ten shillings p. a.); friendship with Gabriel Harvey begins. *Nov.* Northern Rebellion in favour of Mary, Queen of Scots, breaks out.

1570	*Jan.* Execution of 450 rebels.
	July 8 Elizabeth excommunicated by Pope Pius V.
1572	*June 2* Execution of Earl of Norfolk, Catholic conspirator.
	Aug. 24 Massacre of Saint Bartholomew's Day; Huguenots seek refuge in England.
1573	Graduates with BA degree from Cambridge.
	Pierre Ronsard publishes *Sonnets Pour Hélène* in France; Torquato Tasso publishes *Gerusalemme Liberata* in Italy.
1573–5	Attempts to colonise Ulster half-heartedly supported by Elizabeth.
1576	Awarded MA degree.
	March 15 Puritan MP Peter Wentworth imprisoned in the Tower of London after he claims that free speech should exist in Parliament.
	First public theatre built in London.
1577	Possibly in Ireland, as Irenius in *A View of the Present State of Ireland* claims that he witnesses the execution of Murrogh O'Brien at Limerick in July.
	May Archbishop Grindal placed under house arrest after refusal to suppress 'prophesyings' at queen's command.
1578	Secretary to John Young, Bishop of Rochester (Kent).
1578–81	Elizabeth contemplates marriage to François, Duke of Alençon.
1579	In service with the Earl of Leicester as a confidential emissary.
	Oct. 27 Marries Maccabaeus Chylde in Westminster with whom he will have two children, Sylvanus and Katherine.
	Nov. 2 Earl of Desmond proclaimed traitor after his rebellion.
	Nov. 3 John Stubbs loses his right hand after publishing a book arguing against Elizabeth's proposed marriage to Alençon.
	Dec. 5 The Shepheardes Calender is entered into the Stationers' Register and subsequently published.
	Some of Spenser's lost works – *Court of Cupide, Dreams, Pageaunts*, and the critical treatise, *The English Poete* – probably composed at this time.
1580	Publication of correspondence with Harvey in two volumes: *Three proper, and wittie, familiar Letters* and *Two other, very*

commendable Letters, of the same mens writing. Mention of *The Fairie Queene* for the first time, and of other lost works (*Epithalamion Thamesis, Dying Pellicane, Nine Comedies*).
Aug. 12 Arrives in Dublin having become secretary to Arthur Lord Grey de Wilton, the new Lord Deputy.
Nov. 10 Grey massacres Irish rebels at Fort d'Oro, Smerwick. Spenser may have witnessed the event.
Sir Philip Sidney, *Astrophil and Stella* (published 1591) and *Apology for Poetry* (published 1595) in MS circulation.

1581   *The Shepheardes Calender*, second edition.
Appointed to civil service jobs in Dublin and leases land in Wexford.
Munster Rebellion at its height.

1582   Leases more land in Kildare and is accorded the rank of gentleman.
Aug. 31 Lord Grey recalled from Ireland probably because of his harsh methods of dealing with the Munster Rebellion.
Sir Walter Raleigh's poetry circulates at court.

1582–8   Successful career as civil servant. Friendly with other English writers in Ireland (Barnaby Rich, Geoffrey Fenton and Barnaby Googe).

1583   Death of Earl of Desmond and end of Munster Rebellion.

1584   Sir Richard Genville's voyage to establish colonies in the Americas. Elizabeth grants aid to the Dutch against the Spanish.

1586   *Oct. 17* Death of Sir Philip Sidney in Zutphen, Netherlands.

1587   *Feb. 8* Execution of Mary, Queen of Scots.
May 8 Raleigh attempts to establish colonies in the Americas.
Christopher Marlowe's *Tamburlaine, Parts I and II* performed.

1588   Spenser occupies Kilcolman Castle, County Cork, with estate of 3,000 acres from forfeited lands of the Earl of Desmond.
July 28 Spanish Armada defeated.

1588–99   Continues civil service career in Cork with a series of important appointments.

1589	*Oct.* Journeys to England with Sir Walter Raleigh and claims to have read parts of *The Faerie Queene* to Elizabeth. Start of extended lawsuit with Lord Roche over land claims.
1590	Publication of *The Faerie Queene*, Books I–III.
1591	Publication of *Complaints*, *Daphnaïda* and fourth edition of *The Shepheardes Calender*. *Feb. 25* Granted life pension of £50 p.a. by the queen. *Nov. 21* Proclamation against Jesuits. Many Catholics and radical Protestants executed in subsequent years. Sir John Harington publishes his translation of Ariosto's *Orlando Furioso*.
1592	Publication of *Axiochus*, a translation from the Greek (possibly not by Spenser). *Sept.* Fear of second Spanish invasion in England. Shakespeare's *Richard II* and Marlowe's *Edward II* first performed.
1593	*May 30* Death of Christopher Marlowe in Deptford. *July* Henri IV of France converts to Catholicism. Marlowe's *Hero and Leander* and Shakespeare's *Venus and Adonis* published.
1594	*June 11* Marries Elizabeth Boyle, related to Richard Boyle, the Great Earl of Cork with whom he will have one son, Peregrine.
1595	Publication of *Amoretti* and *Epithalamion* as one volume; *Colin Clouts Come Home Againe* and *Astrophel*, a lament for the death of Sir Philip Sidney. *Oct.* Spanish fleet intending to invade Ireland lost at sea. John Donne's early poetry circulates in MS at court. Shakespeare's *A Midsummer Night's Dream* performed. Michel de Montaigne's *Essais* published.
1595–1603	Nine Years' War in Ireland after Hugh O'Neill, Earl of Tyrone, challenges the right of English rule.
1596	Publication of second edition of *The Faerie Queene*, Books I–VI; *Fowre Hymns*, *Prothalamion*. King James VI of Scotland complains that his mother, Mary Queen of Scots, was slandered as Duessa in *FQ*, V, ix, and demands that Spenser be tried and punished.

not privately educated, and who did not go to university, read Spenser at school.[4] He was following in the footsteps of virtually all English poets of significance since the seventeenth century, who read Spenser and, consciously or unconsciously, either imitated or reacted against his work, notable examples being Pope, Keats, Tennyson and Hopkins.[5] Moreover, as these two stories indicate, Spenser was not simply 'the poet's poet', a label which has often reduced him to the marginalised status of an 'unread classic'.[6] His work enjoyed a wider readership until well into the present century, as the thirty or so children's versions of *The Faerie Queene* produced since the mid-eighteenth century indicate.[7] There is also a rather neat coincidence in both anecdotes. They suggest that Spenser, a poet whose work was written at the start of the first English/British empire, assumed a special importance for readers fighting in the war that would effectively end the British Empire for good. As this Companion will demonstrate, Spenser was not able to take the notion of 'Englishness' – his own or that of others – for granted, but subsequently came to represent one of the key figures in a tradition of writing that was felt to express the very essence of the English nation.

The wide readership of Spenser's work was closely related to a series of ideological purposes, which is the second point I would like to make. The children's versions of *The Faerie Queene* were designed 'to introduce young readers to a work of great literature and to afford moral instruction'.[8] Another use to which the work was put can be seen in the image chosen for the stained glass in the tower entrance at Cheltenham Ladies College, an institution which by 1880 had 'emerged as a dominant force in women's education'.[9] The headmistress, Dorothea Beale, wished to provide the young ladies in her charge with suitable images of womanhood to serve as inspirations and exemplars as part of a new architectural programme. She chose the figure of Britomart as an 'Ideal of Woman':

> She is a real woman, propria persona, not merely the usual appendage of a knight. She sets forth alone, and proves herself no mere satellite, for she owns a squire. We are at once interested in her career, and we long to follow her path, but we soon find ourselves in a labyrinth, and we wish for a guide.

The moral instruction Spenser provided was, for Beale, clearly sympathetic to what she saw as legitimate female ideals. Britomart, she explained, 'has learned in the quiet home from the example and teaching of a noble minded father, to form a high ideal of manly perfection'. Men could teach women to be like them, but it was a lonely path. Britomart lets her knight, Artegall, go on his quest and 'bravely, though sadly, she bids him farewell, content to wait till their work is done on earth, for that perfect union which is to be realised only in the peace of heaven'.[10]

Beale's appropriation of Spenser indicates the uncertain and ambivalent sexual politics at work in his writing. If the headmistress of England's premier academy for upper-class young ladies felt that Spenser was a kindred spirit, so did the unnamed officer who read his men portions of *The Faerie Queene* to comfort them in the heat of battle, an act that casts Spenser's poetry as a soothing feminine spirit to inspire men to masculine pursuits. Wilfred Owen is undoubtedly making a pointed contrast between the masculine horror of war and the feminine peace of poetry – especially if what he really has in mind is the barge of Phaedria, one of the most frequently represented episodes from Book II.[11] It seems that while women have read Spenser to make them feel more masculine, men have read him to make them feel more feminine.

The third point I would take from my opening examples is that Spenser's work has often been read in diametrically opposed ways, or as a series of paradoxes – one of these being, of course, centred around the question of gender roles outlined above. Another concerns Spenser's relationship to military culture. Owen cites the joys of Spenser's poetry as a pointed contrast to the aggressive horror of war, thereby escaping from the terrors of the front line. The unnamed officer uses the same opposition to calm his men and so inspire them to greater strength in the fight.

This dichotomy cuts right to the heart of the different ways in which Spenser has been read. If, on the one hand, Spenser has been regarded as the poet of sensuous beauty, gorgeous indolence and tempting luxury by critics and writers from the early seventeenth century to the middle of the twentieth century, others have seen him as the poet of empire, military might and expansionist English puritanism.[12] W. B. Yeats, for example, trying to make sense of his admiration for Spenser as a poet and his hatred of Spenser's share in the oppression of his homeland as a colonial settler, resolves the problem through reading Spenser's work in terms of a fundamental opposition which could not be avoided. Yeats argues that Spenser is at his worst when he is being allegorical, precisely because it 'interrupts our preoccupation with the beautiful and sensuous life he has called up before our eyes'.[13] Spenser is incapable of achieving 'that visionary air which can alone make allegory real' because he has 'no deep moral or religious life' (369). He is really a poet of the charming ways of 'Merry England' (365), but had begun 'to look to the State not only as the rewarder of virtue but as the maker of right and wrong, and had begun to love and hate as it bid him' (371). For Yeats, Spenser was at his least poetic (and virtuous) when writing about Ireland, where he lived almost continuously from 1580 until his death in 1599, employed as a state official, and eventually becoming a wealthy landowner:

> When Spenser wrote of Ireland he wrote as an official, and out of thoughts and emotions that had been organised by the State. He was the first of many Englishmen to see nothing but what he was desired to see. Could he have gone there as a poet merely, he might have found among its poets more wonderful imaginations than even those islands of Phaedria and Acrasia. He would have found among wandering story-tellers, not indeed his own power of rich, sustained description, for that belongs to lettered ease, but certainly all the kingdom of Faery, still unfaded, of which his own poetry was often but a troubled image (372).[14]

Yeats' splitting of Spenser is a brilliant manoeuvre which enables him to separate the wheat from the chaff in Spenser's writings, and then imagine an inspirational exchange between the poets of England and Ireland stripped bare of any political interference. The image of the Englishman blind to the beautiful realities of Ireland recalls Geoffrey Keating's words, targeted at New English historians including Spenser, that they resemble the beetle single-mindedly 'bustling about until it meets with dung of horse or cow, and proceeds to roll itself therein', oblivious to the beauties of 'any delicate flower that may be in the field, or any blossom in the garden'.[15]

However, unlike Keating's harsh comments, Yeats' is a humane, Utopian vision, resolving insoluble problems in the space of cultural encounter, and clearly as much a comment on Yeats' own position in Anglo-Irish politics and letters at the turn of the century as it is a meditation on Spenser himself.[16] Spenser could have been an even greater poet had he paid attention to his surroundings and learnt from them. The bucolic English poet would have learnt from his Irish counterparts who had direct access to the fairyland Spenser conjured up in his imagination.

I have dealt with Yeats' essay at some length because of its perceptiveness and its vast influence. C. S. Lewis, another Anglo-Irishman and probably the most important critic of Spenser in the first half of the twentieth century, made a case similar to that of Yeats, although his political sympathies were rather different. Lewis argued that 'Spenser was the instrument of a detestable policy in Ireland' and that the 'wickedness he had shared begins to corrupt his imagination'.[17] Lewis drew the obvious conclusion that readers should concentrate on the sections of Spenser's poetry which helped them 'grow in mental health', and ignore the nasty Irish parts.[18]

However, looked at another way, Yeats' argument is a clever sleight of hand that cunningly avoids fundamental questions and problems. It is not really possible to divide up Spenser's writing as Yeats – following more than two centuries of critical tradition – wishes to do. Spenser did, in fact, show an interest in Irish poetry, as he acknowledges in *A View of the Present State of Ireland*, in his much-cited passage on the bards. Irenius argues that the Irish bards are excellent poets but that they lead the young to follow vice rather than virtue. More revealingly, perhaps, Irenius notes that poets are 'had in so high regard and estimation amongst them [the Irish], that none dare displease them for feare to runne into reproach thorough their offence'.[19] Given that *A View* was aimed at an *English* audience in England and Ireland (it is, in fact, set in England, as Eudoxus' reference to 'that country of Ireland, whence you [Irenius] lately came' in the first sentence of the dialogue demonstrates), Spenser appears to be making a plea that English poets should have as much influence in England as Irish bards have in Ireland. Yeats' lament for Spenser's ignorance therefore looks somewhat misplaced.

There has been a huge recent upsurge in interest in Spenser's involvement in Ireland and its relation to his writing. Perhaps the keynote was sounded by Stephen Greenblatt in *Renaissance Self-Fashioning*, undoubtedly the most widely read critical work on the English Renaissance in the last twenty-five years, when he claimed that 'Ireland . . . pervades the poem'.[20] Greenblatt's claim has been taken up with great enthusiasm by a host of subsequent scholars concerned to show that Spenser's part in England's imperial ambitions is signalled and shadowed throughout his work.[21] If that is so, readers must face up to the reality that even the most apparently innocent and dream-like sections of the poem may be reflections on contemporary political problems. There can be no obvious escape to the peaceful idyll of fairyland, as Wilfred Owen, lying dazed and battered in a First World War hospital, hoped. Even the most apparently benign fantasies are political.[22]

A further paradox, and one which is in tune with recent reflections on the purpose and origins of national identity in the British Isles at the current moment, is that while Spenser has been read as an exclusively *English* poet, he was clearly centrally concerned with the problem of *Britain*.[23] As Brian Doyle has pointed out, the 'cultural mystique' endowed upon *The Faerie Queene* by the unnamed officer was a central part of the construction of a patriotic, national English literature which was designed to replace the 'cultural authority previously invested in classics'.[24] Yet Spenser only spent one extended period in England after he made his home in Ireland in 1580, a fact he acknowledges in the preface to *Colin Clouts Come Home Againe* (1595), where it is clear that 'home' is Ireland. *The Faerie Queene* opens with the tale of an English Knight, but by Book III concentrates on the adventures of the British woman warrior Britomart, who, significantly, defeats the hero of the first book. The version of the poem published in

Spenser's lifetime ends with the triumph of a monster, the Blatant Beast, first found on the way back from Ireland. The portrait of Duessa as Mary Queen of Scots caused grave offence to her son, the Scottish king, James VI, who wrote to Elizabeth requesting that Spenser be severely punished.[25] Although *The Faerie Queene* allegorically represents the trial of Mary in detail which no reader could have possibly failed to recognise, her execution is not shown. 'Two Cantos of Mutabilitie', which were published posthumously in 1609, seem to represent the threat of Mutabilitie as a legitimate – though patently undesirable – challenge to the rule of Cynthia/Elizabeth. By the late 1590s it was more than likely that the Tudor dynasty would be supplanted by the house of Stuart, most probably through Mary's son, James, who Spenser had so seriously offended, or, less likely, via the claims of Lady Arbella Stuart.[26] The figure of Mutabilitie, who argues that Jove's right to rule the universe is no more valid than her demand that the Titanic forces of chaos be given their due, is judged to be false by Nature. But the unfinished fragment suggests, especially given its setting in the wilds of Ireland, that the wider territories of the British Isles will threaten the stability that an insular England has usually assumed. Moreover, Mutabilitie's claims, like those of the Stuarts, do sound more convincing than those of Cynthia/Elizabeth, who has to rely on Jove's power to maintain her.[27] Spenser's fear that an Anglocentric government might not be able to cope with the demands of governing Scotland, Ireland, and, to a lesser extent, Wales, was, in many ways, a remarkably accurate prediction of the immediate future when James I ascended to the English throne and attempted to unite the British Isles.[28] The Stuarts did indeed succeed the Tudors, as Spenser undoubtedly feared. As is well known, the English parliament threw James' plan out in 1607 and the projected union never succeeded in making disparate peoples feel part of a larger nation.[29] *The Faerie Queene* registers the fear of an integrated Britain, while also providing a strong sense that the disasters inherent in such a union cannot be ignored or avoided.

The purpose of this companion is to guide readers through the fascinating and complex writings of Edmund Spenser, a poet who is at once central to the canon of English literature, and yet distant from England and its traditions. Perhaps this particular paradox is central to the literary tradition in question, where writers are often at odds with their societies, and rarely fit into straightforward, preconceived categories.[30] Spenser is a writer who spent much of his working life representing the queen, yet may have moved towards republicanism at the end of his life; he desired the 'kingdom of our own language', yet did so much to accommodate alien styles that one observer thought that he wrote no recognisable language at all; he seemed to regard himself as an exile in Ireland yet could also refer to it as his home; he produced an enormous volume of work, yet may have been just as interested in his career as a civil servant and landowner; he appears to have started on a Virgilian career path, moving on from the humble form of the pastoral to the major achievement of an epic; but then he moved back again to pastoral and hymns, never completing his *magnum opus*. Interested readers will find more paradoxes and problems in the pages that follow, many of them, it has to be said, recognised by Spenser himself. When the narrator in *The Faerie Queene*, Book VI laments, 'who knowes not *Colin Clout?*' (x, 16), it is clear that Spenser is self-consciously lamenting his own obscurity in the very act of promoting one of his pseudonyms. He was on the one hand an author successful enough to have been granted the rare privilege of a £50 annual pension from Elizabeth (25 February 1591). On the other, he was a minor gentleman official in one of the queen's most remote territories.[31]

The essays in this companion have been commissioned to cover as many aspects of Spenser's work as can be contained within a manageable volume. Obviously some areas have been covered in greater detail than others, reflecting a greater need and demand for these works. The subjects and topics have been selected to be in tune with contemporary critical concerns, as well as trying to form a balanced assessment of the contexts that informed Spenser's writing.

Four essays deal with the corpus of Spenser's works: the pastoral poems, *The Faerie Queene* (two chapters), and the shorter poems. Patrick Cheney analyses *The Shepheardes Calender* and *Colin Clouts Come Home Againe* to show how the questions raised by pastoral poetry shadow Spenser's writing career. Spenser makes himself central to the concerns of the nation, namely 'state, church, university and family, with their corresponding figures and leaders: sovereigns, pastors, wise old men, young men in love' (pp. 79–80). Pastoral, as George Puttenham, argued, is a convenient means of discussing more obvious and dangerous subjects by allegorical or devious means, disguising key subjects in the form of petty debates between shepherds, and so was used by Spenser as a device to frame his life's work.[32] Anne Lake Prescott performs the heroic task of covering the substantial number of Spenser's shorter poems in a single essay. As has often been pointed out, many of these would be much better known had Spenser not written *The Faerie Queene*, and even without his *magnum opus*, Spenser would still have had a legitimate claim to be the most important Elizabethan non-dramatic poet. Prescott discusses the *Complaints*, 'Teares of the Muses', 'Virgil's Gnat', 'Ruines of Rome', 'Muipotmos', 'Visions of the Worlds Vanitie', *Amoretti and Epithalamion*, *Fowre Hymnes*, and *Prothalamion*, showing how carefully and deliberately Spenser made use of his knowledge of classical and contemporary European poetry. While always aware of his debt to other writers, Spenser is often keen to rewrite, rethink and revise previous work, sometimes respectfully, sometimes parodically.

The two essays on *The Faerie Queene* try to cover the vast range of the work to give readers a sense of its overall content and structure. Susanne Wofford analyses the first edition of the poem in terms of its representation of the Faery Queen, an epic and romance tradition, classical and Christian writing, and theories of allegory. Reading a carefully selected series of episodes, as a means of demonstrating the demands Spenser places upon his readers, Wofford shows how both characters and readers become entangled in the poet's 'darke conceit'. The poem's endless deferral of meaning is not simply a sign that we must always fall prey to the wiles of a fallen language that cannot express God's grace and glory, but also a means of representing the attributes of the deity, which is why, according to Wofford, Spenser is so keen to draw attention to his narrative mode. Andrew Hadfield argues that Books IV–VII reveal a funnelling outwards of Spenser's concerns as he revises the conclusions made in the first three books, in accordance with a preconceived plan, as a response to changed circumstances and the development of his ideas, or, most probably, a mixture of both. Often the reader is forced to go back to the first edition of the poem and rethink apparent certainties established there as the poem's unfinished quest advances. Eventually, it is unclear whether Spenser simply ran out of energy and time, or whether he had concluded that the poem was impossible to complete. Whatever the truth, *The Faerie Queene* ends with the real fear that the forces of civilisation may not be strong enough to overcome the forces of chaos and darkness.

There are three chapters dealing with the historical context, the first by David Baker on the English and European social and political context, which highlights political theory as well as individual events. Baker judiciously selects a series of key texts that informed Spenser's political thinking – Machiavelli's *Discourses on Livy* and *The Prince*, and Jean Bodin's *Six Books of a Commonweal* – in order to show how Spenser's political thought processes worked, as well as demonstrating his main influences. Richard McCabe's chapter is concerned with Spenser's relationship with Ireland, which has undoubtedly been the biggest growth area in Spenser studies in the last two decades.[33] McCabe shows how deeply Irish culture – in Irish as well as English – influenced Spenser's writing, as well as illuminating the effects Ireland itself had on English writers who lived there. Linda Gregerson's chapter on the sexual politics of Spenser's writing seeks to locate his work in terms of the Petrarchan poetry which dominated love poetry in Europe in the second half of the sixteenth century. Spenser has been alternately condemned as a misogynist writer by critics, and praised for his subtle understanding of gender. Gregerson argues that while Spenser may have had a sympathetic and complex appreciation of the limited role afforded to women in Petrarchan discourse, he was troubled – as were most of his male contemporaries – by the question of female rule.

Two chapters detail Spenser's literary contexts and influences, while Paul Alpers demonstrates the extent and significance of Spenser's influence on English literature. Colin Burrow shows the vibrancy of the classical tradition with which Spenser worked. Although Spenser cannot be said to have followed a Virgilian literary career path, as some have argued, Burrow makes it clear that he used Virgil and pseudo-Virgilian poems at key points in his writing. Indeed, Spenser was carefully engaged in European debates about the significance of Virgil's works. Equally, he was sympathetic to Ovid, the poet of exile whose work can be balanced against Virgil's poems of empire. Burrow shows how Spenser both used and complicated such obvious divisions. Roland Greene shows how Spenser has been erroneously read as an English poet when he should be read as a central voice in a European tradition, a problem caused by our post-Enlightenment concentration on national boundaries. Spenser read widely in French, Italian, Dutch and Spanish literature from his teenage years onwards, moving happily from one form and style to another as even the most basic comparative investigation will reveal. His work makes use of episodes that are 'the common property of a continuous European literary culture' (p. 241). Paul Alpers, revising Harold Bloom, distinguishes between 'strong' and 'weak' adaptations of Spenser from the early seventeenth century to the twentieth. He shows how Marlowe, Milton, Wordsworth, Keats and Yeats all struggle with Spenser's influence and respond to the ideas, style and form of their illustrious precursor to produce 'strong' re-readings of Spenser's poetry in their own work. In contrast, the seventeenth-century 'Spenserians' (notably Giles Fletcher), James Thomson and William Shenstone produce 'weak' responses to Spenser, often allowing their poetic master to swamp their own individual style.

Richard Rambuss analyses Spenser's life and career in order to demonstrate that Spenser was probably as interested in his professional life as he was in writing poetry. Indeed, there is a symbiotic relationship between the two aspects of his life, as writing poetry was frequently a means of obtaining a job, or a method of advancement.[34] Willy Maley examines the question of Spenser's language and concludes that just as there is a close relationship between Spenser's career as a poet and a civil servant and landowner, so there is between the formal and political concerns of his writing. Maley provides further evidence to complement McCabe's claims, suggesting that Spenser needs to be considered as much in the context of the British Isles and its regions as within the confines of the London court. John King examines the question of Spenser's religious beliefs to show how Spenser's understanding of current theological debates structures many of Spenser's major works. Indeed, poems such as 'Mother Hubberds Tale' have to be read as active contributions to religious controversies.

Edmund Spenser is a major English and European Renaissance poet. His complex and diverse output deserves to be read on a number of counts, leaving aside its formal and aesthetic merits: for what it reveals about the complexities of the intellectual milieu of English writers at the end of the sixteenth century; for its vigorous experimentalism; for its political acumen and involvement in contemporary issues; for its acute and ambiguous analysis of sex and gender; and for its active engagement with a colonised Irish culture, to name but a few of the many strands in Spenser's work. Indeed, it is not surprising that Spenser has been claimed as a central part of an English, Irish and Anglo-Irish literary tradition, nor that the most famous poet writing in English today, Seamus Heaney, has felt the need to respond to Spenser's presence.[35] If this companion helps to persuade readers that Spenser's work has a relevance as part of a living as well as a historical tradition, then it will have served its purpose.

NOTES

1 My thanks to Claire Jowitt and Ray Ryan for comments on an earlier version of this essay. Wilfred Owen to Susan Owen, 10 May 1917; Wilfred Owen, *Collected Letters*, ed. Harold Owen and John Bell (London: Oxford University Press, 1967), p. 457.

2 Owen undoubtedly has in mind the description of the barge of Phaedria (*FQ*, II, vi), or the passage of Guyon and the Palmer onto Acrasia's island (*FQ*, II, xii).

3 Cited in Brian Doyle, *English and Englishness* (London: Routledge, 1989), p. 28.

4 Dominic Hibberd, *Owen the Poet* (Basingstoke: Macmillan, 1986), p. 1.

5 Howard Erskine-Hill, 'Pope, Alexander', in *Spenser Encyclopedia*, pp. 555–6; Aileen Ward, *John Keats: The Making of a Poet* (London: Secker and Warburg, 1963), pp. 28–30; John Killham, 'Tennyson and Victorian Social Values', in D. J. Palmer, ed., *Tennyson: Writers and their Background* (London: Bell, 1973), pp. 147–79, at p. 178; Bernard Begonzi, *Gerard Manley Hopkins* (London: Macmillan, 1977), p. 5.

6 See Andrew Hadfield, ed., *Edmund Spenser*, Longman Critical Readers (Harlow: Longman, 1996), p. 4.

7 See Brenda M. Hosington and Anne Shaver, '*The Faerie Queene*, Children's Versions', in *Spenser Encyclopedia*, pp. 289–91.

8 Hosington and Shaver, '*The Faerie Queene*, Children's Versions', p. 289.

9 Norman K. Farmer, Jr., 'Dorothea's Disagreement', *Country Life*, 14 Jan. 1988, pp. 8–9, at p. 8.

10 Cited in Farmer, 'Dorothea's Disagreement', pp. 8–9.

11 For one representation of Phaedra, see Andrew Hadfield, 'William Kent's Illustrations of *The Faerie Queene*', *Sp. St.* 14 (2000), 1–81, pp. 54–5.

12 For the former view see the essays collected in Paul J. Alpers, ed., *Edmund Spenser*, Penguin Critical Commentaries (Harmondsworth: Penguin, 1967), part 2; for the latter, see, for example, Edwin A. Greenlaw, *Studies in Spenser's Historical Allegory* (Baltimore: Johns Hopkins University Press, 1932); Alastair Fowler, 'Spenser and War', in J. R. Mulryne and Margaret Shewring, eds., *War, Literature and the Arts in Sixteenth-Century Europe* (Basingstoke: Macmillan, 1989), pp. 147–64.

13 W. B. Yeats, 'Edmund Spenser', in *Essays and Introductions* (London: Macmillan, 1961), pp. 356–83, at p. 368. Subsequent references in parentheses in the text.

14 It is notable that Yeats refers the reader to the episodes of Phaedria and Acrasia. Given that the essay was written as an introduction to Yeats' selection of Spenser's poems for Macmillan, it is likely that Owen had this edition in mind when referring to his day out near Amiens.

15 Geoffrey Keating, *The History of Ireland*, ed. and trans. D. Comyn and P. S. Dineen, 4 vols. (London: Early Irish Text Society, 1902–13), I, p. 5.

16 See Roy Foster, *W. B. Yeats: A Life. 1: The Apprentice Mage, 1865–1914* (Oxford: Oxford University Press, 1997), ch. 11.

17 C. S. Lewis, *The Allegory of Love: A Study in Medieval tradition* (Oxford: Oxford University Press, 1979, repr. of 1936 edn), p. 349.

18 Ibid., p. 359.

19 *View*, p. 75.

20 *Renaissance Self-Fashioning: From More to Shakespeare* (Chicago: The University of Chicago Press, 1980), p. 186. See also Willy Maley, '"To Weet to Work Irena's Enfranchisement": Ireland in *The Faerie Queene*', *IUR* 26 (1996), 303–19.

21 A useful overview of recent work is contained in Andrew Murphy, *But the Irish Sea Betwixt Us: Ireland, Colonialism, and Renaissance Literature* (Lexington: The University Press of Kentucky, 1999).

22 See, for example, Louis A. Montrose, 'Of Gentleman and Shepherds: The Politics of Elizabethan Pastoral Form', *ELH* 50 (1983), 415–59.

23 Andrew Hadfield, 'From English to British Literature: John Lyly's *Euphues* and Edmund Spenser's *The Faerie Queene*', in Brendan Bradshaw and Peter Roberts, eds., *British Consciousness and Identity: The Making of Britain, 1533–1707* (Cambridge: Cambridge University Press, 1998), pp. 140–58; and 'Spenser, Drayton and the Question of Britain', *RES* 51 (2000), 582–99.

24 Doyle, *English and Englishness*, p. 27.

25 For fuller details see Richard A. McCabe, 'The Masks of Duessa: Spenser, Mary Queen of Scots, and James VI', *ELR* 17 (1987), 224–42.

26 See Marie Axton, *The Queen's Two Bodies: Drama and the Elizabethan Succession* (London: Royal Historical Society, 1977); Sara Jayne Steen, ed., *The Letters of Lady Arbella Stuart* (Oxford: Oxford University Press, 1994).

27 For details of Mary's claim and its validity, see Howard Erskine-Hill, *Poetry*

and the Realm of Politics: Shakespeare to Dryden (Oxford: Clarendon Press, 1996), ch. 1.

28 For details see Brian P. Levack, *The Formation of the British State: England, Scotland, and the Union, 1603–1707* (Oxford: Clarendon Press, 1987).

29 See Brendan Bradshaw and John Morrill, eds., *The British Problem, c.1534–1707: State Formation in the Atlantic Archipelago* (Basingstoke: Macmillan, 1996).

30 See Annabel Patterson, *Reading Between the Lines* (London: Routledge, 1992); David Gervais, *Literary Englands: Versions of 'Englishness' in Modern Writing* (Cambridge: Cambridge University Press, 1993).

31 See Willy Maley, *A Spenser Chronology* (Basingstoke: Macmillan, 1994), p. 51. On Spenser's role as Colin Clout, see Andrew Hadfield, *Literature, Politics and National Identity: Reformation to Renaissance* (Cambridge: Cambridge University Press, 1994), pp. 170–2. On Spenser's status in Ireland, see Andrew Hadfield, *Spenser's Irish Experience: Wilde Fruit and Salvage Soyl* (Oxford: Clarendon Press, 1997), ch. 1.

32 George Puttenham, *The Arte of English Poesie* (1589), ed. R. C. Alston (Menston: Scolar Press, 1968), pp. 30–1.

33 It is perhaps worth noting that a senior Spenser scholar remarked to me at a conference in 1996 that whilst there had been a large number of papers dealing with Spenser and Ireland, there had been none on the subject of neo-Platonism. The situation neatly reversed that of twenty years earlier.

34 For further details, see Richard Rambuss, *Spenser's Secret Career* (Cambridge: Cambridge University Press, 1993).

35 See, for example, 'Bog Oak', in *New Selected Poems, 1966–1987* (London: Faber, 1990), pp. 19–20.

I

RICHARD RAMBUSS

Spenser's life and career

'Who knowes not *Colin Clout?*' asks *The Faerie Queene* (1596), nodding to the renown of its own author and his poetic alter ego. As posed here, near the conclusion of what was to be the final book of Spenser's epic and the greatest poetic achievement of the sixteenth century, this is surely meant as a rhetorical question. But rhetorical in what way exactly? Does the remark bespeak the bravado of ambition realised, of a career successfully accomplished? Or is it a presage of fame, pointing towards a horizon of celebrity and its rewards: that is, an aspiration not quite yet, but perhaps now at last about to be attained? Or does the rhetorical cast of the query – embedded in the poem's narrative as a parenthetical aside: 'Poor *Colin Clout* (who knowes not *Colin Clout?*)' (VI, x, 16)[1] – mask a more fraught gesture of self-promotion, one borne of the concern that there may indeed still be those who know not Colin Clout, or, in any event, have yet to prize 'Poor Colin' according to his real worth? What does it mean, we should further inquire, that Spenser does not proffer this question from a secure position within or even near Elizabeth's court, the putative epicentre of the courtly values and virtues his nationalistic epic celebrates, and, as a cynosure of elite cultural activity, the seemingly natural home for a poet who presents himself as the nation's laureate? Instead, Spenser's query issues from the outposts of the kingdom, from the 'wilds' of Ireland, where he spent most of the last twenty years of his life pursuing, in tandem with his poetic career, another career as a colonial official and a planter.

Recovered to this context, *The Faerie Queene*'s rhetorical question may not be so simply rhetorical. 'Who knowes not *Colin Clout?*' also opens onto another, more fundamental question: Who *is* Colin Clout / Spenser? Classifying Spenser's identity as a writer is no easy matter. He is one of the great figures of English literature, but much of his *magnum opus*, *The Faerie Queene*, along with the bulk of his major poetry, derives from the decades he spent living, working, and writing in Ireland. Spenser is thus the expatriate author of a national epic, the court poet stationed on the frontier. Do these positions, at once inside and outside his own poetry's chief frames of reference, make Spenser an English poet writing in Ireland, or an 'Irish' poet whose interests are chiefly English, or a hybrid Anglo-Irish poet – an early modern Anglophone writer? There are other, equally tensile borderlines of identity and difference crisscrossing Spenser's station and stature. In *The Faerie Queene* he presumes to school the community of his social superiors in how 'to fashion a gentleman or noble person in vertuous and gentle discipline' ('A Letter of the Authors'), but Spenser himself came from modest, non-gentle stock. His Westminster monument in Poets' Corner posthumously ennobles him as 'the prince of poets', but during his life Spenser had to work for a living, first as a secretary, and then as a career civil servant and public official. As such, Spenser was an upwardly mobile careerist, one who experienced his posting to Ireland as an exile from the centres of power and culture and, at the same time, advantageously parlayed the assignment into opportunities for professional and social advancement unavailable to him back in England. Finally, Spenser was an English émigré who in *Colin Clouts Come Home Againe* (1595) comes home not to England but from it, returning to an estate in Ireland, 'my house of Kilcolman', as he declares in this autobiographical poem's dedicatory epistle (Yale, p. 526). But what kind of homecoming was this? For as a member of an unpopular cadre of New English colonial administrators, plantation makers, and soldiers of fortune, Spenser remained until the end of his life no less estranged from his Irish-born English neighbours in Ireland (the 'Old English,' as these descendants of the original Anglo-Norman conquerors of Ireland were called) than he was alienated from his new home's Gaelic or 'mere' Irish natives. Did the 'barrein soyle' (*Colin Clout*, line 656) of Ireland, then, represent Spenser's home in exile, or his sense of exile at home? As we shall see, it is across these and other competing, shiftingly defined social placements and markers of identity that the life and career of this dually employed poet/bureaucrat took their extraordinary shape.

First things, 1552?–1569

In his 1715 'Life of Mr Edmund Spenser', John Hughes, one of Spenser studies' founding figures, declares that this poet is 'much better known by his Works than by the History of his Life'.[2] As with many other writers of his day and class, history has allotted us too few records to construct Spenser's biography with as much substance and detail as we would like. Even Shakespeare's life, ever the disputed subject of so much speculation and sleuthing, is better documented than Spenser's. Unlike Shakespeare, however, Spenser infused his own voluminous writings with personal references and information, making the poetry itself a tempting autobiographical archive – though one, we need to bear in mind, that would script the story of his life and career to suit Spenser's own interests. It is from his poem *Prothalamion* (1596) that we know that Spenser was born in London, 'my most kyndly Nurse, / That to me gave this Lifes first native sourse' (lines 128–9). The church records that would have told us such particulars as the specific London parish of his birth and baptism (East and West Smithfield have been the locales most often proposed) or his precise birth date were presumably lost in the Great Fire of 1666. The year 1552 is traditionally given as the probable date of Spenser's birth, an assumption based on an indefinite chronological clue offered in one of the poems in *Amoretti* (1595), Spenser's sonnet sequence on his courtship of Elizabeth Boyle, his second wife.[3] He may, in fact, have been born any time between 1551 and 1554. Whatever the exact date, the earliest years of the boy who was to become his nation's first great Protestant poet coincided with a period of extreme religious and political upheaval in England. Upon her accession in 1553, Mary I had sought to turn the country from the Protestantism of her brother Edward VI to Catholicism; Elizabeth I, upon her own accession five years later in 1558, then turned it back.

Few specific details about Spenser's family and origins have survived. Another sonnet in *Amoretti* reveals that Elizabeth was the name of Spenser's mother, just as it was the name of both his monarch and his bride-to-be: 'Ye three Elizabeths for ever live, / that three such graces did unto me give' (*Amoretti* 74, lines 13–14). Spenser's father may have been John Spenser, a weaver from Lancashire who moved to London, became a member of the Merchant Taylors' Company, and was designated a 'free journeyman' skilled in 'the art or mystery of cloth-making'. There are, however, records of several other Spensers who were associated with the guild at this time, some rather more well-to-do than John Spenser of Lancashire and others considerably less so. Which, if any of them, was the poet's father, we do not know. For his own part, Spenser himself says nothing about his father, although in the same passage from *Prothalamion* in which he identifies London as his birthplace, he declares that it is 'from another place I take my name, / An house of auncient fame' (lines 130–1). That ancient house is the baronial Despencer family, and Spenser asserts his kinship with their rich and powerful descendants, the Spencers of Althorp in Northamptonshire, in a number of his other works from the 1590s, including *Colin Clout*. There, in midst of complimenting the accomplished daughters of Sir John Spencer, the poet seizes the opportunity to enlist himself within this 'noble familie': 'Ne lesse praisworthie are the sisters three, / The honor of the noble familie: / Of which I meanest boast my selfe to be, / And most that unto them I am so nie' (lines 536–9). Yet despite the noble ancestry with which he would entitle himself later in life, Spenser was not born a gentleman. This was a prime distinction in a class-conscious early modern culture, and the fact of his lowborn status made the prospects for Spenser's social and professional ascent all the more formidable.

Spenser was a self-made man. The ladder for his eventual climb to the lower ranks of the gentry was his humanist education, which began in 1561, when, it is surmised, Spenser entered the newly founded Merchant Taylors' School as a 'poor scholar' – a student who paid reduced fees or none at all. With an enrolment of 250 boys, Merchant Taylors' School was the second largest in England. Among Spenser's more notable classmates were Thomas Kyd and Thomas Lodge, who were likewise to become significant Elizabethan writers, and Lancelot Andrewes, later the Bishop of Winchester and one of the great sermon writers of the age. The new school's headmaster was Richard Mulcaster, whose two treatises on pedagogy, *Positions* (1581) and *The First Part of the Elementarie* (1582), would earn him prominence as a leading educational theorist and innovator. Mulcaster advocated a broadly based liberal education that included instruction in physical education as well as in music, mathematics and drama. The core of Mulcaster's curriculum was a rigorous training in reading and writing Latin, but he also innovatively established a place in his school for the study of the vernacular alongside the classical languages: 'I love *Rome*, but *London* better, I favour *Italie*, but England more, I honor the Latin, but I worship the *English*', Spenser's headmaster patriotically rhapsodises in *Elementarie*.[4] 'These sentiments', notes William Oram, 'cannot have been lost on a student who would try in his own tongue to surpass or "overgo" the lyrics and the epics of other languages'.[5] Indeed, the introductory 'Epistle' prefacing *The Shepheardes Calender* (1579), the poem that introduces Spenser as England's 'new Poete' and launches his literary literary career, concerns itself with both the proper usage of 'our Mother tongue' (Yale, p. 16) and the promotion of English as a literary language on a par with Latin. But Spenser's aspiration to become England's Virgil – an ambition that was perhaps germinated under Mulcaster's tutelage – was not to be his sole occupation. As I noted earlier, Spenser also sought and secured a succession of private and public bureaucratic offices. His 'second' or other career answered another of Mulcaster's convictions, namely that a principal aim of schooling was to prepare students for a life of public service, whether at home in the commonwealth, or, as in Spenser's own case, attending to the nation's interests abroad.

The single record of Spenser at Merchant Taylors' School appears in the form of an accounting book entry dated 6 February 1569, his final year of attendance.[6] Spenser's name leads a roll of six Merchant Taylors' students who were each given a shilling and a new mourning gown to wear at the funeral of Robert Nowell, a wealthy London lawyer and one of the school's principal benefactors. Spenser continued to receive grants from the Nowell bequest over the next several years, including a stipend of ten shillings upon being admitted to Pembroke Hall, Cambridge in the spring of 1569. A few months later, Spenser, still in his teens, had his first taste of publication, though it was in an unaccredited capacity as a translator – a suitable beginning role according to Renaissance notions of authorship, which stressed the value of imitating other writers over individual invention. For Jan van der Noot's *A Theatre of Worldlings* (1569), Spenser produced an English rendering of Clement Marot's French version of Petrarch's *Rime* 323 in six visionary 'Epigrams', as well as a translation of eleven similarly visionary 'Sonets' from Du Bellay's *Songe*. Spenser may also have provided English translations of the four sonnets van der Noot himself composed as paraphrases of apocalyptic visions taken from the biblical Book of Revelation. A significant Dutch poet and a zealous Calvinist, van der Noot had fled Antwerp to seek religious refuge in England. Spenser's association with him was likely facilitated by Mulcaster, who had acquaintances in London's Dutch community, including van der Noot's cousin, Emmanuel van Meteren, himself a scholar.

The organising theme of *A Theatre of Wordlings*, which had already appeared in London the year before in Dutch and French editions, is the transience and the vanity of all worldly things. The book's *contemptus mundi* moral is advanced by a number of lyrics and their accompanying woodcut illustrations emblematising the fall of the ancient city of Rome. The lengthy prose commentary van der Noot appends to the poetry makes it clear that the book's real energies, however, are invested in an anti-Catholic polemic eagerly foretelling the fall of the contemporary Church of Rome. More than two decades later, Spenser would recycle the work he did in his youth for van der Noot's *Theatre* by publishing reworked versions of the poetry as 'The Visions of Bellay' and 'The Visions of Petrarch, formerly translated'. These re-translations appear in Spenser's volume of *Complaints* (1591), his own poetic miscellany of new and old compositions. It is not surprising that Spenser would lay claim to his juvenilia, given that these visionary lyrics signal in rudimentary form, as we shall see, a number of his poetry's abiding interests. Among them are Spenser's fervent commitment to Protestantism and the Protestant cause in Europe; his engagement with continental, and not only classical, authors; and finally his fascination with the themes of metamorphosis and mutability – a concern that would eventually flower into the fragmentary 'Two Cantos of Mutabilitie' appended to the last book of *The Faerie Queene*.

From Cambridge to Leicester House, 1569–1580

In May of 1569, Spenser went up to university, matriculating at Pembroke Hall, Cambridge, as a sizar. A sizar was a poorer student, who, in return for the cost of his instruction and room and board, performed servant duties in the college, such as waiting table in the dining commons, attending a wealthier fellow student as a valet, or running errands for the college master or fellows. During Spenser's years as a student there, Cambridge was animated by a series of religious disputes over such matters as church government and liturgical ritual. These controversies were provoked by a developing Protestant reform movement later to be known as Puritanism. Although Spenser himself never emerged as the full-fledged Puritan poet and public intellectual Milton was to become a few generations later, Puritanism was a significant religious and political influence on his writing, particularly in *The Shepheardes Calender*, which allegorises a number of the ecclesiastical issues and figures involved in the Cambridge disputes. Spenser's college years were also marked by curricular reform, following upon Elizabeth's approval of a new set of statutes for the university in 1570. The revised, four-year course of study leading to the Bachelor of Arts degree emphasised mastery of dialectic (or logic) and rhetoric. These disciplines were taught by means of lectures, tutorials and debates involving the work of major classical authors such as Cicero, Aristotle, Plato, Virgil and Horace. Spenser took his BA in 1573, ranking eleventh in a class of 120. Three years later he received his MA, this time coming fourth from last in a group of seventy. Although Pembroke Hall remained one of Cambridge's smaller colleges, university enrolments were on the whole rapidly increasing at this time. Among the aims of this expansion was to supply more newly trained humanists to the growing ranks of an increasingly centralised Tudor administration.[7] Perhaps with the objective of securing just such a position for himself, Spenser probably did not spend the entire interval between his degrees in residence at Cambridge. Instead, he may have already been looking beyond the university in search of the patronage that would help him land his own post in public life.

Spenser forged the most important relationship of his early career with one of Cambridge's most notable, even notorious progressives, Gabriel Harvey (1552?-1631), who was a few years Spenser's senior. Harvey, a capaciously learned scholar and bibliophile who enthusiastically contested the intellectual and pedagogical orthodoxies of the day, was elected fellow of Pembroke Hall in 1570, Spenser's second year in attendance. The son of a prosperous master rope maker and local official in Saffron Walden, Harvey, like Spenser, had to rely upon his talents rather than his name to secure the station he wanted for himself in the world. Also like Spenser, Harvey assayed a multidimensional humanist career, pursuing professional advancement and cultural influence as a university professor, a published author of Latin verse and English oratory, a personal secretary, a civil lawyer in the Court of Arches, and perhaps even a reader-scholar for hire.[8] Harvey's career model and early sponsor, as well as a family neighbour in Saffron Walden, was Sir Thomas Smith. The son of a sheep farmer, Smith was another self-made man, whose prodigious learning catapulted him from a professorship at Cambridge to the ambassadorship of France and ultimately to the position of Elizabeth's principal secretary. Most of Harvey's own successes came relatively early during his tenure at Cambridge, where he garnered fame for his masterful, crowded lectures and for his accomplished performances in university disputations. His achievement in the latter forum won him the privilege of meeting the queen when she stopped at Audley End near Cambridge during her summer progress of 1578. On this occasion Elizabeth allowed Harvey to kiss her hand, and she complimented him on his Italianate good looks. In turn, Harvey conferred upon her a handwritten set of encomiastic Latin tributes. Several months later, he presented the queen with an expanded published version of the work, entitled *Gratulationes Valdinenses* ('Joyful Greetings from Saffron Walden').[9]

As this episode indicates, Harvey had been attracting some notice outside the academic world of Cambridge, particularly that of Sir Philip Sidney and his uncle the Earl of Leicester, the leader of a powerful, activist Protestant faction at court. But Harvey accumulated adversaries as well as advocates along his way. Indeed, his Cambridge career was nearly dashed even as it began when a group of Pembroke fellows banded together in an effort to bar him from taking his MA degree in 1573, charging Harvey with nonconformism and a lack of collegiality. This opposition betokened class prejudice against an upstart careerist as much as it did the other fellows' evident dislike of Harvey's self-important, pedantic personal manner – qualities for which he was later to be famously caricatured by Thomas Nashe in a long-running series of merciless satirical jibes. Harvey eventually received his degree, after the intervention on his behalf of John Young, the non-resident master of Pembroke, who in time would also do Spenser's career a good turn. With his adversaries thwarted for a time, Harvey was able to progress through several university positions, including University Praelector of Rhetoric (1573–5) and University Proctor (1583). Yet the pockets of internal opposition to him at Cambridge never fully dissipated. By the mid-1580s, Harvey's academic career had stalled, as did just about any hope he might still have fostered of following in Smith's footsteps by advancing from a university post to one in the Elizabethan civil service. After a brief professorship in civil law at Oxford, Harvey eventually retired to Saffron Walden. He took back with him to his hometown the vast, encyclopedic library he had spent a lifetime assembling and then carefully annotating with the scholarly and personal marginalia for which, along with his relationship to Spenser, he is now most remembered.

During the time they shared together at Cambridge, Harvey's attainments and associations must have duly impressed the younger Spenser. The two men became intimates, literary collaborators, and each other's most avid promoters. In 1580, Spenser and Harvey memorialised their friendship by publishing a series of five letters exchanged between them in a two-sectioned volume entitled *Three Proper, and wittie, familiar Letters: lately passed betwene two Universitie men*, to which is added, with its own title page, *Two Other very commendable Letters, of the same mens writing*. These compendious, highly wrought missives (three from Harvey and two from Spenser) accommodate within their folds an impressive array of formal disquisitions and witty digressions, along with a substantial sampling of each writer's experiments in Latin and English verse. Publication of the letters (for which their authors themselves demurely claim no role) provided Spenser and Harvey with a platform upon which they could at once declare their rising fortunes and display their worthiness of further patronage and preferment. In these patently self-conscious, even self-promotional literary performances, the two correspondents thus hold forth in turn upon subjects ranging from the intellectual fashions and reading lists at Cambridge to an earthquake that had recently rattled London and the protocols for adapting classical meters and poetic forms into suitable English equivalents. Each topic serves as an occasion from these two ambitious 'Universitie men' to flaunt their erudition, their cosmopolitanism and their rhetorical facility – their qualifications, in other words, for either public or private office. The *Letters* also contain the first recorded references to *The Faerie Queene*, as well as an extensive canon of 'lost works' by Spenser that were never published and perhaps not even written. Among these mysterious works are Spenser's 'Dreames, his Legendes, his Court of Cupide, and sondry others', along with 'nine Englishe *Comoedies* and [his] Latin *Stemmata Dudleiana*' (*Poetical Works*, pp. 418, 620).

To foreground the writerly showmanship and careerism of Spenser and Harvey's joint publishing endeavor is not to say that their book of letters is uninflected by what we would think of as more personal biographical textures. The volume's first letter, from Spenser to Harvey, immediately establishes the fondness and closeness of the correspondents' bond. In it, Spenser embeds a quatrain of amatory verse he has recently penned: 'Seeme they comparable to those two', he asks his friend, 'which I translated you *ex tempore* in bed, the last time we lay together in Westminster?' (p. 611). There was nothing unusual in the Elizabethan age about men sharing a bed, and the intimate literary tableau Spenser here conjures evinces the passionate, even amorous homosociality of Renaissance male friendship.[10] Harvey is accorded a similar place in Spenser's affections in *The Shepheardes Calender*. There, under the pastoral guise of a shepherd named Hobbinol, he is singled out as the poet's 'very speciall and most familiar freend, whom he entirely and extraordinarily beloued' (Yale, p. 33). Harvey is, however, not only the poet's 'speciall and most familiar freend'; he also, as Colin Clout rather scornfully reveals in the 'Januarye' eclogue, has been his suitor:

> It is not *Hobbinol*, wherefore I plaine,
> Albee my loue he seeke with dayly suit:
> His clownish gifts and curtsies I disdaine,
> His kiddes, his cracknelles, and his early fruit.
> Ah foolish *Hobbinol*, thy gyfts bene vayne:
> *Colin* them giues to *Rosalind* againe.   (lines 55–60)

Throughout the *Calender* we find Colin looking to leave behind Hobbinol, and the pastoral (university?) world with which he is associated, for Rosalind, a newfound object of desire, or alternately for the attractions of the town. Thus even as Spenser declares Harvey's place in his affections, he signals his desire to displace him.

Correspondingly, even as Spenser addresses Harvey in the *Letters*, they show him looking beyond his familiar friend toward cultivating a closer association with Philip Sidney, around whom had gathered an informal literary circle known as the Areopagus. Among the group's members were the poets Edward Dyer and Fulke Greville. Keen to show off his new acquaintances, Spenser thus informs Harvey that 'the twoo worthy Gentlemen, Master *Sidney*, and Master *Dyer*, . . . have me, I thanke them, in some vse of familiarity' (p. 635). He then provides his friend with a first-hand report of how Sidney and Dyer

> have proclaimed in their *areioi pagoi* [senate councils] a generall surceasing and silence of balde Rymers, and also of the verie best to: in steade of whereof, they haue by authoritie of their whole Senate, prescribed certaine Lawes and rules of Quantities of English sillables, for English verse: having had thereof already greate practise.

Spenser's account concludes with the declaration that Sidney and Dyer have 'drawen mee to their faction'. As attested to by the amount of consideration their letters devote to the topic of quantitative verse, this was a reformatory poetic project with which both Spenser and Harvey were eager to affiliate themselves. At this point in their careers, however, the inroads to Sidney –

as well as, perhaps more importantly, to Sidney's influential uncle the Earl of Leicester – appear to be more open to Spenser than to his friend back at Cambridge. Or at least that is the impression Spenser's own letters, which abound in allusions to his past and prospective future interactions with Sidney, seem intent on conveying. It is unlikely that the relations between this young aristocrat and the lowborn, albeit ambitious, Spenser would have been personally close. Yet however remote the actual associations may have been, Spenser's intimations of rubbing shoulders with his betters reinforce the sense that he had found a place for himself in the Leicester/ Sidney circle and thus a niche at the peripheries of the court. Looking back on this period in 'The Ruines of Time' (1591), Spenser directly claims Leicester as his early patron, recalling how he 'did goodnes by him [that is, the earl] gaine, / And . . . his bounteous minde did trie' (lines 232–3). This poem itself is dedicated to Mary Sidney, the Countess of Pembroke and the older sister of Philip, whom Spenser likewise remembers here as 'the patron of my young Muse' (Yale, p. 230).

Spenser's public courtship of Sidney's notice and favour had commenced with *The Shepheardes Calender* published the year before the Spenser/ Harvey letters, with a title page dedication 'To The Noble and Vertuous Gentleman most worthy of all titles both of learning and chevalrie M. Philip Sidney'. In turn, Sidney mentions *The Shepheardes Calender* in his treatise *An Apology for Poetry* (published 1595), remarking that it 'hath much poetry in his eclogues, indeed worthy the reading if I be not deceived'.[11] Sidney's rather terse acknowledgment underplays Spenser's poetic achievement here, however. Arguably, *The Shepheardes Calender* had already answered Sidney's call in *An Apology* for a neoclassical vernacular poetry, even though Spenser's poem continued to employ rhyme instead of the quantitative meters advocated by Sidney and the Areopagus.[12] Indeed, with its virtuoso display of the possibilities of English as a literary language, *The Shepheardes Calender* had heralded a new movement in English poetry with its appearance in 1579. Composed of twelve individual lyric poems or eclogues (each one corresponding to a month in the calendar), Spenser's debut volume of poetry was unprecedented for its metrical variety, its assortment of poetic forms (including the first English sestina), and its range of topics – literary, religious, and political. In keeping with the social conventions of the period, *The Shepheardes Calender* was first published anonymously, though it is rich in clues ready for deciphering as to the hidden identity of its author. The *Calender*'s 'Dedicatory Epistle' confidently foretells that 'so soone as his name shall come into the knowledge of men, and his worthiness be sounded in the tromp of fame, . . . he shall be . . . beloved of all, embraced of the most, wondred at the best' (Yale, p. 13).

Fulfilling its own prediction of fame, the *Calender* achieved five editions before the century's end.

The physical properties of *The Shepheardes Calender* as a printed book predict – even produce – its stature as an instant literary classic. Only a portion of the material presented between its covers is Spenser's poetry, which is here surrounded by an elabourate scholarly apparatus more befitting a Renaissance edition of the pastorals of Virgil or Mantuan than the debut of an unknown English newcomer. The volume opens with an 'Envoy' or send-off poem, which is signed with another of Spenser's poetic aliases, 'Immerito' ('He who is unworthy'): 'Goe little booke: thy selfe present, / As child whose parent is unkent [unknown]'. Notwithstanding the poet's opening pose of deferential humility, the 'Epistle' that follows boldly situates Spenser and the pastoral inception of his career in the grand tradition of ancients like Theocritus and Virgil, in addition to somewhat more recent continental writers such as Mantuan, Petrarch, Marot, and Sannazaro: 'So finally flyeth this our new Poete, as a bird, whose principals be scarce growen out, but yet as that in time shall be hable to keepe winge with the best' (pp. 18–19). Next we are provided with '*The generall argument of* the whole booke', an essay summarising the meaning and design of the entire work. When we finally reach the eclogues themselves, we discover that they are, like the volume as a whole, comprised of multiple components. Patterned after Francesco Sansovino's illustrated edition of Sannazaro's *Arcadia* (1571), each of Spenser's eclogues is headed by a woodcut print, depicting some aspect of the scenario staged in the poem to follow. Underneath the woodcut is the 'Argument', which offers a prose synopsis of the eclogue. Then comes the poem, followed by one or more verbal 'Emblemes' or capstone mottoes. Finally, a detailed commentary is appended to each eclogue in the form of a scholarly gloss. The identity of the glossator (who is also responsible for the 'Dedicatory Epistle' and perhaps the 'Argument' as well) is one of several secrets theatrically maintained within the pages of *The Shepheardes Calender*. This mysterious figure is demarcated here only by the initials 'E. K.' Some have suggested that E. K. is Edward Kirke, a classmate of Spenser's at Pembroke Hall. Gabriel Harvey is another, perhaps more likely candidate. Even more likely is that Spenser – brandishing the same faculty for self-promotion so evident in the *Letters* – collaborated on, or even himself composed the gloss, thereby providing his poem with both built-in directions for reading and its own pre-scripted critical reception.

Whatever hand was responsible for the annotations to *The Shepheardes Calender*, this kind of scholarly apparatus, by its very presence, accentuates the literary significance and cultural prestige of the work to which it was attached. E. K.'s gloss also served to establish a point of resemblance between Spenser's ready-made classic and the most venerable of all pastoral works, Virgil's *Eclogues*, which was routinely accompanied in Renaissance printed editions by its own scholarly gloss, provided by the fourth-century Latin scholar Servius. Spenser's own eclogues abound in Virgilian allusions and appropriations, from the names of the *Calender*'s shepherds to the situation in which they are placed. These Virgilianisms establish *The Shepheardes Calender* as Spenser's first step in a career patterned upon Virgil's own generic progression, one which took him in time from the humble, introductory form of pastoral to the loftier strains of imperial epic. In the opening stanza of the proem to the first book of *The Faerie Queene*, Spenser explicitly overlays this trajectory – the *rota Virgilii*, as it was called – on his own career path:

> Lo I the man, whose Muse whilome did maske,
>   As time her taught, in lowly Shepheards weeds,
>   Am now enforst a far unfitter taske,
>   For trumpets sterne to chaunge mine Oaten reeds,
>   And sing of Knights and Ladies gentle deeds;
>   Whose prayses having slept in silence long,
>   Me, all too meane, the sacred Muse areeds
>   To blazon broad emongst her learned throng:
> Fierce warres and faithfull loves shall moralize my song.

The Faerie Queene thus fulfills the Virgilian promise of *The Shepheardes Calender*, Spenser's own heroic poem accomplishing for Elizabeth and for England what his epic predecessor's poem *The Aeneid* had achieved for Augustus and for Rome. Notwithstanding Virgil's seminal importance as a model for Spenser in *The Shepheardes Calender*, *The Faerie Queene*, and indeed throughout his career, this revered Augustan Age author is not Spenser's only poetic exemplar. In fact, the first poet named in the *Calender* – and the one to whose work Colin Clout's own endeavours are first compared – is not Virgil, but the native 'maker' Chaucer. What is more, the very name 'Colin Clout', Spenser's most frequently used poetic alias, is derived from Skelton, another English literary predecessor, known for his satirical verse. These English associations, so pronounced from the very inception of Spenser's literary project, indicate that his poetic aims were never exclusively Virgilian, that for him the *rota Virgilii* represented only one course among several literary career paths that he might pursue, indeed pursue simultaneously.

Spenser's secretaryships

Spenser did not rely on poetry for his living. Despite the (self-engendered?) fanfare of his auspicious poetic debut in *The Shepheardes Calender*, the prospect of a single-track career as a writer probably did not even occur to him. If it did, it is unlikely that such a profession, given the modest scale of the literary marketplace and the inconstancies of courtly patronage, would have answered his social, and presumably financial, objectives. Shakespeare earned some fame and enough money to buy New Place, the second largest house in Stratford-Upon-Avon, his hometown, but that was from working in the theatre. Spenser never wrote for the stage. Instead, his literary ambitions were inscribed within an established sixteenth-century career track for humanists, one that projected patronage and preferment by means of a multiform career that combined the profession of letters with other modes of public or private service suitable to the humanist's training and acculturation. The man of letters might thus be additionally employed, for instance, as a tutor, secretary, administrator or statesman. George Gascoigne, who is lauded in the gloss to the 'November' eclogue of *The Shepheardes Calender* as 'the very chiefe of our late rymers' (Yale, p. 197), was a courtier-soldier as well as a writer. Spenser's own 'other' occupation, the one he pursued in parallel with his poetic vocation, was as a secretary and a mid-level government official – a bureaucratic career he conducted principally in the province of colonial Ireland.

Spenser's first secretaryship came not long after he departed Cambridge. By 1578 (and perhaps a few years sooner) he had entered the service of Dr John Young. Young had been master at Pembroke Hall while Spenser was a student and Harvey a fellow there, and it was his intervention that secured the latter his contested MA degree. In April of 1578, Young was installed as the new Bishop of Rochester. We know of Spenser's position in his service because Harvey engraved the title page of a travel book, *The Traveiler of Jerome Turler* (1575), with an inscription indicating that the volume had been given to him by Spenser as a gift: 'ex dono Edmundi Spenserii, Episcopi Roffensis Secretarii, 1578' ('a gift from Edmund Spenser, secretary of the Bishop of Rochester'). Spenser himself publicises his post in the 'September' eclogue of *The Shepheardes Calender*, where Colin Clout is declared to be Roffy's (Rochester's) 'selfe boye' (line 176) or servant. Sometime in 1579, Spenser left Rochester's employment, probably with the ambition of securing another, similar position in or nearer the court. As we considered earlier, the Spenser/Harvey correspondence, which was penned in 1579–80, places Spenser at this time on the margins of the Leicester/Sidney circle and alludes to his attendance at court. We do not know precisely how Spenser was employed by Leicester, but he may have once again occupied some kind of secretarial post. In the letter dated 'Leycester House. This 5. of October. 1579', Spenser informs Harvey that he is 'mox in Gallias navigaturi' ('ready to sail for France') (p. 637) – on some kind of emissary mission for Leicester. He expects to depart 'the next weeke, if I can be displaced of my Lorde'. 'I goe thither', Spenser continues, 'as sent by him, and maintained most what of him: and there am to employ my time, my body, my minde, to his Honours service' (p. 638). Spenser's cryptic declaration keeps the actual designs of the trip grandly veiled, but it might have involved the carrying of letters, a regular charge of secretaries. An even more covert possibility is that the mission entailed some kind of espionage, which was another operation routinely associated in the period with secretaries and couriers. Whatever its purpose, Spenser's confidential expedition to France seems to have been aborted in the end.

On 27 October 1579, an 'Edmounde Spenser' married the twenty-year-old Maccabaeus Chylde at St Margaret's, Westminster. If this Spenser is Spenser the poet, the parish register entry of this wedding is the only extant mention of his first marriage, which we know from later records produced two children: Sylvanus (possibly named after Mulcaster's son) and Katherine (the name of both Mulcaster's wife and his daughter). The next year, Spenser landed another secretaryship – the most important of his career – as a private secretary to Arthur, Lord Grey de Wilton, newly appointed Lord Deputy of Ireland. He arrived there with Grey and a retinue of thirty other attendants on 12 August 1580. For Spenser, this foreign service post was an attractive opportunity, both in terms of career advancement and for the prospect of financial gain. Moreover, like his college mentor and friend Gabriel Harvey, Spenser had issued from an intellectual environment at Cambridge in which colonial theory had been elaborated and debated, with classical precedent for Ireland's subjugation handily being derived from Livy's *Decades* and the long history of Roman imperialism.[13] Harvey's own mentor, Sir Thomas Smith, was a forceful advocate for enhancing the colonial venture in Ireland; he both produced propaganda designed to stimulate an expansion of English operations there and invested his own financial resources in several plantation schemes in the early 1570s. Ireland was also a subject of considerable interest within the Leicester/ Sidney group, to which Spenser had attached himself at this time. Sir Henry Sidney, Philip's father and Leicester's brother-in-law, had served seven terms in Ireland, including three, with mixed success, as Lord Deputy. Philip Sidney joined his father in Ireland for a time in 1576, and then in 1577 composed his own brief on the colonial enterprise, 'A Discourse of Irish Affairs'. In addition to mounting a defence of his father's policies, Sidney's tract urges a strong-armed military campaign that would vanquish Irish resistance once and for all. Spenser would himself later argue a similar position in *A View of the Present State of Ireland* (probably written 1595–6; published 1633), his own treatise on the Irish problem, which renders in dialogue form a decade and a half of his first-hand experience as a government official and planter. Leicester's interest in Ireland is evident from the active role he played in engineering Henry Sidney's appointment as Lord Deputy. Similarly, he successfully lobbied the queen that Grey – like Leicester himself, another hard-line Protestant activist – be appointed as Sidney's replacement. Either Leicester or Sidney may also have been responsible for Spenser being taken into the new Lord Deputy's service.

Spenser's service and duties as one of Lord Grey's personal secretaries (Timothy Reynolds was his other) is amply documented. In the 1920s and 1930s, Spenser scholars H. R. Plomer and Raymond Jenkins identified numerous letters in the State Papers of Ireland written in Spenser's secretary hand or endorsed and addressed by him.[14] Other records indicate that, in addition to penning, verifying and dispatching Grey's official state correspondence (much of which involved defensive justification of his at times quite ruthless military policies and actions, along with pleas for additional troops and money), Spenser also served as paymaster for the Lord Deputy's messengers and spies. Spenser's own salary was £10 paid twice yearly, plus periodic additional allotments for 'paper, ynke, and parchment'. As Jenkins rightly contends, however, 'Spenser was not a modern secretary who sat comfortably at the home office and communicated with his chief by telephone but rather a companion who suffered the moving accidents of flood and field'.[15] It is quite likely, then, that Spenser was in attendance upon his master during Lord Grey's infamous military assault on an enemy fortification at Smerwick. After the surviving garrison of 600 Spanish and Italian papal troops surrendered to Grey on the sole condition that their lives be spared, he summarily ordered them all executed. As Grey's secretary, Spenser scripted the official narrative of the Lord Deputy's victory and the massacre that followed in a letter he penned on 12 November 1580 from Grey to the queen, and in another on 28 November from Grey to Lord Burghley. As a poet, Spenser approvingly retells the event in allegorical form in Book v, canto xii of *The Faerie Queene*. Although it has been the tendency of some Spenser critics to dissociate his literary and bureaucratic careers, we find here, at least with respect to the matter of Ireland, that the writings of Spenser the poet and Spenser the secretary speak in rhyme.

As we have already glimpsed, to serve as a secretary in Spenser's culture was to be much more than a mere amanuensis. The duties of a secretary as his master's nearest and dearest servant, as his right-hand man, were adumbrated in a developing Renaissance discourse on secretaryship that found expression in a variety of proto-professional manuals, letter-writing handbooks and bureaucratic treatises. Among the most important of these works is Angel Day's *The English Secretary* (1599), which insists that the secretary's office is of 'great[er] consequence . . . and more circumstance, than by everie one is considered'.[16] Day expounds on the unique relation of trust and intimacy that binds together secretaries and masters by uncovering the word 'secret' as the etymological root of 'secretary': 'by the verie etimologie of the worde it selfe, both Name and Office in one, doe conclude uppon secrecie'.[17] Day thereby fashions the secretary as the supreme cabinet counsellor, as an inviolable repository for all his master's most private affairs and dealings, as one whose true office is as 'a keeper or conserver of the secret unto him committed'.[18] In his own secretarial treatise, Elizabethan Secretary of State Robert Cecil compares the extraordinary relation that exists between master and secretary to 'the mutual affections of two lovers, undiscovered to their friends'. Notwithstanding the fact that secretaryship was at this time a male office, Cecil goes on to analogise this intimate male–male bond to nothing less than the 'solemnisation of marriage'.[19]

Robert Cecil was the last in a series of Tudor Principal Secretaries – a line that included his father William Cecil (Lord Burghley), Francis Walsingham, Thomas Smith, Stephen Gardiner and Thomas Cromwell – who each in turn had a hand in developing this position into one of he most powerful executive offices in the realm, one that brought with it a place on the Privy Council. Perhaps Spenser had aspirations that his own secretaryships would lead to a position of importance and influence in the Tudor bureaucracy, in the cabinet councils of state. Although he never attained such a lofty office, Spenser's service as secretary to Lord Grey – whom he heralds in one of the dedicatory sonnets attached to *The Faerie Queene* as 'the pillor of my life, / And Patrone of my Muses pupillage' ('To . . . Lord Grey of Wilton', lines 1–2) – did lead to a succession of additional bureaucratic positions, all of them in Ireland. In fact, when Grey was recalled to England in 1582 and replaced as Lord Deputy by the more placatory Sir John Perrot, Spenser stayed in Ireland, perhaps serving for a time as the new Lord Deputy's secretary. The year before Grey's recall, Spenser acquired the additional office of clerk of the chancery for faculties, which were dispensations and licenses granted by the Archbishop of Dublin. In 1583 and again in 1584, Spenser acted as a commissioner of musters in County Kildare; his duties involved taking census of all able-bodied fighting men and available armaments in his region. Sometime in 1583–4, Spenser took on a new position as deputy to his friend Lodowick Bryskett, the recently named clerk of the Council of Munster. In this office, Spenser also rendered secretarial services to Sir John Norris, President of the Council. He attended numerous council sessions at Limerick and Cork, as well as the convening of the Irish Parliament in 1585 and the Parliament of 1586. Furthermore, Spenser was most likely in attendance upon Norris for several military expeditions.

Sometime during this period, Spenser may have advanced from serving as Bryskett's deputy to himself occupying the office of clerk. In 1586 he was named prebendary of Effin, which was attached to Limerick Cathedral; Spenser probably held this non-resident, layman's office as a sinecure. In 1594 he served as the queen's Justice for County Cork. Then in 1598 he was nominated for the post of Sheriff of Cork by the Privy Council, which cited Spenser for being 'a man endowed with good knowledge in learning and not unskillful as without experience in the service of warrs'.[20] Throughout this period, Spenser continued to perform secretarial duties for John Norris, as well as his brother Thomas Norris.

Concurrent with his bureaucratic responsibilities, Spenser was busy throughout this period acquiring Irish real estate. He leased several properties in the 1580s, including a dissolved Franciscan monastery called New Abbey in County Kildare, some twenty-five miles from Dublin. His lease on this estate, signed August 1582, terms him 'Edmund Spenser, Gent.', marking a significant enhancement of his social stature since he left England for Ireland two years earlier. As Louis A. Montrose puts it: 'It was by virtue of his MA that Spenser could begin to think of himself as Master Spenser; however, it was only after he had begun to acquire land and offices in Ireland that he could fully consider himself, and be formally acknowledged as, a gentleman.'[21] Spenser's circumstances were further bettered when he was granted 3028 acres in Cork. His land grant was a small parcel of a vast estate belonging to the Irish rebel Gerald Fitzgerald of Desmond, who, with a price on his head, had been killed in 1583. As part of the Munster Plantation scheme, Desmond's confiscated lands were redistributed to English gentlemen, who were then to settle their plantations with English immigrant families. In May of 1589, Spenser began to occupy his new estate, establishing his own residence at Kilcolman Castle and founding a nascent colony of six English households on his land. Spenser's ownership of a substantial portion of this plantation had been bitterly and litigiously contested by his Anglo-Irish neighbor, Lord Roche, but in October 1590 a royal grant assigned him its possession 'for ever' at an annual rent of about £20. Spenser – perhaps too knowingly – gave his Irish estate the name 'Hap Hazard'. In June 1594 he married his second wife, Elizabeth Boyle, feting his courtship of her and their marriage in a volume of lyric poetry entitled *Amoretti and Epithalamion* (1595). In wedding the much younger Elizabeth, a relation of Sir Richard Boyle, the first Earl of Cork, Spenser became kin to the richest man in all of Ireland. He also continued to accumulate real estate, purchasing the castle and lands of Renny in County Cork in 1597 for £200 as a provision for his son, Peregrine, as well as Buttevant Abbey near Kilcolman.

Spenser in Ireland: Punishment or Preferment?

One of the chief questions animating current scholarship on Spenser's life and career is the meaning of his posting to Ireland in 1580. Was Spenser's appointment to Lord Grey's secretarial corps – a position that entailed trading the attractions of the court, so thrillingly glimpsed by Spenser in his epistolary exchanges with Harvey, for the comparative wasteland of Ireland – an expedient step towards the realisation of his professional and social aspirations? Or did Spenser's Irish assignment signify the diminution, even the frustration of his ambitions? Reformulating an argument that Edwin Greenlaw first posed in 1910, Muriel Bradbrook makes the case in her 1982 essay, 'No Room at the Top: Spenser's Pursuit of Fame', that Spenser, after a promising beginning at court, was dismissed, shipped off to Ireland, due to some kind of political misstep in which he offended either the queen or Leicester, or them both. Whatever the specific cause, the result for Spenser, in Bradbrook's view, was a punishment by exile, leaving the poet, as she memorably puts it, 'buried in a kind of Elizabethan Siberia'.[22] More recent accounts of Spenser's career dispute the notion that his service in Ireland betokened exile. Jean Brink, Christopher Highley, Willy Maley, Andrew Hadfield and others have instead pointed to the ways in which Ireland, despite the inherent perils of this imperfectly colonised colony, could serve as a new frontier of opportunity, especially for an ambitious place-seeker of Spenser's modest social stature.[23] Certainly that was the view of Ireland espoused by Sir Thomas Smith, Sir Philip Sidney and the Earl of Leicester, important figures with whom Spenser had forged political and perhaps personal affiliations early in his career. As Highley sees it, Spenser's relocation to Ireland should thus be regarded 'less an exile from the centers of power, than an opportunity for a man of modest beginnings to fashion more flexibly his social and cultural identity'.[24]

Spenser, as we have already seen, did indeed seize this opportunity, capitalising on the prospects Ireland afforded him for offices, grants and land – and, attendant upon his acquisition of the latter, for his rise to the rank of gentleman. Clearly, these results gainsay the view that his initial posting to Ireland functioned as a form of punitive banishment. It is, however, perhaps another matter altogether that from this point onward Ireland remained the only sphere for Spenser's advancement. That is, neither his bureaucratic service nor his poetic achievements won him a return ticket to England and a place of influence there at court, whether in the office of poet laureate or cabinet counsellor, or in both roles at once. Spenser himself treats the issue of the apparent permanence of his Irish posting in *Colin Clouts Come Home Againe*. The poem recounts in fictionalised pastoral form his trip to England in 1589 to oversee the publication of the first three books of *The Faerie Queene*, and his return a little more than a year later to Ireland. Spenser made this journey in the company of Sir Walter Raleigh (who appears in the poem as 'the shepheard of the Ocean'), his sometime neighbour in Ireland and new friend and patron. Through the offices of Raleigh, then one of Elizabeth's favourites, Spenser was received at court, where he presented the queen with the epic poem he had composed in honour of her reign and dedicated to her. If we credit the account offered in *Colin Clout*, Spenser even had the privilege of reading a portion of his *Faerie Queene* to the queen herself. In about a year's time Elizabeth eventually rewarded him for his efforts by granting Spenser an annual pension of £50. This was a respectable – even, for a poet, a handsome – annuity, especially so in Ireland, where, according to Robert Payne, author of a promotional pamphlet for the Munster Plantation, an Englishman could 'keepe a better house in Ireland for L.li. [£50] a yeare, then in England for CC.li. [£200] a yeare'.[25]

Yet if a £50 pension in Ireland fully answered Spenser's notion of his worth, why does *Colin Clout* protest so ruefully about how poets are under-appreciated and 'meanly waged' (line 382) at Elizabeth's court? Indeed, for a work designed to commemorate the poet's own triumphs – both there at court and upon his heralded return to Ireland – this is a notably ambivalent, even acerbic testimonial. The poem's requisite praise of Elizabeth (or Cynthia, as she is here termed) is crosshatched by its criticism, even repudiation of her court: a place, Colin reports, where art and learning are 'shouldred [thrust aside] . . . , or out of doore quite shit' (line 709). Colin/Spenser thus implies that he comes home to Ireland because there is no home for him at court. Consequently, from its opening lines *Colin Clout* posits an alternative to the English court – an Irish counter-court, one centred not on Cynthia but on Colin himself. According to Louis A. Montrose, part of the work this poem thus sets out to perform is 'to make the author feel at home in Ireland'.[26] Andrew Hadfield intensifies this reading, declaring that the markedly Irish mise-en-scène of Colin's pastoral home-coming suggests 'that the poet considered himself no longer straightfor-wardly English'.[27] Even so, it is important to bear in mind that *Colin Clout* does not show Spenser as completely at home in coming home to Ireland. Rather, the same strain of ambivalence that inflects his feelings of displace-ment from the English court also colours Spenser's response to his appar-ently now permanent placement in Ireland: a situation Colin here depicts as 'my lucklesse lot', as a form of banishment 'Into that waste, where I was quite forgot' (lines 181–3). One wonders where Spenser – an Englishman who is no longer 'straightforwardly English', an Irish homemaker whose homemaking there is a kind of exile – would at this point in his colonial career in fact feel at home.

Judging from the tenor of *Complaints* (1591), the next volume of his poetry to be published after the first instalment of *The Faerie Queene*, Spenser evidently did not regard his 'lucklesse lot' as sufficiently improved by the reward he met with at court. This anthology of new, old and revised works – tonally unified in their elegiac or satiric expression of disillusionment – is an assertively non-laureate career gesture on Spenser's part. Here the laureate's duties of praising the monarch and heralding the nation's imperial destiny are conspicuously neglected. Abandoning the mode of heroic verse to revive various medieval forms (dream vision, fabliau, estates satire, and of course complaint), *Complaints* instead gives voice to what may be Spenser's own professional frustration that he is 'Still wayting to preferment up to climbe' ('Mother Hubberds Tale', line 76). For what form or degree of preferment was Spenser still waiting? Was it a more lucrative pension, a larger estate in Ireland, a more prestigious office in its colonial government, a posting back to England? Whatever the antidote to his frustrations, Spenser's volume of *Complaints* – along with the more personal poetic works that follow in its wake: *Colin Clouts Come Home Againe*; *Amoretti and Epithalamion*; *Fowre Hymnes*; *Prothalamion* – mark a temporary detour from his high Virgilian career. The publication in 1596 of an expanded second edition of *The Faerie Queene* signalled Spenser's resumption of his Virgilian office. His English epic had now grown to six of its promised twelve books. Yet the new legends of Books IV–VI are less sanguine in their blazoning of Elizabethan courtly values and virtues than those of the poem's first instalment. This modulation in Spenser's epic voice may be indicative of the abiding nature of the professional disappointment he first expresses in *Complaints* and *Colin Clout*. It may also reflect alternations in the political climate – including his patron Raleigh's fall from royal grace and the worsening colonial situation in Ireland – that would neither have served Spenser's personal or political interests too well nor enhanced his confidence in an Elizabethan manifest destiny.

Last things, 1598–1599

Perhaps the position of Sheriff of County Cork, to which Spenser had been nominated in September 1598, would have answered his notion of due preferment. This post was more prominent than any Spenser had yet held. Ruth Mohl has suggested that had he been installed in this office and continued from there his rise in the colonial government, Spenser might eventually have been rewarded with a knighthood.[28] During the period in which he was still sheriff-designate, however, the massive revolt against English rule instigated by the Earl of Tyrone had spread from its beginnings in the northern territory of Ulster throughout Ireland. In October 1598, Irish rebels had besieged the Munster Plantation, and Spenser's own Kilcolman was sacked and burned. Along with the other surviving English planters, Spenser and his family sought refuge in Cork. From there, he was dispatched on his final trip back to England. He journeyed there, not as Spenser the poet, but as Spenser the colonial planter and bureaucrat, carrying with him a missive from Sir Thomas Norris, President of Munster. He delivered Norris' letter to the Privy Council while it met at Whitehall on Christmas Eve. On the same occasion, Spenser may also have presented a set of three state papers gathered together under the title *A briefe note of Ireland*. At least one of the papers – 'Certaine pointes to be considered of in the recovering of the Realme of Irelande' – was written by Spenser himself. For his efforts he was paid a fee of £8.

Two weeks later, on 13 January 1599, Spenser died at Westminster. Like so many of the details of Spenser's life, the cause of his death remains unknown. According to William Camden, Spenser's first biographer, his funeral was paid for by the Earl of Essex, another Protestant zealot, whom Spenser had heralded in *Prothalamion* as the nation's brightest future hope. Spenser was buried near Chaucer at Westminster Abbey, Camden further reports, adding that his hearse was 'attended by poets, and mournful elegies and poems, with the pens that wrote them, thrown into his grave'.[29] The poets – Shakespeare himself in their number, according to legend – thus came to honour the 'prince of poets', as Spenser's Westminster memorial entitled him. But this was a 'prince' who also served as a secretary. Ten years after the poet-secretary's death, the first folio edition of *The Faerie Queene* Books I–VI appeared, an epic poem designed by Spenser to teach other gentlemen what it means to be a 'noble person' fashioned in 'vertuous and gentle discipline'. And this from the son of an unknown father, from one who was a gentleman not by birthright, but by his own endeavour and self-fashioning. What is more, Spenser's courtly poem is a lesson in courtesy administered not from the English court, but from the provinces, from Ireland, Spenser's adopted homeland on the margins of the empire. The first folio edition of Spenser's collected works was published in 1611 as *The Faerie Queene: The Shepheardes Calender: Together with the other Works of England's Arch-Poet, Edm. Spenser*. This memorial to Spenser the poet was matched in 1633 by the publication of the work of Spenser the colonial theorist and bureaucrat, when *A View of the Present State of Ireland* appeared in a volume of antiquarian works edited by James Ware.

NOTES

1 Citations of *FQ* are from Hamilton. Thanks to Charles O'Boyle, Jr., for assistance and inspiration.

2 John Hughes, 'The Life of Mr Edmund Spenser', in *The Works of Mr Edmund Spenser*, 6 vols. (London, 1715); excerpted in Cummings, p. 334. The standard modern biography of Spenser remains Alexander C. Judson's *The Life of Edmund Spenser* (Baltimore: Johns Hopkins University Press, 1945). Few new biographical facts have emerged since its publication, and Judson's impressively researched biography remains a landmark work of Spenser scholarship. From its initial publication, however, the story of Spenser's life Judson composes has been roundly criticised for its regular flights into fanciful surmise and conjecture.

3 Spenser alludes to his turning forty in sonnet 60 of *Amoretti*, which was published in 1595. See Donald Cheney's discussion of 'Spenser's Fortieth Birthday and Related Fictions', in *Sp. St.* 4 (1984), 3–31.

4 Richard Mulcaster, *The First Part of the Elementarie Which Entreateth Chiefly of the right writing of our English Tung* (London, 1582), ed. E. T. Campagnac (Oxford: Clarendon Press, 1925), 269.

5 William Allan Oram, *Edmund Spenser* (New York: Twayne, 1997), p. 3.

6 For this and other documentary traces of Spenser's life and career, see Willy Maley's indispensable reference work, *A Spenser Chronology* (Lanham, MD: Barnes & Noble, 1994). Still useful is F. I. Carpenter's *A Reference Guide to Edmund Spenser* (Chicago: University of Chicago Press, 1923), the sourcebook that Maley's *Chronology* updates.

7 See Lisa Jardine's instructive entry on 'Cambridge' in *Spenser Encyclopedia*, pp. 130–31.

8 On Harvey's career and the Cambridge intellectual and political milieu from which he emerged, see Lisa Jardine's important and much-cited essay, 'Mastering the Uncouth: Gabriel Harvey, Edmund Spenser, and the English Experience in Ireland', in John Henry and Sarah Hutton, eds., *New Perspectives on Renaissance Thought* (London: Duckworth, 1990), pp. 68–82; as well as Lisa Jardine and Anthony Grafton, '"Studied for Action": How Harvey Read His Livy', *P & P* 129 (1990), 30–78. See also the useful account of Harvey's life and career provided by Wayne Erickson in *Sixteenth-Century British Nondramatic Writers*, vol. 167 of the *Dictionary of Literary Biography*, 3rd series, ed. David A. Richardson (Detroit: Bruccoli Clark Layman, 1996), pp. 77–93.

9 Harvey's triumph, probably the highlight of his career, is recorded in the gloss accompanying the 'September' eclogue of *The Shepheardes Calender*.

10 On the amorous conventions of male friendship in the Renaissance, see Alan Bray, 'Homosexuality and Male Friendship in Elizabethan England', in Jonathan Goldberg, ed., *Queering the Renaissance* (Durham: Duke University Press, 1994), pp. 40–61. On the erotics of the Harvey–Spenser friendship in particular, see Jonathan Goldberg's chapter on 'Spenser's Familiar Letters', in *Sodometries: Renaissance Texts, Modern Sexualities* (Stanford: Stanford University Press, 1992) and Richard Rambuss, *Spenser's Secret Career* (Cambridge: Cambridge University Press, 1993), pp. 56–9.

11 Sidney, *Apology*, p. 133.

12 The quantitative versification campaign never amounted to much in the end,

and Spenser quickly lost whatever interest he had – or had feigned – in it. Gary Waller offers a helpful discussion of the issue and its attendant cultural politics in *Edmund Spenser: A Literary Life* (London: Macmillan, 1994), pp. 13–16.

13 See Jardine, 'Mastering the Uncouth', p. 73. See also Vincent P. Carey and Clare L. Carroll, 'Factions and Fictions: Spenser's Reflections of and on Elizabethan Politics', in Judith H. Anderson, Donald Cheney and David A. Richardson, eds., *Spenser and the Subject of Biography* (Amherst: University of Massachusetts Press, 1996), p. 36, as well as Jean R. Brink, '"All his minde on honour fixt": The Preferment of Edmund Spenser', in the same volume, pp. 50–3.

14 See, for instance: H. R. Plomer, 'Edmund Spenser's Handwriting', *MP* 21 (1923–4), 201–7; Raymond Jenkins, 'Spenser's Hand', *TLS* 31 (7 January 1932), 12; and Jenkins, '*Newes out of Munster*, a Document in Spenser's Hand', *SP* 32 (1935), 123–30. See also Maley, *Spenser Chronology*.

15 Raymond Jenkins, 'Spenser: The Uncertain Years, 1584–1589', *PMLA* 52 (1938), 350–62, p. 355. For more on Spenser's secretaryships, as well as the ligatures between his career as a secretary and his career as a poet, see Rambuss, *Spenser's Secret Career*, especially ch. 2.

16 Angel Day, *The English Secretary* (London, 1599), part 2, p. 102. Day's handbook is available in a facsimile edition, edited and introduced by Robert O. Evans (Gainseville, FL: Scholars' Facsimiles and Reprints, 1967).

17 Day, *English Secretary*, p. 103.

18 Ibid., pp. 102–3.

19 Robert Cecil, 'The State and Dignity of a Secretary of State's Place, with the Care and Peril Thereof', in *The Harleian Miscellany* 5 (1810), 166–8, p. 167.

20 For a fuller citation of this document, see Maley, *Spenser Chronology*, p. 72.

21 Louis A. Montrose, 'Spenser's Domestic Domain: Poetry, Property, and the Early Modern Subject', in Margreta de Grazia, Maureen Quilligan and Peter Stallybrass, eds., *Subject and Object in Renaissance Culture* (Cambridge: Cambridge University Press, 1996), p. 84.

22 Muriel Bradbrook, 'No Room at the Top: Spenser's Pursuit of Fame', in *Elizabethan Poetry*, Stratford-Upon-Avon Studies 2 (London: St Martin's Press, 1960), p. 103. See also Edwin Greenlaw, 'Spenser and the Earl of Leicester', *PMLA* 25 (1910), 535–61.

23 Among the essays collected in Anderson et al., eds., *Spenser and the Subject of Biography*, see in particular: Carey and Carroll, 'Factions and Fictions'; and Brink, '"All his mind on honour fixed"'. See also in the same volume: Richard Rambuss, 'Spenser's Lives, Spenser's Careers'; and F. J. Levy, 'Spenser and Court Humanism'. Among important recent book-length studies that treat the opportunities for advancement and gain attendant upon Spenser's posting to Ireland are: David J. Baker, *Between Nations: Shakespeare, Spenser, Marvell, and the Question of Britain* (Stanford: Stanford University Press, 1997); Christopher Highley, *Shakespeare, Spenser, and the Crisis in Ireland* (Cambridge: Cambridge University Press, 1997); and Andrew Hadfield, *Edmund Spenser's Irish Experience: Wilde Fruit and Salvage Soyl* (Oxford: Clarendon Press, 1997).

24 Highley, *Shakespeare, Spenser, and the Crisis in Ireland*, p. 4.

25 Robert Payne, *A Briefe description of Ireland: Made in this yeare 1589* (reprinted 1594), *The English Experience* 548 (New York: Da Capo Press, 1937), p. 10; cited in Highley, *Shakespeare, Spenser, and the Crisis in Ireland*, p. 31

26 Montrose, 'Spenser's Domestic Domain', p. 119.

27 Hadfield, *Edmund Spenser's Irish Experience*, p. 15.

28 Ruth Mohl, 'Edmund Spenser', *Spenser Encyclopedia*, pp. 668–71, at p. 670.

29 William Camden, *The Historie of the Most Renowned and Victorious Princesse Elizabeth, Late Queene of England* (London, 1630), cited in Judson, *The Life of Edmund Spenser*, p. 206.

FURTHER READING

Judith A. Anderson, Donald Cheney and David A. Richardson, *Spenser's Life and the Subject of Biography* (Amherst: University of Massachusetts Press, 1996).

Muriel Bradbrook, 'No Room at the Top: Spenser's Pursuit of Fame', in *Elizabethan Poetry*, Stratford-upon-Avon Studies 2 (London: St Martin's Press, 1960).

Frederic Ives Carpenter, *A Reference Guide to Edmund Spenser* (Chicago: University of Chicago Press, 1923).

Patrick Cheney, *Spenser's Famous Flight: A Renaissance Idea of a Literary Career* (Toronto: University of Toronto Press, 1993).

Andrew Hadfield, *Edmund Spenser's Irish Experience: Wilde Fruit and Salvage Soyl* (Oxford: Clarendon Press, 1997).

Richard Helgerson, *Self-Crowned Laureates: Spenser, Jonson, Milton, and the Literary System* (Berkeley: University of California Press, 1983).

Alexander C. Judson, *The Life of Edmund Spenser* in Variorum (Baltimore: Johns Hopkins University Press, 1945).

Willy Maley, *A Spenser Chronology* (Lanham, MD: Barnes & Noble, 1994).

Louis A. Montrose, 'Spenser's Domestic Domain: Poetry, Property, and the Early Modern Subject', in Margreta de Grazia, Maureen Quilligan and Peter Stallybrass, eds., *Subject and Object in Renaissance Culture* (Cambridge: Cambridge University Press, 1996).

David Lee Miller, 'Spenser's Vocation, Spenser's Career', *ELH* 50 (1983), 197–230.

Richard Rambuss, *Spenser's Secret Career* (Cambridge: Cambridge University Press, 1993).

Gary Waller, *Edmund Spenser: A Literary Life* (London: Macmillan, 1994).

2

DAVID J. BAKER

Historical contexts: Britain and Europe

Events and Personages

Edmund Spenser lived at a time when the charged relation between the two 'contexts' of this chapter, Britain and Europe, was changing drastically, and, as we will see, his own relation to these shifting contexts was often equivocal. Inserting Spenser into historical contexts can be problematic, and, certainly, no amount of 'context' can finally decide the meaning of Spenser's life or work. In the several books of *The Faerie Queene* and elsewhere, we find an ongoing mediation on historical contexts that is an index both of Spenser's own uncertain placement within them and his indeterminate effect on them. Sometimes this dialectic can be traced quite clearly: not only can Spenser's work be set 'within' these historical contexts, but these contexts themselves are, to an extent, being defined by him as he writes. In the later years of the sixteenth century, for instance, one of our contexts, that of 'Britain', was not yet assembled as an effective political union. Strictly speaking, 'Great Britain' would not come into existence until 1801.[1] But Spenser invested in the imagining of such a polity throughout his career, and some of our conception of 'Britain' as a splendid fusion of disparate nations we owe to him. 'How brutish is it not to vnderstand', cries Arthur in the second book of *The Faerie Queene*, looking up from a chronicle titled *Briton moniments*, 'How much to [Britain] we owe, that all vs gaue, / That gaue vnto vs all, what euer good we haue' (II, x, 69).[2] In other places, however, the dialectic between Spenser and his contexts is less easy to discern. In the first section of this chapter, we will canvass some of the main political events and salient trends that framed Spenser's endeavours. In the second, we will consider what debt Spenser's writing may have owed to the work of two well-known European thinkers. Although such influences are not determining, they do provide some of the contexts within which and by which Spenser shaped his life and thought in the late sixteenth century.

The European political scene that Spenser knew had changed considerably since the century's early years. Then, England had usually elected to stand by as the Hapsburgs and the Valois, the ruling houses of Spain and France, struggled for territorial advantage. These were contests between large, loosely organised dynastic realms, and were conducted, more often than not, according to the aristocratic code that governed relations between late medieval princes. As one such prince, 'Henry VIII had indulged his fitful impulses towards chivalric fame at vast financial cost and sacrifice of life but without involving the kingdom in life and death struggle'. But by 1570, about a decade into the reign of his daughter, Elizabeth I, these rivalries had been transformed, 'twisted', an historian tells us, 'into a different shape by the presence in all the major courts of elements whose view of international politics was determined by impassioned religious zealotry'.[3] There were now many across Europe – and certainly at the court of England's Protestant queen – who saw political oppositions in stark religious terms, and who, indeed, had little use for a distinction between politics and religion. Catholics and Protestants, 'combatants in a cosmic confrontation between absolute right and absolute wrong',[4] divided Europe along the transnational lines laid down by a conflicted faith.

At the same time, however, there were also many across Europe – and, again, certainly at Elizabeth's court – who derived what was at best a conflicted sense of allegiance from this antagonism. Protestantism had been deployed across the Continent, but 'it lacked any institutional apparatus or . . . general agreement on central doctrinal issues'.[5] Catholics might be fairly united in their abhorrence of Protestantism, but uncertain about the support they owed to co-religionists. Obligations to one's faith could and often did conflict with obligations to one's countrymen, to those of one's 'nation'. And this conflict in itself was a new and potently complicating development. Earlier in the century, territorial disputes had only been 'vaguely nationalistic',[6] perhaps coalescing around a still mostly unformulated notion of what a 'nation' might be. By the latter years, it was increasingly possible to think of oneself as belonging to such an entity and to imagine that others, including one's enemies, did too. This was a period when, as Benedict Anderson puts it in a classic study, an 'older imagining, where . . . borders were porous and indistinct, and sovereignties faded imperceptibly into one another' was gradually giving way to a more 'modern conception', where 'sovereignty is fully, flatly, and evenly operative over each square centimetre of a legally demarcated territory'.[7] Spenser and his contemporaries can be located in the midst of this slow and contingent development. For them, as one theorist puts it, the history of England's formation as a 'nation' is 'half-made because it is in the process of being made'.[8] England, as a proto-nation, was confronted not only with a hostile continent-spanning religious alliance, but with an array of newly arisen polities whose struggles were increasingly, but ambiguously, 'international'.

Perhaps no episode says more about the complications of this European/ British scene and the contradictions of Edmund Spenser's involvement in it than the trial and execution of Mary, Queen of Scots. In 1568, Mary had been driven from Scotland by a clique of noblemen outraged at her domestic conduct and her high-handed treatment of them. When she fled to England for protection, she was imprisoned by a Protestant queen who expected, quite rightly, that her royal cousin would soon become the focus of Catholic resistance. Over the next eighteen years, Elizabeth stayed her hand as Mary was implicated in a number of attempts to oust her. The precise extent of Mary's knowledge and participation in these plots has been debated, but her larger purpose was always clear. And it became exceedingly clear in 1586, when letters from Mary to a band of regicidal conspirators came into the hands of Secretary Francis Walsingham, and her full complicity was revealed. As a confederate in the 'Babington plot' (so called after one of the conspirators), Mary was arrested and tried by a commission of peers, Privy Counsellors, and judges. Intense public outrage against her was fuelled by the conviction that she was a tool of Spain; one of the instigators, a priest, had claimed that sixty thousand troops from abroad were poised to invade after the coup. But Elizabeth's response to this plotting was oddly vacillating. She was extremely chary of taking the life of a fellow prince, even one with such obvious designs on her throne, and delayed giving the order for Mary's execution until she was pressured into it by an indignant Parliament and virtually tricked into it by an impatient Privy Council. The death warrant, which she had signed, was sent (or so she said) without her knowledge. She then denounced the execution – which, in all probability, was the consummation she herself had most devoutly wished.

Mary's death is re-enacted in Book V of Spenser's *The Faerie Queene*, where the false Duessa is condemned and executed with the acquiescence of a benevolent monarch, Mercilla, but never explicitly at her command. Prosecuted by Zele, Duessa is 'damned by them all'. The queen's verdict, though, is

> tempred without griefe or gall,
> Till strong constraint did her thereto enforce.
> And yet euen then ruing [Duessa's] wilfull fall.   V, x, 4

This episode is one of the most notable of Spenser's interventions in the affairs of Britain and Europe. (Mary's son, James VI of Scotland and later James I of England, demanded that Spenser be 'dewly tryed & punished' by

Elizabeth for his 'dishonorable effects . . . against . . . his mother de-ceassed.'[9]) But Spenser's treatment of the incident shows how difficult inserting him into these 'contexts' can be. Here, Spenser certainly seems to be maligning Mary, the Catholic interloper, whose death is seen as just, even self-willed. But what of his stance towards his own Protestant queen? As John Guy notes, Elizabeth's indecisiveness was intrinsic to her political style. For most of her years on the throne, this monarch 'knew her mind even when she procrastinated; her judgement was not infallible, but her instinct was shrewd'.[10] Here, though, is Spenser tacitly condemning Eliza-beth for her pusillanimity or praising her for her (perhaps misplaced) compassion? And, in the fifth book generally, is Spenser writing as a dutiful celebrator of his queen, or, after many years of hard service in Ireland, as an increasingly disgruntled critic of her all too dilatory policies there? As the book's hero, Artegall, enters Mercilla's court, he sees a poet, Bonfont, whose tongue has been nailed to a post. Is this poet Spenser himself, as one critic has claimed, 'his tongue intact, but sacrificed to the queen none-theless?'[11] Or is this silenced poet a figure for the despised traitor whom Spenser has deftly contrived not to be? Readers have not been able to decide such questions finally.

As in this episode, the histories of Britain and Europe impinged on Spenser's works, quite often, through the mediating involvement of the woman he called his 'Glorious Empresse'. But his devotion to her was not entirely constant, nor was it free of ambivalence – and this was hardly surprising. Elizabeth herself, the object of his veneration, was notoriously prone to mutability. Elizabeth governed as she did partly because of who she was: a female monarch who presided over a coterie of restlessly ambitious male courtiers, many of whom were uneasy with her priority, and many of whom disagreed with her on foreign and domestic policy. The queen's royal persona was shaped by her need to accommodate these courtiers and to channel their strivings. The collective fiction that, more than any other, allowed the queen and her court to oblige each other was that they were engaged in a game of 'courtship'. As Guy puts it, 'to succeed at Court politicians had to pretend to be in love with the queen'. The give and take between this monarch and her 'suitors' amounted to a highly eroticised, complex and flexible 'conversation' – at times a rather one-sided conversation, no doubt, but still a conversation. It allowed Elizabeth to be approached, under the guise of a Petrarchan 'mistress', with requests for attention, favour and patronage. It allowed the queen to satisfy those requests, or, under the same guise, to deny them, since 'dithering, prevarica-tion and generally dismissive behavior [were] understood to be archetypical' for such a 'mistress'.[12] It also allowed the court to address the queen in ways that she would not have chosen. Elizabeth's subjects, and especially those of her 'political nation', were constantly in search of ways to make their views, needs and even criticisms known.

Spenser seems to have done this himself in 'Prosopopoia: Or Mother Hubberds Tale' (1591), where he not only took it upon himself to denounce allegorically the queen's impending marriage to a French duke, Alençon, but to depict one of her most beloved counsellors, Lord Burghley, in the aspect of a conniving fox. (The poem, apparently, was confiscated by the government and did not appear in a later edition of Spenser's works.) By doing so, he inserted himself – unsuccessfully, as it turned out – into one of the most potent dynamics of Elizabeth's court: the contest of cliques and favourites. Simplifying considerably, it can be said that, up until the 1580s, the fields of force in court flowed between two magnetic poles: William Cecil, Lord Burghley and Robert Dudley, the Earl of Leicester. The former served Elizabeth in various posts from her accession in 1558 until his death in 1598. His labours for her almost spanned the reign. In their policies, Elizabeth and Burghley were linked closely, though not quite so closely as is sometimes claimed. Guy argues, for instance, that for much of the reign the two differed fundamentally over the political make-up of the kingdom itself. Burghley, along with many on the Privy Council, was an advocate of a 'mixed polity' in which Parliament had its say in governance, if only in assenting to the queen's dicta. Elizabeth 'believed that her *imperium* was ordained by God alone and her prerogative unlimited by her councillors' advice'.[13] In most matters, however, they were temperamentally, if not always ideologically, in harmony. In foreign affairs, Burghley's was a voice of moderation. He sought, like Elizabeth, to avoid open conflict with Catholic Spain. Leicester, on the contrary, adopted firm Protestant views – '[t]here is no man I know in this realm that hath showed a better mind to the furthering of true religion than I have done, even from the first day of her Majesty's reign'[14] – and his foreign policy was shaped to fit. As a confidant (some had said an intimate) of Elizabeth's early years, he had the queen's ear, and he and others of his persuasion made sure that their views were thoroughly aired before her. Although Elizabeth was never comfortable as a champion of militant Protestantism, this was a role that Leicester and his co-religionists urged upon her. In the 1590s – again, simplifying considerably – tensions shifted to the rivalry between Robert Cecil, a younger son of Burghley who had been carefully positioned as his successor, and Leicester's stepson, Robert Devereux, the Earl of Essex. Eventually, in the queen's declining years, Cecil came to exert great power at her behest, while Essex, a proud and flamboyant courtier, would defy her and bring about his own downfall. Essex was immensely popular (Spenser is thought to have been one of his adherents), and he yielded easily to no one. When an Irish campaign failed, he defied Elizabeth's orders to remain in the field, returned to London and staged what amounted to a *coup d'état*. It failed, and he was executed for treason in 1601. His impertinence was the realisation of Elizabeth's abiding fears. From her ascension onward, she had tried to make sure that none of her courtiers would appropriate the influence, much less the sovereignty, that was rightly hers within the kingdom. In her own mind, she was England's sole repository of authority. But the effective reality was that the queen stood at a nexus of intense pressures and that often her success, even her survival, depended on her ability to prevent those pressures from forcing her into any precipitous course of action. Her response to the solicitations of her courtiers, frequently, was to delay, prevaricate and hedge. To keep any one of them from amassing too much clout, Elizabeth encouraged competition among them. When favourites did emerge (Leicester preeminent among them, and later Christopher Hatton), Elizabeth made sure that they were never entirely secure in her approbation, which could easily be withdrawn. Much of the so-called 'factionalism' of her court issued from her shrewd ability to divide her attentions among the many contenders for her favour.

Elizabeth's approach to international affairs, at least in the first half of her reign, was rather similar. In dealing with the great powers of her day, Spain and France, this queen worked to keep all parties – most of them men, of course – off balance and to avoid, as much as possible, direct confrontation. For the most part, these tactics suited the exigencies of a small, vulnerable kingdom that was geographically peripheral to Europe without being detached from its political struggles. When she came to the throne in 1558, England had been engaged in war with France and was allied with Spain. Her Catholic predecessor, Mary Tudor, was espoused to its king, Philip II. At his instigation, England had taken up arms, disastrously, against France and had lost its holdings in Calais. The then reigning French king, Henry II, regarded Elizabeth as the illegitimate offspring of an unsanctified union between her father, Henry VIII, and Anne Boleyn, and had thrown his support behind his daughter-in-law, Mary, Queen of Scots (who at that time was married to the heir to the French throne). The alliance with Spain, which was never popular with most of the English, seemed nonetheless to be prudent diplomatically and militarily prudent, and was in fact so, since it prevented Henry from prosecuting his case against Elizabeth too vigorously. But these foreign relations were to shift dramatically: by the 1570s, Spain was the great enemy and, it was believed, the instigator behind many attempts on the queen's life, while France was England's ostensible ally, bound to her by a treaty in 1572. It was now Spain's ruler, Philip II, who was most adamantly hostile to the 'bastard' queen and her 'heretic' kingdom. Spenser made his own view of Philip II clear enough. In the fifth book of *The Faerie Queene*, Mercilla (as we have seen, one of Spenser's many figures for Elizabeth) is opposed by a 'mighty man' who 'Seekes to subuert her Crowne and dignity, / And all his powre doth thereunto apply' (v, viii, 18). Not only does he intend 'by traytrous traines to spill/her person, and her sacred selfe to slay', alleges Spenser, he is a man of no (true) 'religion': he 'makes his God of his vngodly pelfe' (viii,19). And Philip was in fact both rich and a potent menace to the English queen. His domain was a globally dispersed but well-integrated imperial state, one whose territorial ambitions, religious allegiances and economic policies put England at risk. Since the Papal Bull of 1494, which divided the Americas between Spain and Portugal, Spain had been systematically exploiting its possessions in the 'New World'. The bullion that Philip's galleons brought back was much coveted by many in the English government; they had designs of their own on this wealth and resented Spain's monopoly. English seafarers had been mapping and exploring the Americas since the fifteenth century, and these efforts continued under Elizabeth. In the 1570s, for instance, Martin Frobisher made three trans-Atlantic voyages in the hope of finding a north-west passage that would open up a lucrative trade with the east. When, inevitably, that venture failed, the English planted colonies on the American continent itself. The first two were established in the 1580s by Walter Raleigh. Although these outposts fared poorly – the first was forced to return and the second mysteriously disappeared – they, like the rest of England's explorations, were impelled by a desire to seize a share of the New World resources that were going to Spain. Greed, curiosity and national pride were closely conjoined. When the most notorious of the English 'sea dogs', Francis Drake, set out on a voyage of discovery in 1577, his instructions were to look for fit places for English trading posts. But he ignored these orders and instead set about looting the Spanish possessions on the western coast of South America before sailing west, eventually to circle the globe. He arrived in England three years later. But even this accomplishment was influenced by rivalry with Spain: the safe passage back to England lay across the Pacific, not the Spanish patrolled Atlantic. For his daring (and the shipload of treasure he brought with him) Drake was knighted by Elizabeth, who, to placate Philip, pretended to have no knowledge of his depredations.

The event that sealed English antagonism to Spain occurred in 1588. Until that year, Elizabeth had been trying for an understanding with the king of Spain. But such a *détente* became impossible when Philip tried to send a fleet of about one hundred and thirty ships, the Armada, through the

English Channel. It was to link up with an army deployed in the Netherlands under the command of the Duke of Parma; he was in the Low Countries to suppress Dutch resistance to Spanish rule there. If events went as planned, the combined forces would proceed with an invasion of England. Events, however, did not go as planned. The Armada was intercepted by a much smaller but well-prepared English fleet. Over ten days and in several engagements, they inflicted serious damage on all of the Spanish vessels while incurring no losses to ships themselves. Of the galleons that escaped, many were wrecked on the coasts of Scotland and Ireland. The English cause was aided at various junctures by the weather, which was interpreted as a sign of providential intervention. The defeat signalled the emergence of England as a genuine sea power and demonstrated that England could hold its own against an empire. Though this was not a conflict to Elizabeth's liking, the ideological, commercial and military conflicts between Spain and England were simply too great to be finessed, and by 1588 the queen had been impelled, against her better judgement and her own consistent strategy, into open war.

France, on the other hand, was a more divided state, and Elizabeth adopted her strategies accordingly. In 1563, fighting broke out between French Catholics and Protestants – or Huguenots – and this was to persist, with sporadic eruptions of violence, for the next thirty years. During this time, the Huguenots often asked for help from their English co-religionists, but the help they got was sporadic as well. Elizabeth, characteristically, pursued a temporising strategy, sometimes committing troops, sometimes sending money, and most often trying to maintain more or less amicable relations with all factions. This arrangement was strained by one of the worst of the internecine convulsions. In August 1572, on St Bartholomew's Day, several thousands of Huguenots were struck down in a horrendous massacre, and many were driven from the kingdom. The event was to horrify the English religious imagination for decades. But although this carnage seriously compromised England's relations with France, it did not, as we will see, preclude an *entente* between them. Elizabeth's stance towards France was no more unequivocal then her stance towards Spain. She began her reign at war with the one, and eventually arrived at war with the other. In between, however, her aims were remarkably consistent, although not always obviously so. As one historian puts it: 'The twists and turns of Elizabeth's policy and [her] vacillations . . . reflected her efforts to hold the ring between France and Spain, to ensure that neither became too great a threat to English security.'[15] The queen meant to preclude an invasion of her domain by either of two superpowers and consequently had to deny them both an unencumbered access to the coastline opposite her island state. Her distrust of the French generally, and of anti-monarchical tendencies among the Huguenots specifically, was profound, but in the geo-political contest in which she had staked herself France was a useful counter to Spanish imperialism. Admittedly, the king of France was Catholic (and remained so until the assassination of Henry III in 1589), but a large and demonstrably Protestant community lived within his borders. Above all, France could be counted on to set itself against the hegemony of Spain, and that in itself gave Elizabeth the motive to solicit the support of whatever allies she might find within the kingdom. As one Englishman observed in 1593, 'if the king of Spayne be dead, wee are like enoughe to care little for France'.[16]

Elizabeth also tried, at least at first, to modulate religious tensions in her own kingdom. By all accounts, she herself was never much inclined toward any particular creed and was dismissive of clergymen generally. She was far less driven by religious animus than many of her countrymen, and certainly less than her fervently Protestant counsellors. As in foreign relations, however, she strove to find an accommodation between competing factions. When she ascended the throne, England was emerging from the Catholic rule of her half-sister, Mary Tudor. Her own prerogative as the daughter of Henry VIII depended on the legitimacy of the split with Rome, so that was not allowed to come into question. In 1559, the Act of Supremacy gave Elizabeth the title of 'Supreme governor of the realm in all spiritual or ecclesiastical things as well as civil'. In the same year, an Act of Uniformity mandated a prayer book and required an outward conformity to the established church. The queen's government was tolerant of the Catholics within the realm as long as they were discreet in the practice of their faith. The religious climate changed over the course of Elizabeth's reign, however, in two related ways. First, English Catholicism became progressively more objectionable to the government. As we have seen, Elizabeth was often under threat from Catholic powers abroad, and these were sometimes implicated in internal subversion as well. Mary, Queen of Scots, for instance, was able to garner a good deal of support from among the Catholic earls in the north of the realm. The Papal See also intensified its opposition to the Protestant queen. In 1570, Pius V excommunicated Elizabeth, thereby splitting the loyalties of English Catholics between their sovereign and their church. In response, Parliament passed acts that, over the following years, made it treason to deny Elizabeth's supremacy, to bring papal bulls into the country, or to convert to Catholicism. More than outward conformity was now demanded: church attendance and doctrinal adherence were required as well. In 1580, Jesuit and secular priests were introduced into England. Five years later, all were ordered out, but some remained in hiding to stiffen the resolve of the faithful. Convinced, and not implausibly, that it was under attack from a cabal of foreign and domestic enemies, the government was brutal in its suppressions. From 1581 on, 180 Catholics were executed for treason.

Second, even as Catholicism was being quelled, there were those, pejoratively named 'Puritans', who demanded a yet more radical cleansing, and in the English church itself. They objected to the survival of observances that to them smacked of 'popery': kneeling during communion, the giving of a ring during the marriage ceremony or the wearing of vestments, and this provoked the first sectarian controversy of Elizabeth's reign. In these early days, the queen was not an adamant foe to the 'Puritans', nor they to her. Most of them found that they could live in accord with the doctrines of the English church and could accept even the objectionable practices it imposed as 'things indifferent'. Indeed, it should be said that, well into Elizabeth's reign, most Englishmen were not altogether definite about their religious leanings. They were 'de-catholicized but un-protestantized',[17] not yet convinced adherents of a distinctly 'Anglican' church. By the middle years, however, religious allegiances had taken on greater definition. The established church was now more truly established, both institutionally and doctrinally, and its internal critics more vocal. Elizabeth herself began to see ongoing efforts by 'Puritans' to reform the church as assaults on her prerogative as 'Supreme Governor', and her demands for conformity intensified. In turn, a counter-reaction developed which was to divide the 'Puritan' movement into more and less extreme factions. A minority of 'Separatists', led by Robert Browne, sought to sever itself from the English Church. 'Presbyterians', coalescing around Thomas Cartwright, a Cambridge professor, wanted elected ministers and no bishops. Events came to a head in 1576 when the bishop of Canterbury, Edmund Grindal, long sympathetic to the 'Puritans', refused to obey the queen's directive to quash the 'prophesyings', exercises for the clergy which he saw as a worthy means of promoting zeal among them. For this, Grindal was disgraced and suspended. (In the May and June eclogues of *The Shepheardes Calender*, Spenser has his own say on Grindal's treatment. One 'Algrind' is upheld as an authority on the proper deportment of clergymen.) The aging bishop would have been forced out altogether if not for the reluctance of his eventual successor, John Whitgift, to replace him while he was alive. When Grindal died in 1583, Whitgift quickly set about to suppress the more extreme sects among his predecessor's allies. This was a turning point, and by the closing years of Elizabeth's reign, the 'Puritan' movement as a whole was in abeyance, not eliminated by any means, but consigned to the edges of the sanctioned church.

The confluence of these intersecting developments is aptly illustrated in the previously mentioned Alençon affair. At issue was Elizabeth's stated desire to marry a nobleman who was French and, moreover, Catholic. The queen had been urged to wed by Parliament in 1559, and she had contemplated matrimonial alliances with several leading European figures: Philip of Spain, the Archdukes Ferdinand and Charles, and the Duke of Anjou, who, in 1574, became Henry III of France. At the suggestion of his mother, Catherine de Medici, Elizabeth had also considered his younger brother, the Duke of Alençon (and, in 1576, himself the Duke of Anjou), but little had come of it. In 1578, these negotiations were reopened and the Privy Council took the matter under advisement. In his person, Alençon was not a prepossessing suitor. He was short and swarthy, and his face was pitted by small pox. Elizabeth would come to nickname him her 'frog'. But he was ardent and witty, and he had good reasons to desire the match. Although a nominal Catholic, Alençon had turned from politicking at home and had thrown in his lot with the mostly Protestant leaders of the Dutch revolt against the Spanish. Rebellion had broken out in the Low Countries in 1565, again in 1569, and then yet again in 1576.[18] Alençon was getting little support from his royal brother, and a marriage with Elizabeth would advance him on several fronts. Elizabeth had her own policy considerations. From the beginning of her reign, she had covertly supported the Dutch independence efforts. Her devoutly Protestant counsellors, particularly Leicester and Walsingham, wanted her to intervene more directly. But she preferred to prosecute an alliance with France in a united campaign against Spain, and a marriage to Alençon might make that possible.

The queen's age was probably also on her mind, as, indeed, it was on the minds of most of her subjects, including Spenser. Both the second and the third books of *The Faerie Queene* include long accounts of Elizabeth's dynastic heritage as a 'British' queen. In Book II, as mentioned, Arthur, the 'Briton Prince', comes upon 'An auncient booke, hight *Briton moniments*' (ix, 55) which narrates the fortunes of successive rulers in his 'Deare countrey', and leaves him 'rauisht with delight, to heare / The royall Ofspring of his natiue land' (x, 69). In Book III, it is the aptly named Britomart who shadows Spenser's 'Magnificent Empresse' and presages the harmony her reign will bring. She learns from the enchanter Merlin that when this 'royall virgin' rules,

> eternall vnion shall be made
> Betweene the nations different afore,
> And sacred Peace shall louingly perswade
> The warlike minds, to learne her goodly lore,
> And ciuile armes to exercise no more.   (III, iii, 49)

But both lineages are oddly truncated. The British chronicle of Arthur's 'auncient booke' is literally torn, breaking off abruptly: 'Without full point, or other Cesure right, / As if the rest some wicked hand did rend' (II, x, 68). Similarly, Merlin's prophecy to Britomart ends as the wizard is 'ouercomen', by some 'ghastly spectacle dismayd, / That secretly he saw, yet note discoure' (III, iii, 50). Of both passages it can be said that 'Britain may well become united as the prophetic visions suggest, or all may turn out to be a fantastic chimera.'[19] And if that happens, Spenser seems to be intimating, it will be because the reigning 'British' ruler, the glorious *terminus* to this distinguished line, has yet to produce an heir. As Spenser allowed himself to imply, Elizabeth's sanctifying virginity precluded this outcome, as well as her years. The queen was in her mid-forties when Alençon made his offer. Alençon was some twenty years her junior. But Elizabeth believed, or allowed herself to be convinced, that she was 'a person of . . . the largest and goodliest stature of well-shaped women, with all limbs set and proportioned in the best sort, and one whom, in the sight of all men, nature cannot amend her shape in any part to make her more likely to conceive and bear children without peril'.[20] And, as one historian says, '[o]nce she passed the child-bearing age the diplomatic value of a match vanished, and, equally important, those emotional gratifications which so delighted the Queen.'[21] In this courtship with Alençon, Elizabeth's political designs and her more personal ambitions were, as usual, inextricable. As it turned out, she was to be disappointed in both.

Alençon began his wooing with an intermediary, Jean de Simier, 'a most choice courtier, exquisitely skilled in love-toys, pleasant conceits, and court-dalliances'.[22] He quickly became a favourite and he also received a nickname – '*le petit singe*', the queen's ape. Lavish entertainments were laid on and gifts exchanged. Elizabeth gave every appearance of pursuing a union she meant to consummate. But her subjects, most of them, were not at all enthusiastic. Especially troublesome was the faith and nationality of the prospective groom. Although he was now an ally of the Huguenots, he remained a Catholic and a scion of a long-time foe. The memory of the St Bartholomew's Day massacre was fresh, and his mother was suspected of fomenting it. The Privy Council spent much time debating the match, and was divided: Burghley and Sussex were in favour, but Leicester and Walsingham were opposed, fearing that such a marriage would bring religious strife and nationalist enmity. Several preachers also inveighed against the union, even in the queen's presence, and much to her displeasure. Elizabeth heard as well from Sir Philip Sidney, who sent her a letter detailing his objections, among them that she might lose the love of her people (her anger at thus being addressed led Sidney to avoid the court for a year). In

August 1579, the suitor himself slipped into England for a 'secret' assignation, but after he had departed in October of that year, the affair exploded into public controversy with the publication of a tract entitled *The Discovery of a Gaping Gulf Whereinto England Is Like To Be Swallowed by Another French Marriage; if the Lord Forbid Not the Bans by Letting Her Majestie See the Sin and Punishment Thereof*. In it, a country gentleman of a strictly Protestant temperament, John Stubbs, asserted that the proposed marriage was perverse, politically futile, and detrimental to true religion in England. 'It is natural to all men to abhor foreign rule as a burden of Egypt', he said, and Alençon himself was 'by birth a Frenchman, by profession a Papist, an atheist by conversation, an instrument in France of uncleanness . . . a sorcerer by common voice and fame'.[23] Elizabeth was incensed. At her orders, Stubbs and his publisher were tried and convicted. Each lost his right hand and was imprisoned. But it was becoming clear to Elizabeth that she was not to marry Alençon. The great mass of her people was opposed to the match, and when she tried to coerce her Privy Council into endorsing it, they refused. Alençon continued to court the queen. She reciprocated to a degree – even at one point promising to marry him – and provided him with intermittent military aid. But the affair was effectively over. At the request of the rebels, Alençon returned to the Netherlands, though without much success in the field, and eventually to France, where he died in 1584. The failure of the union with Alençon, and the ill success of Elizabeth's policy of indirect confrontation with Spain, would lead ultimately to the events of 1588. The Armada sailed in the wake of a geo-political love affair gone badly wrong.

Intellectual influences

As we have seen, Spenser condemned the Alençon marriage in 'Mother Hubberds Tale'. He made his views known in another text as well. He was closely associated at this time with the household of the Earl of Leicester, and his agreement with his patron's objections to the match has usually been taken for granted. Leicester himself was in bad odour in 1579. While arguing vigorously against the marriage with Alençon, he had himself married a woman Elizabeth detested, Lettice Knollys, Countess of Essex. (That Elizabeth learned of the clandestine wedding from her 'ape', Simier, made this betrayal all the worse.) Spenser entered the debate indirectly, but, to some readers, quite transparently in his *Shepheardes Calender* (1579). Significantly, he chose as his printer Hugh Singleton, who had just issued Stubbs' *Gaping Gulf* and who had narrowly escaped that author's horrific punishment himself. In the February and November eclogues of the

Calender, Spenser appears to allegorise the still simmering controversy in bucolic terms; shepherds' debates shadow the issues of the day. In the first, by means of the fable of the Oak and the Briar, he may represent a quarrel between Leicester and a bombastic proponent of the marriage, the Earl of Oxford. In the second, he may portray Elizabeth as Dido, and mourn her as 'dead', at least to the coterie centred around his patron. Or he may not. Both interpretations have been advanced,[24] but the eclogues have so far resisted final explanation and no critical consensus has emerged. While we can be sure that Spenser opposed his queen's marriage to a reprobate foreigner, we cannot be sure just how his censure was meant to be read. Quite likely, we are not meant to.

This raises again the problem of Spenser's indeterminate, or perhaps overdetermined relation to the 'contexts' of his writing. As we will see in this section, assigning specific intellectual influences to Spenser can be as hazardous as inferring the exact political import of his texts. Certainly, attempts have been made to show that Spenser is indebted to this or that early modern thinker, that his ideas are variations on their particular themes. But, as Ciaran Brady notes, these attempts have typically 'proved to be . . . contradictory and inconclusive'. At most, they may be said to demonstrate that 'Spenser could be counted among the better-read men of his day'.[25] This poet was thoroughly versed in those works, foreign and domestic, that commanded the attention of the late sixteenth-century English *cognoscenti*. Still, to acknowledge this is not yet to show that some work on his variegated reading list must be counted as a specific influence. In this period, it is often hard to ascribe the 'authorship' of some political doctrine, argument, or phrase to any one pundit. Not only could Spenser have been influenced by notions that he came upon in any number of treatises, but, frequently, their authors had read and cited each other. In his treatise *A View of the Present State of Ireland* (c.1596), for example, Spenser says that English common law ought not to be imposed on the Gaels because 'laws ought to be fashioned unto the manners and condition of the people to whom they are meant, and not to be imposed upon them according to the simple rule of right, for then . . . instead of good they may work ill, and pervert justice to extreme injustice'.[26] The precedent he advances is classical: Lycurgus did not do so to the Lacedea-monians. Yet, as Andrew Hadfield notes, Spenser could have encountered this admonition in texts of 'the French absolutist, Jean Bodin, and the Florentine republican, Niccolo Machiavelli, as well as in native English sources such as Thomas Starkey's *Dialogue between Pole and Lupset* and Sir Thomas Smith's *De Republica Anglorum*'.[27] In what remains of this essay, we will look briefly at the thought of Machiavelli and Bodin, the two figures on this list who are, perhaps, most likely to have influenced Spenser.

Spenser knew of Machiavelli's writings; that we know. Gabriel Harvey, the friend and confidant of Spenser's university days (and possibly the 'E. K.' of *The Shepheardes Calendar*) claimed that Machiavelli's works lay open on the table of every scholar in Cambridge, their *alma mater*. 'I warrant you', he wrote,

> sum good fellowes amongst us begin nowe to be pretely well acquainted with a certayne parlous book callid, as I remember me, Il Principe di Nicolo Machiavelli, and I can peradventire name you an crewe or tooe that ar as cuninge in his Discorsi sopra la prima Deca di Livio, in his Historia Fiorentina, and in his Dialogues della Arte della Guerra tooe, as University men were wont to be in their parva Logicalia and Magna Moralia and Physicalia of both sortes.[28]

Harvey alluded to the Italian in a letter to Spenser, while Spenser himself quoted Machiavelli with apparent approval in the *View*. Discussing the inconveniences that arise when the Lord Deputy in Ireland must wait upon the dictates of the Privy Council in England, Spenser recalls:

> this I remember is worthily observed by Machiavel in his discourses upon Livy, where he commendeth the manner of the Romans' government, in giving absolute power to all their consuls and governors, which, if they abused, they should afterwards dearly answer, and the contrary thereof he reprehendeth in the states of Venice of Florence and many other principalities of Italy, who use to limit their chief officers so straitly as that thereby oftentimes they have lost such happy occasions as they could never come unto again the like.[29]

On the strength of such connections, some scholars have discovered Spenser to be an overt Machiavellian and to have incorporated his teachings, down to their very language, into his texts. Earlier in this century, for instance, Edwin Greenlaw professed to find parallels between the *View* and *The Prince*: '[the first] follows [the second] very closely'.[30] Phrases such as '*medicine forti*' are the same, historical examples similar, arguments seem to march in lock step, and so on. But this almost certainly misstates the relation between these Renaissance writers. Machiavelli's thought permeated the political theory of this period, so much so that 'nearly all political discussions had to take account of his work and orient themselves in relation to it, whether by absorbing him, condemning him, or defending him, or by some more complex placement in relation to him',[31] and so it would be odd indeed if Spenser were altogether untouched by Machiavelli, however mediated that touch might be. Spenser's early exposure to the Italian probably came by way of Harvey's tutelage. Later, in Ireland,

Spenser would fall in with several men whose writings drew extensively on Machiavelli, including two of his neighbours on the Munster plantation: Walter Raleigh, in his *Maxims of State* and *The History of the World*, and Richard Beacon, in his *Solon his Follie* (1594). In the *View*, Spenser deploys this political theorist as only one among many authorities, but it is possible that by doing so he 'signals an awareness of, if not involvement in, the development of a series of alternative political ideas in Irish intellectual society'.[32] As Barnaby Rich once put it, 'thos wordes that in *Englande* would be brought wythin the compasse of treason, they are accounted wyth us in *Ireland* for ordynary table taulke'.[33] This was Spenser's milieu, and, clearly, he took notice of the more radical of Machiavelli's doctrines that circulated there. He may even be detected to have advocated certain of them in his sometimes oblique fashion.

Still it seems closer to the mark to argue, as Richard McCabe has, that '[a]lthough there are many points of contact between Machiavelli and Spenser, their final outlooks are radically different'.[34] In the most obvious way, Spenser is not a Machiavellian. During the sixteenth century, Machiavelli was excoriated for his alleged offences against Christian morality, and with some justification. In *The Prince*, he had notoriously urged that the ruler who wished to govern effectively should learn to 'be a great pretender and dissembler', and to lie, since 'men are so simple and so obedient to present necessities that he who deceives will always find someone who will let himself be deceived'. He must also be capable of cruelty and exemplary punishment, if these are 'well used'. This was not to say that Machiavelli's ideal prince would present himself as an unmitigated tyrant. On the contrary, he might instead elect to appear to be 'merciful, faithful, humane, honest, and religious', and might even adopt these qualities – for a time. But, in truth, this magnate was indifferent to the demands of moral consistency, having learned instead to direct himself according to the demands of Fortuna. As long as she acquiesced, he might display the virtues that elicited the admiration of his subjects. But 'when forced by necessity', it was crucial to 'know how to enter into evil'. 'Hence . . . a prince, if he wants to maintain himself . . . [must] learn to be able not to be good, and to use this and not use it according to necessity.'[35] It was this apparent amoralism that shocked Machiavelli's contemporaries, bringing forth a 'howl of execration that has never finally died away'.[36] Machiavelli's doctrines are nuanced, and their influence was not limited to the political pragmatism that can be read into *The Prince* (his *Discourses*, for instance, were mined for their contributions to a developing tradition of republicanism[37]). But this calculated amorality is what most of Spenser's contemporaries would have recognised as 'Machiavellian'. Spenser's ambitions, though, are larger. As McCabe says, he wants not only to give his prince advice on how to govern, but also to demonstrate that his admonitions are consonant with the purposes of God as well as the principles of 'vertuous and gentle discipline'.[38] This, very broadly considered, is the project of Spenser's *magnum opus*, the six (and more) books of *The Faerie Queene*. And, in the *View* he reaches for a divine mandate for the reforms he offers. One of the marks of Ireland's degradation is that its people 'have not . . . once been lightened with the morning star of truth, but lie weltering in such spiritual darkness, hard by hell mouth, even ready to fall in, if God haply help not'.

Even this, however, needs to be qualified. Spenser is noticeably reluctant to put much emphasis on his religious proposals. 'Little have I to say of religion . . . myself hav[ing] not been much conversant in that calling.'[39] And the treatise itself begins with the suggestion that explanations that look to the 'appointment of God' as the cause of Ireland's troubles should be set aside, since this is a 'vain conceit of simple men'. Instead, the 'unsoundness of . . . counsels and plots' should be scrutinised.[40] Spenser may gesture towards a providential scheme, but in this treatise, he, like Machiavelli, is mostly silent about how it would impinge on his *Realpolitik*. Moreover, like Machiavelli, Spenser sometimes claims that amid the contingencies of early modern politics it is finally the prince's will that ensures stability. 'Even by the sword', answers one of the dialogue's interlocutors when asked how the reformation of Ireland is to begin, 'for all those evils must first be cut away with a strong hand before any good can be planted'.[41] It may well be, then, that Spenser's 'Machiavellianism' is to be located not so much in direct quotations or overt influence, but in a tendency of thought, especially prominent in his later work, to offer princely *virtus* as the solution to otherwise intractable political problems.[42] It was in unhappy Ireland, perhaps, that Spenser found himself moving, late in his life, towards a standpoint that had been reached many years before him by Machiavelli in his *Prince*.

We can also be certain that Spenser knew of the thought of Jean Bodin. A man of affairs as well as a scholar, this prolific and controversial French theorist had a considerable following in England. Harvey claimed that alongside the copies of Machiavelli's works that could be found on every scholar's table at Cambridge, there lay Bodin's *Six Books of a Commonweal* (1576). He had met Bodin there himself.[43] John Dee alleged that he too 'made acquayntance with Joannes Bodinus, in the Chambre of Presence at Westminster.'[44] Both claims are plausible. Bodin was respected in court circles and visited England at least once, possibly in 1579 and then quite certainly in 1581. Both times he would have accompanied Alençon, to whom he had been appointed *maître des requêtes et conseiller*. As his master wooed Elizabeth I, Bodin and the queen spoke often; she 'enjoyed his conversation concerning forms of government and his theory of climate'.[45] We find references to Bodin throughout the writings of Spenser's contemporaries, including Raphael Holinshed and Philip Sidney, although, as it happens, there are none in Spenser's own works. One reason for this might be that Bodin's cordial relation with the English court soured at the close of the Alençon affair. Quite soon thereafter, it may not have been politic for Spenser to invoke Bodin's name. By 1585 the Frenchman was predicting in his correspondence that Elizabeth would be deposed. He appears to have had an insider's knowledge of plots on her life and to have aligned himself tacitly with the conspirators. Not surprisingly, the English authorities wanted Bodin, by now a professed partisan of Mary, Queen of Scots, arrested.

What might surprise us is Bodin's willingness to advocate violence against a reigning prince, since he is best known today as a 'virtually unyielding defender' of royal absolutism.[46] Bodin's pronouncements, though, have multiple emphases, integrally related to one another within the larger unfolding of his thought. In an earlier work, *Method for the Easy Comprehension of History* (1566), Bodin advanced the claims of medieval constitutionalism and was concerned to set limits to the authority of the French monarch. He asserted, for instance, that the king was obliged to abide by his coronation oath, and that the Parliament of Paris could of itself veto legislation the king proposed. But, by the time he came to publish the *Six Books* in 1576, Bodin had witnessed the St Bartholomew's Day Massacre, and, indeed, he had almost been killed in that bloodbath himself. The ongoing Huguenot revolt against the Catholic monarchy of France appalled him. Especially offensive to him was the declaration, heard from some radical Calvinists, that a subject might properly resist a king, even to the extent of committing regicide. In the preface to a later edition of the *Six Books*, he denounces those who 'rebel against their natural princes, opening the door to licentious anarchy, which is worse than the harshest tyranny in the world'.[47] Hoping to counter this dangerous presumption, he set himself the task of erecting a principle of political legitimacy so sacrosanct that any resistance to it must fail of its own patent incoherence and viciousness. '[P]ersons who are sovereign', he said, 'must not be subject in any way to the commands of someone else and must be able to give the law to subjects, and to suppress or repeal disadvantageous laws and replace them with others – which cannot be done by someone who is subject to the laws or to persons having power of command over him.'[48] If someone else has the power to limit and compel you, you are not 'sovereign' by definition. Moreover, says

Bodin, such sovereignty cannot be 'shared by a prince, the nobles, and the people at the same time', in a co-mingling of authority that has never actually been achieved and would in any case be 'impossible and contradictory'.[49] And he was quite clear that 'France . . . is a pure monarchy unmixed with democratic power and still less with aristocracy'.[50]

Bodin's influence on Spenser seems to have been more straightforward than Machiavelli's, although it is mostly homologies between their arguments that can be noted. For instance, 'Spenser's advocation of a ruthless policy in Ireland bears many resemblances to . . . Bodin's proposals for the establishment of an orderly constitution in France.'[51] The poet's plans for the pacification of his adopted kingdom may have been modelled on the theorist's scheme to suppress civil unrest on the Continent. Spenser may also have schooled himself in Bodin's teachings on 'equity', justice tempered with mercy by an intervening magistrate. The dilemmas of this legal doctrine are canvassed in Book v of *The Faerie Queene*, the 'Book of Justice'. But the aspect of Bodin's work that may have especially caught Spenser's attention was its own internal discrepancies. While Bodin was, at least according to his own insistence, entirely committed in his support for monarchical absolutism, he did not posit a monarchy without any restraints on it at all. He set his face against armed resistance to kings, arguing that anyone who even thought of violating his king was worthy of execution. But he also allowed that a *tyrannical* king who was a usurper could be legitimately killed, and even that he could be forcibly deposed by a foreign prince. That he was willing to countenance the death of a prince, Elizabeth I, was perhaps then not so surprising. Bodin was committed to a particularly rigorous form of royal absolutism and stated it, as Skinner says, with 'an epoch-making lack of equivocation',[52] but Elizabeth was a Protestant ruler, and he had moreover declared in the *Six Books* that 'the rule and government of women is directly against the law of nature'.[53] And his 'lack of equivocation', it could be argued, was in part an attempt to clarify out of existence a deeper contradiction between the earlier and later versions of his own thought. The *Six Books*, the work of Bodin's that was perused so widely at Cambridge, was a piece of self-revision. It may have asserted the claims of the absolute sovereign with analytic clarity, but it contained within itself the remnants of counter-arguments Bodin himself had once professed and traces of the resistance theory that it was directed against. It was this ambivalence within Bodin's *oeuvre*, perhaps, that Spenser responded to. By taking up Bodin, Spenser was making use of a thinker who had both dallied with his queen and urged her assassination, an interesting tension given his own equivocal relation with her.

How, asks Ciaran Brady, are we to grasp the Spenserian 'principle of selection' that is at work as this 'eclectic' poet selects from among the doctrines available to him? If he 'chose to be guided by one master and to discount another', what do his choices reveal of the views of the man himself?[54] This short overview of his borrowings from these two writers suggests that this is not a question that can or needs to be answered. In his use of Machiavelli and Bodin, Spenser was what is now sometimes called a *bricoleur*, taking what he needed to fashion a sometimes doubtful 'Allegory, or darke conceit',[55] from authors who were themselves freely taking from each other. Skinner points out, for example, that in his *Six Books* Bodin quotes and rephrases Machiavelli's *Discourses* extensively, especially his 'emphasis on the inexorable tendency of all kingdoms and republics to fall into corruption and collapse'.[56] If influence is to be attributed, then probably it is best to consider Spenser's thought as an often contradictory amalgam of intellectual elements. Recently, for example, Andrew Hadfield has suggested that in *A View* Spenser is 'caught between the politics of Bodin and the republican Machiavelli of *The Discourses* in a double movement simultaneously centripetal and centrifugal'.[57] Operating in such a flux, Spenser does not – and perhaps cannot – hold rigorously to the pronouncements of either of these two Continental savants; he adopts their dictates somewhat loosely and provisionally. This allows him to take from them the emphases that he needs to make his argument of the moment. The influences of Machiavelli and Bodin on Spenser, then, can be understood as opposing pulls exerted by systematic thinkers upon a wide-ranging, politically engaged, but often non-systematic literary mind. That the 'systems' of Machiavelli and Bodin were themselves to shift over the years – the former from the political pragmatism of *The Prince* to the republicanism of *The Discourses*, the latter, in an opposite movement, from constitutionalism to absolutism – only increased the countervailing tensions of their mutual tug upon the English poet.

And if commonality must be found among these thinkers, then perhaps it should be sought not only in the intellectual *topoi* they may or may not share, but also to the more literal 'places' that engendered their various claims, and especially in the 'corruption and collapse' of these locales. Bodin's absolutism was powerfully driven by his revulsion at civil strife, but it was not just in France that he could have found it. Machiavelli's discourses were catalysed by the city-state rivalries of his native Italy, but the lessons he drew from those rivalries would provoke (and appall) the politically minded across Europe for the rest of the century – not least Edmund Spenser, who, living on the conflict-torn Irish frontier, knew very well what turbulence attended the breakdown of constituted authority. If these early modern writers share a concern with internecine violence and its political remedies, it may be because of the diversely troubled circumstances under which each wrote, the turmoil, that is, of their respective 'contexts'.

NOTES

1 James I established a 'union of crowns' among the 'British' kingdoms shortly after he ascended the English throne in 1603; legal consolidation had to wait until the establishment of the 'United Kingdom of Great Britain and Ireland' in 1801.
2 All citations are from Variorum.
3 Wallace T. MacCaffrey, *Queen Elizabeth and the Making of Policy, 1572–1588* (Princeton: Princeton University Press, 1981), p. 157.
4 Ibid., p. 158.
5 Ibid., p. 160.
6 Ibid., p. 157.
7 *Imagined Communities: Reflections on the Origins and Spread of Nationalism* (London: Verso, 1991), p. 19.
8 Homi K. Bhabha, 'Introduction: narrating the nation', in Homi K. Bhabha, ed., *Nation and Narration* (London: Routledge, 1990), p. 3.
9 Jonathan Goldberg, *James I and the Politics of Literature: Jonson, Shakespeare, Donne, and Their Contemporaries* (Baltimore: Johns Hopkins University Press, 1983), p. 1.
10 John Guy, 'Introduction: The 1590s: The second reign of Elizabeth I?', in John Guy, ed., *The Reign of Elizabeth I: Court and Culture in the Last Decade* (Cambridge: Cambridge University Press, 1995), p. 4.
11 Goldberg, *James I and the Politics of Literature*, p. 2.
12 Guy, 'Introduction', in *The Reign of Elizabeth I*, p. 3.
13 Ibid., p. 13.
14 Alan G. R. Smith, *The Emergence of a Nation State: The Commonwealth of England 1529–1660*, (2nd edn, London: Longman, 1997), p. 125.
15 Ibid., p. 158.
16 Paul E. J. Hammer, 'Patronage at Court, Faction and the Earl of Essex', in Guy, ed., *The Reign of Elizabeth I*, p. 74.
17 Christopher Haigh, *English Reformations: Religion, Politics, and Society under the Tudors* (Oxford: Clarendon Press, 1993), p. 290.
18 See Geoffrey Parker, *The Dutch Revolt* (New York: Penguin Books, 1979).
19 Andrew Hadfield, 'From English to British Literature: John Lyly's *Euphues* and Edmund Spenser's *The Faerie Queene*', in Brendan Bradshaw and Peter Roberts, eds., *British Consciousness and Identity: The Making of Britain, 1533–1707* (Cambridge: Cambridge University Press, 1998), pp. 140–58, at p. 155.
20 J. E. Neale, *Queen Elizabeth I* (1938; London: Jonathan Cape, 1943), p. 240.
21 MacCaffrey, *Queen Elizabeth*, p. 254.
22 Neale, *Queen Elizabeth* I, p. 239.
23 MacCaffrey, *Queen Elizabeth*, pp. 258, 261.
24 Notably in Paul E. Lane, *Spenser's Shepheardes Calender: A Study in Elizabethan Allegory* (Notre Dame: University of Notre Dame Press, 1961).
25 'Spenser's Irish Crisis: Humanism and Experience in the 1590s', *P&P* 111 (1986), 17–49, p. 20.

26 *View*, p. 11.

27 'Spenser, Ireland, and Sixteenth-Century Political Theory', *MLR* 89 (1994), 9–10.

28 *The Letter Book of Gabriel Harvey, 1573–80*, ed. E. J. L. Scott (London: Camden Society, 1884), pp. 79–80.

29 *View*, p. 169.

30 Edwin A. Greenlaw, 'The Influence of Machiavelli on Spenser', *MP* 7 (1909), 187–202, p. 194. See also his 'Spenser and British Imperialism', *MP* 9 (1912), 347–70.

31 Peter S. Donaldson, *Machiavelli and Mystery of State* (Cambridge: Cambridge University Press, 1988), p. xi. Amongst a wealth of other work on Machiavelli, see also J. G. A. Pocock's *The Machiavellian Moment: Florentine Political Thought and the Atlantic Republican Tradition* (Princeton: Princeton University Press, 1975).

32 Andrew Hadfield, *Edmund Spenser's Irish Experience: Wilde Fruit and Salvage Soyl* (Oxford: Clarendon Press, 1997), p. 78.

33 E. M. Hinton, 'Rych's Anatomy of Ireland with an account of the author', *PMLA* 55 (1940), 73–101, p. 91.

34 'The Fate of Irena: Spenser and Political Violence', in Patricia Coughlan, ed., *Spenser and Ireland: An Interdisciplinary Perspective* (Cork: Cork University Press, 1989), pp. 109–25, at p. 109.

35 Niccolò Machiavelli, *The Prince*, trans. Harvey C. Mansfield, Jr. (Chicago: University of Chicago Press, 1985), pp. 37, 61, 70.

36 Quentin Skinner, *Machiavelli* (New York: Hill and Wang, 1981), p. 38.

37 On this, see Markku Peltonen, *Classical Humanism and Republicanism in English Political Thought 1570–1640* (Cambridge: Cambridge University Press, 1995). For Spenser's uses of this tradition, see Andrew Hadfield, 'Was Spenser a Republican?', *English* 47 (1998), 169–182.

38 'The fate of Irena', pp. 109–110. The phrase is taken from 'A Letter of the Authors', which prefaces the first book of *The Faerie Queene*.

39 *View*, p. 84.

40 Ibid., p. 1.

41 Ibid., p. 95. Irenius goes on to elaborate: 'by the sword which I named I do not mean the cutting off of all that nation with the sword . . . but . . . I mean the royal power of the prince'.

42 It should be stressed that this tendency co-existed with others that militated against it. As Hadfield points out, 'Spenser's earlier work would seem to imply that he was no friend of absolutist politics within his native land' (Hadfield, *Spenser's Irish Experience*, pp. 67–8).

43 See Leonard F. Dean, 'Bodin's *Methodus* in England before 1625', *SP* 39 (1942), 160–6, p. 161.

44 *The Private Diary of Dr. John Dee*, ed. J. O. Halliwell (London: Camden Society Publications, 1842), p. 10.

45 Marion L. D. Kuntz, 'Introduction' in Jean Bodin, *Colloquium of the Seven about Secrets of the Sublime* (Princeton: Princeton University Press, 1975), p. xxiii.

46 Quentin Skinner, *The Foundations of Modern Political Thought*, 2 vols. (Cambridge: Cambridge University Press, 1978), II, p. 284. See II, pp. 284–310 for a

useful synthesis of Bodin's arguments. See also Julian H. Franklin, *Jean Bodin and the Rise of Absolutist Theory* (Cambridge: Cambridge University Press, 1973).

47 Skinner, *Foundations*, II, p. 285.
48 Jean Bodin, *On Sovereignty: Four Chapters from The Six Books of the Commonwealth*, ed. and trans. Julian H. Franklin (Cambridge: Cambridge University Press, 1992), p. 11.
49 Ibid., p. 92.
50 Ibid., p. 102.
51 Hadfield, 'Spenser, Ireland, and Sixteenth-Century Political Theory', p. 10.
52 Skinner, *Foundations*, II, p. 289.
53 Ibid., p. 293.
54 Brady, 'Spenser's Irish Crisis', p. 20.
55 This phrase too is taken from 'A Letter of the Authors'.
56 Skinner, *Foundations*, II, p. 284.
57 Hadfield, *Spenser's Irish Experience*, p. 77.

FURTHER READING

John Guy, ed., *The Reign of Elizabeth I: Court and Culture in the Last Decade* (Cambridge: Cambridge University Press, 1995).

Andrew Hadfield, *Edmund Spenser's Irish Experience: Wilde Fruit and Salvage Soyl* (Oxford: Clarendon Press, 1997).

Wallace T. MacCaffrey, *Queen Elizabeth and the Making of Policy, 1572–1588* (Princeton: Princeton University Press, 1981).

J. G. A. Pocock, *The Machiavellian Moment: Florentine Political Thought and the Atlantic Republican Tradition* (Princeton: Princeton University Press, 1975).

Quentin Skinner, *The Foundations of Modern Political Thought*, 2 vols. (Cambridge: Cambridge University Press, 1978).

3

RICHARD A. McCABE

Ireland: policy, poetics and parody

During the course of their discussion of Irish customs in *A View of the Present State of Ireland*, Irenius informs Eudoxus that

> the Gaules used to drinke theire enemyes blodd and to painte themselues therewith So allsoe they write that the owlde Irishe weare wonte And so have I sene some of the Irishe doe but not theire enemyes but friendes blodd as namelye at the execucion of A notable Traitour at Limericke Called murrogh Obrien I sawe an olde woman which was his foster mother take up his heade whilste he was quartered and sucked up all the blodd runninge theareout Sayinge that the earthe was not worthie to drinke it and thearewith allso steped her face, and breste and torne heare Cryinge and shrikinge out moste terrible (112).[1]

As the execution of Murrogh O'Brien occurred in 1577 the passage has long been used as evidence for Spenser's presence in Ireland some three years before his officially documented arrival in 1580 as secretary to Lord Arthur Grey, the newly appointed Lord Deputy.[2] But this is to make unwarranted assumptions about the relationship between Irenius and Spenser. *A View* takes the form of a political dialogue, a recognised Renaissance genre, not a personal memoir, and speculations intended to elucidate Spenser's biography may tend to obscure the function of his rhetoric. In the present instance Irenius deploys one of the most potent weapons of colonial polemic, that of alleged 'eye-witness' testimony, a topos used from Herodotus onwards to lend credence to the description of alien civilisations.[3] Generally speaking, the more bizarre or 'barbaric' the perceived divergence from the reader's conception of 'civility', the more effective is the author's appeal to personal experience. As François Hartog observes, 'the eye writes; at least, so the narrative would have us believe'.[4] In the case of Ireland the practice of appealing to 'eye-witness' testimony was established as a rhetorical paradigm in the twelfth century by Giraldus Cambrensis, perhaps the most influential authority to allege that the Irish drank blood.[5] It is entirely consistent with Irenius' characterisation as someone intimately acquainted with the country's customs that he should appeal to personal experience ('so have I sene . . . I sawe') in order to validate what he elsewhere refers to as 'myne owne readinge' (84). A fictitious observer accordingly bears 'factual' witness to the discourse of otherness.

Central to Spenser's colonial argument is the assertion that the Irish, 'thoughe sithens intermingled with manye other nacions repayringe and joyninge unto them' (107), are primarily descended from the Scythians, the blood-drinking barbarians represented in Herodotus' *History* as the antithesis of Greek civilisation.[6] Hence Irenius' earlier, and strategically proleptic, assertion that 'the Scythyans used when they would binde anie solempe vowe or Combinacion to drinke a bowle of blodd togeather vowinge theareby to spende theire laste blodd in that quarrell' (108). The coincidence of customs is seen to argue an identity of race: 'I reasonablie Conclude', Irenius asserts, 'that the Irishe are discended from the *Scythyans* for that they use even to this daie some of the same ceremonies which the *Scythyans* auncientlye used' (107). The implication is plain: for the Irish, as for their Scythian ancestors, the social virtues of friendship and alliance, common to all peoples, are tinged with murderous intent. Vows taken in blood issue in blood. 'How often in the very hour of this alliance has blood been so treacherously and shamefully shed by treacherous blood relations', asserted Giraldus Cambrensis, 'woe to brothers amongst a barbarous people'.[7] For Spenser, such arguments form part of a wider strategy of presenting Celtic society as a sort of criminal confraternity and the Brehon Law, the traditional Celtic code, as an institutionalised perversion of natural justice: 'dwellinge as they doe whole nacions and septes of the Irishe togeather without any Inglishman amongest them they maye doe what they liste and Compounde or alltogeather Conceale amongest themselves theire owne Crimes of which no notice can be had by them which woulde and mighte amende the same by the rule of the lawes of Englande' (48).[8] Eyewitness testimony draws its voyeuristic power from claiming to penetrate such enclosed cabals in order to disclose what no 'Englishman' is supposed to see.

It fell to Celtic commentators such as Geoffrey Keating to rebut the suggestion that Irish society was merely a barbaric inversion of the 'civil' norm by insisting that the colonial frame of reference was entirely inappropriate. From time immemorial, he asserts, 'Ireland was a kingdom apart by herself, like a little world' and its laws, language and culture evolved in coherent unison.[9] For Spenser, however, the need to 'fashion' a 'salvage' was no less pressing than the need to fashion a 'gentleman'. Indeed, to the extent that he increasingly found himself writing a colonial romance rather than a national epic, the one necessitated the other. As both poet and politician, he needed a 'salvage' island – such as might be 'salvaged' by reformers like himself – and duly created one in the official letters written on behalf of Lord Grey, in the pseudo-anthropological speculations of *A View of the Present State of Ireland*, and in the wild, hostile landscape of *The Faerie Queene* which suggests an almost symbiotic relationship between outlaws and outlands, between geographical and social marginality.[10] From the satyrs of book I to the savages of book VI, the work is populated by wild, ill-nurtured sub-races, 'lawlesse people . . . That never used to live by plough nor spade, / But fed on spoile and booty' (VI, x, 39). Outposts of civility, such as the Castle of Alma, are besieged by marauding hordes apparently spawned by the soil itself, 'as when a swarme of Gnats at eventide / Out of the fennes of Allan do arise' (II, ix, 16). In Ireland, both the civil English body and the civil English body politic are seen to be in constant peril of subversion.

The problem, however, was that the racial complexity of the Irish situation resisted reduction to a clear-cut dichotomy between 'self' and 'other'. Many of the descendants of Ireland's first Norman colonisers, later to be known as the 'Old English', had assimilated to Celtic society to such an extent that 'New English' colonists such as Edmund Spenser could scarcely distinguish them from the descendants of indigenous Celtic stock.[11] Lord Grey arrived in Ireland at the height of the Desmond rebellion, a conflict prosecuted by one of the most prestigious of Old English families.[12] Surveying the state of the country just two years previously, Lord Chancellor Gerrard divided the antagonists of the Elizabethan administration into two parties, 'Irishe enymies' and 'Englishe rebells'. The latter, he states, 'are people of our owne nacion' but amongst them are those 'suche as refuzinge Englishe nature growe Irishe in soche sorte as . . . [they are] not be discerned from the Irishe . . . They marrye and foster with the Irishe, and . . . imbrace rather Irishe braghan lawes [Brehon laws] then sweete governement by justice.'[13] They had grown, in Spenser's terms, 'as Irishe as Ohanlans breeche' (117). Owing to this ongoing process of cultural assimilation the polarised categories of 'self' and 'other' (gentleman and savage) threaten to converge. For this very reason the English-speaking denizens of the Pale were at pains to dissociate themselves from their 'degenerate' neighbours. Richard Stanihurst reports that many continental Europeans were 'exceedingly amazed when they converse with someone from Ireland who professes to knowing no Irish'.[14] Regarding Ireland as his 'native' land, Stanihurst coined the term 'Anglo-Hiberni' in an attempt to assert a cultural identity for the English-speaking denizens of the Pale distinct from both the native Irish (the 'antiqui Hibernici') and the native English.[15] Yet, whatever the intention behind it, the term 'Anglo-Hiberni', being itself composite, is more redolent of the culturally hybrid than the culturally autonomous. The dialect of English spoken in the Pale seemed quaintly antiquated to Spenser's contemporaries.[16]

Spenser's moral allegory frequently represents the attainment of self-knowledge, and concomitant selfhood, as the product of struggle between the self and some form of demonic alter-ego: for example, the false Genius who serves as porter to the Bowre of Blisse is described as 'quite contrary' to the true Genius 'that is our Selfe' (II, xii, 47–8). For Spenser, not surprisingly, the hybrid category of what he terms 'the englishe Irishe' constituted an exemplum of moral and civil regression: 'for the moste parte of them are degenerated and growen allmoste meare Irishe yea and are more malitious to the Englishe then the verye Irishe themselves' (96) – and particularly so to 'new Inglishemen' like Spenser (210). When used in such contexts, the words 'degenerate' (115) or 'degendred' (117), being etymologically associated with the Latin 'gens' (race), may be seen to assert a close, and implicitly causal, relationship between racial and moral impurity – a relationship that the phenomenon of cultural assimilation threatens to call into question.[17] Long before Spenser published his account of the Bowre of Blisse, Stanihurst anticipated its central imagery of metamorphosis in his contribution to Holinshed's *Chronicles* when he commented upon the manner in which 'the very Englishe of birth, conversant with the savage sort of that people [the Celtic Irish] become degenerat, and as though they had tasted of Circes poisoned cup, are quite altered'.[18] Similarly, writing in 1612, and possibly influenced by Spenser, Sir John Davies complains of how English colonists 'became degenerate and metamorphosed . . . like those who had drunke of *Circes* Cuppe, and were turned into very Beasts: and yet tooke such pleasure in their beastly manner of life, as they would not returne to their shape of men againe'.[19] As so often in Spenser, the imagery of sexual seduction implies its political equivalent. But the association was more than merely allegorical. The majority of new English colonists were single men of relatively low social status all too likely to intermarry with Gaelic families.[20] In a very real sense, therefore, sex and politics were intimately related. In *The Image of Ireland with a Discoverie of Woodkarne* (1581), John Derricke warned colonists to shun the allure of Celtic women,

> For why should men of Th'englishe pale,
> In suche a Crewe delight?
> Or eke repose suche confidence,
> In that unhappie race:
> Since mischeef lurketh oftentimes
> even in the smothest face?[21]

'How cane suche matching but bringe forthe an evill race', Irenius asks, 'seinge that Comonlye the Childe takethe moste of his nature of the mother besides speache, manners, inclynacion . . . for by them they are firste framed and fashioned' (p. 120). By usurping the Spenserian task of framing and fashioning, Irish Acrasias defeat English Guyons. According to *A View* one of the virtues allegedly lacking in Gaelic society was temperance (105). Read in this context, the process of regressive transformation figured in Spenser's Acrasian metamorphoses problematises the very existence of a national or racial Genius 'that is our Selfe'. Moral allegory has a strong tendency to internalise its enemies whereas colonial allegory is inherently resistant to any suggestion of kinship between 'self' and 'other' for fear of compromising the sense of autonomous identity that the contrast functions to sustain. The tension between the moral and colonial aspects of Spenserian allegory is to this extent intractable.

The Irish context of *The Faerie Queene* is signalled from the outset by the inclusion of dedicatory sonnets to Lord Arthur Grey, the former Lord Deputy, Sir John Norris, Lord President of Munster, the Earl of Ormond, foremost of the Old English peers, and Sir Walter Raleigh, Spenser's fellow planter. As I have argued elsewhere, these poems attest to a desperate sense of cultural isolation in a 'savadge soyle, far from Parnasso mount' (sonnet to Grey), and the implications for *The Faerie Queene*'s avowed intention to 'fashion a gentleman or noble person in vertuous and gentle discipline' are immense. Now it is the Celts who must be 'framed and fashoned' (240) to bring them 'from theire delighte of licentious barbarisme unto the love of goodnes and Civilitye' (54), and the nature of the required 'discipline' alters considerably.[22] Eudoxus suggests that the task may best be accomplished 'by the discipline of the Lawes of Englande' which had brought 'as stoute and warlike a people as ever weare the Irishe' to 'that Civilytie that no nacion in the worlde excelleth them in all goodlye Conversacion and all studies of knowledge and humanitye' (54).

It is at first suggested in *A View*, in a passage reminiscent of the Bowre of Blisse, that it may be 'the *very Genius* of the [Irish] Soile' (43) that frustrates all plans for 'reformacion', but it is later conceded that 'neither is it the nature of the Countrye to alter mens manners, but the bad mindes of the man, who havinge bene broughte up at home under a streighte rule of dutie . . . so sone as they Come thither wheare they see the lawes more slacklye tended . . . they growe more lose and Careles of theire duetie and as it is the nature of all men to love libertye So they become Libertines and fall to all Licentiousnes of the Irishe' (211). Effectively such colonists are seen to become 'Irish' through the lack of what Spenser's 'Letter to Raleigh' terms 'vertuous and gentle discipline': the 'other' is therefore latent in the 'self' and the problem is not racial but moral.[23] Regarded from this viewpoint, 'Irishness' is less an ethnic category than a moral condition. But this contradicts Irenius' prior – and *a priori* – assertion that 'the difference of manners and Customes dothe followe the difference of nacions and people' (97). The contradiction is compounded when Irenius concedes that the original English settlers were 'so rude and barbarous' that it is sometimes impossible to determine whether the 'customes' he deplores were 'Englishe or Irishe' in origin (118). In fact, 'it is but even the other daye since Englande grewe Civill' (118). If anything 'the rude Irishe whiche beinge verie wilde at the firste are now become somwhat more Civill', whereas the descendants of the original colonists 'from Civillitye are growne to be wilde and mere Irishe' (209).

Yet Spenser's anxiety on this score is all the more ironic in that the stated aim of his own colonial policy is one of cultural assimilation: 'since Irelande is so full of her owne nacion that maye not be roted out', he explains, 'I thinke it best by an union of manners, and Comformitye of mindes to bringe them to be one people, to put awaie the dislikefull Conceite bothe of thone and thother' (211–12). Cultural assimilation was adjudged to be 'contagion' only when it favoured the Celts (117). Through the suppression of Irish dress, language, customs and law Spenser believed that the native population would 'in shorte time learne quite to forgett his Irishe nacion' (215). In the new order he envisages, the other would be subsumed into the self. From the Celtic viewpoint, however, this was precisely what had already been achieved through the assimilation of the Old English to Celtic society, and the achievement was duly celebrated by the Celtic bards. Indeed the process of assimilation was so complete as to allow the bards to function with equanimity as spokesmen for both parties. As Gofraidh Fionn O'Dalaigh disarmingly asserted in the fourteenth century: 'In poetry for the English [na nGall] we promise that the Gael shall be banished from Ireland, while in poetry for the Gaels [na nGaoidheal] we promise that the English shall be hunted across the see.'[24]

Though often dismissed as cynical this is rather to be seen as a significant testament to the degree of cultural integration achieved by the Old English families. For Spenser, however, to derogate from one's race or 'gens' is to derogate from one's moral being: racial 'degeneration' (through miscegenation) is equivalent to moral 'degeneration'. Through a process of what he describes as 'licentious conversinge with the Irishe or marryinge and fosteringe with them' (117) the Old English have 'degendred from their antiente dignities'. Just as Gryll prefers his 'hoggish forme' to his 'naturall' state, so they have grown 'degenerate from theire firste natures' (114) and 'now accounte themselves naturall Irishe' (117). A branch of the ancient family of De Vere has even, it is alleged, 'disguised theire names' for 'hatred of the Englishe' and called themselves 'Macswines' or MacSweeneys – or

rather it would be MacSweeneys had Spenser's peculiarly polemic orthography not transformed it into the cultural equivalent of 'MacGrylls'
(115–16). The adoption of an Irish name is regarded as crucial because it
serves as an index to self-perception: thus Eudoxus is horrified 'that an
Englisheman broughte up naturallye in suche swete Civilytie as Englande
affordes can finde suche likinge in that barbarous rudenes that he should
forgett his owne nature and forgoe his owne nacion' (96). Linguistic
intercourse is seen to facilitate sexual intercourse and racial hybridity.
'Wordes', Irenius contends, 'are the Image of the minde So as they proce-
dinge from the minde the minde must be nedes affected with the wordes So
that the speache beinge Irishe the harte must nedes be Irishe for out of the
abundance of the harte the tonge speakethe' (119).

Once Spenser has identified the Irish language as the principal medium of
cultural corruption, it follows that the principal culprits must be the
supreme exponents of that language, the bards, a professional caste widely
believed by New English commentators to act as fomenters of 'rebellion'.[25]
From the outset, therefore, Spenser presents the Celtic bard as a demonic
alter ego of the civil English poet, yet struggling through the vocabulary of
overt condemnation is an undertone of unresolved ambivalence.[26] The very
way in which the bards are introduced suggests a measure of identification
clouding the perception of difference: 'Theare is amongst the Irishe a certen
kinde of people Called Bardes which are to them in steade of Poets whose
profession is to sett fourthe the praises and dispraises of menne in their
Poems or Rymes' (124). Depending upon how one reads the phrase 'in
steade of Poets', the bards are either the Celtic equivalent of the English
poets or an alternative caste of anti-poets. It is uncertain, that is to say,
whether the cultural analogy is positive or negative. In terms of social status
the bards have achieved, by Spenser's own account, more than any contemporary English poet might reasonably expect, for they are 'hadd in soe
highe regard and estimation amongst them that none dare displease them
for feare to runne into reproch . . . for the verses are taken upp with a
generall applause' (124). Judged by the polite standards of Spenserian verse,
the tone adopted by the bards to their patrons is often peremptory. But
what is even more remarkable from Spenser's viewpoint is the apparent
efficacy of the verse itself. Celtic poetry is represented as achieving that
crucial effect of 'praxis', that 'moving' of the emotions, and influencing of
actions, which Sir Philip Sidney identified as central to the moral and
political relevance of poetry.[27] 'With the gaye attire of goodlye wordes',
Irenius argues, the Celtic poets 'easelye deceaue and Carrye awaie the
affeccion of a yonge minde that is not well stayed but desirous by some
bolde adventure to make profe of himselfe' (125). Yet the bards' employ-

ment of what Irenius concedes to be 'goodlye wordes' suggests an uncomfortable element of contact between supposed opposites. Like the young Celtic warriors, Spenser's own St George is anxious 'to prove his puissance in battell brave' (I, i, 3).

Eudoxus' intervention in the dialogue at this point serves to emphasise the dilemma, since he counters Irenius' assault upon the bards' prestige with the assertion that 'in all ages Poets have bene in speciall reputacion' precisely because of their perceived influence upon manners – a bitterly ironic assertion in view of the persistent complaints concerning the neglect of English poetry registered in *The Shepheardes Calender*, 'The Teares of the Muses', *Colin Clouts Come Home Againe*, the fourth and sixth books of *The Faerie Queene*, and *Prothalamion*. To the extent to which literary patronage functions in Spenser as an index of civility, England would seem to be more 'salvage' than Ireland. In *Colin Clouts Come Home Againe* many of the adjectives applied to the indolent courtiers are identical to those applied to the 'wild' Irish: 'foule' (691), 'guilefull' (699), 'ydle' (704), 'wastefull' (762), 'laesie' (766), and even 'lewd' and 'licentious' (787). There exists, it would appear, a sophisticated form of barbarity all the worse for its courtly pretensions. Irenius, however, contends that the Irish bards are 'for the moste parte of another minde' to those Eudoxus has mentioned, 'for they seldome use to Chose out . . . the doinges of good men for the argumentes of theire poems but whom soever they finde to be more Licentious of life . . . moste daungerous and desperate in all partes of disobedience and rebellious disposicion him they set up and glorifye in theire Rymes . . . and to yonge men make an example to followe'. And they do so, he alleges, by attributing to the evil 'the prayses which are proper unto vertue it selfe' (126). Couched in these terms it appears that the bards endeavour to invert the moral programme of *The Faerie Queene* by 'counter-fashioning' a breed of anti-heroes, sinister mirror images of Spenser's questing knights.

In order to support this contention Irenius supplies what purports to be a translation of a bardic poem but what is, in fact, a parodic pastiche. This is a relatively easy effect to accomplish, given the immensely sophisticated nature of bardic verse, because the boundaries between the highly stylised and the parodic are inherently unstable. But since the unfamiliar linguistic and stylistic conventions of bardic verse were perceived to encode a set of correspondingly alien cultural conventions, literary parody inevitably shades into its racial counterpart. Although it takes the form of a dialogue, *A View* admits the Celtic voice only on the level of parody or polemical paraphrase. Irenius is therefore careful to relate literary text to social context by citing the example of 'a moste notorious Thiefe and wicked

outlawe which had lived all his lief time of spoiles and Robberies', of whom
one of the bards is alleged to have said:

> that he was none of those Idle milkesopps that was broughte up by the fire
> side / but that moste of his daies he spente in armes and valiante enterprises
> that he did never eate his meate before he had wonne it with his sword that he
> laye not slugginge all nighte in a Cabbyn under his mantle But used Comonlye
> to kepe others wakinge to defende theire lives and did lighte his Candle at the
> flame of theire howses to leade him in the darkenes.   (126)

'Doe youe not thinke', Irenius concludes, 'that manye of these praises
mighte be applied to men of beste deserte?' The question might well be in
the reader's mind, for the effect of the parody is such that the attempt to
illustrate difference has actually betrayed similarity. Despite the impression
created by Irenius' vocabulary of moral denunciation, the issue is clearly
less moral than political, for the major charge levelled against the bards is
that they produce poems 'tendinge for the moste parte to the hurte of the
Englishe or mayntenaunce of theire owne lewd libertie' (125). The invariably pejorative use of the term 'libertie' – as a synonym for lawlessness –
perfectly encapsulates Spenser's rhetorical strategy. The vocabulary is moral
but the agenda is political. By contrast, or rather by comparison, the bards
may be seen to appropriate to the Celtic cause all of the moral propriety –
and, more importantly for our purposes, all of the language of heroic
endeavour – that Spenser appropriates to the English. Captured in the
'mirror' of Celtic verse the demonic alter ego of the bard reflects a peculiarly
disturbing parody of the self. As Mikhail Bakhtin argues, 'in parodic
discourse two styles, two "languages" . . . come together and to a certain
extent are crossed with each other: the language being parodied . . . and the
language that parodies'.[28] This is particularly true of parodic translation
where the exercise allows the parodist, in a very literal sense, 'to look at
language from the outside, with another's eyes, from the point of view of a
potentially different language and style'.[29] Parody necessitates a fusion of
distinct voices, yet at the point of 'dialogical contact' their very distinctive-
ness threatens to break down, an effect noted by Northrop Frye when he
speaks of 'the constant tendency to self-parody in satiric rhetoric'.[30]
Similarly, when deployed in the cause of colonialism, ethnographic arguments from negative analogy with one's own society are notoriously prone
to implode – as when Irenius can find no better analogy for the ills of the
Church of Ireland than those of the Church of England (139, 141).[31]

Read in this context, Spenser's parody of bardic poetry reveals far more
about his relationship to Celtic society than his more overtly serious
descriptions of Celtic antiquities. He is very conscious of writing from the
margins, rather than the centre, of his society and of the effect that this

must inevitably have upon his own poetic career. As we have seen, he complains in *A View* of how Englishmen domiciled in Ireland 'growe wilde' and 'degenerate from theire first natures' (114), yet in recommending his own poetry to the Earl of Ormond in a dedicatory sonnet to *The Faerie Queene*, he describes it as 'wilde fruit, which salvage soyl hath bred' as though it too were struggling with the 'brutish barbarisme' with which the land is allegedly 'overspredd'. He is all too well aware of how the experience of Ireland has altered the nature of his epic heroes, and epic values, almost to the point of parody. In Ireland, he reports, the '*Jus Politicum* thoughe it be not of it selfe juste yeat by applicacion or rather necessitye is made juste' (66). This is tantamount to admitting that in Ireland justice is not 'it selfe'. Likewise when discussing the 'sinister suggestions of Crueltye' (162) attaching to the reputation of Lord Grey, the prototype for Artegall, Irenius describes how 'the necessitye of that presente state of thinges forced him to that violence and allmoste Changed his verye naturall disposicion' (160). Taken together, the implications of these admissions for 'The Legend of Justice' are striking. In Ireland 'justice' verges on becoming its own antithesis. In Ireland the patron of justice is a strangely hybrid figure, a 'salvage knight' (*FQ*, IV, iv, 42) whose nature partakes of the 'salvage Iland' (v, xi, 39) in which he operates, and whose success depends, as do the policies espoused in *A View*, on the suppression of 'pittye' (159–60) – even though an ability to feel 'pittye' is elsewhere identified as a quality capable of evoking civil acts from 'salvage' natures (*FQ*, VI, iv, 3). It is not that Spenser's policies in this area differ in any significant manner from those espoused in contemporary New English treatises such as Richard Beacon's *Solon His Follie* or Sir William Herbert's *Croftus sive de Hibernia Liber*, but that the highly unchivalric, mechanised violence of Book v, symbolised in the figure of Talus, constantly threatens to distort the epic design as Spenser labours to make a moral virtue of political 'necessitye'.[32] The tenor resists the vehicle. Such discordance is all the more remarkable in that, as Fredric Jameson argues, historical romance generally functions to supply 'a symbolic answer to the perplexing question of how my enemy can be thought of as being *evil* (that is, as other than myself and marked by some absolute difference), when what is responsible for his being so characterised is quite simply the *identity* of his own conduct with mine, the which – points of honour, challenges, tests of strength – he reflects as in a mirror image'.[33] Spenserian romance frustrates such resolution even on a fictional level.

The fact that Detraction and Envie hound Artegall from the 'salvage island' as though he were 'a ravenous Wolfe' (v, xii, 38) – an image associated with the Irish in the 'Cantos of Mutabilitie' (VII, vi, 55) – serves to remind us that Spenser was endeavouring to do precisely what he accuses the bardic poets of doing, namely of making a hero of a figure widely regarded (in England as well as Ireland) as an anti-hero, as someone who 'the sword of Justice lent / Had stayned with reprochfull crueltie, / In guiltlesse blood of many an innocent' (v, xii, 40). It is the strain of this endeavour, I would suggest, that accounts both for the uneasy quality of Book v and for the disconcerting manner in which Spenser's parody of Celtic poetry threatens to turn into self-parody, 'like as two mirrours by opposd reflexion, / Doe both expresse the faces first impression' ('An Hymne in Honour of Beautie', 181–2). The image of Spenserian poetry fleetingly caught in the mirror of Celtic verse serves to remind us that, in the allegory of Book v, the evil poet Malfont and the good poet Bonfont are actually one and the same person (v, ix, 26). In *A View* Spenser defends Grey's 'heroicke spirite' against those 'evill tonges' which 'moste untrewlye and malitiouslye . . . backebite and slaunder' him (162), but at the same time suggests that the methods employed by Grey, and the suppression of 'clemencye' which they entail, must be adopted anew in the 1590s. He twice refers to the more lenient government of Sir John Perrot, Grey's successor, as disastrously 'contrarye' to the country's needs (163), and his opposition was doubtless deepened by Perrot's attempt to cultivate relations with the bards.[34] Yet Irenius' eyewitness account of the disastrous Munster famine, largely occasioned by Grey's policies, surpasses any of the depredations attributed to the heroes of bardic verse:

> Out of euerie Corner of the woods and glinnes they Came Crepinge forthe vppon theire handes for theire Leggs Coulde not beare them, they loked like Anotomies of deathe, they spake like ghostes Cryinge out of theire graues, they did eate of the dead Carrions, happie wheare they Coulde finde them, Yea and one another sone after, in so muche as the verye carkasses they spared not to scrape out of theire graves. (158)

Horrific though it be in human terms, this is presented as an image of Grey's military success ('the profe wheareof I sawe sufficientlye ensampled in Those late warrs in mounster') and consequently of the future success of those who adopt his methods. When Eudoxus first hears Irenius' description of bardic poetry he declares himself at a loss to understand 'what kinde of speaches they can finde or what face they Cane put on to praise suche lewde persones . . . or howe Cane they thinke that anie good minde will applaude or approve the same' (125). Ironically, as it is virtually impossible to represent the defeat of a starving enemy, or indeed the massacre of hundreds of disarmed mercenaries at Smerwick, as chivalric victories worthy of a 'heroicke spirite', Spenser faced much the same problem in his treatment of Lord Grey, and generations of readers have responded with something like

Eudoxus' scepticism.[35] The campaign that, by Spenser's own account, 'allmoste Changed' Grey's 'verye naturall disposicion' effected an assimilation to 'savagery' more damaging to the Lord Deputy's reputation than any of those deplored by Spenser: he and not his Irish or Old English enemies was 'blotted with the name of a bloddye man' (160). In allegorical terms the invention of Talus (whom Artegall is frequently represented as restraining) may serve to distance the violence from the man, but the strategy does not bear close scrutiny. Despite Spenser's optimistic hope that in the future 'the Irishe will better be drawen to the Englishe then the Englishe to the Irishe governemente' (199), the figure of Artegall, who grew 'salvage' in the promotion of English civility, casts considerable doubt upon the worth of the enterprise.

Nor is it at all clear in whose interest such a campaign might be fought. The elated but anonymous crowds who rejoice at the death of Grantorto, often identified in contemporary annotations as the Earl of Desmond, are not, as Elizabethan readers might be led to suppose, the native Irish – except, perhaps, in the realm of wish-fulfilment.[36] Their principal function in the narrative is the proclamation of Irena as 'their true Liege and Princesse naturall' (v, xii, 24). However, as Spenser is committed to the view that Irish sovereignty devolves upon the English crown, the country can have but one true monarch, and Irena, by a highly solipsistic inversion, proves to be yet another pseudonym for Gloriana. In dispatching Artegall to Irena's aid Gloriana champions her own cause by ensuring the elimination of what *A View* terms 'lewde disposed Traitours that shall dare to lifte vp theire heele Againste theire Soueraigne Ladie' (149). In colonial terms Irena's victory encompasses that of Irenius' New English agenda.[37] Ireland has been 'saved' from herself, or might have been saved had not Artegall's recall frustrated his efforts. Not for the first time is Gloriana's court seen to betray Gloriana's cause.

Ideally the movement from justice in Book v to courtesy in Book vi adumbrates the desired progress from war to reconstruction envisaged in *A View*. In point of fact, however, it painfully explores the impediments to such progress. The only 'salvage' capable of nurture is, like the Old English, 'borne of noble blood, / How euer by hard hap he hether came' (vi, v, 3). One recalls Chancellor Gerrard's confidence that 'in theim yet resteth this instincte of Englishe nature, generally to feare justice'.[38] But Serena's noble savage has degenerated to such an extent that he 'cannot expresse his simple minde' (vi, v, 30), in marked distinction to the highly articulate, Irish-speaking families of the Old English. Metaphorically speaking, however, they too are regarded as 'dumb' in the language of civil discourse, 'as it is vnnaturall that anye people shoulde love anothers language more then theire owne' – especially when they have adopted an allegedly 'barbarous' tongue (118). Only by assimilating the Celts to the image of feral man could Spenser transform them into fit objects of the paternalistic imperialism enjoyed by the various foundlings of Book VI who are recovered from the wilderness to be fostered in civility.[39] In reality, however, the Irish were to be 'compelled to sende theire youthe to be dissiplined' in English-speaking schools, 'whearby they will in shorte space growe vp to that Civill Conversacion that bothe the Children will loathe the former rudenes in which they weare bredd and allsoe theire parentes will even by thensample of theire younge Children perceaue the fowlenes of theire owne brutishe behaviour' (218). When Celtic poetry had perished with the Celtic language the 'heart' would perforce be English. It was further hoped that the imposition of English place-names upon newly created counties and shires – from which the indigenous inhabitants had been 'translated' (212) – would be complemented by the enforced abandonment of Irish surnames thereby directly reversing the former process of cultural assimilation (215). As in the days of ancient Rome, imperial cartography would then ideally chart, and draw validation from, the progress of civilisation.[40]

The Celtic bards challenged the validity of the very 'civility' that Spenser espouses. To their way of thinking, assimilation to English culture was itself regressive. In a poem addressed to Brian O'Rourke, a native Gaelic chieftain knighted by Sir Henry Sidney but fated to suffer execution in England, Tadhg Dall O'Huiginn maintains that only the warlike Irish gain the respect of the English, whereas 'the Gaels of civil behaviour' suffer continual harassment.[41] Seen from this perspective the process of 'civilisation' is little more than a strategy of colonial control. O'Huiginn employs a witty beast fable to make his point: the wily Celtic fox must not be deceived by polite, social invitations issued by a ravenous English lion.[42] Similarly Laoisioch Mac an Bhaird deplored what he regarded as the cultural emasculation of the Celtic warrior in a poem which sharply contrasts the careers of two men (probably brothers) one of whom had adopted English manners and one of whom had remained faithful to Celtic mores. In assessing his attitude, it is useful to bear in mind not merely Spenser's parody of bardic verse but also his condemnation of the Irish 'glib' as 'a thicke Curled bushe of haire hanginge downe over theire eyes' (99) which serves as a token of 'salvage brutishnes' (102):

> O man who follows English ways, who cut your thick-clustering hair . . . you are not Donnchadh's good son! . . . *You* think the yellow head of hair unfashionable, *he* detests both wearing locks and going bald after the English style; your characters are different indeed. A man who never loved English ways is Eóghan Bán, beloved of noble ladies. To English ways ['ghalldacht']

he never gave his heart: a savage life he chose ['alltacht rug do roghain'] . . .
He has no longing for a feather bed, he had rather lie upon rushes. Pleasanter
to Donnchadh's good son is a hut of rough poles than the [battlements] of a
tower. A troop of horse at the brink of a gap, a fierce fight, a struggle with
foot soldiers, these are some of the desires of Donnchadh's son – and seeking
battle against the foreigners! How unlike are you to Eóghan Bán – they laugh
at your foot on the stepping stone. Pity that you have not seen your fault, O
man who follows English ways. [43]

In many respects this illustrates the similarity between Spenser and the
bards even better than his parodic translation, for although Eóghan Bán is
praised for choosing a rugged lifestyle the poem is not a defence of
'savagery' but must be interpreted within its own conventions – as must
Spenser's praise of Belphoebe for rejecting court indolence in favour of an
active woodland life. At issue in both cases is a particular concept of
heroism and personal integrity. The sheer craftsmanship and verbal dex-
terity displayed by Laoisioch Mac an Bhaird implies the expectation of a
sophisticated and literate response. The Celtic chieftains, eulogised for their
heroic deeds of arms, fostered bardic literature by maintaining the bardic
schools and lending patronage to individual poets. When Tadhg Dall
O'Huiginn sought a metaphor for the cultural attainments of Celtic courts
he turned, as did Spenser in similar circumstances, to the realm of fairy,
describing the Maguire stronghold of Enniskillen, for example, as a 'fairy
castle of surpassing treasure . . . [thronged with] poets and minstrels, from
one bright, white-surfaced wall to the other . . . a mighty band of elfin
youth . . . such that eye dared not regard them'.[44] When Enniskillen fell
briefly to English forces in 1594 another bard described how it had become
'a den of foreign wolves'.[45] Confronted by such similarity in dissimilarity
Spenser might well say, along with John Donne: 'Oh, to vexe me, contraries
meet in one.'[46] It is suggestive in this respect that in *Colin Clouts Come
Home Againe* he represents Colin (a figure who always hovers between self-
portrait and self-parody) as a denizen of Ireland, almost as though he were
one of Stanihurst's 'Anglo-Hiberni', and allows him to witness the corruption of the Elizabethan court, and its neglect of English poetry, through the
eyes of a stranger whose vocabulary is ironically infused with Celtic
words.[47] It is surely no coincidence that he locates his analysis of the
mutability of the 'self' in Ireland on the summit of Arlo Hill overlooking the
dreaded Glen of Aherlow which 'doth to this day with Wolves and Thieves
abound: / Which too-too true that lands in-dwellers since have found' (*FQ*,
VII, vi, 55).[48]

Though cast in an essentially comic idiom, the fable of Faunus and
Molanna (which, as the narrator recognises, echoes similar aetiological

fables in *Colin Clouts Come Home Againe*) reflects the same sort of anxieties evident in the pseudo-anthropological lore of *A View*. The activities of Faunus, progenitor of 'the Wood-gods breed, which must for ever live' (VII, vi, 50), effectively dispels the civilising influence of Diana 'that is soveraine Queene profest / Of woods and forrests' (VII, vi, 38) and reduces Ireland to barbarity. By becoming a voyeuristic eyewitness to the nakedness of majesty, Faunus undermines the very myth of sacral sovereignty upon which *The Faerie Queene* is premised, degrading epic poetics into parodic fabliau by the simple expedient of laughing at deity.[49] Mutability's attack upon Cynthia points in the same direction: the poem's 'gods', and the cultural and political values they represent, are finally revealed to be remarkably vulnerable to the sheer force of disbelief. As Mutability asks the essential question, 'but what we see not, who shall us perswade?' (VII, vii, 49), it is as though the burden of eye-witness testimony, by which Irenius set such store, has finally begun to work to the detriment of his own policy.

In 'An Hymne of Heavenly Love' the narrator describes how the evil angels 'degendering to hate fell from above'. In response the deity is described as establishing a 'new unknowen Colony' to fill the 'waste and emptie place' they leave behind. But this 'colony' admits the very evil it was meant to supplant as man falls, 'forgetfull of his makers grace, / No lesse then Angels' (92–126). The recurrence of such imagery in a poem so apparently remote from the concerns of colonialism indicates the degree to which such experience had come to inform every facet of Spenserian poetics. Cast as versions of the Fall, the fables of Faunus and Mutability demonstrate Ireland's centrality to the quest for a personal, national and spiritual 'home' to which both Colin Clout and his creator may one day 'come'. Yet the conflation of the colonial and the metaphysical produced no 'pleasing Analysis of all'. On the contrary the attempt to 'moralise' colonialism's 'fierce warres' and miscegenated 'loves' produced a crisis of identity which simultaneously fractured traditional ideologies and vitalised contemporary poetics. A poem intended as an assertion of epic achievement developed into a complex exploration of colonial motivation. The poetry not only survives the policy but draws power from its failure.

NOTES

This essay draws at various points on my previously published work on Spenser and Ireland: *The Pillars of Eternity: Time and Providence in 'The Faerie Queene'* (Dublin: Irish Academic Press, 1989), pp. 39–47; 'The Fate of Irena: Spenser and Political Violence', in Patricia Coughlan, ed., *Spenser and Ireland: An Interdisciplinary Perspective* (Cork: Cork University Press, 1989), pp. 109–25; 'Edmund Spenser, Poet of Exile', *PBA* 80: *1991 Lectures and Memoirs* (1993), 73–103.

1 All quotations of *A View* are from Variorum, *The Prose Works*, IX (1949). the page numbers supplied in the text refer to this edition. Spenser's authorship of *A View* has recently been questioned but the arguments are wholly unconvincing. See Jean R. Brink, 'Constructing the *View of the Present State of Ireland*', *Sp. St.*, II (1990), 203–28; 'Appropriating the Author of *The Faerie Queene*: The Attribution of the *View of the Present State of Ireland* and *A Brief Note of Ireland* to Edmund Spenser', in Peter E. Medine and Joseph Wittreich, eds., *Soundings of Things Done: Essays in Early Modern Literature in Honor of S. K. Heninger Jr.* (Newark: University of Delaware Press, 1997), pp. 93–115. For the contrary arguments see my review of the latter in *RES* 50 (1999), 236–7 and Willy Maley, *Salvaging Spenser: Colonialism, Culture and Identity* (London: Macmillan, 1997), pp. 163–94.

2 The inference was first drawn in the anonymous article 'Edmund Spenser – the State Papers', *Dublin University Magazine* 58 (1861), 131–44, pp. 132–3. For a discussion of Spenser's possible involvement with Ireland prior to 1580 see Maley, *Salvaging Spenser*, pp. 11–33.

3 See François Hartog, *The Mirror of Herodotus: The Representation of the Other in the Writing of History*, trans. Janet Lloyd (Berkeley: University of California Press, 1988), pp. 260–73. See also Michel de Certeau, *Heterologies: Discourse on the Other* (Manchester: Manchester University Press, 1986), pp. 68–9, 73–5.

4 Hartog, *Mirror of Herodotus*, p. 264.

5 Gerald of Wales, *The History and Topography of Ireland*, trans. John J. O'Meara (1951; Harmondsworth: Penguin Books, 1982), pp. 57, 108.

6 For their alleged blood-drinking see Herodotus, *History*, IV, 62.

7 *History and Topography of Ireland*, p. 108.

8 See David J. Baker, '"Some Quirk, Some Subtle Evasion": Legal Subversion in Spenser's *A View of the Present State of Ireland*', *Sp. St.*, 6 (1986), 147–63.

9 *The History of Ireland*, ed. and trans. David Comyn, 4 vols. (London: Irish Texts Society, 1902–14), I, pp. 38–41. See Brendan Bradshaw, 'Geoffrey Keating: Apologist of Irish Ireland', in Brendan Bradshaw, Andrew Hadfield and Willy Maley, eds., *Representing Ireland: Literature and the Origins of Conflict, 1534–1660* (Cambridge: Cambridge University Press, 1993), pp. 166–90.

10 For the letters in the State Papers see Raymond Jenkins, '*Newes out of Munster*, a Document in Spenser's Hand', *SP* 32 (1935), 125–30; 'Spenser with Lord Grey in Ireland', *PMLA* 52 (1937), 338–53; and 'Spenser: The Uncertain Years 1584–89', *PMLA* 53 (1938), 350–62. See also Vincent P. Carey and Clare L. Carroll, 'Factions and Fictions: Spenser's Reflections of and on Elizabethan Politics', in Judith H. Anderson, Donald Cheney and David A. Richardson, eds., *Spenser's Life and the Subject of Biography* (Amherst: University of Massachusetts Press, 1996), pp. 31–44; John Gillies, *Shakespeare and the Geography of Difference* (Cambridge: Cambridge University Press, 1994), pp. 1–39.

11 See Nicholas Canny, *The Formation of the Old English Elite in Ireland* (Dublin: National University of Ireland, 1975), pp. 18–29; Ciaran Brady, 'The Road to the *View*: On the Decline of Reform Thought in Tudor Ireland', in Patricia Coughlan, ed., *Spenser and Ireland: An Interdisciplinary Perspective* (Cork: Cork University Press, 1989), pp. 25–45, at pp. 32–6.

12 See Colm Lennon, *Sixteenth-Century Ireland: The Incomplete Conquest* (Dublin: Gill & Macmillan, 1994), pp. 216–28.

13 *Lord Chancellor Gerrard's Notes of his Report on Ireland, 1577–78*, ed. C. McNeill, *Analecta Hibernica* 2 (1931), 93–291, pp. 95–6.

14 Quoted in Colm Lennon, *Richard Stanihurst, The Dubliner 1547–1618* (Blackrock: Irish Academic Press, 1981), p. 79.

15 Ibid., pp. 72, 82, 126.

16 As, ironically, did his own archaic poetic diction; see Raphael Holinshed, *Chronicles of England, Scotland and Ireland*, 6 vols. (London, 1808), VI, pp. 4, 6. See also Maley, *Salvaging Spenser*, pp. 34–47.

17 For the concept of 'gens' see John Morrill, 'The fashioning of Britain', in Steve G. Ellis and Sarah Barber, eds., *Conquest and Union: Fashioning a British State, 1485–1725* (London: Longman, 1995), pp. 8–39, at p. 11.

18 Holinshed, *Chronicles of England, Scotland and Ireland*, VI, p. 69. See also Stephen Greenblatt, *Renaissance Self-Fashioning: From More to Shakespeare* (Chicago: University of Chicago Press, 1980), pp. 157–92.

19 Sir John Davies, *A Discoverie of the True Causes why Ireland was never entirely Subdued, nor brought under Obedience of the Crowne of England, untill the Beginning of his Majesties happie Raigne* (London, 1612), p. 182.

20 For a full discussion of the Munster plantation see Michael MacCarthy-Morrogh, *The Munster Plantation: English Migration to Southern Ireland, 1583–1641* (Oxford: Clarendon Press, 1986).

21 *The Image of Irelande with a Discoverie of Woodkarne*, with an introduction, transliteration and glossary by D. B. Quinn (Belfast: The Blackstaff Press, 1985), p. 31.

22 For a fuller account see McCabe, 'Edmund Spenser, Poet of Exile', 79–84.

23 See Nicholas Canny, 'The Permissive Frontier: the Problem of Social Control in English Settlements in Ireland and Virginia, 1550–1650', in K. R. Andrews, N. P. Canny and P. E. Hair, eds., *The Westward Enterprise: English Activities in Ireland, the Atlantic, and America 1480–1650* (Liverpool: Liverpool University Press, 1979), pp. 17–44, at pp. 19–24.

24 As quoted in *The Bardic Poems of Tadhg Dall O'Huiginn*, ed. and trans. Eleanor Knott, 2 vols. (1922–6; London: Irish Texts Society, 1984), I, xlvii. See Michelle O'Riordan, *The Gaelic Mind and the Collapse of the Gaelic World* (Cork: Cork University Press, 1990), pp. 51–61.

25 See Brendan Bradshaw, 'Native Reaction to the Westward Enterprise: a Case-Study in Gaelic Ideology', in K. R. Andrews et al., eds., *The Westward Enterprise*, pp. 65–80; T. J. Dunne, 'The Gaelic Response to Conquest and Colonisation: The Evidence of the Poetry', *Studia Hibernica* 20 (1980), 7–30; Nicholas Canny, 'The Formation of the Irish Mind: Religion, Politics and Gaelic Irish Literature 1580–1750', *P&P* 95 (1982), 91–116; Christopher Highley, 'Spenser and the Bards', *Sp. St.* 12 (1991), 77–103.

26 See McCabe, 'Edmund Spenser, Poet of Exile', pp. 78–9.

27 See *The Apology for Poetry*, in G. Gregory Smith, ed., *Elizabethan Critical Essays*, 2 vols. (Oxford: Oxford University Press, 1904), I, p. 171.

28 Mikhail Bakhtin, *The Dialogic Imagination: Four Essays*, ed. Michael Holquist, trans. Caryl Emerson and Michael Holquist (Austin: University of Texas Press, 1981), p. 75

29 Ibid., p. 60.

30 Northrop Frye, *Anatomy of Criticism: Four Essays* (1957; Princeton: Princeton University Press, 1973), p. 234.

31 See Margaret T. Hodgen, *Early Anthropology in the Sixteenth and Seventeenth Centuries* (Philadelphia: University of Pennsylvania Press, 1964), pp. 194–9, 391.

32 See Richard Beacon, *Solon His Follie, or a Politique Discourse, Touching the Reformation of Common-Weales Conquered, Declined or Corrupted* (Oxford, 1594); Sir William Herbert, *Croftus sive De Hibernia Liber*, ed. Arthur Keaveney and John Madden (Baldoyle: Irish Manuscripts Commission, 1992).

33 Fredric Jameson, *The Political Unconscious: Narrative as a Socially Symbolic Act* (1981; London: Methuen, 1983), p. 118.

34 See *The Bardic Poems of Tadhg Dall O'Huiginn*, I, pp. xliv–xlv.

35 For the massacre at Smerwick see Variorum, IX, pp. 524–30.

36 Anonymous, 'MS Notes to Spenser's *Faerie Queene*', N&Q 202 (1957), 509–15, p. 513.

37 See McCabe, 'The Fate of Irena', pp. 120–1. For the queen's alleged part in Grey's failure see also Christopher Highley, *Shakespeare, Spenser, and the Crisis in Ireland* (Cambridge: Cambridge University Press, 1997), pp. 110–33.

38 Gerrard, *Notes of his Report on Ireland, 1577–78*, p. 96.

39 See David Beers Quinn, *The Elizabethans and the Irish* (Ithaca, NY: Cornell University Press, 1966), pp. 106–22; Nicholas Canny, *Kingdom and Colony: Ireland in the Atlantic World, 1560–1800* (Baltimore: Johns Hopkins University Press, 1988), pp. 2, 33, 35.

40 See David J. Baker, 'Off the Map: Charting Uncertainty in Renaissance Ireland', in Brendan Bradshaw et al., eds., *Representing Ireland*, pp. 76–92.

41 *The Bardic Poems of Tadhg Dall O'Huiginn*, I, p. 108; II, p. 72.

42 Ibid., I, pp. 113–4; II, pp. 75–6.

43 See Osborn Bergin, *Irish Bardic Poetry* (Dublin: The Dublin Institute for Advanced Studies, 1970), pp. 49–50, 231–2.

44 *The Bardic Poems of Tadhg Dall O'Huiginn*, I, pp. 73–6; II, pp. 49–50.

45 Bergin, *Irish Bardic Poetry*, pp. 130, 271.

46 John Donne, *Holy Sonnets*, xix.

47 See in particular the use of the term 'bodrags' (line 315), a likely corruption of 'buaidhreach' or 'buadre' (meaning intrusive uproar or disturbance).

48 See Patricia Coughlan, 'The Local Context of Mutabilitie's Plea', *IUR* 26, special issue: *Spenser in Ireland 1596–1996* (1996), 320–41.

49 See Andrew Hadfield, *Spenser's Irish Experience: Wilde Fruit and Salvage Soyl* (Oxford: Clarendon Press: 1997), pp. 192–7.

FURTHER READING

Brendan Bradshaw, Andrew Hadfield and Willy Maley, eds., *Representing Ireland: Literature and the Origins of Conflict, 1534–1660* (Cambridge: Cambridge University Press, 1993).

Patricia Coughlan, ed., *Spenser and Ireland: An Interdisciplinary Perspective* (Cork: Cork University Press, 1989).

Andrew Hadfield, *Spenser's Irish Experience: Wilde Fruit and Salvage Soyl* (Oxford: Clarendon Press: 1997).

Christopher Highley, 'Spenser and the Bards', *Sp. St.* 12 (1991), 77–103.

Colm Lennon, *Sixteenth-Century Ireland: The Incomplete Conquest* (Dublin: Gill & Macmillan, 1994).

Richard A. McCabe, *The Pillars of Eternity: Time and Providence in 'The Faerie Queene'* (Dublin: Irish Academic Press, 1989).

'Edmund Spenser, Poet of Exile', *PBA* 80: *1991 Lectures and Memoir* (1993), 73–103.

Willy Maley, *Salvaging Spenser: Colonialism, Culture and Identity* (London: Macmillan, 1997).

4

PATRICK CHENEY

Spenser's Pastorals: *The Shepheardes Calender* and *Colin Clouts Come Home Againe*

Edmund Spenser is England's first great pastoral poet. In 1579, at about the age of twenty-seven, Spenser inaugurated his literary career by publishing *The Shepheardes Calender*, a collection of twelve pastoral eclogues each named after a month of the year. The poet began with pastoral in imitation of Virgil, who had published his *Eclogues* before his didactic poem, the *Georgics*, and then his epic, the *Aeneid*. In late antiquity, Suetonius, Donatus and Servius all understood Virgil's career model to be identical with his life pattern, as reported in his epitaph: 'Mantua gave birth to me, the Calabrians snatched me away ... I sang of pastures, fields, and princes.'[1] During the Middle Ages, John of Garland accommodated the progressive life-career pattern to a circular cosmic image, the *rota Virgilii* (Wheel of Virgil), which presents a series of concentric circles divided by three spokes, each demarcating a writing style, a life style, a social rank and corresponding imagery (plant, animal, implement) (fig. 1).[2]

In the sixteenth century, Spenser was thus able to understand pastoral as a developmental genre within a Christian universe. His most notable contribution to the form was to yoke the progressive Virgilian career pattern to the circular life pattern of the Christian calendar.[3] Relying throughout on an archaic diction and in each eclogue on a specific (sometimes new) verse form, Spenser uses the twelve-month cycle to record the life-career process by which the young poet comes to write his inaugural pastoral. Hence, his persona, Colin Clout, appears in the opening, middle and concluding eclogues ('January', 'June', 'December'), has his songs sung in the fourth and eighth ('April', 'August'), and is discussed in the ninth and tenth ('September', 'October').[4] In the Colin Clout eclogues, Spenser tells the story of a young poet's preparation to write the very poem we are reading; the crowning event is a solution to his premier problem: just where to locate his private faith as the source and end of his public art. Spenser considers a version of this problem to be plaguing English culture as a whole, and he includes other eclogues that alert the reader to three other,

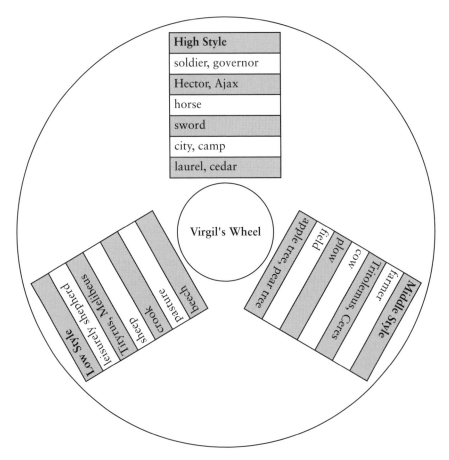

Figure 1   Wheel of Virgil

interrelated patterns: political eclogues, representing a horizontal pattern of the nation's history within time (e.g. 'April'); ecclesiastical eclogues, representing the vertical pattern of Christian salvation in eternity (e.g. 'July'); and social eclogues, often representing the pattern of sexual maturation in the life of the family (e.g. 'March'). Through this innovative set of inter-related patterns, the young poet can relate his own maturation to the primary evolving spheres of the nation – political, religious, educational, erotic – and he can represent a Dantesque solution to the problem of time and death: Virgilian poetic fame mediating Augustinian Christian glory.[5]

Spenser's revolutionary pastoral paradigm presents the poet as important to the nation's institutions of state, church, university and family, with their corresponding figures and leaders: sovereign, pastors, wise old men, young men in love. Simultaneously, he attracts a wide variety of readers to the enjoyment and instruction of the verse: not merely other poets, but the queen and her counsellors, clergymen, educators, and men and women interested in sexuality and marriage. Above all, *The Shepheardes Calender* is a pastoral about the poet's role in the multi-sphered life of the nation.

Perhaps not paradoxically, then, Spenser prints the *Calender* as the product of collaboration, between an anonymous poet, 'Immerito' (Unworthy One); Gabriel Harvey, Spenser's friend from Cambridge University; and 'E. K.', probably Spenser himself.[6] Thus, in an era when modern authorship is emerging in a developing print culture, Spenser surrounds his inaugural poetry with a textual apparatus that communalises his authority: the printer Hugh Singleton's title page, dedicating the work to Sir Philip Sidney; Immerito's prefatory poem, 'To His Booke', which seeks Sidney's patronage; E. K.'s 'Dedicatory Epistle' (DE), which identifies Immerito as the 'new Poete', heir to Chaucer and Virgil (1–21), and introduces his project to 'restore . . . our Mother tonge' (90–3); E. K.'s 'general argument', which divides the eclogues into 'three formes or ranckes' ('plaintive', 'recreative', 'moral') (31–4); an anonymous woodcut and an 'Argument' by E. K. preceding each eclogue; Immerito's emblem and E. K.'s gloss closing each eclogue.

In this quarto-sized 'book', modelled on the *Kalender of Shepherdes* (1506) – an English edition of a French almanac structured according to the Christian calendar (DE, 182–4) – and on Continental publications of famous authors (Virgil, Ronsard), Spenser produces 'the first set of English pastorals in the European tradition' and 'inaugurat[es] . . . the great age of Elizabethan poetry'.[7] Thus, Spenser achieves for England what the inventor of pastoral, Theocritus, achieved for Alexandrian Greece, Virgil for Augustan Rome, and Sannazaro (the Renaissance's first great pastoralist) for fifteenth-century Italy: he invents a native language, art and world that are important to the nation. Subsequent English poets, from Marlowe and Drayton to Milton and Pope, would have to contend with Spenser's national beginning.[8] Having simultaneously inaugurated English pastoral – and thereby his own career and modern English poetry itself – Spenser rightfully assumes the mantle of 'prime Pastoralist of England'.[9]

Yet it is as the prime pastoralist of England that Spenser differs from earlier pastoralists mentioned by E. K.: Theocritus, Virgil, Petrarch, Boccaccio, Sannazaro, Mantuan and Marot (DE, 163–70). In 1595 he published a second completed pastoral by resurrecting his *Calender* persona, Colin Clout, for a title role: *Colin Clouts Come Home Againe*. This second pastoral has other unusual features: it is nearly 1,000 lines long, bears a 1591 'Dedicatory Epistle' to Sir Walter Raleigh, and is followed by seven elegies for Sidney, evidently to memorialise the Sidney circle.[10] *Colin Clout* is important for its record of twelve court poets (376–455) and twelve court ladies (485–583), but also for its imaginative account of Spenser's trip from Ireland to England in 1589–90 under Raleigh's patronage, when he read *The Faerie Queene* to Queen Elizabeth 'at timely houres' (362) and returned 'home' to Ireland.

In this chapter, we might brood more than we have over the peculiarity of England's 'prime pastoralist' penning two pastoral poems. Spenser's second pastoral is peculiar because it appears to confound his self-presentation as 'the Virgil of England', and specifically his self-announced move from pastoral to epic.[11] For in 1590, Spenser published Books I – III of *The Faerie Queene*: 'Lo I the man, whose Muse whilome did maske, / As time her taught, in lowly Shepheards weeds, / Am now enforst a far unfitter taske, / For trumpets sterne to chaunge mine Oaten reeds, / And sing of Knights and Ladies gentle deeds' (I, proem, I). Why would Spenser return to pastoral? Why would he present himself as a pastoral poet from the beginning to the end of his career?[12]

Spenser's use of a pastoral persona throughout his career, his publication of two major pastorals and his penning of an unusually long eclogue mark out a strange place for Spenser's pastoral production. Critics neglect this strangeness; those few who write on both pastorals see *Colin Clout* simply as a return: unlike the *Calender*, 'which was conceived as a *prologue* to heroic poetry, Spenser's late pastorals are *alternatives* to it'.[13] According to this view, Spenser becomes disillusioned with his epic and returns to pastoral in order to entertain the value of private consciousness. Yet Spenser had presented his persona as disillusioned in his inaugural pastoral. Indeed, this condition is Colin's signature stance ('January', 37–38; 'December', 140). Moreover, in 'October' Spenser had built disillusionment with the Virgilian model into the career of the English poet (49–51, 80–4). Most decisively, Spenser's last published poem, *Prothalamion* (1596), shows England's Virgil responding to his disillusionment with renewed commitment to his national epic.[14]

In fact, Spenser did not 'return' to pastoral because he never left it. England's Virgil never progressed from pastoral to epic, for he never completed his epic. Hence, even in the final stanza of the 1596 *Faerie Queene* he still addresses his epic in pastoral terms: 'this homely verse' (VI, xii, 41; see I, proem; III, proem)[15] – the word 'homely' evoking both the title of *Colin Clouts Come Home Againe* and the concept of 'home' that concludes ten of the *Calender* eclogues. Rather than being his solace, pastoral may be Spenser's greatest problem.

To pursue Spenser's representation of this problem, we might divide his career into two phases: pre-epic (*Calender*) and epic (*Faerie Queene*). The four volumes published between the two epic installments – *Complaints*, *Daphnaida*, *Colin Clout/Astrophel*, *Amoretti/Epithalamion* – do not fit into this scheme. Yet the 'October' eclogue extends the Virgilian model by two phases. The first we may call mid-epic: it is derived from the Virgilian georgic that Renaissance poetics ousts and that Spenser enfolds into pastoral and epic,[16] and it shows the poet regenerating his epic strength through 'love' (49–54). The second we may call post-epic: it is derived from Virgil's plan to turn from epic to philosophy,[17] as well as from Du Bartas's rejection of secular for divine poetry, and it shows the poet turning from courtly to contemplative poetry (79–84). While Spenser never reaches this latter phase, he anticipates it in *Fowre Hymnes*. By contrast, the four early-1590 volumes are mid-epic works, as their generally erotic centre confirms, and therefore they may function as regenerative bridges to epic. *Colin Clout* would become not a recursion to pastoral but an excursive step beyond it.

The four-phase division of Spenser's works – pastoral, epic, mid-epic poems, divine poetry – suggests that pastoralism recurs throughout his career not because it is his preferred mode but because it is the form from which he longs to escape. The division identifies Spenser's career as a disciplined struggle to move beyond pastoral, to assume fully the Virgilian mantle. If we seek Spenser's special 'version of pastoral', we need to attend to the site that each poem occupies along the continuum of his career. When we do, we see that he understands pastoral as a genre preparing the young poet to write epic. The *Calender* becomes the inaugural phase of his pastoral progression toward epic, and *Colin Clout* becomes a mid-genre work that bridges that gap.

In particular, then, *Colin Clout* may be less a return to pastoral than a vigorous response to a genre then being invented. According to Clark Hulse, the 'minor epic was . . . the proving ground for . . . epic', a form 'above the pastoral . . . and below the epic, the transition between the two in the *gradus Vergilianus*'.[18] While remaining cautious about classifying *Colin Clout* as an Elizabethan minor epic in the pastoral mode – the one mode Hulse omits (p. 15) – we might consider how intimately Spenser's poem is embedded in the Ovidian genre that produced *Hero and Leander* and *Venus and Adonis* – a genre invented precisely in response to Spenser's epic, as Richard Barnfield announces in his 1595 *Cynthia*, which 'first imitat[es] . . . the verse of . . . [The] Fayrie Queene'.[19] This literary context better explains the relation between the *Calender*, *Colin Clout* and *The Faerie Queene*, including Colin's final appearance in Spenser's epic land-scape (VI, ix-x), to which we shall return at the close of this chapter.

From its inception in Theocritus to its metapoetic reformulation in Virgil and its erotic reconception in Sannazaro, pastoral is inseparable from epic.[20] Theocritus invented pastoral as an alternative to Homeric epic, while Virgil reinvented pastoral as a preparation for epic, and Sannazaro Petrarchized the career principle. The *locus classicus* lies in the opening of late-Augustan, medieval, and Renaissance editions of the *Aeneid*: 'I am he who once tuned my song on a slender reed, then, leaving the woodland, constrained the neighbouring fields to serve the husbandmen, however grasping – a work welcome to farmers: but now of Mars' bristling.'[21] Spenser sanctions this career version in the opening of *The Faerie Queene* quoted earlier. In doing so, he adhered to the dominant theoretical framing of pastoral in Renaissance poetics, which presented the genre as the humble form of the Virgilian triad.[22] In part, this triad was dominant because it had a fundamental place in the English school curriculum, where boys 'proceed[ed] . . . from the lowest kind of verse in the Eclogues, to something . . . loftier in the Georgicks . . . to the stateliest kind in the Aeneids'.[23] While Barnabe Googe and others had written pastorals, Spenser is England's first poet to risk structuring his career on this progressive principle. We might then call his version a 'pastoral of progression': the prime pastoralist of England writes pastoral as a genre in a career pattern progressing to epic.

The framing of pastoral in Spenser's career relates to the two primary versions of pastoral distinguished in modern criticism: the idealistic and the ideological.[24] The idealistic can be traced back to Schiller's *On Naïve and Sentimental Poetry* (1795–6) and receives its definitive statement in Poggioli's *The Oaten Flute* (1957); it defines pastoral as a sentimental longing for the 'ideal' and an escape from the 'actual'. Thus the idealistic version is a pastoral of pleasure that pursues *otium* (leisure) rather than *negotium* (business).[25] The ideological version can be traced back to Elizabethan treatises such as Puttenham's *Arte of English Poesie* (1589) and receives its definitive statement in Empson's *Some Versions of Pastoral* (1935); it defines pastoral as an ideological practice of 'putting the complex into the simple', the gentleman-courtier into the shepherd-poet. Thus the ideological version is a pastoral of power that 'do[es] busily negotiate by colour of otiation'.[26]

Spenser critics now emphasise the pastoral of power over the pastoral of pleasure, but surely the interest of the *Calender* and *Colin Clout* lies in their wonderful fusion of the two. Moreover, both versions proceed along Spenser's pastoral of progression: simple–complex, low–high, country–court, shepherd–gentleman. Both versions imbed epic into pastoral. Empson remarks that his version 'piled the heroic convention onto the pastoral one' (p. 12), and we could extend his point to the Schillerian version.

Spenser's pastoral of progression unfolds the pastoral of power and the pastoral of pleasure into political, social and erotic dimensions, which together serve a religious dimension in a pastoral of contemplation.[27] In the *Calender*, this hierarchy of pastoral versions and their corresponding dimensions coheres with Spenser's emphasis on Colin in relation to the sovereign, pastor, learned father and youthful lover, with their institutions of state, church, university and family. As its title indicates, *Colin Clout* makes the career principle ordering this cultural hierarchy explicit: now the poet is a nationally valuable authority in politics, religion, philosophy and love. Spenser's representation of the poet's multifaceted importance to the nation suggests that England's Virgil pens the *Calender* as a pre-epic work and *Colin Clout* as a mid-epic one.

Consequently, in both poems Spenser foregrounds an experience that solves the premier problem of faith plaguing English culture; this solution forms the source of his cultural authority, the intellectual content of his wisdom, and the linguistic form of his national art. Colin's sublimated epiphany of Dido in 'November' represents the experience that inaugurates his career, and his twin epiphanies of Cynthia and Rosalind in *Colin Clout* represent the experience that bridges pastoral to epic. Both sets of experiences locate wisdom, authority, masculinity and art in the poet's vision of the female, first through Neo-Platonic transcendence, then through Neo-Platonic immanence.

Thus, whereas critics have understood the poet's 'transcendence' (especially in the *Calender*) as either an erotic retreat into classical *otium*, a participation in a Christian contemplation of death, or a hapless escape from harsh political realities,[28] the career principle identifies transcendence as the very prerequisite for national leadership. The audacity of Spenser's pastorals lies in his Dantesque identification of the poet as a model not only for future English poets, but also for all members of the nation who speak the 'Mother tonge'.

Spenser's pastoral nationalism is thus as bold as it is complex. He remains patriotic, but his writerly traverse from Kent to Ireland necessitates a shift in political faith from 'England', not simply to 'Ireland', but to a cultural space linking the two, called 'Britain'.[29] Similarly, his ambivalence towards the Tudor state, his support of a progressive Protestantism memorialising an aristocratic faction, his commitment to the common people and his fidelity to companionate marriage all mark out a pastoral form of nationhood that acknowledges other cultural authorities but advances the poet's own national leadership.[30]

The Shepheardes Calender

In the prefatory material to his first pastoral, Spenser advertises himself as the Christian Virgil of England: he pursues a progressive career in service of an educational programme of national duty and desire mapped onto the cyclical pattern of the Christian calendar and the vertical pattern of Christian salvation.

The title page introduces a pastoral poem serving an epic hero: 'The Shepheardes Calender . . . Entitled to the . . . Gentleman of . . . chevalrie.' The title page relates this chivalric version of Virgilian poetics to the politics of the Sidney faction, which opposed the queen's marriage to the Duke of Alençon. In 1578 Sidney opposed this marriage, while in 1579 Spenser's printer, Singleton, published John Stubbs' *Discoverie of a Gaping Gulfe*, which cost Stubbs his right hand. In 'To His Booke', Immerito repeats this poetics by presenting himself as a 'shepheards swaine' who sings while feeding his 'straying flocke' and dedicates his 'little booke' to the 'president / Of . . . chevalree' (1–10). If the Virgilian epic hero will protect the pastoral poet from 'Envie' (5), Immerito 'will send more [poems]' (18). By reading the Virgilian signs, could Sidney not see a veiled pastoral reference to an epic dedicated to him? Spenser's pun on 'president' – one 'who sits at the head of [chivalry]' and one who 'goes before [chivalry]'[31] – models this Renaissance Virgilian poetics.

In the 'Dedicatory Epistle', E. K. clarifies the Virgilian basis of Immerito's future poems to Sidney. The New Poet chose eclogues to 'follow . . . auncient Poetes, which devised this kind of wryting . . . to prove theyr tender wyngs, before they make a greater flyght' (158–63). Here E. K. authorises Spenser's pastoral of progression as a prophecy for epic. This prophecy emerges in 'the basenesse of the name', Colin Clout, which 'he chose . . . to unfold great matter of argument covertly' (152–4). As E. K. indicates later ('January', 81–4), the name originates with John Skelton and Clément Marot, but it also encloses the Virgilian triad. Since Colin Clout means country lout, he is a pastoral figure. Since *clout* means 'clot of earth' (*OED*, 2nd entry, def. 1), he is a figure of georgic. Finally, since 'Collonnes [comes] of the Latin word *Coloni*', settler, from *colo*, cultivate, from which we derive *colonise*, he is an epic figure for the 'expanding forces of empire'.[32] In 'The generall argument', E. K. Christianises the Virgilian model. He shows Immerito following the two classical precedents for 'Aeglogues' – falsely etymologised as Theocritus' 'Goteheards tales' – about Virgilian 'shepheards' (1–29). Then E. K. justifies Immerito's beginning the calendar with January through Christ's biography: 'we . . . coumpt . . . the seasons from . . . January, upon a more speciall cause, then the heathen

2 'Januarye' woodcut

Philosophers . . . for the incarnation of our . . . Saviour' is the 'eternall monument of our salvation' (56–66). E. K. ends with an advertisement for the Christianised Virgilian model: 'therefore beginneth he, and so continueth he throughout' (109–10).[33]

A reading of the eclogues shows that Spenser holds a complex definition of Virgilian pastoral as a genre of career progression fusing Christianity, nationalism, learning and sexuality. From the first recorded reader (Sidney himself) to today's students, part of the complexity encountered lies in Immerito's 'framing of his style to an old rustic language', which Sidney 'dare[s] not allow'.[34] Yet the fundamental interpretive complexity is that Immerito advertises himself as England's Virgil by presenting a Colin who appears to fail as a national poet: in 'December', Colin hangs up his pipe.

The woodcut to 'Januarye' suggests how to interpret this complexity (fig. 2): as an imitation of Virgil's 'farewell to pastoral' in Eclogue 10.[35] A 'visual announcement of the book', the block depicts the *rota virgilii*: 'Colin stand[s] . . . with his back to the pastoral and his gaze toward [Roman] buildings associated with epic'.[36] Colin's crook-like implement and his position beside his sheep symbolise his correction of wandering members of his community. The broken bagpipe suggests an erotic origin to his art. The pastoral rustic shack and the epic Roman city, with the linking contour line, map the Virgilian path, while the clouds with the zodiacal figure over the city represent the divine sanction of this progress.[37]

While anticipating the Virgilian farewell to pastoral in its climactic event – Colin's hanging up of his pipe – 'Januarye' itself concentrates on the multidimensional problem that threatens the progress of the pastoral poet's career (and hence the growth of his reader). The winter season alerts us to the grounding of the problem in nature. Unlike the locales of Theocritus' first idyll or Virgil's first eclogue, Spenser's natural world is no pastoral of paradisal pleasance, but its inversion. As Harry Berger, Jr., emphasises, Spenser's central principle appears in the pun on 'Art' in line 20: 'Art made a myrrhour, to behold my plight.'[38] Nature is a mirror of Colin's inward condition, but nature is also a mirror of art. Since nature is fallen, so is Colin's subjectivity, and his art mirrors this equation. What secures this complex refraction is a problem with faith, sexual and religious, with hints of a political dimension.

Thus the eclogue opens with the poet's mistaken solution to the problem of faith: 'Pan thou shepheards God, that once didst love, / Pitie [my] . . . paines' (17–18).[39] Colin prays to the Ovidian nature god to help solve his Ovidian problem, begun when Rosalind rejects him. As his 'feeble' flock exemplifies (4–5), his misguided love for Rosalind leads him to misconstrue religious faith as a belief in nature that prevents him from writing communal poetry. Indeed, he conceives of the female as purely a sexual object: 'I sawe so fayre a sight . . . / . . . such sight hath bred my bane' (52–3). Rosalind 'hateth' Colin's 'Shepheards devise . . . as the snake' (65) because she sees his pastoral song as an Ovidian art in search of sexual grace. Colin's faith in Pan leads him to court the female for her physical beauty and thus to train the community to enact a dangerous philosophy, which 'substitute[s] nature for God'.[40] When Rosalind disrupts this poetics, Colin experiences a crisis of faith that both impedes his care for the community and dissolves his naturalist song. To the extent that Rosalind allegorises Queen Elizabeth, Spenser criticizes the monarchy for its own misconceptions about the female and (French) marriage.[41] The Virgil of England is in danger of becoming the exiled Ovid.[42]

While 'Januarye' presents Colin as the young Virgilian poet suffering from an Ovidian problem, 'Februarie' presents a dialogue between shepherds in order to evaluate career models available in the 1570s. The young Cuddie prefers spring, to 'caroll of Love' (61), while the older Thenot prefers winter, to 'tel . . . a tale of truth' (91). Since the weather favours Thenot, he tells Cuddie a tale that he learned of 'Tityrus' (92), an Aesopian fable of the Oak and the Briar (286–7), which plays out the youth–age debate to Thenot's advantage. While critics have seen this eclogue as an allegory of generational strife, 'a broad allegory of competition for power at court', or an allusion to 'the displacement of the Roman church by

Elizabeth's Religious Settlement' (Yale, p. 38), it also transacts a vocational debate. Cuddie models the younger Elizabethan 'amateur' poet in his amorous mode; Thenot, the older Elizabethan amateur in his didactic mode.[43] Both amateurs have faith in Tityrus: 'Many meete tales of youth did he make, / And some of love, and some of chevalrie: / But none fitter then this to applie' (98–100). Tityrus is Spenser's name neither for Virgil nor Chaucer but *Chaucer in 'compari[son]' with Virgil* ('Dedicatory Epistle', 14–15). Thus, Spenser divides Chaucer's 'tales' along transposed Virgilian lines, echoing the three divisions that Dante had outlined for vernacular poetry: 'prowess in arms, kindling of love, rectitude of will'.[44] These three divisions correspond precisely to the three kinds of poetry that critics have determined Spenser found in Chaucer: didactic, erotic, heroic.[45] Spenser's Dantean model of Chaucer contrasts with the models of the Elizabethan amateurs in their amorous and didactic modes, which divide up the Chaucerian model but neglect the chivalric epic.

In Thenot's fable of the Husbandman cutting down the Oak to the Briar's disadvantage, Spenser explodes the Virgilian model. The Oak is the tree of epic: 'With armes full strong . . . / . . . King of the field' (104–8).[46] The Briar is Spenser's tree of pastoral, favoured by Colin ('June', 7–8; 'December', 2), and home to the 'Nightingale' (123), which is Colin's bird ('August', 183–6; 'November', 25–6, 141; 'December', 79). Finally, the Husbandman is a georgic figure, and his destruction of the nightingale's home recalls Orpheus' nightingale-ploughman simile in *Georgics* IV (511–15). As Spenser surveys the landscape, he finds the amorous and didactic amateurs crippling each other. By diagnosing their dangers, he clears a path for himself as the heir to Virgil and Chaucer.

Cohering with 'Februarie', 'March' is not only 'a delightful vignette of befuddled pubescence' (Yale, p. 55), but a mythos about the erotic origin of the pastoral poet's national art. While the eclogue represents Willye and Thomalin as boys discovering desire, E. K.'s 'Argument' introduces a 'speciall meaning': 'to know Cupide the Poets God of Love'. For Spenser, Cupid is the erotic desire creating the art of poetry, and his narrative about the birth of desire aims to help young poets 'know' and order passion. Yet topical allusions indicate that even mature political leaders can bear adolescent desire. Line 59 alludes to the Earl of Leicester's secret marriage to Lettice Knowlles, which angered the queen, while Thomalin's emblem warns Elizabeth about her marriage to Alençon (Yale, pp. 58, 62). Lines 49–51 insert the poet into this allusive politics: 'thilke same unhappye Ewe, / Whose clouted legge her hurt doth shewe, / Fell headlong into a del.' Spenser's word 'clouted' to describe the Ewe's bandage evokes Colin Clout (*clout* = mending cloth, *OED*, 1st entry, def. 1), while the Ewe evokes

Elizabeth, ill in her desire for Alençon. In 'March', Spenser presents himself as a physician who can cure desires affecting national health.

Cohering with 'March', 'Aprill' presents Hobbinol 'record[ing]' (30) Colin's 'laye / of fayre Eliza, Queene of shepheardes all' (33–4). According to E. K. in his 'Argument', 'This Aeglogue . . . prayse[s] . . . Queen Elizabeth'. E. K.'s directive, together with Spenser's imitation of Virgil's Messianic Eclogue IV, advertises the English Christian Virgil preparing to write epic: 'Helpe me to blaze / Her worthy praise' (43–4). Yet Colin is unable to perform this Virgilian role: 'He . . . doth forbeare / His wonted songs' (15–16). Thus, Spenser condemns Elizabeth for sabotaging both national identity and his Virgilian career by proposing to marry Alençon. Spenser's simultaneous praise and dispraise of Elizabeth both advance his pastoral of progression, for he uses an Ovidian erotic myth to identify Eliza as the 'personification' not merely 'of pastoral poetry', but of pastoral in preparation for epic: 'Of fayre Elisa be your silver song, / . . . may shee florish . . . / In princely plight. / For she is Syrinx daughter. . . / Which Pan . . . of her begot' (46, 48–51).[47] Both queen and shepherdess, Eliza embodies the Virgilian topos for generic progression: 'comparing great things with small'.[48] The shepherds' queen both enfolds and unfolds Spenser's future epic.

'Aprill', then, coheres with 'March', 'Februarie' and 'Januarye', in that Colin's song of Eliza illustrates a premature version of the epic that neither Willye, Thomalin, Cuddie nor Thenot sings and that Colin stops trying to sing. Yet Spenser advertises his own ability to write epic, as the woodcut indicates (fig. 3), for Colin plays 'the cornett, a Renaissance instrument used for royal salute in situations inappropriate for the [epic] trumpet [*FQ*, 1, proem, 1]' (Yale, p. 69). The first tetrad of eclogues evaluates competing ideological desires, genres, and career models available in the late 1570s.

'Maye' breeches this vocational program by redefining 'shepherd' as pastor: 'under . . . Piers and Palinodie, be represented two formes of pastoures or Ministers, or the protestant and the Catholique' ('Argument'). Yet the debate seems to be more between two forms of Protestants. Piers represents the faction led by the Archbishop of Canterbury, Edmund Grindal – 'Algrind' (75) – in 'a moderate statement of the progressive Protestants' concern in the 1570s for further church reform'; by contrast, Palinode 'represents the unreconstructed, superficially conforming Elizabethan cleric' (Yale, p. 85). Nonetheless, details reveal that the poet understands the ecclesiastical problem to have a literary cause. Palinode and Piers are not poets, but we might see them as English pastors influenced by poets, especially the amorous and didactic amateurs they resemble. Thus the woodcut (fig. 4) 'centers on bringing home the May with the wagon here

3 'Aprill' woodcut

4 'Maye' woodcut

Virgil is an empty classical temple and an Italianate palace . . . Cuddie rejects Piers' offer by pointing out the figure approaching the temple [of Fame]': Colin Clout (Yale, p. 167). Yet the woodcut does not account for the destiny of the Virgilian model in the eclogue itself. In lines 1–36, Spenser diagnoses the problem plaguing the poet: he who writes 'dapper ditties' (13) to delight the youth suffers from artistic impotence, because he cannot attract patrons. In lines 37–84, Spenser introduces two solutions, both encouraging the poet to attract patronage by moving from lower to higher genres. The first, recognised by Cuddie (55–60) and E. K., are 'the three . . . workes of Virgile' (196). The second is the pattern Piers endorses, which begins by progressing from Virgilian pastoral to epic – 'Abandon then the base and viler clowne . . . / And sing of . . . wars' (37–9) – but then adds the two phases identified earlier: first, 'when the stubborne stroke of stronger stounds, / Has somewhat slackt the tenor of thy string: / Of love . . . sing' (49–51); second, when the poet cannot find a 'place' in 'Princes pallace' (79–80), he should 'flye backe to heaven' (84). The young poet should follow Virgil in moving from pastoral to epic, but when he becomes tired he should follow Chaucer by writing love lyric; finally, when he becomes disillusioned, he should follow Du Bartas in rejecting secular poetry for divine poetry. In lines 85–96, Spenser advertises Colin as the poet who can complete 'such famous flight' (88).[54] Whereas Cuddie thinks Colin's love grounds him (89–90), Piers offers a corrective: 'love does teach him climbe so hie . . . / Such immortall mirrhor . . . / Would rayse ones mynd above the starry skie' (91–4). Spenser represents Colin moving beyond Ovidian love to Neo-Platonic love in order to propel his flight to fame.

In 'November', Colin fulfills Piers' prophecy by singing an elegy that enacts his author's national credentials as the Christian Virgil. The eclogue shows Thenot persuading Colin to break his silence (1–10). For the first time, Colin sings his song himself – not about Rosalind nor Eliza but a 'mayden of great bloud . . . Dido' ('Argument'). As a funeral elegy, Colin's Song of Dido divides in two. In lines 49–162, he mourns the fragility of Dido's care for the shepherds (93–4), expresses contempt for the world (153) and learns that 'nys on earth assurance to be sought: / For what might be in earthlie mould, / . . . did her buried body hould' (156–9). Like Hamlet in the graveyard, Colin witnesses the grim truth about the body's end. Yet as with Hamlet before the fencing match, in lines 163–202 Colin's sight of Dido's body produces the miracle of epiphany: 'Her soule unbodied of the burdenous corpse' (166). His epiphany takes him beyond tragedy into revelation: 'I see thee blessed soule . . . / Walke in Elisian fieldes' (178–9).

Ever since E. K. declared that 'November' 'farre pass[eth] . . . his reache,

5 'October' woodcut

and in myne opinion all other the Eglogues of this booke' ('Argument'), readers have found here the high point of the *Calender*, which Spenser unfolds in religious, political and generic dimensions. First, relying on Scripture, he attempts to demonstrate one of his highest goals: to help the nation pass through mourning to meaning in the face of national tragedy. Hence, Colin's song produces a catharsis both in himself and in his fellow mourner. Thenot has asked Colin to 'bewayle my wofull tene' (41) – put into verse his sadness at Dido's death – and Colin indicates that the song has worked for him: 'my woe now wasted is' (201). Thenot then agrees (203). Second, as E. K. hints by noting the New Poet's imitation of Marot's funeral elegy for Louise de Savoy, 'the frenche queene' ('Argument'), Spenser uses Dido as a 'cult name for Elizabeth' in order to represent her death to him and to the nation if she were to marry Alençon.[55] Yet Spenser softens his criticism: 'Ne would she scorne the simple shepheards swaine, / For she would cal hem often heme / And give hem curds and clouted Creame . . . / Als Colin cloute she would not once disdayne' (97–101). Spenser's 'clouted Creame' and 'Colin cloute' equate the drink Dido gives her shepherds with the identity of her chief pastoral singer. The clotted cream that the queen gives her subjects has evidently been infused into the identity of her poet, who returns the gift by singing of her. Spenser's representation of the intimate relation between poet and queen is a stunning image of the 'reciprocal' self-fashioning ordering his pastoral of progression.[56]

Third, Spenser maps the Augustinian pattern of death and glory onto the Virgilian progression of pastoral and epic. Like Eliza, Dido is that curious amalgam, a sovereign shepherdess, indicating that Spenser imagines her as a personified embodiment of pastoral and epic, symbolised when Thenot identifies her elegist, Colin, as the 'Nightingale . . . sovereigne of song' (25). In this eclogue, Spenser represents the poet's transcendent vision of Dido's apotheosis as the register of his authority, the single experience that allows him to prove his tender wings: he acquires wisdom about the grace ordering nature.

Yet Colin's vision does not lead him to write epic but rather to withdraw from the world. In 'December', is Colin's withdrawal a sign of despondency and death?[57] The career principle suggests an alternative. Colin prays to 'soveraigne Pan . . . God of shepheards' (7) – not to the lover of Syrinx but to the saver of souls (8–10). After reviewing the spring, summer, autumn and winter of his life, Colin 'hang[s his] . . . pype upon this tree' (141), bidding 'Adieu' to delights, lambs, woods, Hobbinol and Rosalind (151–6) – the defining marks of his pastoral art. Thus, anticipating the epic knight of the Red Crosse after his vision of the New Jerusalem (FQ, I, x, 56–64), Colin engages in a preliminary response to the epiphany of Christian grace, in preparation for a renewed return to the world. The Virgilian poet withdraws from nature because he has envisioned grace. Spenser does not show Colin returning to the world because to do so would be to transgress the boundary of pastoral and move into epic. Accordingly, he leaves Colin standing on the threshold of this return; the calendrical pattern literally promises its advent.

In the 'Envoy', Spenser summarises the hierarchical relations among his pastoral of progression, his cyclical pattern of the Christian calendar, his educational programme of national duty and desire, and his vertical pattern of Christian glory:

> Loe I have made a Calender for every yeare,
> That steele in strength, and time in durance shall outweare:
> And if I marked well the starres revolution,
> It shall continewe til the worlds dissolution.
> To teach the ruder shepheard how to feede his sheepe,
> And from the falsers fraud his folded flocke to keepe.
> Goe lyttle Calender, thou hast a free passeporte,
> Goe but a lowly gate emongste the meaner sorte.
> Dare not to match thy pype with Tityrus hys style,
> Nor with the Pilgrim that the Ploughman playde a whyle:
> But followe them farre off, and their high steppes adore.
>
> ('December', 235–45)

By daring to match his pastoral art with those of Virgil and Chaucer, Christian England's national poet announces his plan to 'followe . . . their high steppes' down the path to epic.

Colin Clouts Come Home Againe

Sixteen years later, Spenser makes explicit the *Calender*'s pastoral of progression. In *Colin Clouts Come Home Againe*, the resurrection of his persona shows that his progression to epic is still underway. England's Virgil has not completed his epic. In this poem, Spenser does not pen 'a temporary return to pastoral' in order to 'scrutin[ise] . . . the options available to him' (Yale, p. 524); amid new constraints, he attempts to progress beyond pastoral through epic.

Thus *Colin Clout* reveals the defining paradox of its author's biography: Spenser's writing of *The Faerie Queene* in Ireland dictates that his destiny is to be an exiled shepherd writing national epic from the vantage point of pastoral.[58] Mid-way between the *Calender* and the completed *Faerie Queene*, *Colin Clout* narrates this career-defining paradox.

The biographical interstice within which Spenser writes – between instalments of *The Faerie Queene* – defines *Colin Clout* as generically beyond pastoral, amid-epic. In the Renaissance hierarchy of genres, this production history recalls the recent advent of 'the true avant-garde poetry of the Elizabethan period': the Elizabethan minor epic.[59] *Colin Clout* alludes to two minor epics, Raleigh's *Ocean To Cynthia* (c. 1592) (164–71, 428–31) and Samuel Daniel's *Complaint of Rosamond* (1592) (416–27); it probably also alludes to the genre's inventor, Thomas Lodge, perhaps even his epyllion, *Scylla's Metamorphosis* (1589) (394–5); and finally, it may allude to Shakespeare's two epyllia, *Venus and Adonis* and *The Rape of Lucrece* (1593, 1594) (444–7).[60] In all four cases, Spenser represents the minor epic through the career principle, as this on Daniel: 'Yet doth his trembling Muse but lowly flie . . . / In loves soft laies . . . / Then rouze thy feathers . . . / And to what course thou please thy selfe advance' (420–5). In 1595, Drayton identifies *Endymion and Phoebe*, his pastoral Neo-Platonic chastening of the Ovidian genre, as a companion piece to *Colin Clout*: 'Colin . . . my muse . . . rudely . . . presumes to sing by thee.'[61] Drayton is responding partly to Marlowe, who by 1593 had created the masterpiece of the genre in *Hero and Leander*; this 'Hymn to Earthly Love and Beauty, an anti-Spenserian manifesto',[62] had appropriated Raleigh's identification with Leander from his own minor epic (*Ocean to Cynthia*, 487–91) in order to support Raleigh in his negotiations with the queen after she imprisoned him for secretly marrying her lady-in-waiting, Elizabeth Throckmorton.[63] The minor epic is 'Elizabethan' in daring to represent the queen's courtly sexuality.

In 1591, Spenser dedicated *Colin Clout* to Raleigh. Openly, he built support for the great courtier into his fiction, in *Colin Clout* as in *The Faerie Queene* (e.g. IV, vii–viii). Probably because of the Throckmorton affair, Spenser did not publish *Colin Clout* until 1595. In its formal and thematic features, his second pastoral responds to the 'Elizabethan' minor epic.

In the 'Dedicatory Epistle', Spenser only appears to identify the genre of the poem as pastoral: 'I make you present of this simple pastorall, unworthie of your higher conceipt for the meanesse of the stile.' 'Meanesse' means *lowness* and *in the middle style*.[64] Through this pun, Spenser identifies his poem as a pastoral in the middle style – a significant change from the *Calender* – as John Hughes in 1715 first noted. At lines 616–23, Spenser even narrativises his middle-style pastoral: 'Colin . . . thou hast forgot / Thy selfe . . . to mount so hie' (616–17). Similarly, the poem's verse form marks its mid-level status. The 'decasyllabic cross-rhymed quatrain (abab) . . . constitutes an innovation almost of the order of the Spenserian stanza'.[65] The poem's length also indicates its mid-genre status. At 955 lines, it resembles *Rosamond* (910), *Hero and Leander* (818) and *Venus and Adonis* (1194). Even the narrative mode of *Colin Clout*, complicated by dialogue, allegory and digression, recalls standard features of the minor epic.[66]

Colin Clout begins by introducing Colin's 'song' (51) to his English sovereign from the shores of Ireland: a 'shepheards boy' (1) tells 'the shepheards nation' (17) of Queen Cynthia's national 'glor[y]' (46). Thus, Spenser identifies his 'simple pastorall' as an analogue to *The Faerie Queene*: 'Wake then my pipe . . . / Till I have told her praises lasting long' (48–9).

Unlike the *Calender*, this 'pastoral' centers on the poet in relation to his sovereign. No longer does Spenser use his persona's inability to write epic to predict his own epic; now he records his actual promulgation of epic. Since his days in the *Calender*, Colin has changed considerably. He has left Kent for Ireland, and he has started singing again – before his entire community, which now includes both shepherds and shepherdesses. In Ireland, unlike in Kent, women have a voice. Amid this new companionate community, Colin has become famous, like the Irish bard who is his model.[67] Rather than providing Spenser with 'a space *outside* the Virgilian career model',[68] Colin's new 'home' provides a space that reports his progression through it. Colin Clout has not failed, become disillusioned, or abandoned epic. Printed in England through the publisher of his epic, William Ponsonby, *Colin Clout* navigates a view of the present state of England from the wilds of Ireland. This new 'British' dynamic becomes Spenser's final signature as a national poet.

The opening line – 'The shepheards boy (best knowen by that name)' – emphasises Colin's new fame, while the second line identifies its Virgilian and Chaucerian genealogy: 'That after Tityrus first sung his lay'. The third line then announces the reason for Colin's fame: 'Laies of sweet love, without rebuke or blame'. A reformed poet of eros, Colin now sings delightful love songs consistent with conscience and moral discipline instructive to the nation.

Colin begins his song to Cynthia with 'The shepheard of the Ocean' (66) because Spenser's Irish pastoral friendship with Raleigh led to the epic voyage to their English sovereign's court. After Ocean 'chaunst to find' Colin singing (56–66), they exchanged songs played on one instrument – a harmonious rivalry alien to Theocritus, Virgil and even the *Calender*: 'aemuling my pipe, he tooke in hond . . . He pip'd, I sung; and when he sung, I piped' (72–6). Colin then records the songs the friends composed. Colin's mini-Ovidian epyllion of two Irish rivers, Bregog and Mulla (104–55), mythologises the Throckmorton affair (Yale, pp. 523–4). A cautionary tale to Raleigh about the dangers of 'secret . . . love' (145), the myth also alludes to Spenser's poetic fame, since the Bregog flowed through his Kilcolman estate (92–5).[69] Ocean's brief song (164–7) inscribes *Ocean to Cynthia*, Raleigh's complaint to Elizabeth during the Throckmorton affair: 'His song was . . . a lamentable lay . . . / Of Cynthia' (164–6). Spenser's design – two pastoral shepherds sing minor epics concerning the queen before their epic voyage to her court – models the mid-epic role that *Colin Clout* plays in his pastoral of progression.

Unlike the *Calender*, which placed Colin's isolated Song of Eliza in a lost past, or *The Faerie Queene*, which deferred its representation of Gloriana, *Colin Clout* represents Cynthia in her person and narrates the poet's audience in her presence. Spenser records history, but he also represents a royal version of the artistic experience that bridges pastoral to epic. Colin does not tell us the contents of his epic song to Cynthia (358–67), but he does acknowledge its pastoral origin – 'to mine oaten pipe [she] enclin'd her eare' (360) – and its pastoral effect: she 'joyd that country shepherd ought could fynd / Worth harkening to, emongst the learned throng' (366–7). Spenser presents himself as a pastoral poet writing epic, and what his sovereign enjoys is surely what Colin has just presented: his signature vision of the female, which does not celebrate an abstract Neo-Platonic ideal of beauty, a physically beautiful Ovidian body, or the Petrarchan male's mental image of the beautiful female, but a wondrous immanentist fusion of the three: 'The image of the heavens in shape humane' (351). The poet's perception of the female fills him with 'furious insolence' (622), which makes Cynthia famous within time and glorious through eternity: 'That woods . . . thou hast made / Her name to eccho unto heaven hie' (482–3).

Spenser's mid-level revision of simple pastoral also emerges in Colin's answer to Thestylis' famous question about Colin's return from Cynthia's court: 'Why didst thou ever leave that happie place?' (654). Colin's answer (660–951) divides into three parts. In lines 660–763, he says he leaves because the court violates Christian charity: 'each one seeks with malice . . . / To thrust downe other into foule disgrace' (690–2). As his use of 'tourne' indicates (672), Colin's return 'home' does not mean that Spenser abandons epic for pastoral, but that he rejects the court as the home from which to write epic (as *Prothalamion* confirms). In lines 764–906, Colin offsets courtly pride with his own care for the other, symbolised in his Hymn to Love. And in lines 907–51, he particularises his new poetics of love by generously defending Rosalind.

Here at the close, Spenser consolidates his standing as national 'Priest' of love (832), wise about love's 'mysterie' (833), 'religiously . . . esteemed' (830). Line 788 – '[Love's] mightie mysteries they do prophane' – is general but reads like a veiled criticism of *Hero and Leander*, which presented the female as 'Venus nun' worshipping at Venus' Church.[70] Colin's portrait of Rosalind thus coheres with that of Cynthia: 'of divine regard and heavenly hew' (933).[71] Although Rosalind has not (yet) accepted his love, he cares for her; submitting masculine identity to the dignity of female integrity (911–14), Colin accepts 'blame' for 'look[ing] . . . so hie' and prays that she will 'grant' her 'grace' not to him alone but to the community at large (936–40). If Rosalind figures Elizabeth Boyle, Spenser's wife, his immanentist erotics prepares for *Amoretti/Epithalamion*, published later that year.[72]

Spenser closes *Colin Clout* with a powerful inscription of his pastoral of progression, in imitation of Virgil's conclusion to Eclogue 10, which uses the '*surgamous*' topos (let us rise) to 'imply, allegorically, that the writer will proceed to . . . "higher" poetic forms': Colin 'from ground did rise, / And after him uprose eke all the rest: / All loth to part, but that the glooming skies / Warnd them to draw their bleating flocks to rest' (952–5).[73] This ominous, poignant conclusion identifies Colin as the divinely inspired epic leader of the 'shepheards nation' who cares for both the female and the fold amid the threat of political darkness.

Published the year after *Colin Clout*, Book VI of *The Faerie Queene* extends Spenser's pastoral of progression by inserting his pastoral persona into his epic landscape. In this third or epic phase to his career, Colin combines erotic inspiration for private recreation with public service to his community, which here includes both Irish and English inhabitants (Corydon and Calidore). Thus, Spenser presents Colin performing two pastoral songs within his national epic. In canto x, the second song (the more famous, detailed, complex) shows Colin's pastoral vision of the Graces on Mount Acidale, with a Fourth Grace at its center, interrupted by the Knight of Courtesy. Does this episode validate or interrogate Spenser's pastoral of progression? Colin's neglected first song supplies an interpretive clue. In canto ix, 'the shepheard swaynes' gather on a 'sunshynie' day, 'The whiles their flockes in shadowes shrouded bee', when they 'agree, / That Colin Clout should pipe as one most fit; / And Calidore should lead the ring, as hee / That most in Pastorellaes grace did sit' (41). Finally, Spenser is the prime pastoralist of Britain because he so capaciously envisions the rustic poet of companionate desire to be the engracing conductor of national epic glory.[74]

NOTES

1 Aelius Donatus, *Life of Virgil*, section 123, trans. David Wilson-Okamura, 1996 (at www.virgil.org/vitae/a-donatus.htm, 23 July 1997). See Charles Martindale, 'Green Politics: The *Eclogues*', in Charles Martindale, ed., *Cambridge Companion to Virgil* (Cambridge: Cambridge University Press, 1997), p. 107.

2 John of Garland, '*Parisiana poetria*', ed. and trans. Traugott Lawler (New Haven: Yale University Press, 1974), pp. 38–41.

3 See A. C. Hamilton, 'The Argument of Spenser's *Shepheardes Calender*', in Harry Berger, Jr., ed., *Spenser* (Englewood Cliffs: Prentice, 1968), pp. 30–9; and Donald Cheney, 'The Circular Argument of *The Shepheardes Calender*', in George M. Logan and Gordon Teskey, eds., *Unfolded Tales: Essays on Renaissance Romance* (Ithaca: Cornell University Press, 1989), pp. 137–61.

4 W. W. Greg, *Pastoral Poetry and Pastoral Drama: A Literary Inquiry, with Special Reference to the Pre-Restoration Stage in England* (London: Bullen, 1906), p. 91.

5 See Leo Braudy, *The Frenzy of Renown: Fame and Its History* (New York: Oxford University Press, 1986), esp. pp. 167, 169, 172, 232.

6 Louise Schleiner, 'Spenser's "E. K." as Edmund Kent (Kenned\of Kent): Kyth (Couth), Kissed, and Kunning-Conning', *ELR* 20 (1990), 374–407. Spenser quotations are from *Variorum*; the archaic i-j and u-v are modernised, as are other obsolete typographical conventions such as the italicising of names and places.

7 Paul Alpers, 'Pastoral and the Domain of Lyric in Spenser's *Shepheardes Calender*', *Representations* 12 (1985), 83. See Michael McCanles, '*The Shepheardes Calender* as Document and Monument', *SEL* 22 (1982), 5–19; and Paul Alpers, 'The Eclogue Tradition and the Nature of Pastoral', *College English* 34 (1972), 352–71.

8 Raymond Jenkins, 'Pastoral', in Raymond Jenkins, ed., *The Legacy of Rome: A New Appraisal* (London: Oxford University Press, 1992), pp. 151–75.

9 Michael Drayton, 'To the Reader of his Pastorals' (1619), in Cummings, p. 81.

10 Yale, pp. 524, 563–8. Cf. Sannazaro's pastoral *Arcadia* and his published fragment, *Piscatorial Eclogues*, which follows a similar pattern.

11 Thomas Nashe, *Pierce Penilesse* (1592), in *Works*, ed. Ronald B. McKerrow and rev. F. P. Wilson, 5 vols. (Oxford: Blackwell, 1958), I, p. 299.

12 Colin Clout also appears in the 1580 Spenser–Harvey Letters (G. Gregory Smith, ed. *Elizabethan Critical Essays*, 2 vols. (London: Oxford University Press, 1904), I, p. 114); 1590 *Faerie Queene* (Harvey's 'Commendatory Verse'); 1591 *Complaints* ('Ruines of Time', 225); 1591 *Daphnaida* (229); 1595 *Amoretti/Epithalamion* (G.W. I.'s 'Commendatory Verse'); 1596 *Faerie Queene* (VI, ix–x); 1609 'Mutabilitie Cantoes' (VII, vi, 40).

13 Paul Alpers, 'Spenser's Late Pastorals', *ELH* 56 (1989), 797.

14 Patrick Cheney, *Spenser's Famous Flight: A Renaissance Idea of a Literary Career* (Toronto: University of Toronto Press, 1993), pp. 27–38, 225–45.

15 Andrew Hadfield, *Literature, Politics and National Identity: Reformation to Renaissance* (Cambridge: Cambridge University Press, 1994), pp. 192–3.

16 See Alastair Fowler, *Kinds of Literature: An Introduction to the Theory of Genres and Modes* (Cambridge, MA: Harvard University Press, 1982), p. 240; Jane Tylus, 'Spenser, Virgil, and the Politics of Labor', *ELH* 55 (1988), 53–77.

17 Donatus, *Life of Virgil*, section 123.

18 Clark Hulse, *Metamorphic Verse: The Elizabethan Minor Epic* (Princeton: Princeton University Press, 1981), p. 12.

19 Richard Barnfield, 'Dedicatory Epistle' to *Cynthia*, ed. George Klawitter (Selinsgrove: Susquehanna University Press; London: Associated University Presses, 1990), p. 116.

20 David M. Halperin, *Before Pastoral: Theocritus and the Ancient Tradition of Bucolic Poetry* (New Haven: Yale University Press, 1983), pp. 174–7, 223–30, 237–43, 250–3; Joseph Farrell, *Virgil's 'Georgics' and the Traditions of Ancient Epic: The Art of Allusion in Literary History* (New York: Oxford University Press, 1991), p. 314; Sannazaro, *'Arcadia' and the 'Piscatorial Eclogues'*, trans. Ralph Nash (Detroit: Wayne State University Press, 1966), pp. 9, 14–19.

21 *Virgil*, trans. H. Rushton Fairclough, Loeb Classical Library, 2 vols. (Cambridge, MA: Harvard University Press; London: Heinemann, 1935), I, p. 241.

22 Paul Alpers, *What is Pastoral?* (Chicago: University of Chicago Press, 1996), p. 9.

23 John Brinsley, *Ludus literarius* (London, 1612); repr. English Linguistics 1500–1800, no. 62 (Menston: Scholar Press, 1968), p. 194.

24 Alpers, *What is Pastoral?*, pp. 28–37.

25 Friedrich von Schiller, 'On Naïve and Sentimental Poetry', *German Aesthetic and Literary Criticism*, ed. H. B. Nisbet (Cambridge: Cambridge University Press, 1985); Renato Poggioli, *The Oaten Flute: Essays on Pastoral Poetry and the Pastoral Ideal* (Cambridge, MA: Harvard University Press, 1975). See also Susan Snyder, *Pastoral Process: Spenser, Marvell, Milton* (Stanford: Stanford University Press, 1998), esp. pp. 1–18.

26 George Puttenham, *Arte of English Poesie*, ed. Gladys Doidge Willcock and Alice Walker (Cambridge: Cambridge University Press, 1936), p. 302; William

Empson, *Some Versions of Pastoral* (New York: New Directions, 1974), p. 22; Louis Montrose, '"Eliza, Queene of shepheardes", and the Pastoral of Power', *ELR* 10 (1980), 153–82.

27 John D. Bernard, *Ceremonies of Innocence: Pastoralism in the Poetry of Edmund Spenser* (Cambridge: Cambridge University Press, 1989), pp. 8, 106–7.

28 See, respectively, Hallett Darius Smith, *Elizabethan Poetry: A Study in Conventions, Meaning, and Expression* (Cambridge, MA: Harvard University Press, 1952), p. 2; Isabel G. MacCaffrey, 'Allegory and Pastoral in *The Shepheardes Calender*', in *Critical Essays on Spenser from ELH* (Baltimore: Johns Hopkins Press, 1970), pp. 121, 127–8, 132–3; and Louis Montrose, '"The perfecte paterne of a Poete": The Poetics of Courtship in *The Shepheardes Calender*', *TSLL* 21 (1979), 54.

29 David J. Baker, 'Spenser and the Uses of British History', in Patrick Cheney and Lauren Silberman, eds., *Worldmaking Spenser: Explorations in the Early Modern Age* (Lexington: University Press of Kentucky, 2000), pp. 193–203. See also Andrew Hadfield, *Spenser's Irish Experience: Wilde Fruit and Salvage Soyl* (Oxford: Clarendon, 1997), pp. 13–17.

30 Hadfield, *Literature, Politics and National Identity*, pp. 172, 176, 182, 189–90; Richard Helgerson, *Forms of Nationhood: The Elizabethan Writing of England* (Chicago: University of Chicago Press, 1992), pp. 55, 57, 59. On people power, see Robert Lane, *Shepheardes Devises: Edmund Spenser's 'Shepheardes Calender' and the Institutions of Elizabethan Society* (Athens: University of Georgia Press, 1993).

31 David L. Miller, 'Authorship, Anonymity, and *The Shepheardes Calender*', *MLQ* 40 (1979), 227.

32 For 'Colonnes', see Richard Stanyhurst, *Description of Ireland* (1577), quoted in Willy Maley, *Salvaging Spenser: Colonialism, Culture, and Identity* (Houndmills, Basingstoke: Macmillan, 1997), p. 32; for 'empire', see D. Cheney, 'The Circular Argument', p. 147.

33 Ruth Samson Luborsky, 'The Illustrations to *The Shepheardes Calender*', *Sp. St.* 2 (1981), 29.

34 Sidney, *Apology*, p. 133.

35 Martindale, 'Green Politics', p. 117.

36 Luborsky, 'Illustrations', pp. 24, 29.

37 Ibid.; Yale, p. 27.

38 Harry Berger, Jr., *Revisionary Play: Studies in the Spenserian Dynamics* (Berkeley: University of California Press, 1988), pp. 277–9, 332–3.

39 John W. Moore, Jr., 'Colin Breaks His Pipe: A Reading of the "January" Eclogue', *ELR* 5 (1975), 3–24.

40 John Calvin, *Institutes of the Christian Religion*, ed. John T. McNeill, trans. Ford Lewis Battles, 2 vols. (Philadelphia: Westminster, 1960), I, v, 4 (p. 56).

41 Paul E. McLane, *Spenser's 'Shepheardes Calender': A Study in Elizabethan Allegory* (Notre Dame: University of Notre Dame Press, 1961), pp. 27–46.

42 Hadfield, *Literature, Politics and National Identity*, pp. 178, 181.

43 On amateur poets as precursors to laureate poets, see Richard Helgerson, *Self-Crowned Laureates: Spenser, Jonson, Milton, and the Literary System* (Berkeley: University of California Press, 1983), pp. 21–54.

44 Dante, '*De Vulgari Eloquentia': Dante's Book of Exile*, trans. and ed. Marianne Shapiro (Lincoln: University of Nebraska Press, 1990), II, ii (p. 72).

45 John A. Burrow, 'Chaucer, Geoffrey', in *Spenser Encyclopedia*, p. 145.

46 Marillene Allen, 'Trees,' in *Spenser Encyclopedia*, p. 698.

47 See Montrose, '"Eliza"', p. 167.

48 John S. Coolidge, 'Great Things and Small: The Virgilian Progression', *CL* 17 (1965), 1–23.

49 John D. Bernard, '"June" and the Structure of Spenser's *Shepheardes Calender*', *PQ* 60 (1981), 307.

50 See Farrell, *Vergil's 'Georgics'*, p. 314.

51 W. L. Renwick, ed., *The Shepheardes Calender* (London: Scholaris, 1930), p. 206.

52 See Miller, 'Authorship, Anonymity', p. 229.

53 Cheney, *Spenser's Famous Flight*, pp. 81–6.

54 Ibid., pp. 27–38; Cf. Patrick Cheney, *Marlowe's Counterfeit Profession: Ovid, Spenser, Counter-Nationhood* (Toronto: University of Toronto Press, 1997), pp. 61–5.

55 Douglas Brooks-Davies, ed., *Edmund Spenser: Selected Shorter Poetry* (London: Longman, 1995), p. 172.

56 Louis Montrose, 'Spenser's Domestic Domain: Poetry, Property, and the Early Modern Subject', in Margreta de Grazia, Maureen Quilligan and Peter Stally-brass, eds., *Subject and Object in Renaissance Culture* (Cambridge: Cambridge University Press, 1996), pp. 83–130.

57 See Richard McCabe, '"Little booke: thy selfe present": The Politics of Presentation in *The Shepheardes Calender*', in Howard Erskine-Hill and Richard McCabe, eds., *Presenting Poetry: Composition, Publication, Reception* (Cambridge: Cambridge University Press, 1995), pp. 15–40.

58 See Richard McCabe, 'Edmund Spenser, Poet of Exile', *PBA* 80 (1993), 73–103.

59 Hulse, *Metamorphic Verse*, p. 12.

60 Variorum VII, pp. 568–72; Yale, pp. 532, 541–2.

61 Drayton, *Endymion and Phoebe*, 993–4, in M. M. Reese, ed., *Elizabethan Verse Romances* (London: Routledge and Kegan Paul, 1968), p. 267.

62 Muriel C. Bradbrook, *Shakespeare and Elizabethan Poetry* (London: Chatto, 1961), p. 59.

63 P. Cheney, *Marlowe's Counterfeit Profession*, pp. 240, 246–7

64 Sam Meyer, *An Interpretation of Edmund Spenser's 'Colin Clout'* (Notre Dame: University of Notre Dame Press, 1969), p. 19; Yale, p. 525.

65 David Shore, '*Colin Clouts Come Home Againe*', in *Spenser Encyclopedia*, p. 174.

66 Hulse, *Metamorphic Verse*, pp. 3–34; Shore, '*Colin Clout*'.

67 Christopher Highley, 'Spenser and the Bards', *Sp. St.* 12 (1998), 77–103.

68 Sue Petitt Starke, 'Briton Knight or Irish Bard: Spenser's Pastoral Persona and the Epic Project in *A View of the Present State of Ireland* and *Colin Clouts Come Home Againe*', *Sp. St.* 12 (1998), 133.

69 Thomas R. Edwards, *Imagination and Power: A Study of Poetry on Public Themes* (New York: Oxford University Press, 1971), pp. 48–51.

70 *Hero and Leander* I, 45, in Christopher Marlowe, *The Complete Poems and Translations*, ed. Stephen Orgel (Harmondsworth: Penguin, 1971).

71 J. Christopher Warner, 'Poetry and Praise in *Colin Clouts Come Home Againe* (1595)' *SP* 94 (1997), 368–81.
72 David Burchmore, 'The Image of the Centre in *Colin Clouts Come Home Againe*,' *RES*, NS 28 (1977), 393–406.
73 Martindale, 'Green Politics', p. 113.
74 For helping me think through the topics of this essay, I am grateful to Paul Alpers, Georgia Brown, Clark Hulse, William Oram and Michael Schoenfeldt. For helping with the research and with the checking of quotations and citations, I am indebted to Todd Preston. For judiciously reading drafts, I would like to thank Robert R. Edwards, Andrew Hadfield, David Lee Miller, John W. Moore, Jr, and Anne Lake Prescott. Finally, for a research fellowship supporting the project, I am grateful to Penn State's Institute for the Arts and Humanistic Studies.

FURTHER READING

Paul Alpers, *What is Pastoral?* (Chicago: University of Chicago Press, 1996).

John D. Bernard, *Ceremonies of Innocence: Pastoralism in the Poetry of Edmund Spenser* (Cambridge: Cambridge University Press, 1989).

Harry Berger, Jr., *Revisionary Play: Studies in the Spenserian Dynamics* (Berkeley: University of California Press, 1988), pp. 277–452.

Patrick Cheney, *Spenser's Famous Flight: A Renaissance Idea of a Literary Career* (Toronto: University of Toronto Press, 1993).

Patrick Cullen, *Spenser, Marvell, and Renaissance Pastoral* (Cambridge, MA: Harvard University Press, 1970).

Andrew Hadfield, *Literature, Politics and National Identity: Reformation to Renaissance* (Cambridge: Cambridge University Press, 1994), pp. 170–201.

S. K. Heninger, Jr., 'The Shepheardes Calender', in *Spenser Encyclopedia*, pp. 645–51.

Nancy Jo Hoffman, *Spenser's Pastorals: 'The Shepheardes Calender' and 'Colin Clout'* (Baltimore: Johns Hopkins University Press, 1977).

Lynn Staley Johnson, *'The Shepheardes Calender': An Introduction* (University Park: Pennsylvania State University Press, 1990).

Louis Montrose, '"The perfecte paterne of a Poete": The Poetics of Courtship in *The Shepheardes Calender*', *TSLL* 21 (1979), 34–67.

Annabel Patterson, 'Reopening the Green Cabinet: Clément Marot and Edmund Spenser', in *Pastoral and Ideology: Virgil to Valéry* (Berkeley: University of California Press, 1987), pp. 106–32.

David R. Shore, *Spenser and the Poetics of Pastoral: A Study of the World of Colin Clout* (Kingston-Montreal: McGill-Queen's University Press, 1985).

5

SUSANNE L. WOFFORD

The Faerie Queene, Books I–III

To open Book I of *The Faerie Queene* is to encounter immediately the question of what kind of poem one is reading. A nationalistic panegyric that eulogises Queen Elizabeth I, whom Spenser calls 'O Goddesse heauenly bright, / Mirrour of grace and Maiestie diuine, / Great lady of the greatest Isle' and, perhaps more honestly, 'O dearest dred' (I, proem, 4), *The Faerie Queene* has been described as well-written Elizabethan propaganda or at least as a celebration and extension of the queen's political mythology; as political poetry that is complexly engaged, critical of the queen and her politics; as a Protestant poem more shaped by its Reformation context than by fiction or secular literary ideals; as an inspired Humanist summation of mythology that brings into English a wealth of plot material (*mythoi*) from Irish, Welsh, Scottish, French, Italian, Latin and Greek sources; and as an anatomy of the imagination, a poetic place in which the literary imagination expatiates and dilates to demonstrate how poetry, moral and political value, and literary form intersect. Spenser's great epic-romance is, at some point or another, all of these things. The great challenge for any reader of Spenser, then, is to understand how these different faces of the poem can be brought into one focus.

Some of this multiplicity can be seen in the complex union of genres that the poem creates. Spenser would have seen his poem as a version of 'heroical poetry' (as Sidney calls it in his *Defence of Poetry*), and he identified it with classical epics such as *The Iliad*, *The Odyssey* and especially *The Aeneid*, with romance epics such as Ariosto's *Orlando furioso* and Tasso's *Gerusalemme liberata* (*Jerusalem Delivered*), and with Arthurian romance. (He mentions all of these specifically in his 'Letter to Raleigh', and, perhaps more importantly, demonstrates his allegiance to these literary forms by imitation, allusion, and wholescale appropriation of plot and imagery from all of these sources. All of these intense literary reimaginings of his sources illuminate what was involved for Spenser in 'Englishing' the wealth of epic and romance tradition available on the continent at the time that he began *The Faerie Queene*.

The Faery Queen and the poem's absent centre

Spenser not only entwines epic and romance, two genres which have different historical, formal and political implications, but he builds into the very structure of the poem layers of figurative, symbolic and allegorical meanings. What is sometimes called the allegory of the poem is in fact a weave of several allegories with literary symbolisms of several kinds. A look at the treatment of the Faery Queen can show how Spenser builds multiple readings that substantially qualify the celebration of queen and nation.

Spenser describes in his 'Letter to Raleigh' a typical romance scenario of a Christmas celebration at the court of the Faery Queen in which on each of twelve days a knight would be given a quest, and he assures Raleigh that this scene will be presented in the last book of the poem:

> The beginning thereofe of my history, if it were to be told by an Historiographer should be the twelfth booke, which is the last, where I deuise that the Faery Queene kept her Annuall feaste xii. dayes, vppon which xii. seuerall dayes, the occasions of xii. seuerall aduentures hapned, which being vndertaken by xii seuerall knights, are in these xii. books seuerally handled and discoursed. (Hamilton, p. 738)

This scene, however, never appears in the poem as we have it; it is rather that desired centre and ground of meaning that the poem, as a work written in fallen human language in mortal time, cannot represent. Instead of royal or divine or metropolitan centre, the poem consistently presents a periphery, with knights wandering almost as if in exile in forests and plains, far from the civic and religious centre of the plot or its symbols. We begin Book I only after Red Cross Knight has left the court, for instance; we end it as he heads off towards court, leaving Una behind to mourn the incompletion of her marriage. Similarly, in Books II and III the knights are presented almost entirely in isolated landscapes or, if in more social settings, then in parodies of the Faery Queen's court. In Book III, the absence of that fictional and political centre is particularly felt: although Florimell departs from court to find the wounded Marinell, her headlong rush away from it eventually places her, comet-like, in the middle of the forest of canto i, and the court itself is never shown. The Faery Queen appears only once in the poem, to Arthur in a dream that starts his quest (I, ix) but which leaves him with 'nought but pressed gras' (I, ix, 15) as evidence that she even exists. As the telos of Arthur's quest, and the goal of his epic *labor*, the Faery Queen marks a future promise, a prophesied epiphany, but not one that the poem can bring to fruition in the fictional time of human action. If Aeneas is to travel and fight in order to found Rome, presumably Arthur travels through the poem in an attempt to unite with the Faery Queen and found a lineage, to become a nation under Elizabeth. When Spenser promises to marry Arthur to a Faery Queen named Gloriana, he presents imaginatively a wedding of ancient British myth, legend and lineage with the brilliant reigning queen, modern emblem of British greatness.

What, then, does this absent Faery Queen stand for? 'The Letter to Raleigh' identifies her both with Glory itself – the elusive glory that the poet and characters seek echoes in her name – and specifically with 'the most excellent and glorious person of our soueraine the Queene' (p. 737). Spenser is equally (and unusually) direct in the ending of the proem to Book III, where he invokes Elizabeth, saying that she may see herself either in Gloriana or in Belphoebe (III, proem, 5). If Gloriana is a mirror for Elizabeth, then the poem is placing Elizabeth in the embrace of Arthur, becoming figuratively both his beloved and his descendant. Arthur is seen not only as the ancestor or forerunner of the Tudors, but as the prophetic prefiguration of them – *Rex Quondam Rexque Futurus*, as Malory puts it, the once and future king. The Tudors, and especially in this case Elizabeth herself, are seen as part of a prophetic time scheme in which the current success of the monarchy looks to the past in order to point to a greater glory to come. Richard McCabe reminds us that 'the *Faerie Queene* is future-oriented in the sense that Arthurian heroism is as much an ideal towards which Britain must strive as an image of past glory'.[1] The absent centre represents a union not yet possible, not yet representable, but one towards which Spenser hopes history will move, if the nation is led in the right direction. Readers are urged to recognise the dark guises through which Spenser's poem can speak with 'a critical voice'.[2]

The marriage of Arthur and Gloriana, then, is a union towards which the poem strives. The missing court at the centre of the poem's fiction points forward to a scene also missing, but imagined as the political goal of the poem – the embrace of Arthur and Gloriana, and the specific view of the nation implied in that union. The nationalism of the poem is thus a more serious project than might be suggested by the notion that the poem either praises the monarch (flattery) or reincarnates a Tudor myth of legitimacy. In fact, by importing this secular prophetic dimension the poem is discovering an avenue by which it can articulate what Spenser saw as crucial failings in the Elizabethan political vision and settlement, beginning with the problem of the succession, but going beyond it to the broader issues that connect nationalism with religion and a wider political destiny.

The poem can be seen to locate itself within the politics of courtiership that characterised the 1580s and 1590s. Spenser's images for the human experience contain many images of exile, often explained in religious terms. The knights wandering in the periphery can be read, as Richard Helgerson has done, as figures for the centrifugal feudalism in England itself of the great nobles and their followers who fought to maintain their privilege against the increasingly centralised monarchy. Helgerson sees the poem as siding finally with the rebellious, the wandering, the individually heroic military aristocracy, in spite of its potent praise for the queen. By making Elizabeth I both a muse and the absent but desired centre, Spenser imports a powerful and disruptive set of political meanings into his poem, insisting on both Elizabeth's presence as the very condition of the poem and yet stressing the impossibility of ever representing her, praising her rule yet giving her advice about policy, and satirizing her court. In the House of Pride, for example, Lucifera is 'A mayden Queene' (I, iv, 8) who is described in language very reminiscent of Elizabeth's speeches: 'So proud she shyned in her Princely state' (I, iv, 10). Spenser celebrates female rule and the value of a female separatism that eschews marriage in the figure of Belphoebe, at the same time as he exposes the destructive ravages of a courtiership that provides no place for the male: 'Dye rather, dye, than euer from her seruice swerue' (III, v, 46), laments Timias, Spenser's figure of Sir Walter Raleigh, while the body of the dead Sir Philip Sidney, now turned in Ovidian fashion into a flower, decks the Mound of Venus in the Garden of Adonis, a representation of the body politic of Elizabeth.

The imbuing of the poem with a national prophetic destiny highlights a second, equally important interpretation of the Faery Queen: as a religious symbol of the unrepresentable nature of the divine, an absence that reminds us of the 'vnperfite' (VII, viii) (unfinished, unperfected, non-perfect, fragmentary, ongoing, as in the imperfect tense in romance languages) of human understandings. The Faery Queen points to the transcendent, the arena of divine knowledge and revelation to which no human being can have access. Protestantism from Luther on defined the relation of the believer to the divine as one of faith and faith alone. Arthur's dream vision of the Faery Queene comes to stand as the paradigm of faith, and indeed Arthur's heroism is in part defined by his act of faith: 'But whether dreames delude, or true it were, / Was neuer hart so rauisht with delight' (I, ix, 14). Arthur makes it clear that his decision – 'From that day forth I lou'd that face diuine' (I, ix, 15) – had to be made without the certain knowledge that human beings desire. It has to be based on an act of faith, and even Arthur cannot tell whether his vision is truth or delusion. Moreover, Arthur's dream, which comes to him when he is sleeping, resembles the scenario in which Red Cross is accosted by the false dream sent by Archimago (in I, i), and from this episode we as readers have learned all too well the costs of misidentifying a deluding dream. There is no way around this problem, however: Arthur must make his act of faith without the certain knowledge, in hope and belief that the dream is true. The poem proposes a version of Arthur's act of faith for his readers, a parallel between the knight's experiences and our experiences with our own heroic journey: we cannot really be any more certain than Arthur is of the truth of his vision.

'That face divine' – Arthur's words describing the Faery Queen remind us that the central tropes for the figurative workings of Spenser's poem all come with a strongly Christian and Protestant valence, and it is important to see how often Spenser glosses this distance from the centre in religious terms. One particularly beautiful image early in the poem invokes the sense of exile often seen as characteristically humanist. Spenser here explicitly refers to the excitement of the age of discovery – the navigation of the ship over the whole ocean – yet the gloss he gives to this voyaging is Christian as well as geographical. He describes all of human life as a form of 'wandering' in 'the wide deepe' – one is guided by the light from 'the steadfast star' (I, ii, I) when it is not cloudy, but the image also emphasises the enormous distance from that reliable point of certainty to the wanderers: the 'steadfast star' (the pole star, and also Jesus, the incarnate divine being that 'was in Ocean waues yet neuer wet') 'sendeth light from farre / To all, that in the wide deepe wandring arre' (I, ii, I). Thus for Spenser the distance of wandering knights from the Faery Court is also a figure for the distance of the human world from God. Precisely because Spenser leaves us wandering in the wide deep, we are faced with a poetics of incompletion.

For this reason, Spenser calls his poem a 'darke conceit' ('Letter to Raleigh', p. 737), and identifies the kinds of 'darkness' that characterise his poem with the images of the 'covert vele', the mirror and shadow. In the conclusion to the proem to Book II, Spenser addresses Elizabeth I (and implicitly his future readers), asking Elizabeth's pardon for using allegorical and symbolic imagery to 'shadow' or 'veil' her lineage, the story of her nation and the representation of her brilliance as a leader:

> And thou, O fairest Princesse vnder sky,
> In this faire mirrhour maist behold thy face,
> And thine owne realmes in lond of Faery,
> And in this antique Image thy great auncestry,
>
> The which O pardon me thus to enfold
> In couert vele, and wrap in shadowes light,
> That feeble eyes your glory may behold,
> Which else could not endure those beames bright
> But would dazled be with exceeding light.   (II, proem, 4–5)

These images – mirror, veil and shadow – all are used in biblical episodes and parables to describe the conditions or costs of revelation or epiphany, involving direct vision or understanding of God and the dazzling brightness of the divine. Moses covered his face with a veil after speaking directly to God, because it shone too brightly and frightened the Israelites (see Exodus 34. 30), and during the Middle Ages the veil gained more precise associations with Christian reading practices.[3] But particularly important for Spenser here is the figure of the mirror, because it remains both a religious and a political trope. He takes it from Paul's famous apocalyptic prophecy in 1 Corinthians 13: 'For now we see through a glass, darkly: but then face to face: now I know in part, but then I shall know even as I am known.'[4] The darkness of Spenser's allegory is associated here with the darkness of the fallen, mortal state: just as we cannot see God directly or understand the full meaning of divine matters, so we cannot see the brightness of Elizabeth directly without being dazzled, blinded with the glory that would overcome us. In the terms of the religious allegory, the danger is always one of idolatry: if we see the brightness directly, we will try to worship it, worshipping the vision and not what the vision points to.

The tensions in this trope of the brightness of revelation and the dazzled eyes of the mortal viewer are felt more keenly if we look to see how thoroughly this trope defines Spenser's poetics throughout Book 1, and how it is then rewritten in later books to characterise the experience of love. Whenever Una raises her veil in Book 1, she dazzles viewers, who respond inappropriately or, as in the case of Sans Loy, violently. Most dangerous to her, perhaps, is the Woody Nation in canto vi, whose response to her revealed beauty is to worship her. They 'made her th'image of Idolatryes', and when she tries to prevent their worship 'they her Asse would worship fayn' (I, vi, 19). This episode helps to show how direct revelation will fail in the human world. It reflects what for Spenser was the defining Biblical episode about the human inadequacy to revelation, the transfiguration.

The need to shadow divine brightness is emphasised in the transfiguration, which Spenser places on Mount Tabor (VII, vii, 7). Here the disciples' eyes were dazzled and blinded at the moment when they saw Jesus in his divine glory (Mark 9. 2–8). In the King James version, Jesus' 'raiment became shining' (Mark 9. 3); Matthew in the Geneva Bible tells us that Jesus' face 'did shine as the sunne, and his clothes were white as the light' (Matthew 17. 2). The apostles Peter, James and John respond by wanting to build a tabernacle on the spot, expressing a desire to worship the vision. They are 'overshadowed' immediately by a cloud through which God speaks to them, telling them to listen to the words of Jesus: 'This is my son, Hear him.' Spenser interprets the episode as an example of the dangers to the human believer of revelation so bright that it blinds, leading the viewer to worship that which is revealed in itself. In a stanza identified numerically as a stanza of revelation (associating seven as a holy number because the sabbath is the seventh day, the day when, with his work done, the poet hopes for the great vision), the seventh stanza of the seventh canto of the projected seventh book, Spenser narrates the transfiguration directly for the first time. 'Great dame Nature' is as bright, he tells us, as what the apostles saw on Mount Tabor:

> Her garment was so bright and wondrous sheene,
> That my fraile wit cannot deuise to what
> It to compare, nor finde like stuffe to that,
> As those three sacred *Saints*, though else most wise,
> Yet on mount *Thabor* quite their wits forgat,
> When they their glorious Lord in strange disguise
> Transfigur'd sawe; his garments so did daze their eyes. (VII, vii, 7)

This story defines in specifically religious terms the paradigm of vision that Spenser uses throughout Book I and the rest of the poem. If Spenser did not veil his tale with shadows, and treat it only as an indirect reflection of the truths to which he hopes to give poetic form, we too, like the 'three saints' might be tempted to set up our tents and worship, not remembering that the poem is in every moment pointing beyond itself to a divine truth and power outside the limits of human words.

Epic, romance, nation and religion

Spenser begins his poem by alluding to Vergil, echoing a passage in a medieval manuscript long thought to have been Vergil's actual introduction to the Aeneid: 'Lo I the man . . .' Here he imagines his own career following the path of the famous Roman epic writer, moving from pastoral and georgic poetry to epic.[5] This opening seems clearly to identify the poem as epic, and the ambition to tell his nation's spiritual and political history (a part of the dynastic, national and even imperial legacy of epic) strengthens our sense that the central defining quality of this poem must be epic. Epic aims at a largeness of cultural summation, a sense that all the different sides of a culture will be brought to life in the course of the poem. It is important to remember, then, that epic itself has many purposes and many faces. It is not a single, unchanging entity, but a model for a process of thought. The epic elements of the poem include formal generic traits such as Spenser's frequent and significant use of the epic simile; imitations of the descent to the underworld; reference to the gods and other mythological figures as causes or explanations of action; scenes of prophecy, especially, following

Virgil, dynastic prophecy in the form of epic catalogue; epic realism without recourse to magic as a principal way out of dangerous plot crises; epic invocations; and ecphrastic descriptions of armour and places (compare the description of the Shield of Aeneas or Achilles to the armour of Arthur in I, ix). We might compare the pictures of Troy on the walls of Dido's Temple to Juno in Book I of *The Aeneid* – 'here are tears for passing things' – to the tapestry of Venus and Adonis in the House of Malecasta (III, i), but also to the many ecphrases in which Spenser pauses in his narration to describe the physical appearance of a place (as the description of the House of Pride), descriptions which always convey figuratively to the reader the moral significance of the place, precisely what the characters often miss.

The epic qualities of the poem lead us to expect a stress on the mortality and human limits of heroes, and indeed we find it, articulated powerfully even by semi-mythical figures like Arthur and Belphoebe. Belphoebe was raised, after all, by the goddess Diana and was conceived by a nymph 'Through the influence of th'heauens fruitfull ray' (III, iii, 6), in what seems to be a version of an unfallen birth, without pain for the mother though also without the concomitant human consciousness – 'Vnwares she them conceiu'd, vnwares she bore' (III, vi, 26–7; see III, vi, 6–10, 26–7 for Belphoebe's conception and birth). Belphoebe, in whom Spenser tells us that he has fashioned a mirrour of Elizabeth I's 'rare chastity' and who herself seems a step closer to being a mythological being than some of the fully human characters, nonetheless articulates the significance of the crucial epic limitation of mortality, and of the related need for an heroic code. Confronted with Arthur's wounded squire Timias, who thinks she is more than mortal – 'Angell or Goddesse do I call thee right?' (III, v, 35) – Belphoebe explains that she too is placed under the limit of mortality, and is bound to the mortal world by that limit: 'Ah gentle Squire', she says,

> Nor Goddesse I, nor Angell, but the Mayd,
> And daughter of a woody Nymphe, desire
> No seruice but thy safety and ayd;
> Which if thou gaine, I shalbe well apayd.
> We mortall wights, whose liues and fortunes bee
> To commun accidents still open layd,
> Are bound with commun bond of frailtee,
> To succour wretched wights, whom we captiued see.   (III, v, 36)

Belphoebe's answer is complicated by the classical subtext, for Spenser here alludes to the moment when Aeneas in Book I first sees his mother in disguise as a huntress in the Carthaginian forests. 'O dea certe' (O surely you are a goddess) he says famously to her, and indeed he is right, though she denies it. Belphoebe seems to be a second Diana in her behavior and chastity. Through the allusion to Virgil, Belphoebe is linked to Venus as well, and in a very Elizabethan way combines Venus and Diana (Elizabeth used both Venus and Diana as figures herself), but, unlike Virgil's Venus, who is deceiving her son, Belphoebe is truthful and sincere. She is an embodiment of these goddesses, but is placed on earth under human limitation, and is consistently a spokesperson in the poem for the poem's heroic code (in II, iii for instance).[6] When she appears in front of Timias, then, the poem links her intertextually with an event in which the divine took visible form on the plane of human action, but it uses that allusion to contrast Belphoebe, who is not divine and not immortal and is not in the process of tricking Timias, with Venus, and thereby to define the particular kind of heroism honored in this poem.

Many parts of the poem help to establish an epic context for interpretation. Yet Spenser begins 'singing' of 'Knights and Ladies gentle deeds' (I, proem, I) and of 'A gentle knight' (I, i, I), echoing Ariosto's opening and making the poem sound more like chivalric romance. His narrator seems to be thinking as much of Ariosto, of the vernacular English traditions (of the Arthurian tales, of Chaucer, whom he calls 'the well of English undefyled', of Chaucer's 'gentle knyght' and his son the squire, of Malory) and of romance more generally as he is of epic poetry. This is partly because the blending of epic and romance forms had already occurred in Ariosto and had even been argued out in the fights over the *Furioso* and its genre.[7] Romance sets in motion a different set of principles and expectations, shifting away from epic limitation by imagining a universe more visibly penetrated by spirit, and thus by magic, and also allowing some exceptions to epic linearity: in romance, time is occasionally allowed to turn back, death is not always the absolute human limit, and consequences do not always need to be faced; indeed endings are delayed and with them some of the kinds of recognition and knowledge that might be gained only when finally emerging from the thickets of plot. Don Quixote, an avid reader of chivalric romances, refers to them as *inacabables*, unending and unendable. Even Malory, who wrote of the death of Arthur, retained the story of Merlin living backward in time, and kept the fictional prophecies about Arthur alive. Romance endings allow for the kinds of prophetic return of the hero that made the Arthurian 'matter of Britain' so politically potent in the English sixteenth century.

In Book I a challenge to epic and chivalric behaviour is intrinsic: to try to write an heroic poem about holiness is to confront directly the aggression and violence of the heroic tradition in the service of a faith that is opposed to many of the conventions and values of this kind of story. Perhaps this is why some of the longest extended imitations of epic occur in other books.

In Book II, canto xii, we see a sustained imitation of Tasso that also looks back towards the Circe of *The Odyssey*. In writing his own Circe book, Spenser looks to the ancient world for a culminating quest appropriate for a knight whose Aristotelian virtue, temperance, is explicitly non-Christian. And in Book III, an extraordinary discussion of epic helps to define Britomart's heroism against the fraudulence of Paridell, a mock-epic descendant of Paris who is ready to seduce his Helen and make Troy fall again. The retelling of the Trojan war story with Hellenore and Paridell as its centre is a tour-de-force example of the wit with which Spenser plays with genre to recast the entire epic tradition. In these cantos (III, ix–x), the fall of Troy is told three times: Paridell tells of the fall of Troy as part of his seduction of Hellenore, but he leaves out what is to Britomart the most important part – and to us the most epic part – the events that happen after the fall of Troy, the story of Aeneas, the plot of the *Aeneid*, the founding of Rome, and the eventual founding of Troynovant. In the midst of a seduction scene out of a *fabliau* or novella, Britomart sits naively embodying heroic idealism and asking Paridell how he could have left out the part of the story that moves one to heroism and future deeds. Britomart completes the story, in turn producing a version of the epic, but hers is not the final account of Troy, either. Since the episode plays with the names of Helen and Paris, and thus implicitly makes Malbecco, the cuckolded husband, into the figure of Menelaus, these two cantos can be read as Spenser's own retelling of the fall of Troy, the great epic topic that fills Book II of *The Aeneid* with such grandeur and horror. But Spenser retells the epic as satire and *fabliau*, domesticating the story and reimagining through the *fabliau* the reasons that Helen might have wanted to leave Menelaus. The brilliance of Spenser's retelling of this great epic tale in such a comic and satiric manner is that it presents a critique even of his idealised Britomart. The claims she makes at the banquet with Malbecco, Hellenore and Paridell about epic and national destiny are eloquent summaries of the poem's definition of heroism:

> There there (said *Britomart*) a fresh appeard
> The glory of the later world to spring,
> And *Troy* againe out of her dust was reard,
> To sit in second seat of soueraigne king,
> Of all the world vnder her gouerning.
> But a third kingdome yet is to arise
> Out of the *Troians* scattered of-spring,
> That in all glory and great enterprise,
> Both first and second *Troy* shall dare to equalise.   (III, ix, 44)

This is the serious claim of *The Faerie Queene*: that it is the English equivalent of Virgil's *Aeneid*, and that Britain with its capital of Troynovant

(New Troy, which becomes London) will reach a greatness equal even to Rome's. Spenser founds Britomart's heroism precisely on her understanding of the role of the hero in the post-heroic age: modern heroism as the poem defines it is, as it was for Virgil, a belated heroism coming *after* Troy, after the great ancient warrior heroes, a heroism of prophecy, of foundations and origins, of the building of a new civilisation in the ashes of the old. This is Spenser's project and it is Britomart's, and yet Spenser is willing to satirise her lightly as she sits unaware at the banquet table while Paridell writes in wine his words of seduction to Hellenore and the fall of Troy begins to happen again, but in a private setting. What Britomart articulates here may well be a true ideal for the poem, but it proves remarkably irrelevant to the activities of the scene in which she is in fact participating. Britomart proves as blind as Malbecco to the truth of what is happening around her, and rides to other adventures, a little awkward and naive in her epic idealism. This is not a poem that will ever place itself securely in the epic genre – Spenser invokes a combination of epic, romance and allegory (not to mention fabliau and novella and chronicle) in order to find his path to an epic retelling of British origins.

Allegory and internalisation: a psychological landscape

Spenser's poem employs extensively two kinds of allegorical writing: (1) the use of personification to represent internal states, qualities, ideas or ideals; (2) the use of typology and what medieval exegesis called 'the allegory of the theologians'. Spenser's characters lack what we might feel to be the most important piece of information that would allow them to proceed successfully in their world: that is, the knowledge that they are in an allegory. One of the fictional games that Spenser plays is to present his characters with a situation that appears on the fictional plane of the story to be an external event, while the reader is able to recognise that the poem employs apparently external things or beings as signs of internal psychological events or ideas. Thus the landscape of Spenser's poem is a psychological one: many of its places and commonplaces represent spiritual or emotional aspects of the characters themselves. To learn to read Spenser's poem is to learn that everything – a person in the story, a place, a house, a tree or a giant – can represent an aspect of the hero or heroine's own psyche.

By allegory, modern critics mean theories of how to read figuratively and symbolically – away from the literal meaning – that developed in the ancient world and in the early Christian centuries. The Greek roots of the word allegory suggest that it means 'to speak other', and this 'other-speaking' seems to have been associated with a form of private speech.[8] The

Christian writers of the New Testament began to allegorise in new ways as they appropriated the Jewish Bible and prophetic traditions, claiming that what now became the 'Old Testament' prophecies and events are 'fulfilled' in the life of Christ and, eventually, in the spiritual lives of Christians. The two traditions combined to produce the earliest formal allegory in Pruden-tius' *Psychomachia* (circa 405 BC), a poem representing a war for the psyche or the soul fought between the virtues and the vices, all personified as warriors. The *Psychomachia* represented an important step towards the kind of self-conscious internalising of epic form that characterises *The Faerie Queene*. Spenser both integrates the psychomachian strategies of personifying states and ideas and appropriates the 'allegory of the theologians' in Book I and to some extent throughout the poem.

The Sans brothers – Sans Foy, Sans Loy and Sans Joy – whom the Red Cross Knight encounters in Book I, can serve as an example of psychoma-chian allegory, that is, personification of internal states represented as external, real characters operating in the outer world. The battle with Sans Foy results in a victory for the Red Cross Knight, and yet Sans Foy means 'faithlessness,' and he appears instantly in the narrative the moment after the Red Cross Knight has faithlessly abandoned Una to the wiles of Archimago. Sans Foy is a representation of Red Cross' own faithlessness, yet he is also something bigger – the fact that faithlessness exists as a constant possibility in the world. To meet Sans Foy in battle, then, is already to have succumbed to him: the very fact that the Red Cross Knight has encountered him at all is a sign that he is fast travelling down the broad highway to sin and failure in the quest (a highway that turns out to lead directly to the House of Pride). And indeed the same proves true with all three Sans Brothers. Though the Red Cross Knight appears to conquer Sans Foy, and thus to have taken a small step in the direction of overcoming his faithlessness, many details in the episode hint at a very different story, one that substantiates the allegorical understanding that we gain at the begin-ning – namely, that the Red Cross Knight would never have had to fight Sans Foy had he not already metaphorically become him. Red Cross immediately takes up Sans Foy's lady and his shield after his victory. While this may seem like usual chivalric practice (and it is), this action makes the Red Cross Knight look a lot like Sans Foy. In taking up with Sans Foy's lady, and courting her, he demonstrates that he is faithlessly abandoning Una for Duessa, the woman who will be the greatest threat to the completion of his quest. If anything, then, the Red Cross Knight is worse off, not better, after his so-called victory over Sans Foy, and we are not surprised to learn that Duessa takes him immediately to the House of Pride, proud as he is of his pseudo-victory. Unable to beat Sans Foy by fighting with him, the Red

Cross Knight needs to learn to read his own spiritual and psychological landscape. At the same time, the poem dramatises how difficult this is for anyone by keeping its characters from knowing that these struggles are in fact psychological or internal, rather than simply physical and chivalric.

Examples of psychomachian allegory abound in other parts of the poem as well – in book two, Pyrochles and Cymochles function like the Sans brothers to represent states of mind and being, and the story of Furor and Occasion gives us a vivid picture of the inversions of allegorical logic, with the 'occasion' for the fury, which should come before, instead appearing after Furor. But as we leave the absolutes of the book of holiness, we encounter more and more examples of personifications and psychomachian allegories about whose status as representations of internal states we remain in doubt. An example from Book III suggests the problems for interpretation that the constant possibility of reading internally presents. When Britomart arrives at the House of Malecasta, we are not presumably meant to think, as we are of the Red Cross Knight in the House of Pride, that Britomart has somehow committed a failure of chastity in such a way as to bring her to this place. Perhaps simply falling in love could be construed this way – that Britomart, crossing into puberty (III, ii, 39; and III, i, 65) and having her first erotic passions, has lost a kind of innocence that somehow appropriately places her in this house. But, although there may be some truth to this, as she has experienced the wound of love (III, ii, 26), and her fancy has been shaped by the imagined picture of her beloved, little in the poem suggests that Britomart has any difficulty with chastity, especially if we remember that for Spenser chastity meant more than simple virginity – it meant married, faithful and passionate love. But Britomart does have trouble with a society that associates love with courtly excess, indulgence and sensual extravagance. Spenser begins with a representation not of Britomart's state of mind, but of the literary and cultural conventions that have shaped the discourse of love, literary and cultural conventions that Britomart will have to defeat, and that Spenser will have to overcome, if she is to become a knight who fulfils the highest knightly and romantic ideals. If Britomart is to find her beloved and found a dynasty, as Merlin predicts, then she must conquer any temptation to linger in either a narrative of courtly love, or in lyrical mode that would not give her an heroic and epic destiny. Spenser is challenging the conventions of medieval courtly love and chivalric romance, insisting on a religious and a national as well as a private meaning for his story. In the House of Malecasta, flickers of the more personified sort of place are felt by the reader in the scene in which Britomart is wounded by Gardante (III, i, 65). Placed here on the first step of the ladder of courtly love, and therefore implicitly on the road to 'basciante' (kissing) and 'noctante' (spending the night together) (III, i, 45), Britomart seems momentarily to belong in this house, and her ability to resist the advances of Malecasta, perhaps a figuration of her own wish to climb that same ladder, is profoundly tied to a determination to remain a knight. Britomart seems disinclined to reveal her gender, delays as long as possible taking off her male disguise and when forcibly exposed, fights valiantly against courtly love.

Disciplines of reading in Books I, II and III

So far this account has discussed the 1590 *Faerie Queene* (Books I, II and III with the hermaphrodite ending) as a unit, but each book presents its own special set of allegories and ways of being understood, and it would be useful to describe some of these differences briefly. Book I, the book of holiness, is concerned in a way none of Spenser's other books are with a system of absolutes. As the book of holiness, it is concerned with the relation of 'holiness' to 'wholeness', kinds of unity, 'one-ness' and the lack of self-division (Archimago's effect on Red Cross Knight and Una is to see them 'diuided into double parts' I, ii, 9), and it works with a series of puns on dis-pairing. When one has lost one's unity one 'dispairs' and is 'empaired'; form is associated with wholeness and unity, while being deformed is to invert the synecdoche, moving from whole to part instead of the other way around. One is deformed when one is only a part of a whole human being. Book I also uses as a principal structure the system of typology as we know it from the New Testament, and alludes extensively to the Protestant rereading of the Book of Revelation, finding in its apocalyptic symbolism a main source of inspiration. This system of typology does not work as a structuring principle to the same extent elsewhere in the poem, for the events in Book I happen on a different ontological level from the rest of the story. In Red Cross Knight's encounter with the dragon, then, an apocalyptic tone tells us that this battle is more than just one man's heroic mission.

Book II presents a very different challenge, as it is a book based on a classical virtue, temperance, taken from Aristotle's *Nichomachean Ethics* and depending on a model of balance that resists completely the near-apocalyptic implications of Book I. Perhaps because temperance is not compatible with chivalry, Guyon loses his horse early in the book and remains a pedestrian knight, trying to live up to an ideal of inner balance that consistently proves inadequate to the world he moves in. Throughout the book we are in a place of dualities – no absolutes, no single one thing that sums everything up, but a constant balancing between two extremes or two alternatives in order to find the proper human place in the middle. The iconoclastic explosion that ends the book, which will be examined in the final section of this chapter, provides a useful place to measure the implicit Christian judgement of the ethics being explored in the book, and it suggests that Spenser's view is that in a fallen world 'temperance' often becomes violent repression.

The explosion of eroticism as a principal focus for both human action and mythological imagination is introduced at several points in Book II, most notably in the Bower of Bliss (II, xii), but nothing fully prepares the reader for what is yet again a major shift of gears as we move into a book fully devoted to questions of how to write, and how to act in, a book about love, faithfulness and the body, especially the female body. Book III points towards marriage, as we learn in canto iii when Merlin predicts that Britomart's union with Artegall will eventually produce the lineage of Elizabeth, but it remains nonetheless a book about an unmarried young woman, who begins the story little more than a girl. The book is therefore, perhaps surprisingly, devoted to patterns of three just as the preceding two books explored the varying symbolic meanings of their own numbers: Britomart, Glauce and Merlin together construct the plot of Britomart's quest (no reference here at all to the Faery Queen and her court); while Britomart, Arthur and Guyon begin the book with a joust and form a company. Perhaps the book's most important articulation of this pattern occurs at the end of the 1590 *Faerie Queene*, when Amoret emerges from the House of Busyrane to embrace the waiting Scudamour, forming the ideal union summed up in their names: Scudamour plus Amoret becomes Scudamoret, an emblem of marriage as their bodies entwine. Britomart stands outside this embracing pair, 'halfe enuying their blesse' (III, xii, 46). In part Britomart wishes that the book devoted to her quest had ended with the romantic union represented here. In a book about faithful love and chaste passion, it seems appropriate that we might end up, as in a traditional comic form, with marriage, and Spenser does give us a representation of marriage here in emblematic form. But Britomart only half envies this union, because, as the allusion to the hermaphrodite suggests, there is also something disturbing about the merging of two into one: Scudamour and Amoret have become 'like two senceles stocks' (III, xii, 45a). Book III, for all its interest in love and union, remains finally the book of chastity, and although chastity implies the faithful passion that will lead to marriage, the book remains interested to a significant degree in the way that Britomart holds her body and self separate from the world at large. Whether leaping out of the bed Malecasta has crept into, leaving Marinell on the strand as she rides out of the poem for four cantos, riding away from Malbecco's house before learning the conclusion of the story, or standing outside the embracing lovers here, Britomart remains throughout this book someone apart. Her chaste body is almost always encased in an armour that symbolises not only the metal hard façades and disguises that we wear in the social world once we enter the arena of passion, but the very virgin enclosure that seems the source, magically speaking, of so much of her power. The book ends, then, not with the union of two lovers, but with two united plus one apart, making a threesome to end Book III.

Iconoclasm, idolatry and endings

As we have seen, Spenser calls attention over and over in Books I–III to the incompleteness of his writing, of his vision, of his 'moniments' to time. But *The Faerie Queene* as it was published in 1590 actually has a clear ending in the reference to the hermaphrodite statue and the embrace of Amoret and Scudamour. When he republishes Books I–III in 1596 Spenser has to break this ending for his narrative to continue. In this revision we see that he associated the incompleteness of his work with narrative itself. Just as he has to release Archimago at the beginning of Book II to get the story going again, so he has to eliminate both the closure and the satisfaction of embrace to get the story going in Book IV. The energies of narrative, then, are clearly connected to the poem's near constant frustration of desire, and frustration or at least postponement of desire becomes identified with heroism: 'For dearely sure her loue was to me bent, / As when iust time expired should appeare' (I, ix, 14). These words are Arthur's, describing why the Faery Queen will make him wait for his embrace. But 'just time' never expires within the time of the narrative, which is the time of desire, the time of longing for a full erotic or religious union. The 1590 *Faerie Queene* stands out dramatically against the poem as a whole, then, for having been created and imagined with a definite and celebratory closure.

It is striking to see how many times characters long for ending or closure. Red Cross Knight, as we have seen, wants to give up on life and questing altogether once he sees the vision of the heavenly Jerusalem (I, x, 55). It is interesting to see that Despair plays on this desire for ending, tempting the knight precisely with the thing everyone wants in the poem, and only twisting it very slightly: 'Sleepe after toyle, port after stormie seas, / Ease after warre, death after life doth greatly please' (I, ix, 40), says Despair, and only the last set of the sequence disrupts the rhetoric to reveal Despair's hidden intent. Port after stormy seas: this is what everyone hopes for, including Britomart (III, iv, 8), whose sea is the sea of emotion and grief at not being able to find her beloved. Spenser uses this figure to end Book I; notably some of the readers and characters get off the boat, but the visit to port is short for the poem:

Now strike your sailes ye iolly Mariners,
For we be come vnto a quiet rode,
Where we must land some of our passengers,
And light this wearie vessel of our lode.
Here she a while may make her safe abode,
Till she repaired haue her tackles spent,
And wants supplide. And then againe abroad
On the long voyage whereunto she is bent:
Well may she speede and fairely finish her intent.   (1, xii, 42)

The image as a figure of ending points rather to the temporary nature of the
rest in port, and the uncertainty – the wish – that the 'intent' of the poem
will be reached.

While it is possible to see the incompleteness of the poem as a whole as
simply the result of Spenser's hyperbolic ambition (many readers are not
sorry that he was never able to complete the promised twelve books, given
the length and complexity of what we do have of it), it seems likely that
Spenser himself began to make use of the aesthetics of incompletion – of the
fragment – as a way not only to conclude his mammoth work but to
re-emphasise yet again his central point about the limitations of what can
be represented, especially of the divine or of the transcendent realm, in
human art. The broken ending and the resistance to closure are one of his
two main ways to avoid idolatry; to keep his poem from leading to a
worship of its own images, the poem keeps them dark, broken, incomplete.

Spenser's other solution to the threat of idolatry is represented in the
iconoclasm of the endings of Books II and III. In both books, the titular hero
ends the quest by destroying an erotic place associated in part with lyric
poetry (*carpe diem* lyric for the Bower of Bliss, and Petrarchan poetry,
especially sonnets, in the House of Busyrane), and other threats to the epic
linearity. In Guyon's case, the episode establishes an extraordinary tension
between the virtue of temperance, which presumably should not proceed
with the wrath of a tempest, and the Christian context (of the purging of the
temple by Jesus), which seems to authorise such anger as appropriate,
purgative and health-bringing. In the Bower of Bliss, Guyon could be said
to fail because he cannot keep his balance, cannot maintain the middle way
in the face of a serious erotic temptation. Spenser's iconoclastic zeal seems
to be associated with his love of the fragment and his belief that the
'vnperfite' image will always point beyond itself to the ineffable, and thus
will never become an object of idolatrous desire. In destroying the Bower of
Bliss and the House of Busyrane Spenser is not simply commenting on the
dangers and violence of the literary tradition he has inherited; he is also
celebrating the possibility that, imaginatively, we might find our freedom

from that tradition, using it to reshape the very meaning and purpose of heroic poetry.

NOTES

1 Richard McCabe, *The Pillars of Eternity: Time and Providence in 'The Faerie Queene'* (Blackrock: Irish Academic Press, 1989), p. 51.

2 Andrew Hadfield, *Literature, Politics and National Identity: Reformation to Renaissance* (Cambridge: Cambridge University Press, 1994), p. 200.

3 Notably as a figure for allegory in patristic sources: see John Freccero, 'Medusa: The Letter and the Spirit', in *Dante: The Poetics of Conversion* (Cambridge, MA: Harvard University Press, 1986).

4 On the mirror, see Kathleen Williams, *Spenser's World of Glass: A Reading of The Faerie Queene* (Berkeley: University of California Press, 1966).

5 See Richard Helgerson, *Self-Crowned Laureates: Spenser, Jonson and the Literary System* (Berkeley: University of California Press, 1983), on Spenser's poetic career and claims to the status of poet laureate.

6 See her explanation of the need for heroic *labour* in II, iii, 40–1.

7 See Bernard Weinberg, *A History of Literary Criticism in the Italian Renaissance* (Chicago: University of Chicago Press, 1963), for a detailed account of these debates.

8 Probably the best introduction to theories of allegory is Angus Fletcher, *Allegory: Theory of a Symbolic Mode* (Ithaca, NY: Cornell University Press, 1964).

FURTHER READING

Margaret Beissinger, Jane Tylus and Susanne Wofford, *Epic Traditions in the Contemporary World: The Politics of Community* (Berkeley: University of California Press, 1999).

Elizabeth J. Bellamy, *Translations of Power: Narcissism and the Unconscious in Epic History* (Ithaca: Cornell University Press, 1992).

Harry Berger, *The Allegorical Temper: Vision and Reality in Book II of Spenser's 'Faerie Queene'* (Hamden, CT: Archon Books, 1967 [1957]).

Angus Fletcher, *Allegory: The Theory of a Symbolic Mode* (Ithaca, NY: Cornell University Press, 1964).

John Guillory, *Poetic Authority: Spenser, Milton, and Literary History* (New York: Columbia University Press, 1983).

Isabel McCaffrey, *Spenser's Allegory: The Anatomy of Imagination* (Princeton: Princeton University Press, 1976).

David Lee Miller, *The Poem's Two Bodies: The Poetics of the 1590 'Faerie Queene'* (Princeton: Princeton University Press, 1988).

James Nohrnberg, *The Analogy of the Faerie Queene* (Princeton: Princeton University Press, 1973).

Patricia Parker, *Inescapable Romance: Studies in the Poetics of a Mode* (Princeton: Princeton University Press, 1979).

Mihoko Suzuki, *Metamorphoses of Helen: Authority, Difference, and the Epic* (Ithaca: Cornell University Press, 1989).

Gordon Teskey, *Allegory and Violence* (Ithaca, NY: Cornell University Press, 1996).

Susanne L. Wofford, *The Choice of Achilles: The Ideology of Figure in the Epic* (Stanford: Stanford University Press, 1992).

6

ANDREW HADFIELD

The Faerie Queene, Books IV–VII

The second edition of *The Faerie Queene* was published in 1596. It contained three new books which dealt with the virtues of friendship, justice and courtesy. The ending of the 1590 first edition of the poem was altered so that Amoret and Scudamour were not reunited in a hermaphroditic embrace at the conclusion of Book III. Instead their story ceases to be a tale of private heterosexual bliss and becomes part of a wider focus on love as a social and public force. As in Book III, Scudamour suffers mixed fortunes in war and is afflicted by horrible jealousy, but he eventually manages to lead Amoret away from the Temple of Venus, albeit without the obvious triumph of the ending to the first edition. Amoret, who has been participating in a civilised and modest discussion of love's virtues (reminiscent of Castiglione's *Book of the Courtier*) is terrified at Scudamour's approach. He is criticised by the figure of Womanhood for 'being overbold' (IV, x, 54), words that explicitly recall the motto over the door of the inner chamber in the House of Busyrane that Britomart should '*Be not too bold*' (III, xi, 54).[1] Scudamour has taken on the role of the traditional Petrarchan lover. He displays his shield to Amoret 'On which when *Cupid* with his killing bow / And cruell shafts emblazond she beheld, / At sight thereof she was with terror queld, / And said no more.' In seizing her hand and forcibly removing her from the Temple of Venus he sees her as a 'warie Hynd within the weedie soyle', boasting that 'no intreatie would forgoe so glorious spoyle' (IV, x, 55).

What are the effects of the changes to this episode? The most obvious is that Scudamour and Amoret's union can no longer be read as a romantic conclusion to the poem which is endorsed by the narrator (although one should remember that Britomart, half-intrigued and half-embarrassed, was an awkward witness to their embrace at the end of Book III). Amoret has participated in an all-female court which has discussed the power and forms of love, a striking contrast to the House of Busyrane, most convincingly read as a necessary stage that the lovers have to pass through to achieve

hatred and discord threatened until Cambina intervened and restored a harmonious love between the four, demonstrating all of love's possible forms:

> Where making ioyous feast theire daies they spent
> In perfect loue, deuoide of hatefull strife,
> Allide with bands of mutuall couplement;
> For *Triamond* had *Canacee* to wife,
> With whom he ledd a long and happie life;
> And *Cambel* tooke *Cambina* to his fere,
> The which as life were each to other liefe.
> So all alike did loue, and loued were,
> That since their days such louers were not found elswhere.
>
> (IV, iii, 52)

This concord is contrasted to the strife which accompanies the tournament that Satyrane organises to prevent the knights squabbling over the rights to Florimell's girdle where the false knights Braggadocchio and Blandamour make claims that they cannot substantiate. The result is, predictably enough, a degeneration from order to chaos, with the unnamed salvage knight (Artegall) triumphing until he, in turn is overthrown by Britomart, his future wife. Their union represents a true public bond of military friendship and love in contrast to the knights fighting for the debased currency of false Florimell's honour (although it does not occur until Artegall and Scudamour have fought Britomart once again, a reminder of how fragile human alliances can be and of the delusions that can make us make the wrong choices in life). There is a pointed contrast between the engagement of Artegall and Britomart and the discovery that Florimell cannot wear the girdle she has appropriated as her own.

Artegall and Britomart are parted immediately after their engagement. The stories start to become more fragmented and less obviously interrelated. Amoret is captured by the grossly phallic figure of Lust – a more brutish form than the figures conjured up by Busyrane at the end of Book III. Significantly enough, he lives in an isolated 'caue farre from all peoples hearing' (IV, vii, 8), a reminder that Lust is the 'very antithesis of mutual love'.[13] Fortunately, Amoret is rescued by Timias, Arthur's squire, who has his own problems with lust, bound as he is to a non-sexual relationship with Belphoebe.[14] He is unable to prevent Lust hurting Amoret and so incurs Belphoebe's wrath and rejection. They are soon reconciled, albeit with Timias wounded, having abandoned Amoret and unsure where his master is. Arthur intervenes to rescue Amoret and Aemylia, a foolish lady who has agreed to elope with the Squire of Dames only to be kidnapped by Lust, from Sclaunder, one in a line of figures who damage the reputations of the innocent. The Squire of Dames is taken by Corflambo and is also rescued by Arthur, who kills Corflambo and binds his daughter, Poeana, before calming a series of fights between many of the knights in the story. Scudamour tells the assembled crowd how he rescued Amoret from the Temple of Venus. We are returned to the story of Florimell and Marinell, begun in Book III. Florimell is still imprisoned by Proteus under the sea, a sojourn which recalls Proserpine's period of captivity in Hades, as well as Amoret's trials and tribulations. Her plight is interrupted for the marriage ceremony of the Thames and the Medway, an event that takes place in Proteus' Hall. Despite its magnificent images of harmony and concord, the setting of the nuptials in the domain of the God best known for his shape-shifting and threat to stable order, indicates that we cannot take the event at face value.[15] The stability and order it seems to provide is undercut in a number of ways, not least by the plea of the narrator in the first line of the next canto that he feels unable to complete the 'endlesse worke' of recording the names of the rivers of the world. In the final canto, Marinell, who has discovered Florimell while at the wedding, has his mother, Cymodoce, ask the sea god, Neptune, to release Florimell, and they greet as if betrothed (an image which recalls the projected union of the Red Cross Knight and Una at the end of Book I).

Book IV explores and develops the themes of Book III, opening out and qualifying the discussions of love and chastity into the more social and public arenas of friendship and wider bonds of familial union. Yet if these two books do seem to make a natural pairing, there are numerous signs in Book IV that predict the political emphasis of Books V and VI and which bind the three books together as a sequel to the first edition of *The Faerie Queene*. It is significant that Lust is represented as 'a wilde and salvage man' (IV, vii, 5), 'ouergrowne with haire', representing both the male genitalia and the familiar literary figure of 'the wild man of the woods'.[16] He forces the reader to consider the representation of savages throughout the poem as part of an ongoing debate and sequence of images, qualifying the benign 'salvage nation' who rescue Una in I, vi, and looking forward to the complex juxtaposition of savage men and nations in subsequent books.[17] Equally ominous is the description of the Irish rivers present at the wedding of the Thames and the Medway:

> Ne thence the Irishe Riuers absent were,
> Sith no lesse famous then the rest they bee,
> And ioyne in neighbourhood of kingdome nere,
> Why should they not likewise in loue agree,
> And ioy likewise this solemne day to see?
> They saw it all, and present were in place;

> Though I them all according their degree,
> Cannot recount, nor tell their hidden race,
> Nor read the saluage cuntries, through which they pace. (IV, xi, 40)

The stanza is replete with ironies and portents. It is clear that there is a problem about their inclusion from the rhetorical question which makes up the first six lines. The narrator is defying opposition to their inclusion in the guest list. The last three lines are disingenuous, especially for those who knew anything about Spenser's circumstances, his presence in Ireland since at least 1580, and the fact that he was writing *A View of the Present State of Ireland*, a work that contains copious information on 'the saluage cuntries', at the time that the second edition of *The Faerie Queene* was published. More to the point still, Books V and VI are haunted by the presence of Ireland. What is tactfully excluded in Book IV is just about to loom large.

Book V narrates the quest of Artegall, the Knight of Justice. Traditionally this has been the least popular of the books of the poem.[18] The narrator outlines the problem of contemporary justice in the proem, arguing that the world has decayed from the Golden Age when everything was as it seemed, to the Age of Stone, where 'that which all men did vertue call, / Is now cald vice; and that which vice was hight, / Is now hight vertue, and so us'd of all: / Right now is wrong, and wrong that was is right' (V, proem, 4). There is a strategically placed semantic ambiguity surrounding the verb 'us'd' here: 'us'd' either indicates that everyone has been complicit in the inversion of the moral order and deliberately reverses good and evil, or that no one is capable of understanding the distinction any more. Of course, the distinction is a fine one and the overall effect the same, but the confusion indicates how daunting is the task that faces Artegall in his quest to restore justice. His task is made even harder when we learn that his mentor, Astrea, has found the earth too wicked a place for her to inhabit and has returned to the everlasting security of heaven (V, i, 11). Astrea, one of the many figures of the queen in the poem, is here shown to have abandoned her duties to her subjects in failing to support and instruct the knights in her charge, a clear criticism of Elizabeth's policy in her last years.[19] Given that Artegall's quest is to rescue Irena (Ireland) from Grantorto (great wrong, a figure of Catholic oppression in Europe), the specific allegory points to Elizabeth's neglect of her Irish subjects, specifically 'New English' Protestants like Spenser (Astrea's flight prefigures that of Diana in 'Two Cantos of Mutabilitie'; see below, p. 138). Irena's name carries a pun on Erin (Ireland) and 'irenic' (peaceful), indicating that if Artegall can complete his quest then Ireland can be transformed from a land of war to a land of peace.[20] However, the stress on the need for force in Artegall's upbringing and in his quest illustrates the paradox that true peace will more often than not require war first of all.

Book v can be divided into three sections: the first sees Artegall dealing with problems of the Common Law, concerning a number of specific cases (cantos i–iv); the second requires him to deal with more complex problems which challenge a general understanding of the law and require it to be supplemented by the principle of 'equity', whereby the central authorities can break or reverse the law of statute in the interests of a higher justice (cantos iv–vii); the third shows the operation of the law beyond the boundaries of England itself, in the conflicts in the Netherlands, with Spain, with Scotland (the trial of Mary, Queen of Scots) and in Ireland.[21] Spenser's conception of justice is largely derived from Aristotle and Elizabethan legal discourse. Aristotle argued that justice had to be distributive and commutative. The first principle concerned the correct distribution of honours and wealth among citizens and the establishment of just proportions. The second concerned the need to make punishments fit the crime.[22] The image of the balance appears throughout the Book, Astrea having taught Artegall 'to weigh both right and wrong / In equall balance with due recompence' (v, i, 7). Elizabethan ideals of justice were largely concerned with the need to protect the authority of the state and to prevent it from being undermined or disintegrating. A key issue was the question of true and false pity. The former was a legitimate cause for the intervention of the monarch – or his or her representative – to establish true justice. However, such issues of justice had to be balanced against the even more pressing claim of the citizens to be protected from dangerous enemies. A monarch whose system of justice failed on this count virtually forfeited the right to rule.[23] Artegall has to learn how to administer justice as his quest unfolds, as does the reader, the problems becoming ever more difficult and the gap between virtue and vice ever harder to determine.

The first problem of justice that Artegall has to solve involves a dispute between Sir Sangliere and a squire over the responsibility for the death of a lady. Each claims the lady who remains as his own. Artegall imitates the judgement of Solomon (I Kings 3. 16–28) and offers to divide the living lady in two to provide equal justice, a ruse which enables him to distribute honours properly, i.e., the dead lady to Sir Sangliere and the living one to the squire. Artegall is evidently a magistrate of some wisdom, but he is obliged to sort out his next two problems via the use of force.[24] First, he has to deal with Pollente and Munera, who levy unjust taxes on passers-by; then, the Giant with the Scales who wishes to redistribute wealth along strictly egalitarian lines. Both are dispatched with summary violence by Artegall and his officer of enforcement, the iron man, Talus: Pollente, whose crimes resemble those of contemporary rack-renting landlords, has his head exhibited on his castle walls, as a warning to others; Munera is drowned in the castle moat, having first had her golden hands and silver feet chopped off and nailed on high; the Giant is unceremoniously thrown off the cliff.[25] It may, of course, be the case that Spenser is forcing readers to confront the realities of contemporary violence necessary to implement justice and mercy (and his recommendations for establishing order in Ireland have horrified numerous commentators[26]). Nevertheless, it is by no means obvious that Artegall has the better of the argument at every turn. The giant's assertion that he will curb the excesses of over-mighty subjects is not dissimilar to Artegall's desire to punish Pollente and Munera harshly for their abuse of the commons:

> Tyrants that make men subiect to their law,
> I will suppresse, that they no more may raine;
> And Lordinges curbe, that commons ouer-aw;
> And all the wealth of rich men to the poore will draw.   (v, ii, 38)

Certainly one might suspect that Spenser would have hesitated before endorsing the last statement. But the rights of citizens to resist tyrants had become a commonplace of Protestant political theory, widely available in the circles in which Spenser moved.[27] Artegall's faith in the divine order of the universe argues a more fatalistic approach to human affairs. He argues that 'All creatures must obey the voice of the most hie' (v, ii, 40):

> They liue, they die, like as he doth ordaine,
> Ne euer any asketh reason why . . .
> He maketh Kings to sit in souerainty;
> He maketh subiects to their powre obay;
> He pulleth downe, he setteth up on hy;
> He giues to this, from that he takes away.
> For all we haue is his: what he list doe, he may.   (v, ii, 41)

Numerous ironies surround Artegall's assertions. He sees God as a remote and inaccessible deity whose rule over the universe is incomprehensible to humans.[28] While such a conception appears appropriate in a poem which has moved away from the explicitly Christian imagery of Book I to a universe dominated increasingly by classical gods and pagan deities, it should be remembered that Artegall obtains his power from his sword, Chrysaor, the weapon that Jove used to defeat the Titans (v, i, 9). Jove was, notoriously, a usurper who had overthrown his father Saturn in order to rule in his stead, a stubborn fact that undermines Jove's naïve faith in the legitimately ordained order of the universe. Jove has to rely on his own wiles to perform his duties in his quest – partly a result of the absence of Astrea – and is eventually betrayed by his queen, who calls him back to Faerie Court before he has been able to reform the 'ragged common-weale' of Irena's salvage island (v, xii, 26–7), again an indication that his faith in the order of the universe is misplaced. Moreover, one needs to read Artegall's authority in the light of Mutabilitie's claims in 'Two Cantos of Mutabilitie' (see below, pp. 137–9).

Book v, therefore, presents both author and reader with problems that go beyond the simple implementation of justice and concern its very possibility in the Age of Stone. Canto iii concerns another tournament where Braggadocchio and the false Florimell are finally exposed. In canto iv Artegall has to resolve a dispute between two brothers, Amidas and Bracidas, as to who has rights to land and treasure washed up on the seashore, reinforcing one of the chief puns in the poem, that of law as a means of 'salvaging' civilisation from savage nature (Artegall is the 'salvage knight'). This leads onto the episode that dominates the middle cantos of the book, Artegall's fight with the Amazon, Radigund, which is Spenser's means of exploring questions of the relationships between the sexes, and more significantly, perhaps, the problem of women's rule.[29] First, Artegall and Talus rescue Sir Terpine from Radigund's humiliating rule. He has been trussed up and placed on a gallows where he is taunted by the warrior women who surround him: 'they like tyrants, mercilesse the more, / Reioyced at his miserable case, / And him reuiled, and reproched sore / With bitter taunts, and terms of vile disgrace' (v, iv, 23). The description of the women as 'tyrants' would seem to be an unequivocal condemnation of their government and inversion of the 'natural' order. But who exactly do they represent? A false female state that exists only in legend? Or one of the terrible effects of Elizabeth's rule? As at so many crucial narrative cruxes in *The Faerie Queene*, we are offered two perceptions of the same reality and either asked to choose which is best or decide which describes the situation most accurately. In a sense there are two paths which may be taken or may have been taken already. Both Radigund and Britomart are versions of Elizabeth; the one a type of Boudicca, a virago who will protect her nation, not least through marrying and securing a stable succession; the other, a frustrated and dangerous harpy who, despite her beauty and charms, wrecks the lives of the (male) subjects on whom she should depend. While Britomart is the future wife of Artegall, a union foreseen by Britomart in the Temple of Isis, Radigund becomes his tyrannical mistress, forcing him to become her vassal and perform petty tasks and women's work to earn his keep (v, v, 23). It has often been commented that Spenser goes beyond the cruel and unobtainable lady of the fashionable Petrarchan poetry of the 1580s and 1590s in his *Amoretti* and *Epithalamion* by making the object of his affections his future wife.[30] While Britomart continues this move beyond the confines of that poetic genre, Radigund's enslaving desires signal a return to the terrors exhibited in the House of Busyrane.

Artegall yields to Radigund in single combat, blinded by her beauty when he removes her helmet (v, v, 11–17), a revelation that counterbalances the confusions surrounding Britomart's sex in Book III. Artegall is eventually rescued by Britomart, who beheads her rival, a stark contrast to the false pity that Artegall has shown towards a dangerous woman. Britomart, not Artegall, is the one who has understood the real requirements of justice, to show mercy to a people by dealing harshly with a false tyrant. If Radigund is a nightmare version of Elizabeth herself, she is also a form of Mary, Queen of Scots, a dangerous queen who starts to take on a more significant role as the book moves into international politics.

In canto viii, Arthur and Artegall kill the Souldan who threatens the subjects of Mercilla, a straightforward allegory of Philip II's attempts to invade England in the 1580s and 1590s, principally through the disastrous Armada of 1588. Arthur, having blinded the Souldan and his horses with his shield, hangs his broken shield and armour on a tree 'to be a moniment for euermore' (v, viii, 45). Seeing this 'moniment', the Souldan's wife, Adicia (from the Greek 'adikia', lawlessness), becomes a savage tiger in her angry despair, providing a neat thematic link to the discussion of savagery throughout the later books of *The Faerie Queene* as well as demonstrating the effect such displays of power were supposed to have. Arthur and Artegall head on to the Palace of Mercilla destroying the shape-shifting Malengin – usually taken to be an Irish rebel or a Jesuit priest – on the way.[31] In Mercilla's court they pass by the gruesome image of the poet, Bonfont, whose tongue has been nailed to a post and his name changed to Malfont because he 'falsely did reuyle, / And foule blaspheme that Queene [Mercilla] for forged guyle' (v, ix, 25). The image is a complex one, especially if we note that Malengin, clearly a dangerous creature, is glossed in the headnote to the canto as 'Guyle'. It is easy to argue that Spenser sympathises with the mutilated and silenced poet, but his crime links him to a dangerous rebel. On the other hand, one needs to note that the court falls into uneasy silence when Arthur and Artegall pass through to the queen's chamber, because they are horrified at the sight of knights in armour: 'Ne euer was the name of warre there spoken, / But ioyous peace and quietnesse always' (24). This comment is as double-edged as the image of Mal/ Bonfont. If the courtiers cannot tell the difference between 'forged guile' and honest speech it may well be the result of their distance from the dangerous parts of the queen's realms. They have little knowledge of the grim events and struggles that provide them with comfort and security.[32]

Equally problematic is the representation of the trial of Duessa, an allegory of the trial of Mary, Queen of Scots, which takes place at Mercilla's court.[33] James VI was seriously offended by the allegory and demanded that

Spenser be punished. Elizabeth as Mercilla is opposed by her male courtiers who demand Duessa's execution, notably Artegall, fortified after his unhappy imprisonment by Radigund, who 'with constant firme intent, / For zeale of Iustice was against her bent' (v, x, 49). Eventually, Mercilla, despite her pity for Duessa, accepts the verdict of guilty and agrees to the death sentence (significantly enough, not carried out within the poem). The reader is forced to decide whether the queen has acted justly, or whether she has actually demonstrated false pity – as Artegall did to Radigund – putting her own tender feelings before the needs and rights of her subjects.

The threats to Elizabeth's subjects grow towards the end of Book v. At first all goes well as Arthur manages to defeat Geryoneo and protect Sir Burbon (Henri IV of France) against a swarm of his enemies after he has foolishly thrown away his shield (an allegory of Henri's changing from the Protestant to the Catholic faith). In the final canto Artegall defeats the most fearsome of the giants who threaten Elizabeth, Grantorto, and so achieves his quest by liberating Irena. However, the Book ends disastrously, with Artegall and Talus called away mysteriously by Gloriana, before he has had time to impose true justice in Irena's land (Ireland). On the way back, he is attacked by two hideous hags, Envy and Detraction, the latest in a line of treacherous female figures. They unleash the Blatant Beast, a monster with a multitude of tongues, who can make the very woods and rocks 'quake and tremble with dismay' (v, xii, 41), a parody of Orpheus, the harpist who could commune with nature through his playing.

The issues dealt with in Book v become more significant as the narrative continues. Artegall learns from his mistakes in ways that are much more impressive than the parallel educational journeys of earlier heroes such as the Red Cross Knight and Guyon. However, as the last canto demonstrates, he fails through no fault of his own, a sign that political events have become too overwhelming for the individual to cope with, or to be contained within the confines of individual behaviour, no matter how morally responsible that individual is. The book ends without Justice having been established, a sign that Courtesy, the virtue explored in Book vi, has no foundation on which to establish itself. In this way, the book is doomed to failure.[34]

The proem to Book vi provides a definition of 'courtesy' which makes it clear that not only does the virtue have the inverse of its true meaning in the modern world, but it cannot really be defined. Courtesy is derived from 'court' and is the 'roote of ciuill conuersation' (vi, i, 1). However, as everything is a forgery today, the 'vertues seat is deepe within the mynd' (proem, 5). The metaphor used to describe 'courtesy' suggests that it will be found in the places furthest away from the court. The narrator argues that in the nursery of virtues:

Amongst them all growes not a fayrer flowre,
Then is the bloosme of comely courtesie,
Which though it on a lowly stalke doe bowre,
Yet brancheth forth in braue nobilitie,
And spreds it selfe through all ciuilitie.   (VI, proem, 4)

Courtesy may have derived its definition from the court, the apex of
political and social power, but now the cultural traffic is the other way
round and virtue travels from the country to the city. It is no wonder that
Calidore, the Knight of Courtesy, is so often confused and unsure of his
role, and disappears from the book for half the narrative (cantos iv–ix). It is
hardly surprising that, in sharp contrast to Book v, very little time is spent
on Calidore's quest. The capture of the Blatant Beast is dealt with in 20
stanzas at the end of canto xii and ends in failure. As with Artegall, Calidore
is not to blame for this. It is also noteworthy that the book is full of aimless
and wandering characters of uncertain origins and destinations: Serena,
Calepine, the Salvage Man, Pastorella. Book VI can be described as a
pastoral tragedy. There are richly comic moments, notably when Calidore
disturbs yet another pair of lovers, blunders into the clearing to interrupt
Colin Clout's vision of the Graces dancing (x, 17–20), or hopelessly
misinterprets Meliobee's praise of the shepherd's life and disquisition on the
roles and stations each has in life (ix, 16–33). Equally, there are moments of
rural contentment and tranquillity. However, the predominant image of
Book VI is that of the pastoral world left unprotected and constantly
threatened by evil figures lurking in the woods because law and order have
not been properly imposed by the authorities, a theme that becomes more
horrifying and urgent as the narrative continues. While the first few episodes
do involve the problem of courtesy as commonly understood – good
manners, politeness and the proper treatment of others – the second half of
the book sees the pastoral retreat overwhelmed by cannibals and then
brigands before the Blatant Beast escapes to roam at large and threatens the
very world of the poem itself: 'Ne may this homely verse, of many meanest,
/ Hope to escape his venemous despite' (VI, xii, 41). Calidore, like Artegall,
is simply unable to complete the quest assigned to him. If he appears
ridiculous at times, it is generally not his fault, but is because he has been
asked to perform things which are not humanly possible. Courtesy has no
meaning in a world without justice. Calidore's sojourn with the shepherds is
on one level a grave error as it is he who should be preserving them from
harm (as Meliboee's words make clear to the wary reader), so that it is
largely his fault when their rural idyll is destroyed. On another, it is no
wonder that he fails. If Gloriana prevents Artegall from completing his
quest, then Calidore has no chance with his. The allegory shuttles back and

forth between contingent and cosmic significance. The Blatant Beast first appears when Artegall is returning from 'the saluage island' (VI, i, 9), slandering his attempts to establish justice in Ireland. It soon becomes a representation of falsehood, making Calidore, like the Red Cross Knight in Book I, a figure of truth.[35] The implication is that Book VI is a nightmare vision of rural Ireland and/or rural England. The lack of definition is crucially important as it indicates that the failure to sort out the Catholic threat to Ireland may well result in the destruction of England too. Individual historical events, such as the premature recall of Lord Grey de Wilton, Spenser's erstwhile patron, can have cosmic significance.[36]

Calidore's quest begins with an easy problem to solve when he has to prevent Crudor and Briana from stripping the hair from passing knights. The episode points out the close link between courtesy and justice in its echoes of Artegall's treatment of Pollente and Munera, although the eventual punishment meted out is less harsh (they are both instructed in eloquence and civilised behaviour). He then makes Tristram his squire after he sees him killing a discourteous knight, and saves the lovers Priscilla and Aladine, an event which leads to his first problem: he has to lie about Priscilla's whereabouts to her parents in order to save her honour, a sign that courtesy may be impossible to carry out in a difficult world. He then manages to disturb Serena and Calepine, and while the two knights rest, Serena is attacked and wounded by the Blatant Beast and the two lovers have to face the discourteous Turpine. Calidore now disappears from the narrative and the action centres on Calepine. Calepine and Serena are rescued by a benign Salvage Man. He takes them to a hermit who helps to cure them of their wounds. The Salvage Man represents a primitive, amenable form of humanity, unable to speak (iv, 11), but naturally kind and courteous who 'neither plough'd nor sowed, / Ne fed on flesh, ne euer of wyld beast / Did taste the bloud, obaying natures first beheast' (14). This Salvage Man is one form of natural humanity found in recent reports of the Americas; unfortunately, his influence is overwhelmed later in the book by the other, hostile type of natural man.[37]

Arthur manages to defeat and then kill the discourteous Sir Turpine, and Calepine rescues Serena from a band of cannibals after her aimless wandering had exposed her to danger. They represent the other pole of primitive humanity from the Salvage Man with their debased and vicious religion of human sacrifice, but also the perverse sacrilege of false religion.[38] Calidore's absence is clearly significant, but he returns in the next canto (ix), decides to abandon his quest and remain with the shepherds, and falls in love with Pastorella. He then witnesses Colin Clout's conjuring up the three Graces with his pipes, but unfortunately his entrance causes the Graces to disappear. Colin explains that they have now gone forever and that their nakedness was a representation of the truth; their purpose was to teach mankind courtesy (x, 23–4). The mysterious fourth Grace was a 'countrey lasse' (25), a fact that forces Colin to apologise to Gloriana for seemingly ignoring her (28). Yet again, the episode provides a sign that true courtesy is now separated from the court and occurs only in obscure country areas (like Spenser's Munster).[39] Calidore's clumsiness is comic, given that the Knight of Courtesy has actually made the manifestation of courtesy disappear. Again, though, one might ask who is really at fault. The knight? Or the queen who has failed to establish the true ground ready for the virtue to flourish and who is specifically *not* a Grace?

The Book draws to a close when a band of Brigands kidnap Pastorella and destroy the rural idyll of the shepherds. This last group of savage people are explicitly compared to the Salvage Man as they, like him, do not 'liue by plough or spade'. Whereas he ate only the fruits of the forest, they 'fed on spoile and booty, which they made / Upon their neighbours' (x, 39). The Salvage Man can be integrated into society easily enough as he is keen to learn the rudiments of civilisation. The Brigands need to be controlled with force, or they will overrun and loot their neighbours. Clearly Calidore has been at fault here, although it should be added that the book provides enough clues to suggest that he is right to assume that he will find courtesy in rural retreats.

The Brigands are defeated after they fall out among themselves, this time with the help of Calidore who reunites Pastorella with her parents and finally resumes his quest. He manages to subdue and bind the Blatant Beast, but the beast mysteriously escapes to run riot throughout the world, another sign that Calidore has been asked to accomplish impossible feats. The text of *The Faerie Queene* published in Spenser's lifetime ends on a distinctly gloomy note with the beast 'Barking and biting all that him doe bate, / Albe they worthy blame, or cleare of crime' (xii, 40). In the nightmare world of the present, as Books V and VI have outlined, it is impossible to distinguish truth from falsehood.

In 1609, a fragment of a seventh book was published by Matthew Lownes, entitled 'Two Cantos of Mutabilitie', supposedly forming the core of a Book of the Legend of Constancy.[40] It is not clear how Lownes came into possession of the work, but he may have found it among the papers he inherited from William Ponsonby, Spenser's main publisher, after Ponsonby's death.[41] Although most scholars agree that these cantos were probably composed just before Spenser's death, opinion is divided as to their status or purpose. The two cantos, vi and vii, tell the story of the challenge made by Mutabilitie to Jove, chief of the Gods, as to who should really rule the universe. They meet on Arlo Hill in Ireland to present their cases and Nature awards victory to Jove, arguing that Mutabilitie is hoist by her own petard because she too is subject to the wiles of change she claims as her own. There are two extant stanzas from an eighth canto which appear to accept Nature's conception of eternity in mutability. Mutabilitie may hold sway in the sphere under the moon, but the narrator turns his attention to

> That same time when no more *Change* shall be,
> But stedfast rest of all things firmly stayd
> Upon the pillours of Eternity,
> That is contrayr to *Mutabilitie*. (VII, viii, 2)

While these words may reassure and comfort on the one hand, on the other they hint at an imminent end to the world, a sense of the hastening Apocalypse inaugurated by the chaotic rule of Mutabilitie. It is at least arguable that Mutabilitie, although undesirable, gets the better of the argument with Jove. He is, after all, a usurper who overthrew his father, Saturn, demonstrating that Mutabilitie is not the only deity who has challenged the order of the universe. Jove's anger at her challenge and claim that he rules by dint of force would appear to bear out Mutabilitie's claim rather than refute her: 'For, we [i.e., Jove] by Conquest of our soueraigne might, / And by eternall doome of Fates decree, / Haue wonne the Empire of the Heauens bright' (VII, vi, 33). Furthermore, the setting of the debate in Ireland, and the myth of Faunus, the foolish God who sees Diana naked and so drives her away from her favourite holiday island, is full of references to recent events and attaches these to grander themes. Diana is, of course, a figure of Elizabeth (identified as Cynthia in the 'Letter to Raleigh', another name for Diana) so that her abandoning Ireland refers to Elizabeth's lack of military aid to the English settlers there (as well as alluding to Astrea's abandonment of Artegall). The fact that she is seen naked suggests that Ireland is the place where her masks of power slip away and she needs to act more – rather than less – resolutely. Her curse on Ireland, transforming it from the fairest of the British Isles (vi, 38) to a wilderness where wolves and thieves threaten loyal subjects in the extensive forests there, accurately describes the situation of the English in Ireland as colonists like Spenser saw it. Although the story of Faunus, based largely on the legend of Acteon, has been described as 'a comic minor plot', it can be seen as a founding myth for the whole of *The Faerie Queene*.[42] Spenser's harsh criticisms of the queen (elsewhere Cynthia is reminded that she is old, will soon die and is subject herself to the wiles of Mutabilitie (vii, 50)) perhaps ensured that the fragment would not be published in his lifetime (or Elizabeth's). In the absence of further discoveries, it is quite possible to argue that 'Two Cantos of Mutabilitie' do not form part of a larger work, but represent the fundamental struggle between constancy and change at the heart of *The Faerie Queene*. Furthermore, they locate that struggle in Ireland.

NOTES

1 The numerological parallel of stanza 54 reinforces this parallel. On Spenser's keen interest in numerology, see A. Kent Hieatt, *Short Time's Endless Monument: The Symbolism of the Numbers in Edmund Spenser's 'Epithalamion'* (New York: Columbia University Press, 1960); Alastair Fowler, *Spenser and the Numbers of Time* (London: Routledge, 1964). For a reading of these words in the light of the Bluebeard legend, see Dorothy Stephens, *The Limits of Eroticism in Post-Petrarchan Narrative: Conditional Pleasure from Spenser to Marvell* (Cambridge: Cambridge University Press, 1998), pp. 79–84.

2 See Lauren Silberman's excellent reading in *Transforming Desire: Erotic Knowledge and Books III and IV of The Faerie Queene* (Berkeley: University of California Press, 1995), pp. 58–70.

3 Ibid., p. 63.

4 See Andrew Hadfield, 'Introduction', in Andrew Hadfield, ed., *Edmund Spenser* (London: Longman, 1996), pp. 15–7; Richard T. Neuse, 'Adonis, Gardens of', in *Spenser Encyclopedia*, pp. 8–9.

5 See Andrew Hadfield, 'The "sacred hunger of ambitious minds": Spenser's savage religion', in Donna B. Hamilton and Richard Strier, eds., *Religion, Literature and Politics in Post-Reformation England, 1540–1688* (Cambridge: Cambridge University Press, 1996), pp. 27–45.

6 See Jonathan Goldberg, *Endlesse Worke: Spenser and the Structures of Discourse* (Baltimore: Johns Hopkins University Press, 1981).

7 On the problematic status of the letter, see Darryl J. Gless, *Interpretation and Theology in Spenser* (Cambridge: Cambridge University Press, 1994), pp. 48–9. For an argument that the ending of Book VI was Spenser's intended conclusion to the poem, see Richard T. Neuse, 'Book VI as Conclusion to *The Faerie Queene*', *ELH* 35 (1968), 329–53.

8 Hamilton, p. 738.

9 See Thomas H. Cain, *Praise in 'The Faerie Queene'* (Lincoln, Nebraska: University of Nebraska Press, 1978); Philippa Berry, *Of Chastity and Power: Elizabethan Literature and the Unmarried Queen* (London: Routledge, 1989).

10 See Andrew Hadfield, '"Who knowes not Colin Clout?": The permanent exile of Edmund Spenser', in *Literature, Politics and National Identity* (Cambridge: Cambridge University Press, 1994), pp. 170–201.

11 For details, see Willy Maley, *A Spenser Chronology* (Basingstoke: Macmillan, 1994), pp. 16, 28; J. W. Bennett, *The Evolution of 'The Faerie Queene'* (Chicago: Chicago University Press, 1942). Bennett suggests that Book IV contains the leftovers from Book III, a sign that the second edition of the poem was written in haste. Both Books date from the same period and were re-used in 1596 (ch. 12).

12 '*The Faerie Queene*, Book IV', *Spenser Encyclopedia*, pp. 273–80, at p. 273.

13 Elizabeth Heale, *The Faerie Queene: A Reader's Guide* (Cambridge: Cambridge University Press, 2nd edn, 1999), p. 111.

14 Timias' relationship with Belphoebe is easily recognisable as an allegory of Sir

Walter Raleigh's troubled relationship with his queen after his marriage to Elizabeth Throckmorton in 1592, a match that Queen Elizabeth abhorred; see James P. Bednarz, 'Raleigh in Spenser's Historical Allegory', *Sp. St.* 4 (1983), 49–70.

15 On Proteus as a 'shape-shifter', see A. Bartlett Giamatti, *Play of Double Senses: Spenser's 'Faerie Queene'* (New Jersey: Prentice Hall, 1975); Supriya Chaudhuri, 'Proteus', in *Spenser Encyclopedia*, pp. 560–1; Ovid, *Metamorphoses*, trans. Mary M. Innes (Harmondsworth: Penguin, 1955), pp. 198, 252–3.

16 On 'wild men of the woods', see Richard Bernheimer, *Wild Men in the Middle Ages: A Study in Art, Sentiment, and Demonology* (Cambridge, MA: Harvard University Press, 1952).

17 For comment see Andrew Hadfield, *Spenser's Irish Experience: Wilde Fruit and Salvage Soyl* (Oxford: Clarendon Press, 1997), chs. 4–5.

18 'The fifth book is the least popular in *The Faerie Queene*. This is partly the poet's fault, for he has included in it some flat and uninspired passages; but in part it results from the differences between his conception of justice and ours' (C. S. Lewis, *The Allegory of Love: A Study in Medieval Tradition* (Oxford: Oxford University Press, 1958, repr. of 1936), p. 347). Jane Aptekar's *Icons of Justice: Iconography and Thematic Imagery in Book v of 'The Faerie Queene'* (New York: Columbia University Press, 1969), is a good guide to the book. See also T. K. Dunseath, *Spenser's Allegory of Justice in Book v of 'The Faerie Queene'* (Princeton: Princeton University Press, 1968).

19 On Elizabeth as Astrea, see Frances A. Yates, *Astraea: The Imperial Theme in the Sixteenth Century* (London: Routledge, 1975); Helen Hackett, *Virgin Mother, Maiden Queen* (Basingstoke: Macmillan, 1995).

20 Medieval Ireland had traditionally been divided into a 'Land of War' where the Irish held sway, and a 'Land of Peace', where English rule had been established by the English authorities.

21 Michael O'Connell, '*The Faerie Queene, Book v*', in *Spenser Encyclopedia*, pp. 280–3, at p. 281.

22 See Aristotle, *The Nichomachean Ethics*, trans. David Ross (Oxford: Oxford University Press, 1980), Book v.

23 See Heale, *Faerie Queene*, pp. 123–4. Quentin Skinner, *The Foundations of Modern Political Thought*, 2 vols. (Cambridge: Cambridge University Press, 1978), II, part 3.

24 Elizabeth Fowler points out how the landscape of Book v is littered with dismembered corpses, tortured victims and parts of bodies. See 'The Failure of Moral Philosophy in the Work of Edmund Spenser', *Representations* 51 (1995), 47–76.

25 For details of the violence involved in Elizabethan punishments and executions, see John Bellamy, *The Tudor Law of Treason: An Introduction* (London: Routledge, 1979), pp. 191–210.

26 See, for example, Ciaran Brady, 'Spenser's Irish Crisis: Humanism and Experience in the 1590s', *P&P* 111 (1986), 17–49.

27 See Skinner, *Foundations of Modern Political Thought*, II, pt. 3; *Vindiciae Contratyrannos, or, concerning the legitimate power of a prince over the people, and of the people over a prince*, ed. George Garnett (Cambridge: Cambridge University Press, 1994).

28 The lines may be based on Saturn's description of his awesome power in Chaucer's *The Knight's Tale* (in *The Riverside Chaucer*, ed. Larry D. Benson (Oxford: Oxford University Press, 1987)), lines 2453–78.

29 For comment, see Sheila T. Cavanagh, *Wanton Eyes and Chaste Desires: Female Sexuality in The Faerie Queene* (Bloomington: Indiana University Press, 1994), pp. 164–9; Clare Carroll, 'The Construction of Gender and the Cultural and Political Other in *The Faerie Queene* 5 and *A View of the Present State of Ireland*: The Critics, the Context, and the Case of Radigund', *Criticism* 32 (1990), 163–91.

30 For a recent commentary on readings of the *Amoretti* and *Epithalamion*, see *Edmund Spenser's Amoretti and Epithalamion: A Critical Edition*, ed. Kenneth J. Larsen (Tempe: Medieval and Renaissance Texts and Studies, 1997); Germaine Warkentin, '*Amoretti, Epithalamion*', in *Spenser Encyclopedia*, pp. 30–8.

31 See Harold Skulsky, '*Malengin*', in *Spenser Encyclopedia*, p. 450.

32 For a perceptive recent analysis of this passage, see M. Lindsay Kaplan, *The Culture of Slander in early Modern England* (Cambridge: Cambridge University Press, 1997), pp. 39–42.

33 See Richard A. McCabe, 'The Masks of Duessa: Spenser, Mary Queen of Scots, and James VI', *ELR* 17 (1987), 224–42.

34 Useful accounts of Book VI can be found in Donald Cheney, *Spenser's Image of Nature: Wild Man and Shepherd in 'The Faerie Queene'* (New Haven: Yale University Press, 1966); Arnold Williams, *Flower on a Lowly Stalk: The Sixth Book of the 'Faerie Queene'* (East Lansing: University of Michigan Press, 1967); Humphrey Tonkin, *Spenser's Courteous Pastoral: Book Six of 'The Faerie Queene'* (Oxford: Clarendon Press, 1972).

35 See Hadfield, 'Spenser's Savage Religion', pp. 33–4.

36 Richard A. McCabe, 'The Fate of Irena: Spenser and Political Violence', in Patricia Coughlan, ed., *Spenser and Ireland: An Interdisciplinary Perspective* (Cork: Cork University Press, 1989), pp. 109–25.

37 See Peter Hulme, *Colonial Encounters: Europe and the Native Caribbean, 1492–1797* (London: Methuen, 1986), ch. 2.

38 See Kenneth Borris, '"Diuelish Ceremonies": Allegorical Satire of Protestant Extremism in *The Faerie Queene*, VI, viii, 31–51', *Sp. St.* 8 (1987), 175–209; Anne Fogarty, 'The Colonisation of Language: Narrative Strategies in *A View of the Present State of Ireland* and *The Faerie Queene*, Book VI', in Coughlan, ed., *Spenser and Ireland*, pp. 75–108.

39 See Stella P. Revard, '*Graces*', in *Spenser Encyclopedia*, pp. 338–9; Edgar Wind, *Pagan Mysteries in the Renaissance* (Harmondsworth: Penguin, 1967, repr. of 1958), ch. 2.

40 For commentary see Sheldon P. Zitner, '*The Faerie Queene, Book VII*', *Spenser Encyclopedia*, pp. 287–9; Hadfield, *Spenser's Irish Experience*, ch. 6.

41 Colin Burrow, *Edmund Spenser* (Plymouth: Northcote House, 1996), p. 41.

42 Zitner, '*Faerie Queene, Book VII*', p. 288.

FURTHER READING

Jane Aptekar, *Icons of Justice: Iconography and Thematic Imagery in Book V of 'The Faerie Queene'* (New York: Columbia University Press, 1969).

A. Bartlett Giamatti, *Play of Double Senses: Spenser's 'Faerie Queene'* (New Jersey: Prentice Hall, 1975).

Thomas H. Cain, *Praise in 'The Faerie Queene'* (Lincoln, Nebraska: University of Nebraska Press, 1978).

Donald Cheney, *Spenser's Image of Nature: Wild Man and Shepherd in 'The Faerie Queene'* (New Haven: Yale University Press, 1966).

Jonathan Goldberg, *Endlesse Worke: Spenser and the Structures of Discourse* (Baltimore: Johns Hopkins University Press, 1981).

Elizabeth Heale, *The Faerie Queene: A Reader's Guide* (Cambridge: Cambridge University Press, 2nd edn, 1999).

Humphrey Tonkin, *Spenser's Courteous Pastoral: Book Six of 'The Faerie Queene'* (Oxford: Clarendon Press, 1972).

7

ANNE LAKE PRESCOTT

Spenser's shorter poems

This essay discusses the shorter poems that Spenser published in the 1590s with the exceptions of 'Mother Hubberds Tale' and *Colin Clouts Come Home Againe*. Do they have anything in common aside from authorship and relative brevity? Perhaps so. All concern love or sorrow, and some explore the often tense relation of those two energies that Spenser variously locates in the psyche, the state and the cosmos. True, much human life can be read as a dialectic of desire and melancholy (in Elizabethan terms, 'forward' and 'froward' passions), but Spenser's focus on the dialectic is particularly sharp. These poems are by definition non-epic ventures. Yet awareness of *The Faerie Queene* is never far away, sometimes detectable in verse on the collapse of greatness, sometimes, more obliquely, in echoes of Virgil or Ovidian subversions of the *Aeneid*, and sometimes audible as references to the national epic on which Spenser the lover knows, or says he knows, he should be working.

Complaints (1591) was published by William Ponsonby, publisher of the 1590 *Faerie Queene*.[1] Much remains mysterious about this venture. Did Spenser oversee its printing? In a preface Ponsonby reports that he has collected the contents, extracting poems from those owning copies, retrieving others 'purloined' from Spenser, and failing to obtain some others.[2] Spenser had been in England, so it is possible that he oversaw the printing or at least authorised the volume's arrangement. Debate continues. In any event, the order of poems shows signs of thought, even if the thought was Ponsonby's. As the title suggests, all the collection's poems complain about something, whether elegiacally, satirically, or in the lachrymose vein that baffles or bores modern readers. Perhaps Spenser hopes to subject the psychology and discourse of grief to cool scrutiny even as he indulges a current taste for moans, tears, shrieks and sententious remarks on Fortune and change. Many Elizabethans enjoyed the rhetoric of grief even when condemning unstinted tears as womanish or impious. Like erotic discourse, complaint – exhortations to *contemptus mundi*, images of mutability, or estates satire – affords opportunities for clever conceits, elegant tropes and elabourate rhetorical patterns that stop the verse from dissolving into mere puddles of emotion. 'Complaint' as a genre has medieval precedent, but Spenser's volume is hardly old-fashioned, for the poetics of lamentation interested fashionable Renaissance poets on the Continent, to say nothing of Ovid grieving in his *Tristia* and longing for Augustus to summon him home.

Complaints begins and ends with visionary poetry that commemorates lost greatness, particularly that of ancient Rome. 'The Ruines of Time', which opens the volume, owes much to two sonnet sequences by Joachim Du Bellay. The first is 'Les Antiquitez de Rome' (1558). Translated as 'The Ruines of Rome', it appears towards the middle of *Complaints*. The second, Du Bellay's appended 'Songe' ('Dream Vision'), comprises such images of ruination as a fallen oak or spoiled fountain. Spenser's translation of eleven of these, together with his version of Petrarch's *Rime 323* on the death of Laura, had appeared without credit in the 1569 *Theatre for Voluptuous Worldlings*, an illustrated tract by a Protestant refugee from Antwerp, Jan van der Noot, that denounces Catholic pride and corruption. These translations, polished up and without pictures, conclude *Complaints* as 'The Visions of Bellay' and 'The Visions of Petrarch'.

Dedicated to Mary Sidney, Countess of Pembroke, 'The Ruines of Time' tells how the narrator was walking by 'silver streaming Thamesis' when he meets 'Verlame', a personification of the now vanished Roman-British city, Verulamium (in cold fact never on the Thames). In a long complaint about the slipperiness of earthly glory Verlame remembers the imperial capital whose very name, in its Elizabethan pronunciation ('Room') encouraged puns on space and on earth's rheumy matter that flows down Time's slipstream: 'O Rome thy ruine I lament and rue.' Her tears recall weeping biblical cities as well as the fashion for overheard laments by such fallen women as Jane Shore in 'A Mirror for Magistrates'.

Verlame has more to regret than her dimmed glory as a particle of empire, for she thinks modern England, after the recent deaths of Philip Sidney and the Earl of Leicester, a wasteland infested by ominous screech-owls and crafty foxes. Raw power remains: one statesman, 'broad spreading like an aged tree, / Lets none shoot up, that nigh him planted bee' (452–3). This egoist, in effect a one-tree Rome, sounds like William Cecil as Spenser saw him: an aged and selfish muse-scorner. How unlike Essex and Raleigh, Spenser would have thought or hoped. A set of visions follows, indebted to Petrarch and Du Bellay: an altar decays, a tower collapses, a paradise is trashed, a giant tumbles, a bridge fails, and white bears (recalling the Dudley crest) are buried. At least the dead Dudleys are in the skies. Stella-loving Sidney, with 'sid' (Greek 'star') in his name, is a celestial swan and 'signe', a fine pun on the constellation 'cygnus', or 'cygne' in French. An envoy to Sidney concludes the poem. Are we to pity Verlame? Some would say no; given to more self-pity than most modern critics can stand or than many Elizabethans would approve, she represents an empire toward which any Englishman might well feel as much resentment as awe. On the other hand, she is also British; and Spenser, although Christian, valued as well as mistrusted worldly glory.

The grandeur that was Rome had more than antiquarian interest for Spenser's generation. Rome's fall, the theory ran, had allowed a divinely sanctioned *imperium* to continue its ancient western path from Asia Minor (or, more literally, to make a right turn north). The Holy Roman Emperor, Charles V, and then his son, Philip II of Spain, laid claim to it, Trojan ancestors and all. But England, to whom legend also gave Trojan ancestry, insisted on sharing in this *translatio imperii*.[3] The elegiac treatments of Rome, of which there were many in Renaissance poetry and art, are deeply ambivalent: the not-so-eternal city's ruins are sad but can also be recycled as new walls and houses, new nations, new texts.

This ambivalence was especially complicated in Protestant countries, where Roman pride seemed to anticipate global pretensions by the papacy and Spain. Similarly, Roman civil wars warned that disunity makes a people vulnerable to foreign invasion, as happened in France and as many feared might happen in England should the Spanish repress the Netherlands or capture Ireland. Rome's ruins are thus a 'moniment' in every sense. They are a monument, if a dusty one, to a towering greatness for which a modern poet like Spenser might long, with which he might compete, and allusions to which could give epic resonance to love poetry and complaint. But they also admonish would-be empires, as do the prophecies of ruination in Daniel and Revelation, even while signifying that there is now space, Rome/room, for new poets and new societies. Terror of Spain and relief at England's defeat of the Armada in 1588 generated a large number of sermons, tracts and poems anticipating the fall of Spain's and the popes' Babylonish power in terms of ancient Rome's conquest by northern 'barbarians'. The Geneva Bible (1560) provides an apocalyptic version of this fall in a picture of the restored Temple, all rectilinear stability and proportion, erected against a distant jumble of ruined earthly power. Compare the 'pillours of Eternity' at the end of *The Faerie Queene*.

Sidney's soul now sparkles as a sign/cygne, but in the next poem English culture is moribund. All nine muses gather in 'Teares of the Muses' by the 'silver Springs of Helicone' (like many sorrowing figures, they gravitate to running water) and mourn its condition in a hundred sad sixains that

Spenser dedicates to Alice Spencer, Lady Strange. The introduction has nine stanzas; the fourth muse, Erato, has eleven; the others each have nine stanzas of sorrow followed by a tenth that makes a transition to the next complaint. The pattern is thus not quite consistent, although it is unclear if this indicates trouble on Parnassus or a sophisticated taste for slight asymmetry.

English aristocrats, says Clio, neither patronise the arts intelligently nor do deeds worth the singing. Some are so 'puft up with sdeignful insolence' that they 'underkeep' what grows beneath them and destroy its buds. Do they not know that without poets whatever is good will 'die in darknesse, and lie hid in slime'? Melpomene argues that without learned understanding there can be no true tragedy, and Thalia, who used to 'maske in mirth', cannot inspire comedy now that 'ugly Barbarisme, / And brutish Ignorance' entertain the vulgar with 'vaine toyes'. Euterpe finds Helicon dirty and her groves a wilderness; Terpsichore complains of poets who have 'usurped' her realm by flattery, corrupt 'fooleries' and 'newfanglenesse'. Erato sees dung-hill 'leawdnes' (ignorance and indecency) where once Love was 'school-master of my skill'. Calliope grieves that noblemen give her no reason to use her epic 'golden Trompet of eternitie'. Nobody, says Urania, will follow her to the skies to 'behold the heavens great Hierarchie' in 'contemplation of things heavenlie wrought'. Polyhymnia says that poetry, once the darling of princes and priests, is now profaned by the 'vulgar, that with hands uncleane / Dares to pollute her hidden mysterie', although she rejoices that Elizabeth (the 'Pandora of all heavenly graces') writes poetry.

Modern scholars themselves often find cause for complaint when discussing this poem. It is 1591: why is Spenser discouraged about a nation in which Marlowe and Shakespeare have been writing plays, Watson and Lodge have been writing verse, and he himself has just published *The Faerie Queene*? Can the muses not read? Was the literature effervescing around Spenser not elite and erudite enough for him? There may be something subtler at work. If the muses represent, as for many they did, the whole 'encyclopedia' or circle of learning, then it is not enough to write or patronise pretty lyrics, the popular stage, or even hortatory laments like those in 'A Mirror for Magistrates'.[4] True poets, said Spenser's friend Gabriel Harvey, are not 'superficial humanists' (students of good letters) but 'curious universall scholars'.[5] When the language in 'Teares of the Muses' is pressed, moreover, it becomes ambiguous. It is not mere cynicism to say that grief, like generosity, can be aggressive.[6] Spenser's images of aspiration blocked by the great and female secret bowers or groves violated by baseness set up an unstable dynamic involving gender and class. In this dynamic the place of middle-class male poets can be hard to locate, but we can still hear the resentment that gives urgency to the muses' tears and the faint implication that there is something futile about inspiration so secret, so embowered. If muses and good poets need the aristocracy, they probably need the base vulgar too, especially if they venture out of Parnassian groves and into print.

After the complaining muses comes a complaining insect. 'Virgils Gnat', in eighty-six pretty octava-rima stanzas, is an amplified and more sententious version of the 'Culex', a semi-serious poem once ascribed to Virgil. The subtitle specifies that 'Gnat' is 'Long since dedicated To the most noble and excellent Lord, the Earle of Leicester, late deceased', which implies that Spenser wrote all or most of it between 1580 and 1588. Addressed to Augustus, 'Culex' tells of a shepherd who swats a gnat that stung him awake so as to save him from a serpent. Understandably upset, the gnat's ghost returns in 'Virgils Gnat' to report on the underworld and reproach his now repentant murderer, who then dedicates a flowery monument to his saviour's memory. The poem reads like a comment on the tendency of the powerful to kill the messenger rather than attend to the message. Spenser strengthens this impression in a preliminary sonnet to Leicester: 'Wrong'd, yet not daring to express my paine / To you (great Lord) the causer of my care, / In clowdie teares my case I thus complaine / Unto your selfe, that onely privie are'. May readers who guess the secret not 'further seeke to glose upon the text'. Despite efforts to link the poem with some political event such as Elizabeth I's marriage negotiations with the Duke of Alençon, nobody knows how Leicester wronged Spenser, if he did and if Spenser is not generating an inky cloud of seeming secrecy so as to appear well connected. Being wronged by an earl is a social accomplishment of sorts. Even Spenser's request to the reader is cryptic: if 'glose' meant 'write an interpretive gloss', it also meant 'lie'. As so often, the fear of being misread – or read too perceptively – haunts Elizabethan texts. Some readers could arrange for the writer to share the gnat's fate.

'Virgils Gnat' is followed by 'Mother Hubberds Tale', discussed elsewhere in this volume. Estates satire in the form of an animal fable told in the person of a 'good old woman', it notices a range of social types including upstart malcontents – a group that probably includes a disguised version of Cecil. This imprudently courageous tale of the ape and fox who usurped a kingdom while the lion(ess) slept led the authorities to have *Complaints* called in, although so far as we know Spenser himself went unpunished.[7]

The ape and fox had aspired to greatness, an ambition with which Spenser sympathised somewhere in his imagination or he would not have written so bitterly about big trees that overshadow shrubs or statesmen who stifle the hopes of others. The most notorious instance of aspiration not just to govern the world but to *be* the world is Rome, so it is fitting that Spenser's 'Ruines of Rome' comes next. The topic had particular significance for Protestants, but one may doubt that Spenser departs far or disapprovingly from Du Bellay. The 'Antiquitez' is a brilliantly complicated exploration of pitying regret, punitive triumph and paradoxical wonder. Although a Catholic, Du Bellay's loyalties were more Gallican than papist; he had scant love for modern Rome and felt considerable ambivalence toward the old. As a fellow poet, Spenser would also have perceived the aggressive affection with which Du Bellay, writing in what felt like exile in Rome, managed to create a non-epic that parallels, in its fragmentary fashion, the Virgilian *Franciade* that his friend Ronsard was failing to complete. 'Ruines' also has a convoluted relation to Petrarchan love poetry: ruined or corrupt cities can resemble proud, lost, or fallen beloveds.

The most likable poem in *Complaints*, one with its own relation to Virgil and imperial pride, is the mock-epic 'Muiopotmos' ('The Fate of a Fly'; 'fly' meant any airborne insect). It is also the most puzzling. The title page is dated 1590 (i.e., before March 25, 1591), which could suggest that it was typeset before the rest of *Complaints*. Spenser dedicates it to Lady Elizabeth Carey, daughter of Sir John Spencer of Althorpe and related by marriage to Essex. Spenser thanks her for past favour and vows to honour the name that her 'brave deserts' have 'purchast' for her. That the poet would want to please a lady to whom as a Spens/cer he claimed alliance is unsurprising. More enigmatic is the request 'to make a milde construction' of his poem: to take it in good part. Any such request, however, is an invitation to 'construe'. Some have obliged by finding allegories in this story of a malicious spider's brutal murder of a careless butterfly, but their failure to agree upon one dominant meaning has led others to take the poem as more general satire and complaint, a delicate comment on mutability, mortality, and the constrictions put on innocently self-pleasing if imprudent desire by envy, slander, fate and chance.

The narrative recalls Chaucer's 'Nun's Priest's Tale' and, thanks to the opening alliteration ('I sing of deadly dolorous debate'), the by now slightly musty 'Mirror for Magistrates' with its stories of greatness crushed under Fortune's wheel. Renaissance readers would also identify 'Muiopotmos' as rhyprography, the paradoxical treatment of insignificant or unpraiseworthy topics, and would classify it with the 'Battle of the Mice and Frogs' ascribed to Homer, Lucian on the fly, Erasmus' *Praise of Folly*, or the many Renaissance poems on insects, baldness and the like.[8] In many ways, though, the poem is an 'epyllion': a little epic, often indebted to Ovid, that treats a mythical or erotic topic in sensual language. Generically and stylistically, the poem thus stages a conflict between public epic aspirations (the second stanza's astonished query, 'And is there then / Such rancour in the harts of mightie men?' parodies *Aeneid* I, II: 'Tantaene animis coelestibus irae', while the last stanza parodies Virgil's concluding lines on the death of Turnus) and the Ovidian seriousness with which Spenser describes pleasure and metamorphosis.[9] Spenser's epic aspirations were now obvious, yet 'Muiopotmos' shows that he was capable of ironic distance from that project. Butterflies should take more care than does Spenser's hero as he cavorts in his Edenic garden of earthly delights – spiders and worse lurk there with mortal sting and perhaps forked tongue – but the poem's skeptical humor, elegiac melancholy, and pleasure in private sensual liberty offer an alternative to epic, martial and imperial ambitions.

The tale opens, after an invocation to the mournful muse Melpomene, with the arming of the princely hero, Clarion, pride of his aged father Muscaroll. Clarion's name suggests brightness and Fame's trumpet, while his position as heir to the 'Empire of the aire' evokes dynasties and conquest.[10] This send-up of epic convention has disquieting aspects, for Clarion's breastplate and helmet, like his Herculean 'hairie hide of some wilde beast' and the lances he carries on his head (his antennae), are in fact his body. Except for his painted wings, this butterfly *is* his military equipment. What is inside? His enemy the spider at least has an abdomen full of thread. The narrator explains the wings with a story in the Ovidian manner. While Clarion's ancestress Astery, a nymph whose name suggests 'star', gathers flowers, her jealous companions slander her to Venus.[11] Giving 'hastie credit to th'accuser' (compare the ass-eared judge in Apelles' famous painting of Calumny and the fable in Spenser's 'Februarie' eclogue), the goddess changes Astery to a butterfly. On flowery wings inherited from her, Clarion sports with 'kingly joyaunce' through what Judith Anderson, alluding to Book I of *The Faerie Queene*, wittily calls a 'garden of Error'.[12] He observes its delights with a 'curious busie eye', which some might call the sin of 'curiosity', a prying into God's secrets; this butterfly cares more for seeing beauty than for hearing truth. 'Greedily' preying on nature's variety, much of it – a proto- or anti-colonialist touch? – 'fetcht from farre away', Clarion is glad to 'enjoy delight with libertie, / And to be Lord of all the workes of Nature, / To raine in th'aire from earth to highest skie'. Such confidence is dangerous in Spenser, although his mind was also clearly moved by thoughts of soaring flight and riotous plenitude.

At the poem's pivotal centre, the narrator comments on Fortune and the need for divine guidance to survive the fate 'woven' by Jove (in this context probably not God but a subordinate power). The fate comes in a form suiting a poem so fascinated by textiles and texts: the web spun by the spider Aragnoll. Many readers will take this web as involving calumny spun by malice.[13] In Elizabethan England calumnies need not be false, when told of the powerful and great, to count as *scandalum magnatum*, slander of the great. To explain why spiders would want to kill butterflies, although wealth, beauty and happiness tend in any case to attract envy, the narrator revises Ovid's story of Arachne's and Athena's weaving contest. Spenser makes important changes: the defeated Arachne's own inward rage, not divine will, causes her metamorphosis into a spider. Her image of Jove and Europa may allude, granted how the myth was read in the Renaissance, to imperial conflicts between east and west, while Athena's evocation of the time her invention of the olive tree outdid Poseidon's invention of the war-horse has been taken as complimenting Elizabeth's recent victory over Spain and her preference for peace.[14]

With force and craft – Aragnoll is both 'Foxe' and 'Lyon' – the Machia-vellian spider traps Clarion in a subtle web that reminds the narrator of the net in which Vulcan caught, and exposed to scandal, his wife Venus and her lover Mars. Becoming more entangled the more he struggles (an astute comment on how slander works), Clarion is stabbed to death, and as his groaning spirit flees to the air his body remains 'the spectacle of care'. Had he shown more 'care', a moralist might note, he would not have come to this pass.

One can understand the temptation to read 'Muiopotmos' as allegorising a political event (although nobody knows which), the nature of art (although butterflies create nothing except caterpillars), or the struggle between soul – *psyche*, Greek for butterfly – and flesh (although it seems unlike Spenser utterly to denigrate the body).[15] Aragnoll certainly has a trace of Satan, but also a trace of the author: mendacious or magical weaving of lies and spells disconcertingly resemble the delightful or instruc-tive weaving of a text.[16] The poem is also anti-court satire, for Clarion is pretty, imprudent and pleasure-driven, and bears arms useless against 'policy'. And, as a parody of dynastic epic, 'Muiopotmos' concerns itself with ancestral grudges, origins, generations. Most relevant to *Complaints*, however, and visible even on the poem's surface, is the spectacle of bright-ness darkened, empire humbled, and improvident pleasure denied. One critic has called Clarion 'desire on the wing, a veritable *Eros*'.[17] His flutterings may be vain in every sense, and his fate may make us smile, but he has the poet's sympathy. Spenser disliked the somberly dressed spiders of his age who might enviously destroy those who, with whatever sage and serious purpose, wrote of fairyland and dreamed of airy empires.

The volume concludes with three short sonnet sequences. 'Visions of the Worlds Vanitie' recounts various instances of small creatures that bring down the mighty. The last sonnet calls these 'sad sights', but the lesson it deduces is mixed: 'Thenceforth I gan in my engrieved brest / To scorne all difference of great and small', yet we are also told, with less than perfect logic, to 'love the low degree'. The sight of eagles, lions, elephants and cedars brought low is sobering but not, unless one is an eagle, lion, elephant or cedar, entirely displeasing. Indeed Erasmus, whose essay 'The dungbeetle seeks the eagle' (in *Adages*) Spenser may have been reading, drew from such reversals quasi-republican and anti-imperial conclusions. Next is Spenser's translation of Du Bellay's 'Songe'. Spenser follows Du Bellay fairly closely, the first sonnet preserving the pious moral given by a sort of Ghost of Empires Past who appears on the 'great rivers banck, that runnes by Rome' to warn the sleeping poet that 'onely God surmounts all times decay'. Last come the sonnets from *Rime* 323 that allegorise the death of Laura. Van der Noot had read them as images of papal Rome's fate and hence, although hardly a matter for laughter, not entirely a matter for tears. Here, in *Complaints* in 1591, they seem once again entirely elegiac.

Probably in 1591 (or in 1592 before the legal new year, March 25) Spenser published another complaint: *Daphnaïda* recounts, and may partly condemn, the sorrow of Alcyon (Sir Arthur Gorges, himself a poet) for his dead Daphne (Douglas Howard, Lady Gorges). The poem's obsession with the number seven (there are eighty-one seven-line stanzas) may intimate that Alcyon's comprehension is as yet limited to the days of the week, that he ignores the dying Daphne's plea that he remember eternity. In 1595 came *Astrophel*, a belated elegy for Sidney. Spenser reworks Bion's 'Lament for Adonis' (the youth loved by Venus who, like Sidney, died from a wound to the thigh). Although warm in its praise of the dead hero, now thoroughly mythologised by his family and by those in authority whom his political militancy no longer vexed, the poem may also insinuate that Sidney too lightly threw away his life through foolish heroics. The elegy is followed by 'The Doleful Lay of Clorinda' in the person of Astrophel's sister (Mary Sidney). There is still no consensus on who – Spenser, Mary Sidney, or both – wrote it; the poems are certainly related by tone, style, and – with 216 and 108 lines respectively – numerical patterning that may gesture at the analogous numbers of Philip Sidney's *Astrophil and Stella*.

In 1595, the same year that saw *Colin Clouts Come Home Againe* (discussed elsewhere in this volume), Ponsonby published a handsome octavo entitled *Amoretti and Epithalamion. Written not long since by Edmunde Spenser.* It was entered in the Stationers' Register on November 19, 1594. According to Ponsonby's preface, the author had sent the manuscript from Ireland. A sonnet by 'G. W.' (Geoffrey Whitney?) tells Spenser to 'hie' him 'home' so poetry's sun will shine again in England, and G. W. Junior (who, if Whitney, compiled *A Choise of Emblemes*, 1586), promises 'endles honor' to Colin, writer of pastoral, epic and exercises 'in thy lovely mistris praise'. The volume memorialises Spenser's courtship of Elizabeth Boyle, a young, well-born Anglo-Irish woman, and the couple's wedding on June 11, 1594 – St Barnaby's day, which in the Julian calendar is the summer solstice. Spenser was by now a widower in his forties.

Amoretti comprises eighty-nine sonnets, printed one to a page. Sonnets 35 and 83, associating the lover with Narcissus, are nearly identical, but the repetition may be deliberate. The various patterns that many perceive require both poems and, in any case, words in one context cannot mean quite the same thing as they mean in another. Spenser makes no effort to conceal the lady's identity – not for him names like 'Idea' or 'Stella' – but he had composed *Amoretti* 8 and perhaps others too before courting Elizabeth Boyle. This may be one reason for the sonnets' variety: they range from the abjectly Petrarchan to the amused and mellow, the lightly parodic, the religious and the violent. Most express praise, longing or complaint. Sonnet 33 addresses a friend, Lodowick Bryskett. Several glance at the epic Spenser has interrupted. And a few record (or say they do) Elizabeth's own thoughts on, for example, a laurel leaf, the waves' erasure of her name after her suitor has traced it on the strand, her fears and her pride. Her high spirits frustrate yet amuse her suitor; *Amoretti* makes better poetry when read with an ear for its quiet humour. It is hard to take very seriously the image of the reluctant lady as a stubborn dolphin in sonnet 38, for example, and the allegation in sonnet 54 that if she cannot pity his theatrics she is a 'sencelesse stone' seems more self-mocking than truly derogatory.

Amoretti is loosely Neo-Platonic: as the Idea of Beauty and Goodness, Elizabeth lifts her lover above the mundane and, says sonnet 8, 'fashion[s]' him 'within'. But Spenser can treat such language with witty exaggeration. Whatever his attraction towards blissful flight into the empyrean, Spenser shared the more strictly Christian conviction that God and his grace descend to us. Compare Prince Arthur going *down* through the muck to liberate the Red Cross Knight in *FQ*, I, viii, 40 like Christ harrowing Hell.[18] The sequence is also Petrarchan, for it was hard to write amatory sonnets in the Renaissance without recollecting the *Rime* and its imitators. Even to reject Petrarchism was to be Petrarchan: the first poet to call Petrarch foolish was none other than Petrarch, and to insist, like Shakespeare, that a 'mistress' eyes are nothing like the sun' must summon up remembrance of sunny-eyed mistresses. Spenser can use this discourse seriously, knowing that Eros really can cause anguished desire, inward confusion, pained resentment of the beloved's failure to be or do what the lover wants, and even – to the exasperation of critics who read it as dismemberment or fetishising – fixation on eyes, lips and hands. Yet Spenser also mocks such language and, engagingly, shows his beloved mocking it too. Although she may well enjoy being praised, understanding that a little Petrarchism never hurt a real lady, at least not one with wit and literary taste, she knows that Petrarchan mood swings are often theatre. Indeed, her laughter at both comic and tragic performances in sonnet 54 suggests show her poised scepticism (and perhaps the anti-theatrical prejudice widespread at the time). The idealisations and self-pity of the Petrarchan tradition yield to a mutual affection suited to marriage, but then to separation, misunderstanding and gloom.

Spenser's love sonnets demonstrated his mastery of a conventional discourse now, if fleetingly, at the height of English fashion. But *Amoretti* is profoundly revisionary. The lover in virtually all such sequences longs for a sexually unavailable beloved. Such desire, aside from risking idolatry, conflicts with love of God and, often, with the seventh commandment (Renaissance commentators tended to assume that Laura was married, and Sidney's puns allow that 'Stella' is married to Lord Rich). Spenser's innovation was to dedicate an entire sequence to a woman he could honorably win. When in sonnet 68 Spenser writes, 'So let us love, deare love, lyke as we ought, / love is the lesson which the Lord us taught', he leaves the dominant sonnet tradition and shows how an English Protestant poet can outdo the Petrarchans. If Petrarch is a tempest-tossed ship, in sonnet 63 Spenser 'descr[ies] the happy shore'. If Petrarch makes a fool of himself by vainly pursuing a fleeing white hind, Spenser's deer in *Amoretti* 67 yields itself. It does so 'beguyld' by 'her owne will' (which then could mean sexual desire, even genitalia) and only after the lover has stopped his rhetorical posturing, hard work, reproaches and badgering. Just as God will not be bullied or bribed, ladies accept lovers only when free to choose and urged by desire. The lover's triumph, moreover, shows a Protestant preference for the natural heat of chaste marriage over cool virginity, although some Catholic poets also wrote affectionately of their spouses.

In his first sonnet Spenser says these 'leaves' are 'happy' to be in the lady's 'lilly' hands, but he then compares them to 'captives trembling at the victors sight'. The sonnet hints at one way to read *Amoretti*: as a wreath of pages/ leaves and an engagement ring anticipating the wedding ring, circles and garlands of the wedding poem to come. As Alexander Dunlop first argued, *Amoretti* makes a triptych paralleling a segment of the liturgical year, and may glance at an entire calendrical circle.[19] In brief: after twenty-one sonnets that include a reference to January comes a sonnet on the 'holy day' of Ash Wednesday in which, with more than a touch of Catholic 'idolatry', the lover worships in the lady's temple; next come as many sonnets as there are days in Lent, counting Sundays; then, right after the lady lets herself be caught, there is a shout of triumph at Easter, an explicitly Christian poem (with no papist flummery, sterner readers might note approvingly); and finally come another twenty-one sonnets, with indications at the end of coldness and separation. Spenser would have found something approaching a precedent for this pattern in Du Bellay's 1550 *Olive* (and he might have been fascinated, had he read her in manuscript, to see how Anne de Marquets arranged her 480 *Sonets Spirituels* (1605) according to the liturgical year). But Spenser gives *Amoretti* more precise personal relevance by referring in sonnet 62 to the start of a new year. He probably means not the liturgical year that begins in late autumn, or the one in Elizabethan almanacs that starts on 1 January, but the equally traditional legal year commencing on March 25, date of Gabriel's annunciation to Mary. The addition of this sonnet identifies the year as 1594, when Easter fell on 31 March, six days/sonnets later.

Why would Spenser want such a pattern, to say nothing of others even more complex? For the same reason he both uses and revises Petrarchism: *his* love can be reconciled with and even represent the love between Christ and Church. But that love is not yet a marriage: Christians still endure separation and alienation in a long anticipatory and autumnal season of Advent. For this reason, and perhaps because Renaissance sonnet sequences have a generic distaste for happy endings, the cycle ends with Spenser as a slandered and lonesome dove moping in the cold.

The sequence's troubled ending is not the only darkness of *Amoretti*. Some of the most interesting recent work on Spenser's love poetry has shown how disturbing it can be. This should not be surprising in a mature poet: sexual and romantic desire are not carefree instincts but inspire or derive from much that is dangerous, aggressive, predatory, evasive and ambivalent. There is probably no sexual triumph without loss, if only the loss of the lover's status as longing pursuer and the beloved's sacrifice of the power always to refuse. No wonder that the tapestry of images in *Amoretti* includes eyes, smiles, temples, ships and so forth, but also prisons and bonds, cruel animals, bloodshed and warfare. The captive 'leaves' that Spenser offers Elizabeth Boyle 'tremble' no more than the very real captives Spenser had seen in Ireland. Worse, when he reminds her in sonnet 20 that killing 'yelled pray' is shameful, we may wonder if he remembers the English massacre of prisoners at Smerwick and, if so, what the memory is doing here. It is well to remember that *Amoretti* was put together in Ireland during a cruel time by one whose exact view of that cruelty is being debated.[20]

After the sonnet sequence come four untitled light-hearted poems that modern editors call 'Anacreontics', the second and third derived from epigrams by Clément Marot. Their role is unclear. Does their erotic tone prepare for the wedding hymn? Do they show off Spenser's ability to write in this fashionably elegant manner? Do they serve some structural pattern? Or do they provide a tonal modulation, a sorbet to clear the palate for the next course? Other love poets also published sonnets followed first by something light and then by a long poem in a different tone. Daniel's *Delia* (1592) has this pattern, as do Fletcher's *Licia* (1593), Lodge's Phillis (1593) and, if we count its poems on Cupid, Shakespeare's *Sonnets* (1609).[21]

Spenser's wedding song, a *canzone* with stanzas and lines of varying length and a concluding envoy, adapts a genre, the epithalamion, with classical and Continental precedents. Traces of these, together with language from the Song of Solomon and the prayerbook, are evident in the poem's phrasing, but Spenser's poem is an original performance of astonishing tonal and structural complexity.[22] Its predominate note is triumphant and some would say even egotistic joy. Spenser sings of his own wedding and not, like Catullus or Du Bellay, of someone else's (to be sure he was the first to do so: in the late 1520s Jean Salmon Macrin's *Livre des épithalames* had offered his wife love poems, a wedding hymn, and a celebration of the couple's new baby). Spenser even shifts the prayer for offspring from the altar, where the priest would recite it, to the bedroom, where he is alone with his wife, one who seems more subdued, now, than she had been in *Amoretti*. And although imperative verbs are traditional in epithalamia, Spenser's seem bossier than most as he adds the part of master of ceremonies to his other roles. Some readers feel restive; others hesitate to begrudge a groom his self-pleased jubilation or to reject his plea in stanza 7 to 'let this day let this one day be myne'.

Recent criticism has tended to focus on either the poem's ingenuity or its dissonance. As Kent Hieatt first demonstrated, the structure of *Epithalamion* imitates several circles ('rings' echoed by the poem's many references to garlands and even by the refrain's reiterated words 'echo rings'). The poem's twenty-four stanzas parallel the hours and its 365 long lines a year's worth of days. Moreover, by noting nightfall and by changing the refrain of stanza 17 from a request that woods resound with celebratory noise into a request for silence, Spenser breaks the poem into two parts with the same ratio, according to his almanac, that day had to night, in Ireland, on 11 June.[23] There may be other ingenuities. Hieatt thinks that the 359 long lines before the concluding stanza and its mention of 'short time' alludes to the sun's incomplete daily circle around an imperfect world. John Gleason, counting all the lines and even the envoy's letters finds a double allusion to the traditional Platonic marriage number, 216, and an additional One, the monad.[24] Cutting against these circles are the events of the wedding day, a linear movement with its own symmetry.[25] First we hear of cosmic energies as symbolised by pagan figures; next the groom summons a few human beings, including the bride, and then an increasing crowd; at the poem's centre is the wedding, described now in overtly Christian terms that part the veil of metaphor and myth; festivities follow, then the couple's quiet solitude, and finally the mythological imagery again – but also a Christian hope for babies to increase the count of Heaven's 'saints' (in Protestant terminology, the elect).

What is the point of this cleverness, aside from the pleasure of making a wedding poem a miniature cosmos? Spenser's poem may so insistently recall Time – the hours, the sun's circles, the zodiac, the days that will now shorten – because procreative marriage can be a consolation for grief at death and loss. Another consolation is the building of what Spenser's envoy calls an 'endlesse moniment': the poem itself. Numbers are again relevant, if David Chinitz is right that the poem inscribes an architect's 'golden section'.[26] Considering he wrote a 'moniment' in words, Spenser could also have recalled an epigram by Daniel Rogers in William Camden's *Britannia* (1586, sig. I3v) that says Salisbury cathedral has 365 days, twelve months, and as many pillars as a year has hours. If architecture can be 'frozen music', as it is sometimes called, why can poetry not be frozen time?

Like *Amoretti*, *Epithalamion* allows and even encourages unease. Marriage, even if the groom's second, is a transition in which much is left behind: virginity or singleness, and liberty (a wedding ring shows one is bound, bonded, wedlocked). The bride's premarital identity is now gone, and until recently her sexual initiation meant not only blood and pain but, should she conceive, significant danger later. That may be one reason people cry at weddings, that flowers deck both brides and graves, and that many wedding customs are designed to ward off evil.

Spenser acknowledges these discomforts in several ways. The groom's sexual pride is not without hints of violence and violation, while some mythological allusions, despite the positive spin one can put on them, are startling: in Renaissance mythography, to compare a lady to Medusa is to admire her chastity, and yet . . . those snakes! The Medusa of stanza 11 redeems – but also recalls – *Amoretti*'s 'viper thoughts'.[27] Similarly, when in stanza 1 Spenser compares himself to Orpheus we think of the poet who moved trees and stones but also the husband who lost his wife (indeed, Spenser had already lost one). And allusions to Jove's love affairs, even if pagan analogues of Christ's marriage to his church, can make uncomfortable reading for mortal women who remember the god's habitual failure to ask permission of his partners. The most explicit recognition that risks, as well as little cupids, attend the marriage bed is in stanza 19, with its semicomic shooing away (and hence, inevitably, the invocation) of goblins, frogs and 'things that be not'. Spenser did not invent this ritualistic expulsion of (non-)imaginary threats; here, in fact, he maybe adapting an obsolescent Catholic rite in which the priest prayed that the wedding bed be free from the 'demons of illusion'.[28]

Spenser may have one more reason for unease: the unfinished *Faerie Queene* on his desk. Does the 'Cynthia' who 'peeps' through his window in stanza 21 wonder why he is ignoring his other Elizabeth so as to attend to his private happiness? Perhaps. But probably we should not exaggerate his turn to the personal: early modern notions of privacy are distinct from our own and weddings were social, even cosmic affairs. Although Protestants do not think it a sacrament, the wedding service, which also mentions worldly goods, witnesses and biblical history, still says that it represents the union of Christ and his church. Spenser himself stresses the event's public nature, summoning local 'merchants daughters' as well as inwardly imagined nymphs.

The next year, 1596, Ponsonby published Spenser's *Fowre Hymnes*, dedicated to the countesses of Cumberland and Warwick. Each of these hymns consist of several seven-line sonnets, powered by images of flight and related to each other by verbal echoes. Spenser first addresses Love (Cupid) and Beauty (Venus). Then, in hymns he says he wrote as retractions of the first two, he praises Heavenly Love (Christ, whose loving descent into flesh counteracts the other hymns' levitations) and Heavenly Beauty (Sapience, traditionally female and hence offering a way to acknowledge God's femininity). The hymns, as is typical of Spenser, are a mix-and-match exercise in having it all: first Petrarch, pagan myth, Plato, and the Homeric or Orphic hymns, then the Bible and Christian Platonism. Two issues are particularly worth noting: first, the disjunction between Spenser's rueful assertion that he wrote the first two hymns in his 'greener times' and the unlikelihood that these idealistic if 'green' poems would redden the cheeks of even the most respectable countess; and second, the possible role the hymns have in Spenser's sense of a poetic career. To move from pastoral to epic (by way of a georgic hero in Book 1) is Virgilian.[29] To move on to Christian hymnody does more than add an Orphic or Homeric spoke to the Virgilian 'rota', for it allows poetry to soar on the wings of the Dove, to surpass mere pagans. Divine poetry like that advocated in Guillaume Du Bartas' 'Uranie' was becoming fashionable, although a better model for Spenser may be the powerful hymns of Ronsard that likewise merge Christianity and classical myth.

Some time in the late summer or early fall of 1596 Elizabeth and Katherine Somerset, daughters of the (Catholic) Earl of Worcester, celebrated their betrothals to Henry Guildford and William Petre respectively. Their double wedding took place on November 8. Apparently the Earl of Essex, recently returned from a successful expedition to Cadiz, attended the betrothal. Essex was young, splendid and arrogant (and was to die on the scaffold in 1601 after an attempted coup). Spenser may have hoped for Essex's favour, although just how *Prothalamion*, the exquisite 'Spousall Verse' written on or for the betrothal, relates to issues of patronage is unclear. Indeed, much about the poem's ten eighteen-line stanzas can seem mystifying.

Spenser's narrator tells how, hoping to ease the 'discontent' brought on by the frustration of his 'idle hopes' at court, he walked along the flowery banks of 'silver streaming Themmes'. There he sees a 'Flocke of Nymphes' (green-haired, like the virginal nymph Chloris before Zephyr impregnated her, thus turning her into Flora, goddess of spring). They are gathering flowers, not unlike Europa and Proserpine before Jove and Pluto carried them off. Now the narrator sees two white swans swimming down the river Lee, whiter than Jove as the swan who raped or seduced Leda, and whiter than Leda herself. Running to gaze on these birds/brides (not the only wordplay in this poem, which offers puns on 'Somers-heat' and 'Somerset' and juxtaposes 'fair', 'foul' and 'fowl'), the nymphs cast garlands on the swans and one sings a 'lay' wishing them peace, pleasure, happiness, babies, and the confounding of their 'foes', this last a reminder that all is not serenity in England. The swans now turn to swim up the Thames to 'mery London, my most kyndly Nurse', landing at Exeter House, former home of Spenser's dead patron, the Earl of Leicester. This gives Spenser an opportunity to praise the new owner, 'Whose dreadful name, late through all Spaine did thunder, / And Hercules two pillors standing neere, / Did make to quake and feare'. Not only a compliment to Essex, the lines reinforce Elizabeth's defiant appropriation of the Hapsburg impresa, the Pillars of Hercules that mark the passage from the Mediterranean to the Atlantic. Perhaps, says the narrator in lines that have led some readers to see that *Prothalamion* is as much job application as encomium, 'some brave muse' may sing of these victories and make the queen's name ring 'Through al the world'. Essex comes forth to greet the brides like flaming 'Hesperus' fresh from the 'Ocean'. Spenser probably means the evening star: it appears in the west (where Essex had just been) at the end of the half-day that the poem's 180 lines may also represent, and it attends upon the greater light of the moon. Thus Spenser flatters Essex yet subordinates him to Elizabeth.

It should be clear why the poem has occasioned debate. Once more Spenser creates an elabourate structure, although theories concerning it vary.[30] The 180 lines suggest half a zodiac as well as half a day: the springtime constellation Gemini – Leda's sons – appears in the poem's complex of mythological and astronomical allusions. Leda's double set of twins is relevant to a poem on a double betrothal, but one child, Helen, helped bring about the supposed Trojan origin of Britain and Troynovant, later called London. In this very public poem Spenser has not forgotten the myths sustaining *The Faerie Queene*, and he is still a national poet. The poem's tone remains elusive. For a 'Spousall' poem it has a surprising degree of anger, as though the prickly satire becoming popular in London's smarter, young male circles had started to slouch its malcontented way into Spenserian verse.

The touches of elegy are not astonishing in a (pre)marriage poem, for, as I have argued, a rite of passage records both loss and accomplishment. But Spenser seems again to go out of his way to add such touches. Note, for example, the role of Leda's story, so filled with memories of sexual and military violation (what Yeats was to call, in 'Leda and the Swan', 'The broken wall, the burning roof and tower') or danger. And then there is the haunting refrain, 'Sweete Themmes runne softly, till I end my Song'. As the swans, ancient symbols of poetry, swim down one river and up another, Spenser hushes the great river, one he associates with the Tiber through faint echoes of the *Aeneid*. If the Tiber in 'The Ruines of Rome' is, like Adonis in his garden, paradoxically eternal in its mutability, so too the Thames will flow on after Spenser has fallen silent and the birds/brides have gone grey. Symbols of time, and also of the wet rush of desire, the poem's two rivers bring together pairs of brides and grooms, troubled poet and wedding party, the prospect of satisfied longing and the intimations of mortality. The poignancy of living and writing in a flowing world remains: for Spenser, the pillars of eternity are not found in London, not even at Essex House.

NOTES

1 For extensive secondary material on the poems, see *Spenser Encyclopedia*; *Spenser's Selected Shorter Poems*; and the MLA database.

2 These works remain lost. One, 'The Dying Pellican', sounds like a poem in Marguerite de Navarre's *Chansons spirituelles* in which a dying pelican (Christ) serenades his bride (the Church); it follows one on a deer (Christ) that submits to capture after the hunter gives up (cf. *Amoretti* 67).

3 See Marie Tanner, *The Last Descendant of Aeneas: The Hapsburgs and the Mythic Image of the Emperor* (New Haven: Yale University Press, 1993). Spenser accepts the legend in his poetry, not in *View*; educated Elizabethans knew it was debatable at best.

4 Gerald Snare, 'The Muses on Poetry: Spenser's *The Teares of the Muses*', *TUSE* 17 (1969), 31–52.

5 Gabriel Harvey, *Marginalia*, ed. G. C. Smith (Stratford-upon-Avon, 1913), p. 162, written in his copy of Dionysius Periegetes' *Survey of the World* (1572).

6 I follow Mark Rasmussen, 'Spenser's Plaintive Muses', *Sp. St.* 13 (1999), 139–64.

7 Richard Peterson, 'Laurel Crown and Ape's Tail: New Light on Spenser's Career from Sir Thomas Tresham', *Sp. St.* 12 (1998), 1–35.

8 Rosalie Colie, *Epidemica Paradoxia* (Princeton: Princeton University Press, 1966).

9 Clark Hulse, *Metaphoric Verse: The Elizabethan Minor Epic* (Princeton: Princeton University Press, 1981), ch. 6.

10 Michael West, 'Spenser's Art of War', *RQ* 41 (1988), 654–704, notes the similarity between Aragnoll's web and Renaissance military diagrams. The image of aristocracy caught in a snare of malice is relevant to the slander, as Spenser thought it, that greeted Lord Grey in Ireland.

11 'Virgil's Gnat' mentions an 'Astery': when Jove pursued her in the form of an eagle she turned to a quail and then to a rock, providing one derivation of the name of Delos, Diana's birthplace.

12 '"Nat worth a boterflye": *Muiopotmos* and *The Nun's Priest's Tale*', *JMRS* 1 (1971), 89–106.

13 Ronald Bond, '*Invidia* and the Allegory of Spenser's *Muiopotmos*', *ESC* 11 (1976), 144–55.

14 West, 'Spenser's Art of War', pp. 692–3.

15 On butterflies as *psyche*, see D. C. Allen, *Image and Meaning: Metaphoric Traditions in Renaissance Poetry* (Baltimore: Johns Hopkins University Press, 1968), ch. 2.

16 Cf. Pamela Royston Macfie, 'Text and *Textura*: Spenser's Arachnean Art', in D. B. Allen and R. A. White, eds., *Traditions and Innovations: Essays on British Literature of the Middle Ages and the Renaissance* (Newark: University of Delaware Press, 1990).

17 Judith Dundas, '*Muiopotmos*: A World of Art', *YES* 5 (1975), 30–8.

18 Some critics, most persuasively William Johnson in *Spenser's Amoretti: Analogies of Love* (Lewisburg: Bucknell Univ. Press, 1990), think the lover learns to deserve the lady. Yet *unearned* victory better suits Protestant theology and a genre that subordinates narrative to variety and the fragmentary.

19 'The Drama of Spenser's *Amoretti*', *Sp. St.* 1 (1980), 107–20. Kenneth Larsen's edition of *Amoretti and Epithalamion* (Tempe: MRTS, 1997) elaborates on this, if sometimes implausibly.

20 See an essay by James Fleming forthcoming in *Sp. St.* 15. On tonal complexities see also Roger Kuin, *Camber Music: Elizabethan Sonnet-Sequences and the Pleasure of Criticism* (Toronto: University of Toronto Press, 1998).

21 For background, see Janet Levarie, 'Renaissance Anacreontics', *CL* 25 (1973), 221–39. Cf. four 'fescennine' poems accompanying Claudian's epithalamion for Honorius.

22 The fullest survey remains Virginia Tufte, *The Poetry of Marriage: The Epithalamium in Europe and Its Development in England*, Studies in Comparative Literature 2 (Los Angeles: University of Southern California, 1970).

23 *Short Time's Endless Monument* (New York: Columbia University Press, 1960).

24 'Opening Spenser's Wedding Poem', *ELR* 24 (1994), 620–37.

25 Max Wickert, 'Structure and Ceremony in Spenser's *Epithalamion*', *ELH* 35 (1968), 135–57.

26 'The Poem as Sacrament: Spenser's *Epithalamion* and the golden section', *JMRS* 21 (1991), 251–68.

27 Mentioned by Joseph Loewenstein, 'A Note on the Structure of Spenser's *Amoretti*: Viper Thoughts', *Sp. St.* 8 (1990), 311–23. See also Celeste Schenck, *Mourning and Panegyric: The Poetics of Pastoral Ceremony* (University Park: Pennsylvania State University Press, 1988).

28 See my 'The Thirsty Deer and the Lord of Life', *Sp. St.* 6 (1986), 33–76.

29 Patrick Cheney, *Spenser's Famous Flight: A Renaissance Idea of a Literary Career* (Toronto: Toronto University Press, 1993).

30 See Alastair Fowler, *Conceitful Thought* (Edinburgh: Edinburgh University Press, 1975).

FURTHER READING

Richard Danson Brown, *'The New Poet': Novelty and Tradition in Spenser's Complaints* (Liverpool: Liverpool University Press, 1999).

Kent A. Hieatt, *Short Time's Endless Monument: The Symbolism of the Numbers in Edmund Spenser's Epithalamion* (New York: Columbia University Press, 1970).

Clark Hulse, *Metamorphic Verse: The Elizabethan Minor Epic* (Princeton: Princeton University Press, 1981).

William Johnson, *Spenser's Amoretti: Analogies of Love* (Lewisburg: Bucknell University Press, 1990).

Theresa Krier, 'Generations of Blazons: Psychoanalysis and the Song of Songs in the *Amoreh*', *TSLL* 40 (1998), 293–327.

Kenneth Larsen, ed., *Amoretti* and *Epithalamion* (Tempe: MRTS, 1997).

Judith Owens, 'The Poetics of Accommodation in Spencer's *Epithalamion*', *SEL* 40 (2000), 41–62.

Anne Lake Prescott, *French Poets and the English Renaissance: Studies in Fame and Transformation* (New Haven: Yale University Press, 1978).

Virginia Tufte, *The Poetry of Marriage: The Epithalamion in Europe and its Development in England*, Studies in Comparative Literature 2 (Los Angeles: University of Southern California, 1970).

8

WILLY MALEY

Spenser's languages: writing in the ruins of English

The recent turn towards historicist criticism in Spenser studies, exemplified by the fashion for placing the poet in an Irish context, has inhibited studies of a more formal kind. Critics like S. K. Heninger and Jean Brink have tried to rein in readers bent on contextualising Spenser to death.[1] The last major work on Spenser's language was Herbert Sugden's *The Grammar of Spenser's* Faerie Queene, first published in 1936 and reissued thirty years later. Sugden's findings – that Spenser's style was cramped by his approach to poetic diction, his desire to enhance poetic language, the limitations of theme and the constraints of his chosen verse form – have found general acceptance. In her contribution to *The Spenser Encyclopedia* Barbara Strang pointed out the paradox that despite universal acknowledgement of Spenser's facility for language, this aspect of his work 'has received practically no attention during the last thirty years, when items for the Spenser bibliography have been pouring off the presses at an average rate of three a week'.[2] It is a measure of the richness and complexity of the subject that Strang's comprehensive entry on this topic is supplemented by separate essays on dialect, etymology, glossing, morphology and syntax, names, neologisms, pronunciation, puns, rhyme and versification.[3] The problem is that all of these features overlap. Dialect cannot be discussed without reference to archaisms, puns depend to a large extent upon etymology, and rhyme is influenced by pronunciation. It may come as a crumb of comfort to new readers trying to get tongue and teeth round Spenser's language sandwich to learn that critics are as confused as they are, though there is broad agreement on the general features of Spenser's style: deliberate borrowings from Chaucer, Langland, Lydgate, Malory, Skelton and others; the favouring of conventional, rather than imaginative, epithets; a penchant for word compounds; varying and patterning of vowel sounds and sibilant consonants; a bias towards alliterating pairs; arcane orthography aimed at enhancing visual rhyme; regular inversion of customary word order; the frequent use of figures and forgings aimed at metrical regularity; the structural simplicity of syntax; and a tendency for iambic pentameter to contain an internal pause after the second foot.[4]

Since the premise of this essay is that Spenser had several languages at his disposal, including competing varieties of English, it may make sense to begin with the assertion that he had none, that is, with the two quotations most likely to be cited in any discussion of Spenser's language: the poet's own complaint to Gabriel Harvey in a letter pleading for 'the kingdom of our own language' and Ben Jonson's notorious barb that he 'writ no language'. There is a curious complicity between these two famous phrases. Spenser aspires to the kingdom of his own language, while Jonson apparently considers him to have none.

So famous is Jonson's phrase that it is rarely set in its own immediate context or that of Jonson's wider attitude to Spenser. The authors of *Jonson's Spenser* take it to mean that Spenser wrote 'no [spoken] language', while Paula Blank reads in it a denial 'that the diction of the *Shepheardes Calender* was English at all'.[5] In the passage in question Jonson is reflecting on what sort of reading makes a good writer, and recommends 'the openest, and clearest' to begin with:

> and beware of letting them taste Gower, or Chaucer at first, lest falling too much in love with antiquity, and not apprehending the weight, they grow rough and barren in language only. When their judgements are firm, and out of danger, let them read both, the old and the new: but no less take heed, that their new flowers, and sweetness do not as much corrupt, as the other's dryness and squalor, if they choose not carefully. Spenser, in affecting the ancients, writ no language: yet I would have him read for his matter; but as Virgil read Ennius.[6]

David Hill Radcliffe points out that although Jonson would have Spenser 'read for his matter', elsewhere he announced that 'Spenser's stanzas pleased him not, nor his matter'.[7] In any case, reaching Spenser's 'matter' entails working through his language, its layers and lairs, in order to arrive at something approaching the truth. Jonson approves of reading the ancients, but favours a mix of 'old' and 'new'. Later, in a phrase that could have been lifted from the preface to *The Shepheardes Calender*, Jonson remarks: 'Words borrowed of antiquity, do lend a kind of majesty to style, and are not without their delight sometimes. For they have the authority of years, and out of their intermission do win to themselves a kind of grace like newness. But the eldest of the present, and newest of the past language is the best.'[8] And this was precisely Spenser's policy, for despite his final equivocation, Jonson's charged advocacy of a combination of past and present forms, and his accompanying emphasis on 'the consent of the learned', are quite in keeping with Spenser's approach. After all, it is E. K., the ghost-editor of *The*

Shepheardes Calender, who suggests that the poet's language, though 'being so auncient', is 'yet both English, and also used of most excellent Authors and most famous Poetes', adding that these old words 'bring great grace and, as one would say, auctoritie to the verse'.[9] The title of Spenser's pastoral is itself an instance of Jonson's principle of 'something old, something new' in action, since E. K. describes it as 'applying an olde name to a new worke' (p. 418). Moreover, in the lines that precede the claim that archaisms 'lend a kind of majesty to style', Jonson stresses the importance of 'custom':

> Custom is the most certain mistress of language, as the public stamp makes the current money. But we must not be too frequent with the mint, every day coining. Nor fetch words from the extreme and utmost ages; since the chief virtue of a style is perspicuity, and nothing so vicious in it, as to need an interpreter.[10]

It could be objected that the glossary to *The Shepheardes Calender* illustrates the need for an interpreter, but in fact both E. K. and Spenser share Jonson's emphasis on 'use'. In his letter to Harvey, Spenser says the new versification 'is to be wonne with Custome, and rough words must be subdued with Use' (p. 611). That one literary coterie's archaisms are another speech community's dialect is made clear by E. K.'s remark that 'olde and obsolete wordes are most used of country folke' (p. 417). But even this is ambiguous, since it implies both that country folk employ archaisms, and that a writer representing country folk ought thus to deploy such terms.

Spenser's own terms are as loaded as Jonson's. In *Three proper wittie familiar Letters*, he asks Harvey 'why a Gods name may not we, as else the Greekes, have the kingdome of oure owne Language'. Richard Helgerson took this sentence as the starting-point of his groundbreaking study of English identity formation, *Forms of Nationhood*, delicately unpeeling its layers of meaning.[11] Helgerson rightly points to the centrality of language in forging a national culture to rival that of Greece and Rome, a key component of English Renaissance literature, but if we set Spenser's question in its original context, we can see that its supposed subject is, like Jonson's, very specific. Spenser is addressing Harvey's efforts at quantitative verse:

> I like your late Englishe Hexameters so exceedingly well, that I also enure my Penne sometime in that kinde: whyche I fynd indeede, as I have heard you often defende in worde, neither so harde, nor so harshe, that it will easily and fairely, yeelde it selfe to oure Moother tongue. For the onely, or chiefest hardnesse, whych seemeth, is in the Accente: whyche sometime gapeth, and as it were yawneth ilfavouredly . . . But it is to be wonne with Custome, and rough words must be subdued with Use. For, why a Gods name may not we, as else the Greekes, have the kingdome of oure owne Language, and measure our Accentes, by the sounde, reserving the Quantitie to the Verse.　(p. 611)

It is clearly a question of civilising a barbarous tongue, but one problem with Helgerson's critique is the tendency to think singularly of English sovereignty and to underestimate the part played by the non-English nations of the emerging British state. As Patricia Ingham notes, speaking of *The Faerie Queene*: 'The kingdom about which and in which this strange and exotic language is used is ambiguously located.'[12] It is not just England whose nationhood is being formed. The point is that technical arguments about reading and poetic form always impinge upon larger questions of culture and identity.

Most criticism of Spenser's language takes as its text *The Shepheardes Calender* – and with some justification, for it is in this first major work that Spenser most explicitly discusses his choice of language, and it is here that the questions of archaism, dialect, diction and neologisms are most provocatively posed. The 'dialect' of *The Shepheardes Calender* has been the subject of intense debate. It has been seen as a new national language in waiting, a literary dialect drawing directly on Chaucerian English, a regional form deriving chiefly from the North of England, and a colonial variety surviving among the descendants of the medieval English colony in Ireland, the 'Old English'.[13] There is no reason to suppose that we must choose between these perspectives. Chaucer is praised, the sorry state of the English language is lamented, and Northern words appear, as do Irish ones. The word 'kerne', glossed in the 'July' eclogue as 'a Churle or Farmer', is treated as an Irish word in *A View of the Present State of Ireland*.

Questions of form and context, as well as perceptions of poetic personae, are instrumental in dictating language choice. Jonson's appropriation of Spenser even as he distances himself from him may come down to a difference in approaches to poetry. Sheldon Zitner crucially distinguishes between the 'occasional' poet (Jonson) and the 'mythic' poet (Spenser):

> The mythic or epic poet celebrates the experience of a race or culture, gathering it up in a vast and lofty retrospect. And as he does so he gathers up the language in whose unique history that experience has been deposited. He records the achievement and the presence of the past in the echo and allusion of language and letters . . . And the longer his work, the more its composition tends to the rapidity of improvisation. Thus both elevation and extent, given the restrictions of meter, argue the logic of metaplasm, archaism, and other departures from currency.[14]

In writing an epic, improvisation and variation are essential, as is openness to other languages. *The Shepheardes Calender* differs from *The Faerie Queene* in that dialect terms are dispersed in the latter. The politics of geography and genre dictated Spenser's linguistic choices in *The Faerie Queene*. If in his pastoral Spenser could afford to be provincial, then in his epic he was forced to abandon that earlier chauvinism when faced with the necessity of shoring up English ruins with foreign fragments. As well as scale and setting, theme and topic exert an influence over the linguistic choices animating Spenser's epic. Bruce McElderry observes: 'The subject matter of *The Faerie Queene* is itself the most powerful factor in creating the impression of archaism.'[15]

As with the observation that Jonson was a 'classicist', the attribution of archaisms to Spenser is so common as to demand no further explanation. Yet once one looks a little closer it becomes harder to tell the neologisms from the archaisms and either from the dialect. Reports of Spenser's archaisms have been greatly exaggerated, likewise his reliance on dialect, which is minimal in *The Shepheardes Calender* and negligible in his later work. Thomas Warton was one of the first influential readers of Spenser to challenge the line established indirectly by E. K. and by Jonson, namely that Spenser needed an interpreter. Warton argued that Spenser's usage was essentially Elizabethan. The accepted view now is that in terms of grammar, syntax and vocabulary Spenser is a late sixteenth-century writer.

Spenser is best viewed as a poet caught between classes, cultures and countries, one for whom the time is out of joint. Samuel Daniel spoke of Spenser's 'aged accents and untimely words'.[16] Archaisms may lie in the eye and ear of the beholder, but by the end of the seventeenth century there is evidence to suggest that E. K.'s glosses to *The Shepheardes Calender*, far from becoming superfluous, were actually insufficient. The 1679 folio edition of Spenser's works was supplemented by 'A Glossary, or An Alphabetical Index of Unusual Words Explained', while the edition of 1750 comes 'With a glossary explaining the old and obscure words'.

Critics disagree as to when a standard language was available. Was Spenser writing at a time when a standard language and orthography had not fully emerged, giving him great flexibility when it came to style and spelling, or had the imposition of a standard already rendered him anachronistic? According to Patricia Ingham: 'By the early sixteenth century, there existed a standard type for both written and spoken English.'[17] But others are less sure. Avril Bruten maintains that 'Spenser wrote in a period in which there was no single "correct" pronunciation of English.'[18]

There is also the vexed question of the relationship between a standard and its dialects. An old saying has it that language is a dialect with an army and a navy. It is rather too convenient to superimpose retrospectively a fixed standard from which other varieties deviate. Steven Ellis has pointed out that in 1500 half of the British Isles were Celtic speaking. By 1650 the figure was a tenth.[19] The English standard was raised at the expense of dialects deficient in armies and navies. Spenser participated both in the ruin and the resurrection of other cultures, through his uneasy reliance on Celtic myth and Old English language.

In *A View*, Irenius is often at pains to convince Eudoxus that words – and practices – deemed Irish are in fact Old English. Spenser's own ambivalence about old words – that they can ruin as well as raise – reflects his anxiety about the Old English, who can claim to be more English than the English themselves since they have preserved customs and forms of speech long since abandoned in England and abroad, and in Spenser's own view, abandoned at a cost. Spenser's journey through the available varieties of English reflects his passage from the 1570s, when his patrons were closely connected to the Geraldine cause in Ireland and identified with Old English figures like Stanihurst and the Earl of Kildare (himself a patron of Spenser), to the 1580s and 90s, when he became disaffected with that community. The rupture occurred between 1579 and 1583, when the Desmond Rebellion finally put paid to the Leicester-Sidney support of the Geraldines. *The Shepheardes Calender* was composed while the Geraldine branch of the Old English was still allied to Leicester's faction at court, indeed, while the Earl of Kildare, as good a contender for 'E. K.' as any, was staying at Leicester house – and it is essentially an Old English work. Thereafter, Spenser found himself at odds with a colonial elite whose language and ideas he had borrowed. *The Faerie Queene* is a New English epic literally erected on the site of Old English power.

There is a tension throughout Spenser's work, and a productive and structuring one, between respect for the old and fear of innovation on the one hand, and anxiety about hauntings and survivals – Englishness and Catholicism – that threaten to undermine his New English community in Ireland, on the other. Spenser was caught between a push to experiment in the vernacular and the pull of an older generation of writers in English, including Chaucer. By imitating Chaucer, Spenser was following the Old English, for it was among the inhabitants of the English Pale in Ireland that, as Stanihurst informed readers of Holinshed's *Chronicles*, 'to this daie, the dregs of the old ancient Chaucer English are kept as well' as in the rest of the English Pale.[20] The so-called marginal forms of English lent themselves better to creative translation. Regional and national varieties of English could confer authenticity and authority upon a writer ostensibly alienated, disenfranchised or exiled, as well as serving as a site of critical resistance.

Spenser criticism has tended to be both court-centred and Anglocentric, which means that critics, even though they are aware that Spenser was a colonist who spent the majority of his literary career in Ireland, find it hard to think outside quite narrow metropolitan terms. *The Faerie Queene* is not a 'courtly epic'. Precious little action occurs at court. It is rather a colonialist epic. Indeed, it is one of its central paradoxes that one looks beyond the court for any semblance of civility: Book VI begins with the uncontroversial claim that 'Of Court it seemes, men Courtesie doe call' (VI, i, 1), but Spenser goes on to confound this etymology and show that courtesy is to be found in the country, far from the court.

Ingham describes Spenser's style in his epic poem as 'a strangely mixed language as fitted to his Fairyland as newspeak is to Airstrip One in Orwell's *Nineteen Eighty-Four*'.[21] Spenser's language is 'oldspeak', a conscious turning back to an established archive with Chaucer at its centre that simultaneously conjures up the speech of the Old English in Ireland. Spenser was colloquial and colonial rather than courtly. Blank sees Spenser 'as a dialect poet, a "regional" author who . . . self-consciously defined his work in terms of a marginalized provincial culture. Instead of the courtly London poet we recognise at first glance, I would like to present a different Spenser, one who, like his protagonist Colin Clout, made a home in the north country.'[22] Blank and I disagree only on the precise location of the margins, whether in Northern England or in Southern Ireland. But why not both, and more besides? Spenser is a colonial poet rather than a court poet, a country poet rather than a city poet. He is a Cambridge poet, a Kent poet and a Cork poet, a strolling bard or wandering minstrel of the Celtic fringe and the English Pale, a poet of the provinces, scribbling on the sidelines of English society. His problematic relationship to any putative cultural centre, whether the court or the city of London, is what makes his language so remarkable.

Critics have not acknowledged sufficiently the extent to which Spenser was influenced by Scots like William Dunbar and Gavin Douglas, by Irishmen like Stanihurst, and by English contemporaries with Irish connections, such as Barnaby Googe and Edmund Campion. Some of the most interesting work on the 'English' language in the early modern period was being undertaken in the margins of English culture. It was Campion – like Stanihurst, a member of the Leicester-Sidney circle before he was executed as a Jesuit in 1581 – who, in his *Two Bokes of the Histories of Ireland*, emphasised custom as the key to language development, 'considering the course of enterchanging and blending speeches together not by invention of arte but by use of talke'.[23] The Tudor borderlands were at the cutting edge of linguistic innovation and variation. The translations of Virgil by Stanihurst and Douglas are cases in point, as are the pastoral eclogues of Googe, Googe's translations and those of Lodowick Bryskett and Geoffrey Fenton, and the Chaucerian imitations of Dunbar. In *A View* Spenser acknowledged the Scottish humanist George Buchanan as a key intellectual influence, lending further weight to the argument that he looked to the margins for inspiration. Irish and Scottish Virgilians and Chaucerians pointed the way for Spenser.[24] Kim Hall points out that in *A View*: 'Cultural and political differences between the English, the Scottish, and the Irish are distilled to problematic linguistic differences, the overcoming and assimilation of which is the first step in an imperialist project.'[25] Blank shares the view that Spenser and his contemporaries were engaged in an enterprise of 'overcoming and assimilation':

> Many Renaissance English writers were preoccupied not so much with the language of the 'wild Irish', but with the English of those countrymen who lived alongside a people considered barbaric. For these writers, the 'broken English' of the Anglo-Irish demonstrated the threat of cultural and racial degeneration, the possibility that not only English customs and forms, but Englishmen themselves, might 'become' Irish. Their preoccupation, in other words, was not so much with the 'Anglicisation' of the Irish as with the 'Gaelicisation' of the English.[26]

This assumes that 'Renaissance' and 'English' are settled terms, and ignores the extent to which Spenser drew on an archive of English in Ireland, ignores too the case that could be made for the Old English as the guarantors of an ancient Englishness, a liberty of language and politics, liberties surrendered in England itself. This is the real crux of Spenser's Irish sojourn, the degree to which he came round to the Old English view that Englishness in its purest expression was best preserved in the colonial margins rather than the cosmopolitan centre. Spenser is deeply ambivalent about the Irish in *A View*, and in the 'Two Cantos of Mutabilitie' that close *The Faerie Queene*. The same could be said of his position with regard to the Old English community. Politically, he opposed them, but culturally and linguistically he made use of them. Old English language and Celtic mythology were his two great storehouses.

As well as being influenced by Celtic mythology and by his Irish residence, Spenser may have been versed in Welsh.[27] If, like Shakespeare, Spenser had little Latin and less Greek, he possibly had a working knowledge of Welsh, Scots and Irish through his use of Celtic sources for his poetry and prose. Rather than seeing Spenser's language as 'broken English', or as a well of English undefiled, we ought to view it as brogue-ken and Brit-tell, drawing on a living archive of English in Ireland in order to pave the way for a British future.

The Renaissance was also a Ruinaissance, a sifting through the residue of the classical tradition, and Spenser remains a poet of ruins, raking in the ashes of English in order to remember the cinders of his heritage. He ruinates and ruminates. Maryclaire Moroney has treated Spenser's ambivalent attitude to ruins in *The Faerie Queene* and *A View*, observing that

'Renaissance meditations on the ruins of antiquity are a more familiar component of this early modern concern with the remains, physical and otherwise, of a past they wished to emulate and transcend'.[28] The Reformation was built on the ruins of Rome, and Spenser himself made his home among the ruins of Kilcolman Castle, where he deformed as well as reformed the English language.

As well as being a poet of ruins, Spenser is a poet of exile and empire.[29] The boldness of his borrowings and burrowings marks him out as unique among English writers. He is, in Colin Burrow's words, a figure 'who makes writing out of loss and who makes something new by emphasizing the pastness of the past'.[30] Writing in the ruins, among the relics and remains of an earlier English civilisation, Spenser salvages something from sediments and secretions. In the preface to *The Shepheardes Calender*, E. K. warns against the ruination of dialect: 'Yet nether every where must old words be stuffed in, nor the commen Dialecte and maner of speaking so corrupted therby, that as in old buildings it seme disorderly and ruinous.' Spenser is, in E. K.'s phrase, a poet of 'disorderly order' (p. 417). E. K.'s insistence that archaisms must not be allowed to corrupt dialect offers an interesting analogue to the argument that dialect corrupts an emerging standard. Spenser made his home literally among the ruins of the original English colony in Ireland, where he found the time and space, and most important of all, the rich reserves of language, to write in the ruins of a genre, and in the ruins of an earlier form of English.

Spenser is an arch-etymologist. With regard to etymology there are two rival theories. Conventionalists believe the relation between a word and its object is arbitrary. Naturalists hold that words accurately represent the essences of objects. K. K. Ruthven argues that 'naturalist etymologizers like Spenser regard etymons as vehicles of truths obscured by the duplicities of everyday language; etymology therefore promises linguistic restitution, the consequences of which are moral and epistemological'.[31] Spenser's etymologising extends to *A View*, where his meditations and musings on the origins of customs and colloquialisms are as inventive as anything in his poetry. They restore the roots of words that have been rerouted by history. Irenius derives 'pale', as in the 'English Pale' in Ireland, from the Latin *palare*, 'that is, to forrage or out-run, because those marchers and borderers use commonly so to doe. So as to have a County Palatine is, in effect, to have a priviledge to spoyle the enemies borders adjoyning.'[32]

Ruthven cites 'universe' as the turning point of Book VII of *The Faerie Queene*. 'Universe' derives from Latin *unus*, 'one', and 'versus' from *vertere*, 'to turn'. Puttenham (1589) falsely glossed it as 'the whole of created or existing things regarded collectively'. As Ruthven says: 'Etymologically, a *universe* is a "one turning", a derivation which raises the question of whether or not the word matches the thing.'[33] 'Universe' translates best as both 'overturn' and 'turnover'. Spenser has Nature tell Mutabilitie that things change, but only to turn back to themselves. In other words, heads you win, tails you don't lose.

Variety is the spice – and sometimes the vice – of Spenser's verse. He mingles his measures, mixes his metaphors, and gets more mileage out of his metre than any other poet writing in English. He is both an archaiser and a moderniser who exploits a dazzling array of rhyme schemes. *The Shepheardes Calender* has '16 different units of verse (2 in "Aprill" and "November", and at least 4 in "August"), with very little overlap in form'.[34] The minor poems are a veritable panorama of poetic forms: 'Ruines of Time' and *Fowre Hymnes* are in rime royal (5*ababbcc*); 'Teares of the Muses' and *Astrophel* are in ballad stanzas (5*ababcc*); 'Ruines of Rome', 'Visions of Bellay' and 'Visions of Petrarch' are all in Surrey's English sonnet form (5*abab cdcd efef gg*); 'Mother Hubberds Tale' is composed of iambic pentameter couplets; and 'Virgils Gnat' and 'Muiopotmos' are in the Italian epic and epigram stanza, ottava rima (5*abababcc*).[35]

The focus on *The Shepheardes Calender* and its archaisms and dialect forms obscures the fact that Spenser's greatest gift to poetry was the Spenserian stanza, 'probably the most brilliantly original exploitation of the inherent possibilities of the language in the history of English versification'.[36] The stanza is a nine-line unit, with a rhyme scheme of ababbcbcC, ending in a great alexandrine. Spenser's sense of variation is crucial, and 'derives from something far less formal than a theory of language', namely 'a context of assumptions – the atmosphere his actual use of language breathes'.[37] That phrase – 'a context of assumptions' – is a useful one, because it embeds the idea of 'context' within a textual poetics. Spenser's own immediate context throughout the composition of *The Faerie Queene* was Ireland, and if this fact has lent itself to ideological and cultural criticism rather than readings of a more formal or textual kind then that does not mean that Ireland merely affected Spenser's life and attitudes, and not the intricacies of his work. That said, some of the most interesting treatments of Spenser's language in recent years have come from critics who focus on the Irish angle.[38] It is a question of emphasis. Some critics contrast the clarity of *A View* with the complexity of the poetry. Strang speaks of Spenser's prose as 'classically correct sixteenth-century English', and Bruten is similarly convinced of *A View*'s simplicity and directness.[39] But *A View* is as preoccupied with the twists and turns of language as the poetry.

Spenser made a name for himself by making names, and naming is a crucial component of his linguistics. Spenser had several. As well as signing himself both "Edmond' and 'Edmund', he styled himself 'Colin Clout', 'Immerito', 'E. K.', 'Irenius' and 'Eudoxus'. Spenserian names can function as nouns or adjectives, narratives or aspirations. Names in Spenser can take the form of personifications (the Salvage Man); compounds (Kirkrapine); narrative names (Duessa); classical or Romance monikers (Radigund); bilingual hybrids and paronyms (Scudamour and Belphoebe); mythological and literary names (Hellenore and Tristram); pseudomythical coinages (Phao and Poris); pastoral appellations (Coridon and Meliobee); Irish toponyms (Arlo and Mulla); feigned names of public persons (Gloriana, Hobbinol and Rosalind); or serials produced from the same base (Sans Foy, Sans Loy, Sans Joy).[40] From medieval romance Spenser borrowed the practice of postponing the attribution of a name until a character had come to represent a specific action or quality in the reader's mind. Spenser must first unravel names to show how the characters originated and developed. This deferral becomes part of the reader's own self-fashioning, a test of attentiveness. Names are earned and learned, and go to the heart of a person's identity.

As well as being an incurable name-dropper, Spenser is a compulsive coiner of phrases, an 'archae-neologist', one who mines and undermines, like an old mole working at the wellhead of English. Alan Ward concedes that archaisms and neologisms blur in Spenser's writings, so that 'it is often difficult to know whether we are dealing with new formations or archaic survivals'.[41] There are two principal groups of neologisms, new terms based on existing English words, and lexical items borrowed from other languages. The chief source of foreign loan words is French, but there are also extensive appropriations from Latin and Italian, as well as 'Celtic' loan words. From Latin Spenser takes the word *subverse*, 'to subvert' (*FQ* III, xii, 42 'Mother Hubberds Tale' 1234). And in a sense the Spenserian stanza is a 'subverse' that overturns expectations. Two examples of Spenserian coinages that have entered the language are *blatant* and *derring-do*, the latter based on an archaic form of 'daring to do', and these are fitting phrases to characterise Spenser's boldness and clarity of vision.[42]

Spenser's tutor, Richard Mulcaster, used the term 'enfranchisement' to describe the patriotic practice of adding new words to the language. Mulcaster may have been a crucial influence in convincing Spenser that English, bolstered by the classics, could be the bearer of a national literature. 'Enfranchisement' is a somewhat ironic expression since it suggests French-ification, and as it happens both Du Bellay's *Deffence de la Langue Francoyse* (1549) and Ronsard's *Abrege de l'Art Poetique François* (1565) influenced Spenser's championing of the English vernacular. Du Bellay favoured archaisms and neologisms while Ronsard advocated technical language associated with new industries and professions, as well as provincial dialects. Meanwhile, Mulcaster argued that new words must be assimilated 'as the stranger denisons be to the lawes of our cuntre . . . If we mean to make them ours, then let them take an oath to be trew to our tung, and the ordinances thereof.'[43] Interestingly Spenser uses the word 'franchisement' of the personification of Ireland in Book v: 'To weet to worke *Irenaes* franchisement' (*FQ* v, xi, 36.4).

Spenser provided a running glossary for all his work, but the precise purpose of the gloss to *The Shepheardes Calender* is still debated. E. K. justifies his editorial apparatus thus:

> Hereunto have I added a certain Glosse or scholion for thexposition of old wordes and harder phrases: which maner of glosing and commenting, well I wote, wil seeme straunge and rare in our tongue: yet for somuch as I knew many excellent and proper devises both in wordes and matter would passe in the speedy course of reading, either as unknowen, or as not marked, and that in this kind, as in other we might be equal to the learned of other nations, I thought good to take the paines upon me. . . .   (p. 418)

Gerald Snare argues that E. K.'s glosses are 'conventional', despite the fact that *The Shepheardes Calender* is not a classical or canonical text.[44] The habit of glossing texts, the editorial practice of supplementing the work with notes explaining alien or awkward words and phrases, dates from classical Greece and Rome. It had its heyday with the late Roman Empire in the third and fourth centuries AD, when Servius glossed Virgil and Porphyrion glossed Horace, and the practice continues today. But E. K.'s glosses, like T. S. Eliot's notes on *The Waste Land* (1922) and Alasdair Gray's marginal annotations on *Lanark* (1984), may be seen as highly selective, ironic, punning, playful and parodic, sending up classical scholarship – and academic politesse generally – rather than merely imitating it. Critics and readers sometimes overlook the fact that one of the words glossed – 'unkent' – appears in the verse 'To his booke' preceding the epistle, and that E. K. also uses archaisms and dialect terms. Moreover, the short text that follows the epistle, 'The generall argument of the whole booke', begins with an attempt to arrive at the proper meaning of 'eclogues', a word 'I know is unknowen to most, and also mistaken of some the best learned', and so constitutes an exercise in etymology and glossing itself (p. 419).

Critics warn against deducing contemporary pronunciation or even Spenser's own from literary texts, and especially from poetry. As Avril Bruten argues: 'His decorum is not that of phonological exactness but of aesthetic verisimilitude.'[45] It is a matter of poetic license, but even in his prose Spenser takes liberties with language. In his propensity for punning he is second only to Joyce. Maureen Quilligan has argued that Spenserian allegory is generated through wordplay, giving the example of Book I of *The Faerie Queene* as constructed on the foundation of 'error'. Quilligan attributes to Spenser 'a kind of wordplay which, by its subliminal fluidity, resembles Freud's theory that the truth of the unconscious can be revealed through word association'.[46] Spenser's puns are etymological and homophonic, founded on meaning or musicality. Debra Fried speaks of Spenser's rhyme puns as 'broodingly encyclopaedic and etymologizing' and argues that the poet at times 'provides a rhyming dictionary'.[47] Spenser's puns carry weight. Quilligan suggests that his wordplay may be less a contemporary craze than a habit of mind 'caught from his medieval precursors in allegorical narrative'.[48] The first and last lines of *The Faerie Queene* are puns: 'A gentle knight was pricking on the plaine' is a sexual/textual play on words ('prick' for penis but also for needlework), and the 'Sabbaoth's sight' longed for at the end of the Mutabilitie cantos plays on 'Elizabeth' (Eli-zabeth / Eli-sabbath), so that the poet, in keeping with the theme of Diana's discovery, anticipates a sighting of his sovereign. Even if we take a different ending and beginning we find puns propping up the project. The opening lines of the Proem to Book I play on 'low':

> *Lo* I the man, whose Muse whi*lo*me did maske,
> As time her taught, in *lo*wly Shepheards weeds[.]

There is also, among others, a pun on 'whilome' (while home) and 'blazon broad' (abroad), recording the poet's own flight from England to Ireland. The last lines of Book VI, the ending published in Spenser's own lifetime, contains a priceless pun on Lord Burghley even as its author ostensibly absolves himself from culpability for offending Elizabeth's chief advisor:

> Therfore do you my rimes keep better measure,
> And seeke to please, that now is counted wisemens threasure.
>
> (VI, xii, 41.8–9)

As well as an allusion to the three wise men there is a sly reference to the fact that Burgley was Lord Treasurer ('threasure'), and an insinuation that what was treasured at court was not 'homely verse', but the desire to please and to measure merit through money. Spenser's puns and anagrams are politically charged. They should not be relegated to wordplay as they do a job – 'workplay' is a better description.

E. K. insists archaisms have the sanction of nation and tradition:

> For in my opinion it is one special prayse, of many whych are dew to this Poete, that he hath laboured to restore, as to theyr rightfull heritage such good and naturall English words, as have ben long time out of use and almost cleane disherited. Which is the onely cause, that our Mother tonge, which truely of it self is both ful enough for prose and stately enough for verse, hath long time ben counted most bare and barrein of both.　(p. 417)

According to E. K., there are two ways of dealing with the neglect of pure and proper English. One is the painstaking salvaging project undertaken by the new poet, and the other is a cut-and-paste job that relies on foreign implants to bolster the body of the language:

> Which default when as some endevoured to salve and recure, they patched up the holes with peces and rags of other languages, borrowing here of the french, there of the Italian, every where of the Latine, not weighing how il, those tongues accorde with themselves, but much worse with ours: So now they have made our English tongue, a gallimaufray or hodgepodge of al other speches. (p. 417)

Jonson's phrase disparaging Spenser is analogous to E. K.'s phrase disparaging those who undervalue the native English tradition. Critics attribute to Spenser precisely the 'gallimaufray or hodgepodge of al other speches' that E. K. derides in other writers (p. 417). The demands of epic and the disaffection with (the) Old English compels Spenser to supplement his provincial patchwork with exactly the continental quilt ridiculed by E. K., and to fleece foreign fields for additional material. Salvaging and ruining are the two main processes in which Spenser is engaged. The result of this 'gallimaufray or hodgepodge' is that English speakers and writers may be more familiar with foreign languages than with past forms of their own:

> Other some not so wel seene in the English tonge as perhaps in other languages, if they happen to here an olde word albeit very naturall and significant, crye out streight way, that we speak no English, but gibbrish . . . Whose first shame is, that they are not ashamed, in their own mother tonge straungers to be counted and alienes. The second shame no lesse then the first, that what so they understand not, they streight way deeme to be sencelesse, and not at al to be understode . . . The last more shameful then both, that of their owne country and natural speach, which together with their Nources milk they sucked, they have so base regard and bastard judgement, that they will not onely themselves not labor to garnish and beautifie it, but also repine, that of other it shold be embellished. (p. 417)

Ironically, 'embellish' is included in the gloss to the 'April' eclogue, where it is defined as 'beautifye and set out' (p. 434). In A View, in terms that echo those of E. K., Irenius draws a direct link between Old English degeneration and Irish language acquisition:

> I suppose that the chiefe cause of bringing in the Irish language, amongst them, was specially their fostering, and marrying with the Irish, the which are two most dangerous infections; for first the childe that sucketh the milke of the nurse, must of necessity learne his first speach of her, the which being the first inured to his tongue, is ever after most pleasing unto him, insomuch as though hee afterwards be taught English, yet the smacke of the first will

allwayes abide with him . . . for the minde followeth much the temperature of the body: and also the words are the image of the minde, so as they proceeding from the minde, the minde must needes be affected with the words. So that the speach being Irish, the heart must needes bee Irish: for out of the abundance of the heart, the tongue speaketh.   (p. 71)

There is arguably a tension, going back to Spenser's letter to Harvey, between 'oure Moother tongue' and 'the kingdome of oure owne Language', for there will be times when mother tongue and kingdom are at odds, most obviously in the case of Irish subjects of an English crown, but also with regard to an Old English community disenfranchised by the Reformation and the attendant process of New English recolonisation. For a poet like Spenser, born in England but based in Ireland, there could be no simple relationship between language and politics.

Spenser's attitude to language in general was eclectic, eccentric and idiosyncratic. Dispensing with decorum, he trawled for words in places other poets had long since abandoned or never quite reached. He drew extensively on his experiences in Ireland and in the archives of English, as well as on classical, continental and Celtic/British sources. Clare Carroll remarks that 'Spenser's use of Irish traditional lore enacts his ambivalent attitude to Irish language and literature – poised between its preservation and destruction'.[49] Stephen Greenblatt closed his seminal essay on Spenser by saying that the 'final colonialism [is] the colonialism of language'.[50] Other aspects of Greenblatt's essay on Spenser have been much debated, but it is this final fraught and fleeting phrase that ought to supersede those of Spenser and Jonson with which I began, as the starting-point of any future study. As well as running away with the garland from Apollo, Spenser stole the land and language of his Irish and Old English neighbours and made it his own.

NOTES

1 Jean Brink, 'Who Fashioned Edmund Spenser?: The Textual History of *Complaints*', SP 88 (1991), 153–68, p. 153; S. K. Heninger, 'Spenser, Sidney, and Poetic Form', SP 88 (1991), 140–52.

2 Barbara M. H. Strang, 'Language, General, and Resources Exploited in Rhyme', in *Spenser Encyclopedia*, pp. 426–9, at p. 426.

3 Avril Bruten, 'Morphology and Syntax', pp. 480–1; Pronunciation', pp. 558–9; William Harmon, 'Rhyme', pp. 604–5; Patricia Ingham, 'Dialect', pp. 215–16; Herbert Marks and Kenneth Gross, 'Names, Naming', pp. 494–6; Noel Osselton, 'Archaism', pp. 52–3; Maureen Quilligan, 'Puns', pp. 570–3; K. K. Ruthven, 'Etymology', pp. 255–6; Gerald Snare, 'Glossing', p. 334; Alan Ward, 'Neologism', pp. 508–9; Susanne Woods, 'Versification', pp. 710–13.

4 See the summary by A. C. Partridge in *The Language of Renaissance Poetry: Spenser, Shakespeare, Donne, Milton* (London: Deutsch, 1971), pp. 97–8.

5 Paula Blank, 'The Dialect of *The Shepheardes Calender*', *Sp. St.* 10 (1992), 71–94, p. 74; James A. Riddell and Stanley Stewart, *Jonson's Spenser: Evidence and Historical Criticism* (Pittsburgh, PA: Duquesne University Press, 1995), pp. 22–7. That Jonson admired Spenser is evident from his annotations to the 'First Folio' of Spenser's *Works* (1617).

6 *Ben Jonson: The Complete Poems*, ed. George Parfitt (Harmondsworth: Penguin, 1984), p. 428.

7 David Hill Radcliffe, *Edmund Spenser: A Reception History* (Columbia, SC: Camden House, 1996), pp. 16–17.

8 Parfitt, ed., *Jonson: Complete Poems*, p. 432.

9 *Poetical Works*, pp. 416–17. All references to Spenser's poetry are to this edition and will be given by page number in the text.

10 Parfitt, ed., *Jonson: Complete Poems*, p. 432.

11 Richard Helgerson, *Forms of Nationhood: The Elizabethan Writing of England* (Chicago and London: University of Chicago Press, 1992), pp. 1–3.

12 Ingham, 'Dialect', p. 215.

13 See, for example, Blank, 'The Dialect of *The Shepheardes Calender*'; Willy Maley, 'Spenser's Irish English: Language and Identity in Early Modern Ireland', in *Salvaging Spenser: Colonialism, Culture and Identity* (London: Macmillan, 1997), pp. 34–47.

14 Sheldon P. Zitner, 'Spenser's Diction and Classical Precedent', *PQ* 45.2 (1966), 360–71, pp. 369–70.

15 Bruce Robert McElderry, Jr., 'Archaism and Innovation in Spenser's Poetic Diction', *PMLA* 47.1 (1932), 144–70, p. 159.

16 Cited by E. de Selincourt in *Poetical Works*, p. lxii.

17 Ingham, 'Dialect', p. 215.

18 Bruten, 'Pronunciation', p. 558.

19 Steven Ellis, '"Not Mere English": The British Perspective, 1400–1650', *History Today* 38.12 (1988), 41–8, p. 41.

20 Stanyhurst, 'Description of Ireland', in Raphael Holinshed, ed., *Chronicles of England, Scotland and Ireland*, 6 vols., VI: *Ireland* (London: J. Johnson, 1807–8), p. 4.

21 Ingham, 'Dialect', p. 216.

22 Blank, 'The Dialect of the *Shepheardes Calender*', p. 72.

23 Edmund Campion, *Two Bokes of the Histories of Ireland*, ed. A. F. Vossen (Assen, Netherlands: Van Gorcum, 1963), p. 17.

24 On Gavin Douglas and the Scottish Renaissance see Robert Cummings, '"To Cart the Fift Quheill": Gavin Douglas' Humanist Supplement to the *Eneados*', *Translation and Literature* 4 (1995), 133–56; R. D. S. Jack, '"Translating" the Lost Scottish Renaissance', *Translation and Literature* 6 (1997), 66–80.

25 Kim F. Hall, *Things of Darkness: Economies of Race and Gender in Early Modern England* (Ithaca: Cornell University Press, 1995), p. 146.

26 Paula Blank, *Broken English: Dialects and the Politics of Language in Renaissance Writings* (London: Routledge, 1996), p. 145.

27 Donald Bruce, 'Spenser's Welsh', *N&Q* NS 32.4 (1985), 465–6. Conversely, John Draper maintained that 'the author of *The View of the Present State of Ireland* knew very little Welsh'. See John W. Draper, 'Spenser's Linguistics in *The Present State of Ireland*', *MP* 17.8 (1919), 111–26, p. 123.

28 Maryclaire Moroney, 'Spenser's Dissolution: Monasticism and Ruins in *The Faerie Queene* and *The View of the Present State of Ireland*', *Sp. St.* 12 (1991; 1998), 105–32, p. 129, n. 14.
29 See Richard McCabe, 'Edmund Spenser, Poet of Exile', *PBA* 80 (1991), 73–103.
30 Colin Burrow, *Edmund Spenser* (Plymouth: Northcote House, 1996), pp. 20–1.
31 Ruthven, 'Etymology', p. 256.
32 *State*, p. 37. Further references will be given by page number in the text.
33 Ruthven, 'Etymology', p. 256.
34 Woods, 'Versification', p. 711.
35 Ibid., pp. 711–12.
36 Strang, 'Language, General, and Resources Exploited in Rhyme', p. 426.
37 Ibid.
38 Recent examples include Clare Carroll, 'Spenser and the Irish Language: The Sons of Milesio in *A View of the Present State of Ireland*, *The Faerie Queene*, Book v and the *Leabhar Gabhála*', *The Irish University Review* 26 (Autumn/Winter, 1996), special issue: *Spenser in Ireland: 'The Faerie Queene', 1596–1996*, ed. Anne Fogarty, 281–90; Anne Fogarty, 'The Colonisation of Language: Narrative Strategies in *A View of the Present State of Ireland* and *The Faerie Queene*, Book vi', in Patricia Coughlan, ed., *Spenser and Ireland: An Interdisciplinary Perspective* (Cork: Cork University Press, 1989), pp. 75–108; Eamonn Grennan, 'Language and Politics: A Note on Some Metaphors in Spenser's *A View of the Present State of Ireland*', *Sp. St.* 3 (1982), 99–110. These critics were able to draw on an earlier generation of Spenserians who explored Spenser's linguistics from an Irish perspective. See, among others, Frank F. Covington, 'Another View of Spenser's Linguistics', *SP* 19 (1922), 244–8; John W. Draper, 'Spenser's Linguistics in *The Present State of Ireland*', *MP* 17 (1919) 111–126; 'More Light on Spenser's Linguistics', *MLN* 41 (1926), 127–8; Roland M. Smith, 'More Irish Words in Spenser', *MLN* 59 (1944), 472–7; Smith, 'Irish Names in *The Faerie Queene*', *MLN* 61 (1946), 27–38.
39 Strang, 'Language, General, and Resources Exploited in Rhyme', p. 426; Bruten, 'Morphology and Syntax', p. 480.
40 Marks and Gross, 'Names, Naming', p. 494.
41 Ward, 'Neologism', p. 509.
42 Ibid.
43 Richard Mulcaster, *The Elementarie*, ed. E. T. Campagnac (Oxford: Clarendon Press, 1925), p. 175. Cited in Blank, 'The Dialect of *The Shepheardes Calender*', p. 77.
44 Snare, 'Glossing', p. 334.
45 Bruten, 'Pronunciation', p. 558.
46 Maureen Quilligan, *The Language of Allegory: Defining the Genre* (Ithaca: Cornell University Press, 1979), pp. 33–5.
47 Debra Fried, 'Rhyme Puns', in Jonathan Culler (ed.), *On Puns* (Oxford: Blackwell, 1988), pp. 83–99, at pp. 85–6.
48 Quilligan, 'Puns', p. 571.
49 Carroll, 'Spenser and the Irish Language', p. 290.
50 Stephen Greenblatt, 'To Fashion a Gentleman: Spenser and the Destruction of the Bower of Bliss', in *Renaissance Self-Fashioning: From More to Shakespeare* (Chicago: Chicago University Press, 1980), pp. 157–92, at p. 192.

FURTHER READING

Paula Blank, 'The Dialect of *The Shepheardes Calender*', *Sp. St.* 10 (1992), pp. 71–94.

  Broken English: Dialects and the Politics of Language in Renaissance Writings (London: Routledge, 1996).

John W. Draper, 'The Glosses to Spenser's *Shepheardes Calender*', *JEGP* 18 (1919), pp. 556–74.

  'Classical Coinage in the *Faerie Queene*', *PMLA* 47.1 (1932), pp. 97–108.

Anne Fogarty, 'The Colonisation of Language: Narrative Strategies in *A View of the Present State of Ireland* and *The Faerie Queene*, Book VI', in Patricia Coughlan, ed., *Spenser and Ireland: An Interdisciplinary Perspective* (Cork: Cork University Press, 1989), pp. 75–108.

Eamonn Grennan, 'Language and Politics: A Note on Some Metaphors in Spenser's *A View of the Present State of Ireland*', *Sp. St.* 3 (1982), pp. 99–110.

Richard Helgerson, 'Barbarous Tongues: The Ideology of Poetic Form in Renaissance England', in Heather Dubrow and Richard Strier, eds., *The Historical Renaissance: New Essays on Tudor and Stuart Literature and Culture* (Chicago and London: Chicago University Press, 1988), pp. 273–92.

Bruce Robert McElderry, Jr., 'Archaism and Innovation in Spenser's Poetic Diction', *PMLA* 47.1 (1932), pp. 144–70.

Willy Maley, 'Spenser's Irish English: Language and Identity in Early Modern Ireland', in *Salvaging Spenser: Colonialism, Culture and Identity* (London: Macmillan, 1997), pp. 34–47.

Roland M. Smith, 'Spenser's Scholarly Script and "Right Writing"', in D. C. Allen, ed., *Studies in Honor of T. W. Baldwin* (Urbana, Illinois: University of Illinois Press, 1958), pp. 66–111.

Barbara M. H. Strang, 'Language, General, and Resources Exploited in Rhyme', in *Spenser Encyclopedia*, pp. 426–9.

Herbert W. Sugden, *The Grammar of Spenser's* Faerie Queene (New York: Kraus Reprint Corp., 1966; first published Philadelphia: Linguistic Society of America, 1936).

Sheldon P. Zitner, 'Spenser's Diction and Classical Precedent', *PQ* 45.2 (1966), pp. 360–71.

9

LINDA GREGERSON

Sexual politics

When Elizabeth Tudor was seven months old, she was displayed naked to the French ambassador and two other special envoys, so they might see and report that the marriage of the King of England and his new queen had been sanctioned by the birth of a child who was free from physical deformity.[1] During the early decades of her reign, the Spanish ambassadors bribed Elizabeth's laundresses so that they might know if she had regular menstrual cycles. When the second round of French marriage negotiations began in 1579 (the queen was then 45 years old), Lord Burghley consulted her female servants and physicians in an effort to determine whether she was still capable of bearing children (he decided that she was).[2] Attention to the monarch's body, to even its most intimate functions, was nothing new in early modern Europe. When that body was female, however, the scrutiny was different in kind.

The powers ascribed to male and female were asymmetrical in sixteenth-century law, in sixteenth-century physiology, in sixteenth-century social life; when a female prince inherited the throne of England, she constituted both a practical and a representational crisis. The state was considered to hold a large proprietary interest in sexuality and procreation. Female chastity was the bearer of formidable ideological and practical significance; it was the indispensable guarantor of social coherence, legitimate title and the orderly maintenance and transfer of material wealth, including land tenure. Marriage alliance and marriage negotiation were major instruments of foreign and domestic policy. Ambition of every sort, private and public, secular and spiritual, could and did put forth its claims in the vocabularies of sexual desire. Edmund Spenser did not invent the complex, eroticised vocabularies that permeated Tudor politics, but he was a key figure in their elabouration. He was also their most penetrating expositor and critic.

The basic idiom was Petrarchan. The lyric poem in Spenser's era, and by extension the whole high-cultural field of compliment, was habitually treated as a vehicle for male desire. Lyric praise involved close focus on the isolated parts of feminine beauty: eyes, hair, lips, etc. Lyric tension derived from proprietary competition for access to the female body, and made this competition the ground for masculine career. Spenser openly modelled his *Amoretti* (1595) on Petrarch's sequence of love poems to Laura, but Spenser's most extensive and profound investigation of Petrarchan poetics takes place within *The Faerie Queene*. When Sir Walter Raleigh composed commendatory verses to accompany the 1590 publication of *The Faerie Queene*, he did not, as might have been expected, compare the poet's achievement to that of Virgil or Ariosto or Tasso. The poet he singles out as the key predecessor, the poet most conspicuously displaced (and thus celebrated) by *The Faerie Queene*, is Petrarch, love's consummate lyricist.[3]

> Me thought I saw the graue, where Laura lay,
> Within that Temple, where the vestall flame
> Was wont to burne, and passing by that way,
> To see that buried dust of liuing fame,
> Whose tombe faire loue, and fairer vertue kept,
> All suddenly I saw the Faery Queene:
> At whose approch the soule of Petarke wept,
> And from thenceforth those graces were not seene.
> For they this Queene attended, in whose steed
> Obliuion laid him downe on Lauras herse:
> Hereat the hardest stones were seene to bleed,
> And grones of buried ghostes the heauens did perse.
> Where Homers spright did tremble all for griefe,
> And curst th'accesse of that celestiall theife.[4]

Weighed in the balance with Petrarch, even Homer merits a mere two lines of Raleigh's poem.

When the Petrarchan sonnet was imported into England from Italy in the early decades of the sixteenth century, it was understood to comprise not only a set of prosodic features (the eleven-syllable Italian line became iambic pentameter; the octave-plus-sestet became fourteen lines of variable subdivisions), but also a set of thematic and rhetorical conventions. Sonnets came in groups and told a story. Or rather, they refused to tell a story outright but were built around a story that took place in the white space between individual lyrics. The story was of love: love unrequited, love requited but unfulfilled, love so fleetingly fulfilled as merely to make suffering keener, love thwarted by the beloved's absence or aloofness, her prior possession by another, her mortal decline and death. Impediment was as central to the sonnet as was love. Impediment produced the lyric voice. Without impediment, the lover would have no need to resort to poetry; he would have something better to do.

Petrarchism afforded sixteenth-century England its foremost paradigm of literary subjectivity. That subjectivity was always predicated upon absence: the lady refuses, the lady sickens or dies, the lady's remoteness makes her a perfect site for erotic and poetic ambition. The vacancy at the heart of love is the lover's provocation and anxiety – he longs to have that which he fears to lose – but absence is also his opportunity. Deprived of full presence, the lover writes. The differential or gap between lover and beloved (a differential crucial even to the consummated sexuality of courtly love) is rehearsed again and again in the gap between words and referents, the gap that fuels continuing linguistic production. Writing to fill and preserve the gap, the poet invents a vocation. That vocation is at once a compensation for erotic longing and an aggravation or reenactment of it: hence the complex resonance in Petrarch's conspicuous punning on Laura and laurel, the elusive beloved and the civic crown the poet is given in her stead.

Again and again in *The Faerie Queene*, Spenser lays bare the oppositional dynamics of Petrarchan sexuality, the erotic economy within whose bounds the lover and beloved can only prosper at one another's expense. But nowhere is his critical anatomy so explicit as in his violent inversion of an image from Petrarch's *Rime* 23. The Italian poet describes his amatory suffering thus:

> *Questa che col mirar gli animi fura*
> *m'aperse il petto el' cor prese con mano*
>
> (She, who with her glance steals souls,
> opened my breast and took my heart with her hand)[5]

In Spenser's version, the heart torn out of its breast is not the lover's but the lady's. In the culminating canto of Book III, Spenser's Knight of Chastity has fought her way through walls of flame to rescue captive Amoret. She finds the maiden led in allegorical procession as the 'spoyle' of Cupid:

> Her brest all naked; as net iuory, . . .
> And a wide wound therein (O ruefull sight) . . .
> At that wide orifice her trembling hart
> Was drawne forth, and in siluer basin layd,
> Quite through transfixed with a deadly dart,
> And in her bloud yet steeming fresh embayd . . .
>
> (III, xii, 20–21)

The trope is lurid, inscribed in female flesh, but its logic is partly obscure until Britomart makes her way to the inner chamber where Amoret's tormentor can be seen at work:

> And her before the vile Enchaunter sate,
> Figuring straunge characters of his art,

> With liuing bloud he those characters wrate,
> Dreadfully dropping from her dying hart,
> Seeming transfixed with a cruell dart,
> And all perforce to make her him to loue.   (III, xii, 31)

Two decades ago, Nancy Vickers published a classic essay on the fragmentation of the female body so central to Petrarchan poetics.[6] Tracing the recurrent appearances of the Diana/Actaeon myth in the *Rime sparse*, Vickers argues that Petrarch's fetishisation of feminine body parts – his isolation of those parts for the purpose of erotic contemplation and praise – enacts a preemptive reversal of Actaeon's fragmentation as the Renaissance came to construe it. That fragmentation begins, in Ovid's tale, when Actaeon beholds Diana naked in her bath. So that he will not be able to talk about what he has seen, the angry goddess sprinkles him with water and changes him to a stag, and he is subsequently torn to pieces by his own hounds. The female body in this parable is a body withheld; the gaze is male and transgressive; desire tears one apart. Spenser's critique of Petrarch is of a piece with Vickers' Ovidian reading of the *Rime Sparse*: Spenser literalises, and thus reveals in all its disturbing hostility, the adversarial structure of erotic desire. When Spenser casts Busyrane as an avatar of the Petrarchan poet, he exposes the harsh foundations of a lofty aesthetic formation: the penman visits upon the lady the fate he fears she spells for him; he writes in the beloved's blood.

Spenser did not build the House of Busyrane to stand for a rare aberration in heterosexual love as his culture had encoded it: his critique is far more sweeping; his poem is full to bursting with variations on chronic abuse. Two further examples will have to stand in for the scores that might be adduced: when, in the Book of Courtesy, a group of cannibals discovers the sleeping Serena, they resolve 'to make a common feast' of her (VI, viii, 38). While awaiting their feast, they visually and verbally savour the delicacies they plan to consume:

> Some with their eyes the daintest morsels chose;
> Some praise her paps, some praise her lips and nose;
> Some whet their kniues, and strip their elbows bare. (VI, viii, 39)

The sequence is part burlesque: the cannibals allow Serena to finish her nap, the better to fatten ('battill') her for slaughter, and the cannibals debate the relative merits of one large feast or 'many meals'. But the sequence is also explicit about its sources in Petrarchan habits of speech and mind, and it submits these habits to a reading both ruthless and political. Serena's 'yuorie necke, her alabaster brest, / Her paps, which like white silken pillowes were' (VI, viii, 42), each separate beauty comes straight from the stock inventory of the sonneteers, where voyeurism breeds carnivorous appetite. Serena's genitals 'hang' like the 'spoiles of Princes' (VI, viii, 42), ripe for violent seizing. Petrarchan praise affords a thin veneer for the predations of the gaze.

In a complementary sequence, and as part of the same critique, the poet causes False Florimell to be built before our eyes:

> The substance, whereof she the bodie made,
> Was purest snow in massie mould congeald, . . .
> And virgin wex, that neuer yet was seald, . . .
>
> In stead of eyes two burning lampes she set
> In siluer sockets, shyning like the skyes, . . .
> In stead of yellow lockes she did deuise,
> With golden wyre to weaue her curled head.   (III, viii, 6–7)

The golden wires and starry lamps, drawn from the standard inventory of Petrarchan simile, are made to undergo a ghoulish transformation here, becoming the raw materials for the manufacture of a 'carckasse' whose only animation derives from the 'wicket Spright' who takes up lodging within it. In the same idiom that governs the imaginative disassembly of Serena's body by ravenous spectators, False Florimell's body is assembled by a witch to placate her ravenous son. That son quickly loses his trophy to Braggadocchio: false lady is fit partner for false knight. The two anatomies, Serena's and False Florimell's, share a single moral. The falseness at stake is not the falseness in women but the falseness in male appetite, whose creatures they are. Nor does Braggadocchio's bad judgement absolve true knights. To a man, the knights of Fairyland are 'ravished' by False Florimell: she out-shines, in their view, all other womanhood, outshines even her 'true' original. The remarkable feature of Spenser's sexual polemic is the consistency with which 'false women' invariably turn out to be not independent agents but the distillations of false desire. Like the episode of Serena and the cannibals, the construction of False Florimell and her subsequent career seem to speak with great clarity: men, you are to blame.

The Petrarchan is not the only sexual/political economy subjected to radical exposition in *The Faerie Queene*. Drawing upon the templates of wedding masque and epithalamion, Spenser looks more broadly at the fetishisation of female virginity so central to the symbolic and material continuities of early modern patriarchy. Amoret's vulnerability to torment appears to be a correlative of her transition to married life: she has been abducted by Busyrane during her own bridal feast, under cover of a masque (IV, i, 3). Amoret's lurid sufferings in the House of Busyrane have been widely construed as a kind of psychomachia, representing the new bride's fear of defloration[7] or her 'obsession' with the warlike codes of courtly love.[8] Thomas Roche interprets the Masque of Cupid as a kind of refracting mirror: an object of terror for the bride, whose fearful vision governs the House of Busyrane as we see it, but a 'jovial' celebration of love's triumph for the wedding guests, whose perspective parallels that of the Renaissance sonneteers.[9] While subsequent readers have generally found it right and necessary to construe the House of Busyrane as a complex locus for multiple points of view, they have not always subscribed to Roche's mapping of its contents. Harry Berger points out that the 'celebratory' perspectives attributed to wedding guests, groom and sonneteers appear to include a significant portion of sadism.[10] Is that sadism entirely to be discounted as the symptom of female sexual panic, as the bride's lurid misconstruction of an institution (marriage) that is otherwise benign?

When George Puttenham describes the epithalamion or 'bedding ballad' in *The Arte of English Poesie*, he describes a raucous music intended to cover (and surely to approximate) the 'skreeking and outcry' of the bride during defloration. 'For which purpose also they used . . . to suppresse the noise by casting of pottes full of nuttes round about the chamber vpon the hard floore or pauement'. With the light of day, the musicians return in a gentler mode to call the bride forth from the bridal chamber, 'no more as a virgine, but as a wife', so that her parents and kinsmen may judge whether she be 'dead or aliue, or maimed by any accident nocturnall'.[11] The cruel 'penning' of Amoret, like the savage incision that opens her breast, is the mark of male prerogative; Spenser's culture encoded these phenomena in the ritualised outcry of epithalamion. Spenser stages the virgin's terror amidst the reign of terror made (and enjoyed) by those who dispose of her; the proliferating nightmare allegorised in the House of Busyrane is a social as well as a psychic phenomenon.

Dividing the newlyweds' exchange of vows from their retirement to the bridal chamber, the wedding feast and the attendant celebration interpolate public claims into the midst of private union and, much like the epithalamion, establish the public share in propagation. Community and custom defer the rites of intimacy, thus establishing that intimacy is theirs to bestow. Amoret's suspended status as a 'virgine wife' (IV, i, 6) unfolds the tensions and danger inherent in an all-but-universal moment of transition. That Busyrane has found his opening at Amoret's own wedding feast is highly apt; his abduction of the bride merely takes to a malevolent extreme the proprietary challenge that nuptial festivity advances as a matter of routine. The Masque of Cupid, scripted by Busyrane, is a complex variation on that other masque, the usual one, from whose midst Amoret is stolen. Were it simply the pathologised antithesis of a bland and uncontested social practice, we would not find so much 'skreeking and outcry' in Puttenham's epithalamion. Nor would we find in traditional cultures that wedding nights end with a public display of bloody sheets.

To counter the debasements of Petrarchan discourse and fetishised virginity, Spenser proposes a corrective paradigm in the person of his female Knight of Chastity. The 'Letter to Raleigh' describes the love of Britomart as an 'Accident' rather than an 'intendment' of the poem.[12] The third adventure brought before the court of the Faerie Queene, as was to have been revealed in the poem's twelfth book, was not the search for Artegall but the rescue of Amoret, and this adventure properly belongs to Scudamour, not Britomart. But the story as we have it begins with Britomart's gaze in a glass, and her quest for the face she has seen in the glass takes her well beyond the bounds of the book that is named for her and well beyond a merely private destiny. Britomart's charge is to seek out the knight who will rescue her father's kingdom and secure its posterity, which posterity includes the sixteenth-century English queen. Her search is conducted on two simultaneous grounds: on the fortuitous terrain of Fairyland and in her own evolving person. For Artegall is not merely elusive; he is also, left to his own devices, unstable. Britomart will have to maintain the exemplary figure of knighthood when Artegall himself has lapsed from it. She will hold the man's place so that he, beholding this remedial reflection, will have a place to return to. She will keep his proper likeness when even he abjures it.

That Britomart can so effectively function as a mirror for emulation, a paradigm of knighthood and of womanhood at once, rather than falling under suspicion as another usurping female and therefore an affront to Justice, is the product of complicated narrative and symbolic plotting. Britomart's first state, her maidenly freedom from love and use under the protection of her royal father, is irrevocably dismantled after she looks upon a face in a glass; her final state, as mother to a line of royal and national heroes, exists as vision only, prophesied by the magician who made the glass and again by a dream in the Temple of Isis. Between these two sanctioned and stable states, in the meantime of poetic action, Britomart searches for her knight through half the books of *The Faerie Queene* and through numerous tests of faith. As we have seen in the story of Amoret, the passage from virgin to bride, from one closed circle of possession to that other contradictory one, is fraught with proprietary tensions in the patriarchal world of chastity; the creature is never her own but on sufferance. Intact, the virgin is held in trust for her new life; enfolded in her husband's arms, the bride is his path to generation. In either state, her surest possessions are her absences – the absence of sexual experience, which leaves the lines of generation unmuddied, and the anatomical 'absence' that signifies subordinate gender. When Britomart sets forth in male disguise, therefore, she enters a realm of considerable sexual ambiguity. Her achievement will be to hand herself over to Arthegall and to sexual generation, but her progress will expose the boundaries and the ideologies of gender to considerable strain.

Narrative surrogacy is chronic in *The Faerie Queene*: knights are perpetually standing in for one another on the field of battle and in the layered progress of allegorical quest; Britomart herself stands in for Scudamour at a crucial juncture. But the surrogacy at the heart of the Book of Justice is more momentous than that which has gone before: it presses harder on the differential orders of sex and gender, and it violates the tacit decorums that govern principal virtues in *The Faerie Queene*. Britomart not only fails to stay put in a book of her own, but she plays the part of Justice better than Justice himself, and she does so for several crucial cantos in the book that bears his name. Spenser has complained in the proem to Book v that it is virtually impossible to write about Justice in the present era because men have declined so since antiquity, have been so utterly 'degendered' (v, proem, ii). And Britomart's continuing invention and impersonation of Justice threaten to undermine the very authority they consolidate.

Britomart has throughout the middle books of *The Faerie Queene* negotiated a double lineage. She has adopted the armour and the example of an enemy (the Saxon warrior Angela) in order to invent a beloved foe who will become the protector and progenitor of her native race. She has revived the lineage of female warriors in order to defend the prerogatives of patriarchy. And, in a scene that brings to crisis point her competing affiliations, she is forced to turn so fiercely against her kind that she nearly undoes the sources of generation. In Britomart's battle with Radigund, both warriors hack and hew at one another without remorse, not sparing even those 'dainty parts' which nature meant '[f]or other vses' (v, vii, 29). They perform a ghastly inversion of the fecundity attributed to their sex: 'that all in gore / They trode, and on the ground their liues did strow, / Like fruitless seede, of which vntimely death should grow' (v, vii, 31). The savagery is great because the threat is great: in Radigund the book of chastity must confront one of its own most plausible extrapolations. Radigund can very nearly pass for Britomart, and she tampers very closely with Britomart's betrothed. She is brave and skilled in battle. She may bind her martial opponents to shameful and unchivalrous pledges of servitude, but she can behave in exemplary fashion on the battlefield: while Artegall allows a dependant to be shamefully hanged (v, v, 18), Radigund steadfastly protects her fellows, ordering all of the weak and wounded to safety before she retreats (v, iv, 45). Founding and defending a martial state, she simply takes to a further extreme the revolution that begins with a girl who steals from her father's house in armour.

Or does she? The Knight of Chastity bears arms and endures adventure, but rather than construing her powers as the foundation for gynocracy, she submits to the fortuitous path of chivalric romance. And according to the logic of romance, she is confronted at every turning with the wrecks and perversions of her allotted quest. She is told by vision, by prophecy, by every literary and social code that her proper role is that of consort and catalyst, of helpmeet and tempering influence, but the man who gives coherence to the network of obeisance and desire is one she finds in a state of abjection. Beholding 'her owne Loue' as Radigund's thrall – a beloved and a love in which self and other, man and woman, intrinsic and imposed are confounded – Britomart turns her head aside in 'secret shame' (v, vii, 38). The spectacle cuts close, in other words: the transformations that began with a borrowed suit of armour and the imprint of a face in a glass find in the Amazonian state and the imprisonment of Artegall a powerful line of fulfilment. But Radigund's political and erotic example is one that Britomart is made to recoil from. Radigund lays claim to means that Britomart, in Spenser's world, must choose to lack: hence the Amazon's summary execution.

The decisive combat has been twice rehearsed – once in the battle between Britomart and Artegall (IV, iv, 44–8), once in the battle between Artegall and the Amazon (v, v, 1–18). During each rehearsal, the unveiling (or more properly, the unvisoring) of the feminine face has been fatal to martial action; Artegall will not strike his revealed opponent. Unlacing Radigund's helmet and taking pity on what he beholds, Artegall has abandoned knightly prerogative and submitted to the disfiguring 'shame' of feminine dress and feminine occupation. But Britomart, tellingly, is free to be more ruthless than the man. At just that juncture where narrative precedent and the conventions of single combat would dictate that she unlace the Amazon's helmet and gaze on the face of the enemy self, Britomart severs the head and the helmet with a single stroke (v, vii, 34). Spenser cannot allow the reciprocal gaze of gendered common cause to disrupt his narrative and ideological imperative.

Gender in *The Faerie Queene* is emphatically hierarchical. Artegall dressed as a woman is a scandal and a figure of shame; Radigund empowered as a man is a usurper. A knight may not surrender his lawful prerogatives; a woman may not grasp what is beyond her. Britomart has had to train in arms and erotic improvisation only to censure and suppress analogous presumption in another of her sex. Without the special dispensation of fate, even a Faery Queene would be a usurper:

Such is the crueltie of womenkynd,
When they haue shaken off the shamefast band,
With which wise Nature did them strongly bynd,
T'obay the heasts of mans well ruling hand,
That then all rule and reason they withstand,
To purchase a licentious libertie.
But vertuous women wisely vnderstand,
That they were borne to base humilitie,
Vnlesse the heauens them lift to lawfull soueraintie.　(v, v, 25)

The sweep of the narrator's proscription is no more breathtaking than the abruptness of his single exception.[13] Gloriana is a law unto herself; she can therefore be no precedent. Britomart borrows manly garb and manly mobility, but she preserves her symbolic and procreative capacities only by foregoing the earthly middle ground of direct political power, the corporate, as opposed to the corporal and allegorical, realm of influence.

Spenser waves the flag of patriarchy, as did his female monarch, at particularly trying junctures. When Britomart decapitates Radigund on the battlefield, she cuts off the recognition scene that Elizabethan sovereignty will not bear and cuts off too the abominable precedent of the Amazonian state: 'And changing all that forme of common weale, / The liberty of women did repeale, / Which they had long vsurpt; and them restoring / To mens subiection, did true Iustice deale' (v, vii, 42). Justice – Tudor justice – requires the subject formed by subjection. Britomart can do better for justice than Justice himself not because she is a woman but because she is not hampered by a female prince. And here, perhaps, is the real significance of the narrative conundrum that distinguishes Spenser's poem from the outline addressed to Raleigh: Britomart's quest, whether construed as the 'invention' of Artegall or as the rescue of Amoret, neither originates nor concludes, not even hypothetically or 'offstage', in the court of Gloriana. Britomart restores the body politic to its proper shape by insisting that liberty and subjection are gendered attributes: she separates male from female, legitimate freedom from 'vsurpt'. Redivided and regrouped around a venerable asymmetry of power, 'all' members of the commonwealth adore their conquering Reformer and treat her 'as a Goddesse' (v, vii, 42).

And thou, O fairest Princesse vnder sky,
In this faire mirrhour maist behold thy face,
And thine owne realmes in lond of Faery,
And in this antique Image thy great auncestry. . .
The which O pardon me thus to enfold.
In couert vele, and wrap in shadowes light,
That feeble eyes your glory may behold,

> Which else could not endure those beames bright,
> But would be dazled with exceeding light.   (II, proem, 4–5)

The tradition of combining encomium and tutelage in courtly address is as old as monarchy itself. What distinguishes the public ceremonies of praise and petition in England during the second half of the sixteenth century from those of parallel cultures and times is first and foremost the sex of the reigning monarch. Those accustomed to speak and be heard in Tudor England, to voice opinion on matters of state and religion, to urge action and shape popular sentiment, to seek and bestow public favour, all, with one notable exception, were male. And this, rhetorically, made all the difference. Addressing his monarch, the Elizabethan courtier spoke across a gender divide, and spoke in a language heightened not merely with the usual doses of deference and hyperbole but with the fervour of eros. 'While your majesty gives me leave to say I love you', wrote Essex in 1591,

> my fortune is as my affection, unmatchable. If ever you deny me that liberty, you may end my life, but never shake my constancy, for were the sweetness of your nature turned into the greatest bitterness that could be, it is not in your power, as great a Queen as you are, to make me love you less.[14]

When Sir Walter Raleigh, another of Elizabeth's favourites, was imprisoned in the tower for impregnating one of the queen's maids of honour, he wrote to Robert Cecil, trusting that his letter would be shared with Cecil's mistress:

> My heart was never broken till this day, that I hear the queen goes away so far off, whom I have followed so many years with so great love and desire, in so many journeys, and am now left behind her in a dark prison all alone. . . . I that was wont to behold her riding like Alexander, hunting like Diana, walking like Venus, the gentle wind blowing her fair hair about her pure cheeks like a nymph, sometime sitting in the shade like a Goddess, sometime singing like an angel, sometime playing like Orpheus; behold! the sorrow of this world once amiss hath bereaved me of all.[15]

Access to the person of the queen was not simply the stuff of high-flown erotic compliment; it was a very real material advantage, even a necessity, for those who sought political advancement. The centres of cultural, legal, economic and military power were far more diffuse in early modern England than the long tradition of top-down, court- and London-centred narrative history would have us believe, but the Elizabethan court was indeed the country's single most impressive fount of patronage and visibility. Certainly it was the only context in which a man could leap from relative obscurity, as Raleigh had, to possession of £3,500 a year and 42,000 acres of Irish land.[16] Christopher Haigh estimates that two-thirds of the English nobility were part- or full-time courtiers during the early part of Elizabeth's reign, and that another fifty or sixty leading gentry were resident courtiers.[17] This company was overwhelmingly male: in a household that numbered well over a thousand courtiers and retainers, Elizabeth kept fewer than twenty women of the Chamber – some dozen matrons of distinguished family and half as many maids of honour. Men of means and consequence sustained large ranks of followers with gifts of money, office and occupation. These great men in turn had constantly to sue for the wardships, leases, titles and monopolies that enabled them to dispense munificence on such a scale. Their suits proceeded on the dance floor, in the privy chamber, in letters, masques and lyric poems, in emblems and impresas, in exchanges of gifts and the wearing of 'favours', in ceremonial pageants on the tilting grounds, at entrances to great estates in the course of the queen's summer progress. She was Cynthia holding sway over the ocean, she was Perfect Beauty in a fortress, she was the queen of Love. 'Some call her Pandora', says one of the characters in Dekker's *Old Fortunatus*; 'some Gloriana: some Belphoebe: some Astraea: all by several names to express several loves: Yet all those names make but one celestial body, as all those loves meet to create but one soul.' 'I', says his interlocutor, 'am of her country, and we adore her by the name of Eliza'.[18]

Elizabeth spoke too, of course: sometimes coyly, sometimes sternly, and always, when it came to love, enigmatically. For there was a literal ground. From the very beginning of her reign, Elizabeth was expected, and urged in the strongest possible terms, to marry. She was urged by Parliament within weeks of her coronation. She was urged by her closest councillors. She was urged by the House of Lords in 1563 (let it 'please your Majesty to dispose yourself to marry, where you will, with whom you will, and as shortly as you will') and by the House of Commons ('God incline your Majesty's heart to marriage').[19] She was urged again by Parliament in 1566 and yet again a decade later, every time she allowed that body to assemble. She was urged by ambassadors on behalf of foreign suitors: Philip II of Spain, Prince Eric of Sweden, Archdukes Ferdinand and Charles of Austria, the Dukes of Holstein and Saxony, and much later, but repeatedly, the Duke of Alençon. She was urged by suitors at home: the Earl of Arundel, Sir William Pickering, and lengthily, disturbingly, by Robert Dudley. 'Her majesty visits him in his chamber day and night', reported the Spanish Ambassador.[20] 'She is going to marry her horse-keeper', said Mary Stuart, 'who has killed his wife to make room for her'.[21]

Certainly this pressure to marry reflects a number of narrowly paternalistic motives: those accustomed to power were uneasy with a woman on the throne; they wanted Elizabeth bound in the customary ties of matrimony; they wanted their prejudices confirmed. But the question of royal succession was not abstract. Disputed succession had plunged the country into generation upon generation of civil war in the previous century. The founding of the Tudor monarchy had reconciled competing factions, but stability was tenuous, as fragile as the link between father and offspring. When Elizabeth's father put aside one wife in favour of another whom he judged to be more capable of bearing him a son, he opened the way to a massive reconfiguration of English polity and English church. Four wives later he died, and England under his three surviving heirs went through a dizzying succession of official religions, from the zealous Protestantism of young Edward VI, to the 'bloody' counter-insurgency of Roman Catholicism under Mary, and thence to the ambiguous Anglicanism of Elizabeth. Elizabeth's was the longest of the Tudor reigns and looks in retrospect like a period of remarkable stability, but from a contemporary perspective her forty-five years on the throne unfolded as one long succession crisis, for Elizabeth never produced an heir; nor, until the very end, did she agree to name a successor. As long as it seemed as though she *might* produce an heir – and she let it seem so for a very long time – her possible marriage was a subject of intense political interest.

Elizabeth's personal preferences and private intentions in the nuptial sphere are quite simply unavailable to us, as they were to her contemporaries. She may well have contemplated marriage to Dudley in the earliest part of her reign; she may well, against all probability, have contemplated marriage to the Duke of Alençon. But she deflected direct petition with great resourcefulness. She professed herself happy to live and die a virgin, though willing to take the question of marriage under consideration. She professed herself already married to her kingdom. She professed herself a loving mother: 'charge me not with the want of children, forasmuch as everyone of you, and every Englishman besides, are my children and relations';[22] 'after my death you may have many stepdames, yet shall you never have a more natural mother than I mean to be unto you all'.[23] Her death was all too palpable a possibility. After the unmarried queen, the last of her line, fell dangerously ill with smallpox in 1562, the petitions from Parliament on the subject of succession were renewed with ever greater urgency:

> Most gracious sovereign Lady, the lamentable and pitiful state and condition wherein al your nobles and counsellors of late were, when it pleased God to lay his heavy hand over you, and the amazedness that most men of understanding were, by the bruit that grew by that sickness, brought unto, is one cause of this petition. [Your death in the present circumstances would bring] very evident and great danger and peril to all states and sorts of men in this

realm, by the factions, seditions and intestine war that would grow through want of understanding to whom they should yield their allegiances and duties.[24]

The queen was immovable: 'I know now as well as I did before that I am mortal.' And she maddeningly returned one of her 'answers answerless':

> Think not that I, that in other matters have had convenient care of you all, will in this matter, touching the safety of myself and you all, be careless. For I know that this matter toucheth me much nearer than it doth you all, who, if the worst happen, can lose but your bodies; but if I take not that convenient care that it behoveth me to have therein, I hazard to lose both body and soul.[25]

Elizabeth's multiplication of gendered roles – marriageable maiden, goddess of love, implacable virgin, mother, wife – allowed her crucial leverage in a multidimensional contest of wills and expectations. Modern critics, eager to locate a site of legible 'agency' for the queen, have sometimes professed to find this elusive trace in the oppositional rhetoric of virginity. As an alternate ideology, virginity had great advantages – it spared the queen subjection to any man of flesh and blood – and Elizabeth invoked it with alacrity. But she also conducted marriage negotiations, with differing degrees of earnestness, until well into her forty-eighth year. The virgin cult was one of several deft and overdetermined strategies for keeping calculations and alliances in motion. To entertain multiple offers of marriage, to vacillate, to lengthily consult, spared the queen the necessity of choosing one suitor over others and thus alienating several factions (Spanish, French, domestic, Protestant, Catholic) by favouring one. To argue that she was already bound in mystic contract (to God, to nation) symbolically stabilised her position and put her beyond the reach of importunate petition or too-literal courtship. And complicating the mix yet further, the queen could invoke her masculine authority as well, could stage her sex as double in its warrants and its aptitudes. 'Though I be a woman', she said to a Parliamentary delegation in 1563, 'yet I have as good a courage answerable to my place as ever my father had'.[26] 'I have', she said to the assembled troops at Tilbury, 'the heart and stomach of a King'.[27] These triangulations are not, nor could they be, the record of linear will. Their efficacy inheres in their responsiveness to changing circumstance, factional pressures, a shifting population of policy- and image-makers, as also in their ability to *deflect* change, faction and shifting populations. The queen's sex and sexuality constituted a mobile, and highly contested, field. That it accommodated so much contest was its genius.

Not everyone agreed to play. William Cecil, Lord Burghley, gave ample evidence of his devotion to the queen and was for forty years her most trusted advisor, first as Principal Secretary and later as Lord Treasurer, but he did not take it as part of his brief to address her in the language of erotic compliment. Indeed, he spent much of his career as a counterbalance to (and counter-conspirator against) the most avid and impetuous of Elizabeth's suitors. When Spenser published the second instalment of *The Faerie Queene* in 1596, he introduced the new books with stanzas that are commonly read as a reproach to Burghley, who had proved no more sympathetic to England's chief poet than to England's chief romantic heroes:

> The rugged forhead that with graue foresight
> Welds kingdomes causes, and affaires of state,
> My looser rimes (I wote) doth sharply wite,
> For praising loue, as I have done of late.   (IV, proem, I)

And on behalf of his heroes, and the vested vocabularies in which they and he had found most license to pursue their cultural and political work, the poet counterattacks:

> Such ones ill iudge of loue, that cannot loue,
> Ne in their frosen hearts feele kindly flame . . .
> To such therefore I do not sing at all,
> But to that sacred Saint my soueraigne Queene,
> In whose chast breast all bountie naturall,
> And treasures of true loue enlocked beene,
> Boue all her sexe that euer yet was seene;
> To her I sing of loue, that loueth best,
> And best is lou'd of all aliue I weene.   (IV, proem, 2,4)

Spenser was himself no courtier, and criticism has begun to question the assumption that courtly promotion must inevitably have been his lifetime aspiration, so it is worth observing that erotic address to the queen was not the exclusive preserve of Whitehall or Richmond Palace. There was for most of her reign a thriving market in portable, and wearable, images of the queen that portrayed her as eternally youthful (the Privy Council ordered unflattering portraits destroyed). There was an even wider circulation of popular ballads and love songs, like the following from 1559:

> Come over the born, Bessy,
> Come over the born, Bessy,
> Sweet Bessy come over to me;
> And I shall thee take,
> And my dear lady make
> Before all other that ever I see.[28]

Fragmentary evidence suggests that the language of erotic liberty had some power to penetrate the imaginative life of Elizabeth's subjects high and low.

When the astrologer Simon Forman confided to his diary a dream about the queen, he rendered her in tantalising and unseemly disarray and open to sexual insinuation. When a sailor named Abraham Edwardes was arrested for drawing his dagger in the presence of the queen after sending her a passionate letter, the Clerk of the Privy Council judged him to be suffering from love madness.[29] Both the dream and the more extravagant fantasy occurred during the last years of the reign, when the queen was in her sixties. And both derive their charge, or a major portion of it, from social and political transgression. The fantasy is of crossing uncrossable lines. Its motives and effects are as varied and capacious as the nation it defines: pleasurable trespass, narcissistic torment, misogynist aggression, class revenge, every permutation of differential sex and power.

The pithiest retrospective analysis of these dynamics comes from the pen of Francis Bacon. 'The reigns of women are commonly obscured by marriage', he wrote,

> their praises and actions passing to the credit of their husbands; whereas those that continue unmarried have their glory entire and proper to them-selves. . . . As for those lighter points of character – as that she allowed herself to be wooed and courted, and even to have love made to her; and liked it; and continued it beyond the natural age for such vanities – if any of the sadder sort of persons be disposed to make a great matter of this, it may be observed that there is something to admire in these very things, which ever way you take then. For if viewed indulgently, they are much like the accounts we find in romances, of the queen in the blessed islands, and her court and institutions, who allows of amorous admiration but prohibits desire. But if you take them seriously, they challenge admiration of another kind and of a very high order; for certain it is that these dalliances detracted but little from her fame and nothing from her majesty, and neither weakened her power nor sensibly hindered her business.[30]

'And thou, O fairest Princess vnder sky, / In this faire mirrhour maist behold thy face.' The lineaments of the English queen are rendered in shadows and light throughout *The Faerie Queene*: in the poem's presiding monarch, who is everywhere implicit and everywhere withheld; in Brito-mart, her mythic ancestor; in the virgin Belphoebe and her twin the married Amoret; in 'Dread' Astraea and 'Angel-like' Mercilla, whose overlapping spheres are the domains of Justice; in every patron virtue and in virtue's grounding anti-types, the female figures of pride and lust and nature-deforming power. Those who seek to understand the poet's ideological engagement with his female prince, his judgment on the varieties of female rule and female modes of action, quite naturally turn to the third book of *The Faerie Queene*, where female exempla abound. But Spenser addresses these questions with comparable urgency, and with greater evidence of conceptual disruption over time, in Books v and vi.

In the allegorised Book of Justice, Artegall's reversal stands in stark and painful contrast to Britomart's earlier, more freely fictive reformation of the Amazonian state. Radigund's innovations have been 'repealed' and her realm restored to the coherence of patriarchal rule, but the triumph is short-lived. Book v ends in frank dismay, its hopes aborted and its hero undermined not by hostile fate, nor by planets 'runne quite out of square' (v, proem, 1), nor by a secret fault in human will, but by the faulty judgement of a woman on top.

In Book vi, Spenser returns to the longer view and to the intensified mediation of pastoral romance. He returns in some disillusion. 'Of Court it seemes, men Courtesie doe call' (vi, i, 1). The etymological derivation appears to rehearse a compliment and a model of cultural production: courtesy in action circulates the image of the court. But just what court is that? For courtesy in the present age has declined so far from its full flowering in antiquity

> That it indeed is nought but forgerie,
> Fashion'd to please the eies of them, that pas,
> Which see not perfect things but in a glas.   (vi, proem, 5)

The paradigma, or mirror of courtesy, is now no more than the darkened, distorting glass of the Pauline epistle. The present age is an age of exile from true forms. So the poet must attribute to his Lady Queen a 'selfe' from which he will derive the lost pattern, a self 'in whose pure minde, as in a mirrour sheene' (vi, proem, 6), the paradigm may be rediscovered.

> Then pardon me, most dreaded Soueraine,
> That from your selfe I doe this vertue bring,
> And to your selfe doe it returne again   (vi, proem, vii)

Not the court as it exists, then, but the court as a projection of the inner world of the queen, who is thus made subject of and to the Book of Courtesy. We return in a different key to the proprietary struggle we have witnessed in Petrarchan lyric between 'you as you are' and 'you as you are to me'.

Elizabeth's last decade was a time of widespread disaffection – her subjects were burdened with oppressive taxation, successive years of crop failure and plague visitation, with costly and indecisive wars, factionalism at court, depressed trade, and recurrent social instability. Elizabeth was less often to be seen in public in these later years; Raleigh called her 'a lady whom time had surprised'.[31] Spenser was not alone in his strategic disengagement from the monarch's waning personal cult. Nor was he alone in pinning his hopes on a masculine alternative: 'suche an one I Coulde name', he wrote, 'vppon whom the ey of all Englande is fixed and our laste hopes

now rest'.[32] A vision of the same great lord secures a social blessing in the
Prothalamion: 'a noble Peer',

> Great *Englands* glory and the Worlds wide wonder,
> Whose dreadfull name, late through all *Spaine* did thunder,
> And Hercules two pillors standing neere,
> Did make to quake and feare:
> Faire branch of Honor, flower of Chevalrie,
> That fillest *England* with thy triumphes fame,
> Joy have thou of thy noble victorie,
> And endlesse happinesse of thine owne name
> That promiseth the same:
> That through thy prowesse and victorious armes,
> Thy country may be freed from forraine harmes:
> And great *Elisaes* glorious Name may Ring
> Through al the world, fil'd with thy wide Alarmes.   (Yale, p. 768)

Essex, in the end, was not the solution these passages envision, neither for
Ireland nor for England.[33] But the longing for a simplified, consolidating
hero is telling in and of itself. The poet, retrenching, wishes to imagine a
masculine bearer for Elisa's fame. The weariness this wish bespeaks is not, I
suspect, the weariness of material adversity alone, but is also a kind of
ideological exhaustion: when a patriarchal culture must sustain at its centre
a female prince for forty-five years, the labour is great.

NOTES

1 Retha M. Warnicke, *The Rise and Fall of Anne Boleyn: Family Politics at the
   Court of Henry VIII* (Cambridge: Cambridge University Press, 1989), p. 179.
2 Christopher Haigh, *Elizabeth I* (London: Longman, 1986), p. 16
3 Petrarch's literary output included a large body of work in Latin: letters in prose
   and verse; autobiographical, polemical, historical and philosophic writings;
   penitential psalms; pastoral poems; and an unfinished epic, the *Africa*. It was his
   sequence of vernacular love poems that dominated Petrarch's reputation in
   Renaissance Europe and was responsible for his vast literary and cultural
   influence.
4 The text of Raleigh's sonnet, one of two commendatory poems he composed to
   accompany the 1590 *Faerie Queene*, can be found in the second appendix to
   Hamilton.
5 *Rime* 23, lines 73–4. Text and translation are those of Robert M. Durling's
   edition: *Petrarch's Lyric Poems* (Cambridge: Harvard University Press, 1976).
6 Nancy Vickers, 'Diana Described: Scattered Woman and Scattered Rhyme', *CI*
   8 (1981), 265–79.
7 See James Nohrnberg, *The Analogy of* The Faerie Queene (Princeton: Princeton
   University Press, 1976), p. 475.
8 See Isabel G. MacCaffrey, *Spenser's Allegory: The Anatomy of Imagination*
   (Princeton: Princeton University Press, 1976), pp. 112–13.

9 Thomas P. Roche, Jr., 'The Challenge to Chastity: Britomart at the House of Busyrane', *PMLA* 76 (1961), 340–4, pp. 340–41.

10 Harry Berger, Jr., 'Busirane and the War between the Sexes', in *Revisionary Play: Studies in the Spenserian Dynamics* (Berkeley: University of California Press, 1988), pp. 172–94, at p. 183.

11 George Puttenham, *The Arte of English Poesie* (London, 1589; repr.. Kent, Ohio: Kent State University Press, 1970), pp. 68, 66 and 67.

12 The 'Letter to Raleigh' appears as Appendix 1 in Hamilton, p. 738.

13 Cf. John Knox's attack on female government as an unholy aberration in *The First Blast of the Trumpet against the Monstrous Regiment of Women* (1558). When Elizabeth acceded to the throne mere months after the *Blast* appeared in print, Knox hastened to qualify: although female rule was unnatural on the whole, he wrote, 'God had made an exception so that Elizabeth might restore the Gospel' (quoted in Haigh, *Elizabeth I*, p. 10).

14 Cited in J. E. Neale, *Queen Elizabeth* (London: Jonathan Cape, 1934), p. 324.

15 Ibid. pp. 328–9.

16 Lacey Baldwin Smith, *Elizabeth Tudor: Portrait of a Queen* (Boston: Little, Brown, 1975), p. 94.

17 Haigh, *Elizabeth I*, p. 87.

18 Thomas Dekker, *Old Fortunatus* (1599); cited in Roy Strong, *The Cult of Elizabeth* (London: Thames and Hudson, 1977), p. 15.

19 Cited in Haigh, *Elizabeth I*, p. 11.

20 See Neale, *Queen Elizabeth*, p. 85.

21 Smith, *Elizabeth Tudor*, p. 124.

22 George P. Rice, Jr., ed., *The Public Speaking of Elizabeth I: Selections from her Official Addresses* (New York: Columbia University Press, 1951), p. 117.

23 J. E. Neale, *Elizabeth I and her Parliaments*, 2 vols. (London: Cape, 1957), I, p. 109.

24 Cited in Haigh, *Elizabeth I*, p. 17.

25 Neale, *Parliaments*, p. 108.

26 Haigh, *Elizabeth I*, p. 21.

27 Neale, *Queen Elizabeth*, p. 298.

28 Haigh, *Elizabeth I*, p. 149.

29 Both episodes are cited and discussed in the earlier version of Louis A. Montrose's work on *A Midsummer Night's Dream*. See '"The Shaping Fantasies": Figuration of Gender and Power in Elizabethan Culture', in Stephen Greenblatt, ed., *Representing the English Renaissance* (Berkely: University of California Press, 1998), pp. 31–68.

30 *In Felicem Memoriam Elizabethae, The Works of Francis Bacon*, ed. James Spedding et al., 15 vols. (Boston, 1860), XI, pp. 425–61, at pp. 450, 460.

31 'Trial of Sir Walter Raleigh', in *Criminal Trials*, ed. David Jardine, 2 vols. (London, 1832–5), I, pp. 400–76, at p. 413.

32 *View*, p. 228.

33 On Robert Devereux, Second Earl of Essex, and *The Faerie Queene*, see Linda Gregerson, 'Narcissus Interrupted: Specularity and the Subject of the Tudor State', in *The Reformation of the Subject* (Cambridge: Cambridge University Press, 1995), pp. 80–110.

FURTHER READING

Marie Axton, *The Queene's Two Bodies: Drama and the Elizabethan Succession* (London: Royal Historical Society, 1977).

Harry Berger, Jr., 'Busirane and the War between the Sexes', and 'Pan and the Poetics of Misogyny', in *Revisionary Play: Studies in the Spenserian Dynamics* (Berkeley: University of California Press, 1988), pp. 172–94, 347–77.

Philippa Berry, *Of Chastity and Power: Elizabethan Literature and the Unmarried Queen* (London: Routledge, 1989).

Sheila T. Cavanagh, *Wanton Eyes and Chaste Desires: Female Sexuality in* The Faerie Queene (Bloomington: Indiana University Press, 1994).

Jonathan Crewe, 'Spenser's Saluage Petrarchanism: *Pensées Sauvages* in *The Faerie Queene*', in Jonathan Crewe, ed., *Reconfiguring the Renaissance: Essays in Critical Materialism* (Bucknell Review 35, no. 2) (Lewisburg, PA: Bucknell University Press, 1992), pp. 89–103.

John Freccero, 'The Fig Tree and the Laurel: Petrarch's Poetics', in Patricia Parker and David Quint, eds., *Literary Theory/Renaissance Texts* (Baltimore: Johns Hopkins University Press, 1986), pp. 20–32.

Susan Frye, *Elizabeth I: The Competition for Representation* (New York: Oxford University Press, 1993).

Linda Gregerson, *The Reformation of the Subject: Spenser, Milton, and the English Protestant Epic* (Cambridge: Cambridge University Press, 1995), pp. 9–147.

Christopher Haigh, *Elizabeth I* (London: Longman, 1988).

Louis Adrian Montrose, 'The Elizabethan Subject and the Spenserian Text', in Patricia Parker and David Quint, eds., *Literary Theory/Renaissance Texts* (Baltimore: Johns Hopkins University Press, 1986), pp. 303–40.

'The Shaping Fantasies of *A Midsummer Night's Dream*', in *The Purpose of Playing: Shakespeare and the Cultural Politics of the Elizabethan Theatre* (Chicago: The University of Chicago Press, 1996), pp. 109–205.

'The Work of Gender in the Discourse of Discovery', *Representations* 33 (1991), 1–41.

Maureen Quilligan, 'The Gender of the Reader', in *Milton's Spenser: The Politics of Reading* (Ithaca: Cornell University Press, 1983).

Dorothy Stephens, *The Limits of Eroticism in Post-Petrarchan Narrative: Conditional Pleasure from Spenser to Marvell* (Cambridge: Cambridge University Press, 1998).

Nancy J. Vickers, 'Diana Described: Scattered Woman and Scattered Rhyme', *Critical Inquiry* 8 (1981), 265–79.

10

Spenser's religion

Edmund Spenser lived during an era of chronic religious anxiety. He was born at about the time of the accession to the throne of Mary I (1553–8), the Catholic queen who attempted to reverse Henry VIII's schism from the Church of Rome and the Protestant religious settlement of her late brother, Edward VI (1547–53). Too young to remember Wyatt's Rebellion (1554), which triggered persecutions that earned the queen her reputation as 'Bloody Mary', Spenser would compose lines that allude at some level to burnings of Protestant heretics: 'holy Martyrs often doen to dye, / With cruell malice and strong tyranny' (*FQ*, I, viii, 36). Surely he read sensational accounts of religious persecution in John Foxe's *Acts and Monuments of These Latter and Perilous Days* (1563), known popularly as the *Book of Martyrs*. The most influential book of its age, other than the English Bible, that monumental collection exerted a profound influence upon the formation of English Protestant identity and nationhood.

Coming of age under Elizabeth I (1558–1603), the poet served the Virgin Queen who attempted to resolve religious discord with an ecclesiastical settlement that fused Catholic ritualism with codification of Protestant theology in the 'Thirty-Nine Articles of Religion' (1563). For hundreds of years, patriotic citizens celebrated the 17 November, the anniversary of her sister's death and her own Accession Day, as a national triumph over Catholicism. Nonetheless, the Elizabethan Compromise spawned both Catholic recusancy (refusal to attend church services) and rancorous Puritan attacks on vestiges of 'popery'. Both groupings disagreed with the imposition of state religion by means of the formulaic liturgy and authorised sermons contained respectively in the *Book of Common Prayer* and the *Book of Homilies*.

In order to enroll as a poor student in Merchant Taylors' School, young Spenser had to recite the catechism, a brief outline of officially authorised religious principles. The school's headmaster, Richard Mulcaster, enjoyed a reputation both as an educational reformer and as a zealous Protestant ideologue. At the outset of Elizabeth's reign, Mulcaster provided a narrative record of pageantry in celebration of the young queen's pre-coronation entry into the City of London. The scholar described her performance as that of a heroine who embraced a folio Bible symbolic of nationalistic faith. That gesture accorded with Protestant belief that lay people are entitled to read the Bible in the vernacular, a privilege revoked during Queen Mary's reign.

Surely the young queen embraced a copy of the Great Bible, the officially authorised translation based upon the work of William Tyndale and Miles Coverdale. The Royal Injunctions of 1559 ordered every church in the land to make a Bible available to parishioners. Matthew Parker, Archbishop of Canterbury, organised compilation of a new version, the Bishops' Bible (1568), for use in church services and in response to the popularity of the Geneva Bible (1560), a text whose polemical annotations held out special appeal to Puritan readers.[1] Spenser's verse draws on all three English translations.

Spenser appeared before the aged Coverdale when the latter visited Merchant Taylors' School as a public examiner in November 1564. With him on that occasion were distinguished ecclesiastics: Edmund Grindal, Bishop of London, and Alexander Nowell, Dean of St Paul's Cathedral. Spenser's grammar school years coincided with the first outburst of Puritan protest during the Vestiarian Controversy (1566). Radical ministers opposed the wearing of clerical vestments as a 'popish' vestige, whereas defenders of the church establishment declared that they were 'indifferent things' subject to state control.

In 1569 the youthful poet contributed verse translations to *A Theatre for Voluptuous Worldlings* by Jan van der Noot, a Calvinist who fled from Antwerp to London after the invasion of the Low Countries by the Duke of Alva, commander-in-chief of the forces of the Hapsburg Emperor. That action entailed widespread persecution of Protestants. It is likely that Mulcaster recommended his student to van der Noot or his publisher, Henry Bynneman, thus becoming the first among many patrons who advanced Spenser's career. Charged with a hostility towards Roman ecclesiastical hegemony shared by all Protestants and some Catholics, the *Theatre* attacks the pope as 'the Roman Antichrist', a medieval apocalyptic theme embraced by Martin Luther. The text rejects practices that are anathema to Protestants: pardons, indulgences, relics, purgatory, pilgrimages, religious images and clerical celibacy. Although Spenser's translations of 'Sonnets' that van der Noot drew out of the Book of Revelation are non-polemical, they paraphrase texts commonly associated with apocalyptic conflict between the 'true' Christian Church and the 'false' Church of Rome. They include the seven-headed Beast from the Sea, the Whore of Babylon, the Man on a White Horse, and New Jerusalem (Rev. 13, 17, 19, 21). That these figures held a long-term attraction for Spenser may be noted from their eventual reconfiguration in the ecclesiastical allegory found in Book 1 of *The Faerie Queene*.

During the same year, Spenser began his studies at Pembroke Hall, Cambridge. Cambridge was a hotbed of religious controversy inspired by Thomas Cartwright's attack on the episcopal hierarchy of the Church of England (1569–70). Puritan criticism of the official worship service, of clerical vestments and of the hierarchical structure of the church enjoyed a strong following at Pembroke. Presbyterians such as Cartwright advocated substitution of congregational control of individual churches by bodies of elders (presbyters) for the centralised government of the church by bishops appointed by the Crown. Bishop Grindal joined another former Master of Pembroke Hall, John Whitgift, in censuring Cartwright, whose attack on the Elizabethan religious settlement resulted in his deprivation from the Lady Margaret Professorship of Divinity and exile to Calvin's Geneva.

Patronage must have played a role in Spenser's receipt of a poor student's scholarship during John Young's tenure as Master of Pembroke Hall (1567–78). Funding came from an endowment established by the will of Alexander Nowell's brother. It may be that Bishop Grindal joined Mulcaster in advancing Spenser's university career. A protégé of Dean Nowell, Young received the mastership of Pembroke on the recommendation of Grindal, who had joined Nowell as an examiner at Merchant Taylors' School during Spenser's childhood. Grindal had served as Master of Pembroke Hall in succession to his own patron, Bishop Ridley, who had been burnt alive as a heretic during Queen Mary's reign.

Controversy thickened during the early 1570s, when Puritans in Parliament failed in their attempt to pass legislation to amend the *Book of Common Prayer*. They had wanted the wearing of surplices and kneeling at communion abolished, on the grounds that these practices hinted at transubstantiation of the elements of bread and wine into the body and blood of Christ during the Lord's Supper. Unalterable opposition to transubstantiation permeated Protestant hostility to the Roman Catholic Mass. John Field and Thomas Wilcox stirred up the Admonition Controversy by publishing a first and second *Admonition to Parliament* (1572). Their advocacy of Presbyterianism countered the queen's insistence upon episcopacy and royal prerogative in ecclesiastical affairs.

The government's sense of imperilment at the other end of the religio-political spectrum worsened with the Northern Rebellion of 1569, which demanded restoration of Roman Catholicism, and the promulgation by

Pope Pius V of a 1570 bull that excommunicated Queen Elizabeth and urged English Catholics to overthrow her regime. Intensified hostility to the papacy in John Foxe's revision of the *Book of Martyrs* (1570) reflected this renewed sense of endangerment. Copies of this text were available for reading at cathedral deaneries, guildhalls and other locations. During succeeding decades, authorities accused Catholics of launching a series of intrigues including the Babington Plot to assassinate Elizabeth and place her Catholic rival, Mary, Queen of Scots, on the throne. During two decades of imprisonment, Mary threatened the legitimacy of the Elizabethan regime as a claimant to the Crown. Spenser's unflattering portrayal of the Scottish queen and allegorisation of her execution in Book v of *The Faerie Queene* drew protest from her son, James VI of Scotland, later James I of England.

Spenser's life history colours the allegorisation of ecclesiastical contro-versy in his early poetry. When Edmund Grindal, by now Archbishop of Canterbury, consecrated John Young as Bishop of Rochester in 1578, the new bishop at once appointed Spenser as his private secretary. We know this because a copy of Jerome Turner's *Traveler* (1575) owned by Gabriel Harvey, a fellow of Pembroke Hall who befriended Spenser, is inscribed: 'Ex dono Edmundi Spenserii, Episcopi Roffensis Secretarii. 1578' ('A gift from Edmund Spenser, secretary of the Bishop of Rochester. 1578').

That Spenser worked on the dozen pastoral eclogues in *The Shepheardes Calender* during residence in Young's household at Bromley in Kent is suggested by localised topographical references. Of the eclogues 'mixed with some Satyrical bitternesse', three deal with ecclesiastical affairs: 'the fift of coloured deceipt, the seventh and ninth of dissolute shepheardes and pastours' ('General Argument'). Identification of herdsmen with clerics in 'May', 'July' and 'September' is grounded upon pastoral satires written in Latin by the influential Italian poets Petrarch and Mantuan.

The 'September' eclogue's representation of John Young as an ideal bishop dramatises a response to Presbyterian agitation. Hobbinol's praise of 'meeke, wise, and merciable' Roffy (or Roffyn), a figure for Young as *Episcopus Roffensis*, identifies him as Spenser's patron: 'Colin clout I wene be his selfe boy' ('September', lines 174–6). The poet used that pen name throughout his career, just as he identified Hobbinol with his friend Harvey. A tale told by Diggon Davie praises 'Argus eyed' Roffy (203) as a watchful shepherd-pastor who protects his flock by killing a predator, 'a wicked Wolfe . . . / Ycladde in clothing of seely sheepe' (184, 188). Just as Roffy functions as a type of Christ as the Good Shepherd in protecting the laity from a wolf in sheep's clothing, a Gospel figure for 'false' clerics, Diggon Davie plays the role of a prodigal son recently returned from 'a farre countrye' where he became disillusioned by the prideful greed of bad shepherds. Reference to the 'abuses . . . and loose living of Popish prelates' (argument for 'September') identifies that remote place as Rome, thus associating Roffy's vigilance with a hunt for a crypto-Catholic cleric within the Church of England. Hunts for overt wolves or covert foxes were a conventional element in anti-Catholic polemics.

Although there is general agreement concerning the reformist Protestantism of Spenser's satirical eclogues, a common view persists that the satirical eclogues afford evidence of Spenser's youthful Puritanism.[2] Broadly construed, that view is indisputable. Virtually all Elizabethan Protestants with a rigorous faith strove to return to the purity of Gospel worship. A narrower identification of Puritanism with anti-Catholicism is not useful because all Protestant groupings were hostile to 'popery'. (The term Anglican is anachronistic because it defines a state of the Church of England born during the nineteenth century.) The view that the Protestant pastors in Spenser's *Calender* speak the 'idiom . . . of Elizabethan Puritan propaganda' familiar from the Admonition Controversy of the 1570s[3] is unhelpful because it ignores the text's silence concerning disputes over church government, use of candles, kneeling during communion, and other controversial issues. That interpretation collapses distinctions between Presbyterian separatists such as Wilcox and Field and non-separatist Episcopalians who opposed them. The latter included Edmund Grindal and John Young, persecutors of both Catholic priests and separatist Presbyterians. Sympathetic voices in the *Calender* articulate views closely aligned with progressive Episcopalians. Indeed, Diggon Davie's praise of Roffy for good *oversight* involves a bilingual play on words, because the Greek word *episkopos* defines *bishop* as 'overseer'.

Via the thinly veiled allegorical figure of Algrind, an anagram of Grindal, the 'July' eclogue considers the aftermath of a confrontation between archbishop and queen concerning ecclesiastical control. His disgrace resulted in the failure of efforts to neutralise religious tensions by fostering reform from *within* the Church of England. Grindal's appointment had stirred up expectations of continued reform of the ministry and church discipline at a time when a progressive faction within the Privy Council, at court, and among the bishops favoured the eradication of surviving Catholic practices and the encouragement of Pelagianism (belief in free will and denial of original sin). Grindal's support for gospel preaching, cooperation between gentry and clergy, and evangelical episcopacy devoted to pastoral care rather than prelatic prerogative accommodated the views of non-separatist Puritans.

The 'Argument' situates 'July' within contemporary ecclesiastical debate: 'This Aeglogue is made in the honour and commendation of good shepheardes, and to the shame and disprayse of proude and ambitious Pastours. Such as Morrell is here imagined to bee.' That hill-dweller represents John Aylmer, Bishop of London, the only notable alluded to in the *Calender*, other than the queen, who did not sympathise with Grindal. The debate between goatherd Morrell and shepherd Thomalin mirrors Jesus' distinction between souls of the reprobate and of the elect (Matt. 25. 32–3). Inverting the Parable of the Good Shepherd (Matt. 18. 12–14), Morrell's association with the purchase of sheep by false shepherds indicates that he is loyal to Pan, the shepherd god whom E. K., the anonymous commentator, identifies with 'the Pope, whom they count theyr God and greatest shepheard' (line 179 and gloss). Morrell's attire associates him with Romanism:

> They bene yclad in purple and pall,
> so hath theyr god them blist,
> They reigne and rulen over all,
> and lord it, as they list:
> Ygirt with belts of glitter and gold . . .   (173–7)

These lines recall the Vestiarian Controversy, but festering discontent with prelatical pomp predates the Reformation.

Despite the daring allusion to Grindal, pastoral dialogue and disguise furnish the poet with a self-protective means of addressing highly charged topical issues without endorsing fixed positions. Algrind combines both the high position of Morrell and the simplicity of Thomalin, who herds sheep in 'the lowly playne' (line 7). Thomalin's fable about Algrind alludes to Archbishop Grindal's suspension from duties and the seizure of his property for refusing to execute Queen Elizabeth's order to suppress the 'prophesyings', in which clergy without licenses to compose their own sermons expounded biblical texts outside the context of the official *Book of Homilies*. The prophesyings compensated for deficiencies in the education of clergy.

The tale dramatises the thwarted yearnings of Protestant progressives of the 'Grindalian' era (1575–7) for a learned and humble ministry and episcopacy devoted to pastoral care. Grindal's quasi-Puritan commitment to increased emphasis upon Bible preaching and continuing ecclesiastical reform resulted in the defiance of royal prerogative, but he also attacked the nonconformity of Presbyterians and radical Puritans. Although the high-flying Eagle (a mythological figure for Queen Elizabeth) brains Algrind with a shellfish, the fable does not attribute to him the manifest flaws of goatherd Morrell, nor does it blame the Eagle.

By inviting the reader to identify the interlocutors in 'May', Piers and Palinode ('countersong'), with 'two formes of pastoures or Ministers, or the

Protestant and the Catholique', the 'Argument' indicates that the eclogue addresses the controversial survival of Roman Catholic practices. Piers' tale concerning the Kid who foolishly falls victim to a 'false Foxe' (279) assimilates the satirical tradition of Catholic clerics concealing themselves as wily Foxes under Protestant monarchs. According to E. K., the Kid's predicament exemplifies the dangers of religious backsliding, warning 'the protestaunt beware, howe he geveth credit to the unfaythfull Catholique' (gloss on line 304).

In his railing attack on Maying customs, Piers articulates fundamental questions concerning the ignorance and avarice of clerics concealed under the guise of hireling shepherds who 'playen, while their flockes be unfedde' (44):

> Perdie so farre am I from envie,
> That their fondnesse inly I pitie.
> Those faytours little regarden their charge,
> While they letting their sheepe runne at large.　　(37–40)

His diatribe against hireling shepherds and those who abandon their flock by putting them out for hire (i.e., nonresident holders of benefices) attacks a long-standing clerical abuse. Piers subscribes to the position of Archbishop Grindal in subjecting clergy to a higher standard than laity: 'But shepheards (as Algrind used to say,) / Mought not live ylike, as men of the laye' (75–6).

The negative position taken by Piers concerning Maying customs reflects the emergence of English Sabbatarianism, a movement to observe Sunday strictly as a day of worship, Bible reading and rest. Sabbatarians regarded the pursuit of such practices as sports, games, dancing and visiting alehouses while church services were in progress as vestiges of Roman Catholicism. Articulating concerns that predate the Reformation, they did not call for an outright ban on May games, play-going and other pastimes. By contrast, Palinode favours the proliferation of saints' days in the sacred calendar of the Roman church and the merrymaking that attended them (lines 15, 310). E. K.'s biases weight the 'May' eclogue in favour of Piers's strident attack, but that shepherd is neither flawless nor a simple mouthpiece for the poet's religious opinions. Palinode's call for tolerance approaches that of Hobbinol, who opposes the unbending rigorism of Diggon Davie, a visionary cousin of Piers ('September', 68–73).

At some point prior to the publication of *The Shepheardes Calender* in 1579, presumably at the recommendation of Bishop Young, Spenser moved into Leicester House, the London establishment of his new patron, Robert Dudley, Earl of Leicester, the most powerful noble in the land. In the pseudonymous guise of Immerito, Spenser dedicated the *Calender* to Leicester's nephew, Sir Philip Sidney, who joined Dudley as a leader of nobles and courtiers disaffected with what they perceived as Queen Elizabeth's flirtation with Catholicism. They opposed her disengagement from the fate of beleaguered Protestants in the Low Countries and apparent desire to marry the Duke of Anjou. As heir apparent to the throne of France, Anjou was implicated in the notorious St Bartholomew's Day massacre (24 August 1572), which broke the force of the Huguenot movement. For militant Protestants, the marital ambitions of an aging and childless queen raised the spectre of engulfment by Continental Catholicism.

Publication of the *Calender* during the heated marriage controversy accords with the delicate ambiguity of the 'April' eclogue's praise of Eliza as a marriageable virgin. Homage paid by Colin Clout, the absent singer whose song of praise is delivered by Hobbinol, enhances the queen's standing as an eligible woman at virtually the last moment when she is still remotely capable of childbearing. Colin's song delivers what may be the earliest comparison of Elizabeth to Cynthia or Phoebe, virgin goddess of the moon: 'Tell me, have ye seene her angelick face, / Like *Phoebe* fayre?' (64–5). In so doing, it praises her in a manner that echoes the views of powerful Protestant lords who wished that she retain her unwedded state.

Further indication of the poet's engagement with the religious politics of the late 1570s is provided by *Prosopopoia: Or Mother Hubberds Tale* (published in 1591), a beast fable in which the adventures of a Fox and an Ape expose the failures of different social estates. Punning allusion to Jean de Simier, the French ambassador who advanced marriage negotiations on behalf of the Duke of Alençon, as one of several topical identifications of the Ape, seems to tie composition of the poem to the same time period as the *Calender*. Indeed, the dramatisation of a catalogue of clerical abuses (353–574) recalls Spenser's satirical eclogues. In particular, the hypocritical yearning of the Fox to become a parson recalls the dissimulating Fox in the 'May' eclogue. Nevertheless, the variety of disguises assumed by that beast makes it difficult to reduce it to a stock type for a crypto-Catholic cleric. On the contrary, the recommendation of the corrupt Priest that the Fox 'fashion eke a godly zeale' in order to curry favour with a noble patron of 'a zealous disposition' (491–3) sounds very much like a slap against the fervency of religious enthusiasts. The well-fed Priest's dedication to an 'easie life' in which play-going follows reading of 'Homelies upon holidays' (393–5) personifies clerical laxity.

In 1580 Spenser moved to Ireland as secretary to a Dudley protégé, the Lord Deputy, Arthur, Lord Grey of Wilton. Spending the rest of his life as a civil servant in an alien colony, with the exception of occasional trips to

London, the poet witnessed relentless conflict between English colonists and the Catholic Irish. He was probably present at the Smerwick massacre, where hundreds of Italian and Spanish supporters of the Munster Rebellion, in addition to some Irishwomen and children, were slaughtered by Grey's forces. One of two interlocutors in Spenser's *View of the Present State of Ireland*, a dialogue that explores prospects for reform in the administration of Ireland, Irenius describes that event in detail. His critique of Irish religion alleges that the prevalence of 'popish trumperie' (i.e., rubbish) throughout the land has seduced ignorant Catholics into accepting the Roman-rite Mass by drinking 'of that Cupp of fornication, with which the purple harlott [the Whore of Babylon] had then made all nations drunke'.[4] His recommendations for religious reform include the establishment of an Irish church staffed by native Protestant clerics.

Having started work on *The Faerie Queene* prior to departure from England, Spenser granted religion a central position in a poem that begins with a book entitled the 'Legend of Holiness'. As a member of the Anglo-Protestant minority in Catholic Ireland, the poet composed the romantic epic against a backdrop of reports concerning developments in England: the beginning of the Jesuit Mission to England in 1580; persecution of recusants and clandestine priests; the collapse of the Puritan movement during the mid-1580s, when the queen arrested prospects for further ecclesiastical reform; and the development of the nationalistic myth of a zealously Protestant queen, which took on special force following the destruction of the Spanish Armada (1588), despite widespread discontent with the inflexibility of the aging queen among progressive Protestants.

More than the satires concerning ecclesiastical affairs in *The Shepheardes Calender*, the puzzling religious allegories in *The Faerie Queene* have elicited a wide range of conflicting interpretations. Despite the indeterminate open-endedness of Spenserian allegory, consensus exists concerning the reformist Protestantism of Spenser's romantic epic. Critics who discover an engagement with Reformation theology set the poem within multiple and overlapping frames of reference including Elizabethan Protestant politics;[5] the native tradition of Reformation literature and iconography;[6] the adaptation of reader-response interpretation to the pluralistic views of reformed Protestant and post-Tridentine Catholic theologians;[7] post-Armada apocalypticism;[8] or the interrogation of Protestant discourses concerning the body, sex, marriage and free will.[9] Those who attempt to bring the poem into simple conformity with the *Book of Common Prayer* and other formularies of the Church of England[10] have returned to an uncomplicated belief in 'Anglicanism' which has been challenged as anachronistic by ecclesiastical historians.[11] Focusing on apparent Catholic survivals in the poem, a provocative claim that the text versifies pre-Augustinian patristic theology and liturgy constructs an image of Spenser as a Greek Orthodox poet who presumably transported a library of esoteric religious texts to Ireland and wrote under the influence of Greek Fathers of the Church such as Tertullian, John Chrysostom and Clement of Alexandria.[12]

Like succeeding books of *The Faerie Queene*, Book 1 operates at multiple levels of moral, romantic, historical and theological allegory.[13] At the levels of historical and theological allegory, which do not exclude other layers of meaning, it considers the shifting phases of the English Reformation and questions concerning individual salvation. Spenser's version of the legend of St George represents the Red Cross Knight variously as the human soul, lover of Una, England and Christ. The knight's identity as St George is apparent from the beginning, because of the bloody cross on his shield, even though the crucial element of his popular image, the dragon battle, is postponed until canto xi. His status is problematic, however, because Protestants rejected veneration of the saints as a medieval tradition lacking in biblical foundation. When he arrives at the House of Holiness, Dame Caelia's expression of surprise, 'Strange thing it is an errant knight to see / Here in this place' (1, x, 10), calls attention to an uneasy fusion of quest romance with saint's life. That moment reflects the way in which the cult of St George survived the iconoclastic attack on that hero's unique status as patron of both England and its monarchy. It also acknowledges the Protestant redefinition of sainthood in terms of testimonial of faith in Jesus Christ by ordinary individuals, to the point of death if necessary, rather than the miraculous intercessions that fill medieval saints' legends.

Even though the Red Cross Knight is initially ignorant of his own identity, his allegorical armament suggests that he functions as a Protestant Everyman. Spenser's 'Letter to Raleigh' announces that the knight wears the 'armour of a Christian man specified by Saint Paul'. It includes the Girdle of Truth, Breastplate of Righteousness, Footwear of the Gospel of Peace, Shield of Faith, Helmet of Salvation, and Sword of the Spirit, 'which is the worde of God' (Eph. 6. 1–17). Embracing Paul rather than Peter, Luther led Protestants in applying the Pauline Epistles as the basis for belief in justification by faith, as opposed to the Roman Catholic doctrine of justification by good works. The knight's incapacity to wield his symbolic weapons effectively accords with the doctrines of human depravity and irresistible grace. Although the Shield of Faith is all-important, the prominence of the Sword of the Spirit calls attention to the role of Bible reading in salvation theology. The complementary operation of scriptural revelation and a justifying faith affords a basis for Protestant theology.

At the outset of his quest to save Una's imprisoned parents, Adam and

Eve, the Red Cross Knight has not yet learned to surrender confidence in human power and rely unquestioningly, as an instrument of grace, upon the Shield of Faith and Sword of the Spirit. Just as Una personifies the oneness of 'truth', the Dwarf who accompanies her may personify the operation of human reason subordinate to Christian faith. In the opening encounter with Error, the knight wins a clumsy victory. Even though Una exhorts him to 'Add faith unto your force, and be not faint' (1, i, 19), he strangles the monster with his bare hands in a striking departure from the traditional saint's legend. Only then does he employ the sword to deliver the coup de grâce. The dragonets who 'sucked vp their dying mothers blood' (1, i, 25) may recall Jesuits or clandestine priests. Their cannibalistic feast upon the body and blood of their monstrous parent parodies the doctrine of transubstantiation and Mass offered by the Roman Church, itself parodied as an unholy mother.

That the Red Cross Knight has erred in battle with Error is apparent in the ensuing encounter with Archimago, a more deceptive enemy to holiness whose friar's habit of 'long blacke weedes' and seclusion in a 'little lowly Hermitage' convey an external appearance of austere piety. Although that arch-magician and maker of dissimulating images deceives both Red Cross and Una, his tales of popes and saints and studies in 'Magick bookes and artes of sundry kindes' invite the reader to identify him with the Roman Antichrist and with reformist stereotypes concerning Roman Catholic hypocrisy and superstition (1, i, 29, 34–6). During the Elizabethan age, Protestant polemicists vilified recusant priests as wizards and necromancers.

Readers have long recognised that the Book of Revelation affords a model for the apocalyptic conflict in Book 1 of *The Faerie Queene*. The Red Cross Knight is a variation of a warrior named Faithful and True (i.e., Christ), who rides upon a White Horse and defeats the forces of Antichrist (Rev. 19). The contrasting figures of Una and Duessa invoke interpretation of the Woman Clothed with the Sun, the apocalyptic figure who flees into the wilderness under attack from the demonic dragon (Rev. 12), and the Whore of Babylon (Rev. 17) in terms of the prophecy of conflict between 'true' and 'false' churches. The knight's incapacity to differentiate between the respective claims of Una, whose black mantle conceals radiant beauty, and Duessa, whose gaudy costume misrepresents her as Fidessa ('faith'), dramatises the individual Christian's difficulty in differentiating between 'images' of competing churches. Nonetheless, Duessa's parentage clearly identifies her with the papacy:

> Borne the sole daughter of an Emperour,
> He that the wide West vnder his rule has,
> And high hath set his throne, where *Tiberis* doth pas.   (1, ii, 22)

The Red Cross Knight's inconstancy towards Una, a surrogate for Elizabeth I, who employed the motto, *Semper Una* ('always one') and the heraldic colours of white and black, allegorises apostasy.

Following Una's abandonment by Red Cross, her sojourn at the house of Corceca dramatises abuses associated with 'blind' devotion and monasticism. That sightless mother performs ceaseless acts of formulaic religiosity:

> that old woman day and night did pray
> Upon her beades devoutly penitent;
> Nine hundred *Pater nosters* every day,
> And thrise nine hundred *Aves* she was wont to say. (I, iii, 13)

Her incessant telling of rosary beads, like those carried by Archimago, link her to Catholic devotion. Corceca's deaf daughter, Abessa, personifies incapacity to hear 'truth'. As *abbess* at a disorderly house, she alludes to monastic corruption. Her failure to observe her vow of celibacy links her to Duessa, just as it embodies Protestant allegations that the religious orders nurtured sexual immorality.

Abessa's lover, Kirkrapine ('church robbery'), personifies the alleged failure of the Church of Rome to devote alms and church wealth to preaching and the charitable care of the poor and needy. Instead, he robs

> Churches of their ornaments,
> And poore mens boxes of their due reliefe,
> Which given was to them for good intents. (I, iii, 17)

The episode alludes obliquely to Henry VIII's Dissolution of the Monasteries when the Lion, a personification of monarchical power, suppresses the disorderliness of Corceca's household. Nonetheless, Kirkrapine's appropriation of church 'ornaments' and other 'holy things' is problematic because it also gives him the appearance of a Protestant iconoclast. He symbolises a complex cluster of allegations concerning misappropriation of ecclesiastical wealth, indiscretions of Catholic religious orders, and excesses of Protestant iconoclasts.

A variety of adventures experienced by the Red Cross Knight and Una personify other religious concerns. Like the Woman Clothed with the Sun, Una flees into the wilderness where she encounters fauns and satyrs, whose ignorance of 'truth' leads them to worship her like an idol (canto vi). She in turn strives to inculcate Christian faith in them. The knight encounters Sans Foy, Sans Joy and Sans Loy, Saracen knights who consort with Duessa and personify faithlessness, joylessness (i.e., despair) and lawlessness. His encounter with humans metamorphosed into trees, Fradubio ('Friar Doubt') and Fraelissa ('Sister Frail'), affords an ironic mirror image of the knight's own predicament. Fradubio had lost human form through dalliance with Fidessa-Duessa. As a variation of faithlessness attacked in Jesus' Parable of the House on the Rock and the House on the Sand (Matt. 7. 24–7), the House of Pride draws the Red Cross Knight in as one guilty of pride (canto iv). He witnesses the pageant of the Seven Deadly Sins: Idleness (who wears a monklike habit), Gluttony, Lechery, Avarice, Envy and Wrath, with Satan (Pride) driving the team. The tableau is presided over by Lucifera, a feminine variation of that foremost sin.

The low point of the Red Cross Knight's fall into sin comes at the Castle of Orgoglio, an embodiment of pride tied more specifically to alleged failures of Roman Catholicism. Willingly removing the Armour of God in order to lie with Duessa, the knight suffers defeat by a giant who represents a projection of the knight's own sinfulness. Orgoglio's liaison with Duessa identifies the monster with human depravity, the 'pride' of carnal desire, and theological error. Aligned with the worldly kings who commit fornication with the Whore of Babylon (Rev. 17), he appears to personify Spanish Catholicism in the historical allegory. Duessa's wearing of a papal tiara (I, vii, 16) associates the golden cup that she holds aloft (I, viii, 14), as she rides her Seven-Headed Beast, with the doctrine of transubstantiation and Roman-rite Mass. Imprisoned in Orgoglio's dungeon, the Red Cross Knight is rescued by Prince Arthur, who here personifies unalloyed Holiness, only to flirt with suicide when Despair plays the role of a parodic preacher, in the manner of Archimago, by distorting Paul's Letter to Romans to suggest he is eternally damned.

Following Una's intervention to express what Despair has suppressed, the promise of salvation contingent upon the unmerited gift of divine grace, the scene shifts to the House of Holiness (canto x). Offering an antithesis to the ignorance of both Archimago and Corceca, the household of Dame Caelia (Heavenly) affords a compressed summary of religious doctrine. Her three daughters personify the theological virtues according to St Paul. The seniority of Fidelia (Faith) and Speranza (Hope) over their fecund sister, Charissa (Charity), accords with Protestant understanding that divine grace saves believers when it operates through inward faith rather than charitable works in the external world. Under tutelage from Fidelia, who holds aloft a book symbolic of the Bible (or the New Testament or Book of Revelation), the Red Cross Knight moves beyond conviction of sin to faith that divine grace has imputed him righteous. The previously inarticulate and illiterate knight comprehends fundamental theological truths.

Having encountered the Seven Bead-Men, who personify charitable deeds contingent upon faith, the knight ascends Mount Contemplation. He there encounters Contemplation, blind to this world but possessing spiritual insight, who affords a corrective alternative to the formulaic devotional practices. The antithesis of Archimago, this 'true' hermit enables the Red Cross Knight to attain the high point of his spiritual progress in an apocalyptic vision of the New Jerusalem (heaven), before instructing him to descend from the mountaintop to complete his obligation of active service in the world.

Controversy exists concerning Red Cross' climactic victory over the great Dragon (Satan according to Rev. 20) in canto xi. Because of the indeterminacy of Spenserian allegory, definitive interpretation of the knight's relationship to Christ, or whether, indeed, he actually becomes Christ during that apocalyptic conflict, is elusive. Nevertheless, scholars agree that the well of life and tree of life (Rev. 22. 1–2) that succour the knight during the three-day battle involve sacramental allegory. His 'baptised hands' identify immersion in the well (1, xi, 36) with baptism. Dispute focuses on the salvific balm that flows from the tree: does it warrant comparison with the Eucharist or extreme unction? Argument based upon Spenser's presumed reading of Greek patristic sources has led one scholar to conclude that the Red Cross Knight reenacts the Easter liturgy whereby communicants undergo deification, receives chrismation with sacramental balm, and typifies the Harrowing of Hell by Christ resurrected.[14] Nonetheless, reference to only two sacraments seems conclusive. Protestants reduced the seven sacraments of medieval Christendom to the pair that possess scriptural warrant: baptism and the Lord's Supper.

Although religious allegory occupies a lesser place in the remainder of Spenser's romantic epic, Holiness affords a foundation for the succeeding books, which concern Temperance, Chastity, Friendship, Justice and Courtesy. In Book II, for example, Mammon recalls Despair as a parodic preacher who offers counsel on intemperance. In the key episode of the Bower of Bliss in canto xii, the seductress Acrasia is far more alluring than Error or Duessa, but her personification of intemperance also hints at a satirical portrayal of the Roman Church as a devouring mother who preys upon her offspring.[15] Books III and IV are deeply implicated in Reformation discourses concerning sex and marriage; indeed, an ongoing series of violent failures of wedlock interrogates, or subverts, Protestant idealisation of married chastity.[16]

Building upon the 'Legend of Holiness' in the most extensive religious allegory in *The Faerie Queene* other than Book I, Book V is imbued with apocalyptic rhetoric familiar from patriotic sermons and commentaries before and after the destruction of the Spanish Armada. Britomart (Chastity) affords a flattering representation of Queen Elizabeth in rescuing Artegall (Justice) and slaying Radigund, an embodiment of female misgovernment associated with the Catholic Queens, Mary I and Mary, Queen of Scots.

Duessa's trial at the court of Mercilla (Mercy), another personification of Queen Elizabeth, and the ambiguous circumstances of her execution drama-tise the demise of the queen of Scotland (canto ix). Isis Church, where Britomart experiences a prophetic vision of her marriage to Artegall, shelters vegetarian priests whose avoidance of flesh and wine parodies the Roman-rite Mass (canto vii).

Book v addresses the beleaguered Protestant cause both at home and abroad. Arthur's defeat of the Soldan, a figure that refers to alleged Islamic despotism and Philip II of Spain, alludes to the destruction of the Spanish Armada as a providential deliverance of England. The flight into the wilderness of widow Belge (Belgium and Holland) marks her, like Una, as a type of the Woman Clothed with the Sun. Belge's territory has fallen under the dominion of Geryoneo, whose Inquisition allegorises the tyrannous sway of the Spanish Hapsburgs. As Governor General of the Netherlands, the Duke of Alva engaged in a notorious reign of terror.

Anti-Mass satire represents Geryoneo as a monstrous double of Orgoglio. The slaughter of widow Belge's sons (i.e., provinces) upon an idolatrous altar recalls martyrdoms at Orgoglio's Castle, just as the 'sinfull sacrifice' of the 'flesh of men' and the 'powring forth their bloud' at Geryoneo's Church functions as an anti-Mass allegory (v, x, 28). Prince Arthur's bloody slaughter of Idol at Geryoneo's idolatrous shrine concludes with an out-rageous pun: 'Then downe to ground fell that deformed *Masse*' (v, xi, 32; my emphasis). Related puns mock the Roman-rite Eucharist by association with Orgoglio's laughable lack of substance as a 'monstrous *masse* of earthly slime, / Puft vp with emptie wind, and fild with sinfull crime' (I, vii, 9). Anticipating the death of Geryoneo's Idol, Arthur's decapitation of Orgoglio constitutes a lurid parody of the transubstantiation of the elements of bread and wine into the body and blood of Christ. Wallowing in gore, the giant's headless body vanishes away at the moment of death: 'and of that monstrous *mas* / Was nothing left, but like an emptie bladder was' (I, viii, 24).

Allegorisation of affairs in France and Ireland concludes Book v. Burbon's abandonment of the Shield of Faith that he received from the Red Cross Knight represents the recent conversion to Catholicism of Henri du Bourbon in order to gain the throne of France, personified as Flourdelis. Artegall's continued quest to rescue Irena (Ireland) fails to resolve the discord with which the poet was all too familiar. Although the knight rescues Irena and decapitates Grantorto, a personification of injustice associated with Roman Catholic tyranny, his effort to bring justice to Irena's land breaks off with his recall to the court of Gloriana. Artegall's encounter with Envy, Detraction and the Blatant Beast allude to the scandal that destroyed the career of Spenser's patron, Lord Grey de Wilton, following the Smerwick massacre.

The ensuing 'Legend of Courtesy' closes with renewed apocalyptic onslaught by the Blatant Beast. Returning to issues encountered at Corceca's irreligious abbey, the text seems to endorse destruction of Catholic 'idolatry' at the same time that it attacks the excesses of Protestant iconoclasm. The depredation of the Blatant Beast thus reveals depravity concealed within a monastery, 'In which what filth and ordure did appeare, / Were yrkesome to report' (VI, xii, 24). The double-edged satire attacks both monastic abuses and the failure of iconoclasm, when the monster

> robd the Chancell, and the deskes downe threw,
> And Altars fouled, and blasphemy spoke,
> And th'Images for all their goodly hew,
> Did cast to ground. (VI, xii, 25)

Destruction of the old religion did not ensure that 'pure' religious practices would replace it.

Although Calidore as the Knight of Courtesy succeeds in restraining the Blatant Beast, its escape postpones resolution of apocalyptic expectations. The ending of the entire poem in the fragmentary 'Cantos of Mutabilitie' looks towards the end of time in a way that recalls the unresolved conclusion of the 'Legend of Holiness':

> But thence-forth all shall rest eternally
> With Him that is the God of Sabbaoth hight:
> O that great Sabbaoth God, grant me that Sabaoths sight. (VII, viii, 2)

This profound yearning for release from worldly corruption represents a fitting conclusion to a body of poetry that returns again and again to devotional failures of both individuals and churchmen who should minister to their spiritual needs, but rarely do so.

NOTES

1 Quotations are from *The Geneva Bible*, facsimile edn, ed. Lloyd Berry (Madison: University of Wisconsin Press, 1969).
2 For a review of scholarship on the subject, see John N. King, 'Was Spenser a Puritan?', *Sp. St.* 6 (1985), 1–31.
3 Anthea Hume, *Edmund Spenser: Protestant Poet* (Cambridge: Cambridge University Press, 1984), pp. 14, 21–3.
4 Ed. by W. L. Renwick (London: Eric Partridge, 1934), p. 110.
5 David G. Norbrook, *Poetry and Politics in the English Renaissance* (London: Routledge and Kegan Paul, 1984), pp. 106–56; John N. King, *Spenser's Poetry and the Reformation Tradition* (Princeton: Princeton University Press, 1990), esp. pp. 110–47.
6 King, *Spenser's Poetry*, esp. pp. 183–232.

7 Darryl J. Gless, *Interpretation and Theology in Spenser* (Cambridge: Cambridge University Press, 1994).

8 Kenneth Borris, *Spenser's Poetics of Prophecy in* The Faerie Queene v, English Literary Studies Monograph Series, no. 52 (Victoria: University of Victoria, 1991), esp. pp. 19–35.

9 Richard Mallette, *Spenser and the Discourses of Reformation England* (Lincoln: University of Nebraska Press, 1997).

10 Virgil K. Whitaker, *The Religious Basis of Spenser's Thought* (Stanford: Stanford University Press, 1950); John N. Wall, *Transformations of the Word: Spenser, Herbert, and Vaughan* (Athens: University of Georgia Press, 1988), pp. 88–127.

11 E.g. Patrick Collinson, *The Religion of Protestants: The Church in English Society, 1559–1625* (Oxford: Clarendon Press, 1982), pp. 107–111, 138.

12 Harold L. Weatherby, *Mirrors of Celestial Grace: Patristic Theology in Spenser's Allegory* (Toronto: University of Toronto Press, 1994).

13 For readings of Book I, see King, *Spenser's Poetry*, pp. 183–231; Gless, *Interpretation and Theology*, pp. 48–171; Mallette, *Spenser and Discourses*, pp. 17–49.

14 Weatherby, *Mirrors of Celestial Grace*, pp. 38–43.

15 King, *Spenser's Poetry*, pp. 101–2.

16 Mallette, *Spenser and Discourses*, pp. 113–42.

FURTHER READING

Kenneth Borris, *Spenser's Poetics of Prophecy in* The Faerie Queene v. English Literary Studies Monograph Series 52 (Victoria: University of Victoria, 1991).

Patrick Collinson, *The Elizabethan Puritan Movement* (London: Jonathan Cape, 1967).

Darryl J. Gless, *Interpretation and Theology in Spenser* (Cambridge: Cambridge University Press, 1994).

Christopher Haigh, *The English Reformations: Religion, Politics, and Society under the Tudors* (Oxford: Clarendon Press, 1993).

John N. King, *Spenser's Poetry and the Reformation Tradition* (Princeton: Princeton University Press, 1990).

Richard Mallette, *Spenser and the Discourses of Reformation England* (Lincoln: University of Nebraska Press, 1997).

David G. Norbrook, *Poetry and Politics in the English Renaissance* (London: Routledge and Kegan Paul, 1984).

John N. Wall, *Transformations of the Word: Spenser, Herbert, and Vaughan* (Athens: University of Georgia Press, 1988).

Harold L. Weatherby, *Mirrors of Celestial Grace: Patristic Theology in Spenser's Allegory* (Toronto: University of Toronto Press, 1994).

Virgil K. Whitaker, *The Religious Basis of Spenser's Thought* (Stanford: Stanford University Press, 1950).

11

COLIN BURROW

Spenser and classical traditions

'Classical traditions' is a less than appealing title. In fact, the phrase conjures up a whole gallery of misery: an unhealthy subservience to Virgil, Ovid, Homer and the rest, an unquestioning regard for the authority of antiquity, a failure to value individual creativity, and a lack of responsiveness to the immediate pressures of the present. What could be worse?

Spenser's response to classical traditions is usually exempted from these strictures. His eighteenth-century admirers often characterise his response to his reading as dreamily eclectic, in a manner which enabled him to make something entirely his own out of his classical reading. He is also often said to have lacked a very precise understanding of the classics. Thomas Greene, for example, suggests that Spenser lacks the awareness of anachronism – that is, a sense of how his culture differs from that of ancient Rome – which was the central emerging element in the ways Renaissance poets responded to their classical predecessors. In *The Faerie Queene*, Greene claims, 'historical self-consciousness seems sporadic and dim'.[1] The chief aim of this chapter is to destroy once and for all this vision of Spenser as a happy anachronist, and to show how Spenser responded in highly sophisticated ways both to the complexities of his classical originals and to the uncertainties of his time. From the interplay of these two forces Spenser generates some of his most subtle and topical writing.

First though it is necessary to get a sense of what 'classical traditions' were in Spenser's period, because they were not then what they are now. At the Merchant Taylors' School Spenser would have been required to speak Latin even during breaks from lessons, and to spend the majority of his time in the classroom translating classical texts of gradated difficulty, from grammatical text-books such as Erasmus' *De Copia* to the giddy heights of Homer. Latin was for him a language in which you joked with your friends as well as one in which you performed for your schoolmaster. The statutes of his school required students to endure a gruelling timetable which began at 7 am, and even specified where they should pee,[2] but they omitted details of the curriculum. It is likely, though, that he was required to memorise at least twelve lines of Ovid a week, and he would have read Ovid, Terence, Horace and Virgil as models for verse composition. Virgil's *Eclogues* and *Georgics* were favoured starting-points for the study of Latin, and were read side by side with post-classical imitations of them, such as the Eclogues of Mantuan.[3] A list of books from Merchant Taylors' in 1599 shows that mythological handbooks and dictionaries were also a major part of the apparatus of learning.[4] This work on classical languages was not cut off from the vernacular: Spenser's schoolmaster, Richard Mulcaster, was keen that English language and literature should be enriched by absorbing classical words and texts.

Students of the classics were also encouraged to make their reading contribute to their writing by constructing 'common-place books' for themselves as they read. These were notebooks divided by headings, or 'loci communes' such as 'death', 'marriage', 'chastity', under which readers would record passages from ancient and modern literature. At a later point, if they were to compose an oration or a poem on one of these topics, they would return to the appropriate page in their common-place book, which might record the thoughts of a whole variety of authorities, and selectively adapt what they found there to the occasion in hand. The textual integrity of literary authorities was in this culture secondary to present rhetorical needs: if you wanted to write about rivers you might find a passage of Horace and a piece of Ariosto and a section of Ovid all on the same page of your common-place book, and you might fuse them. If you needed (as Spenser's friend Gabriel Harvey did) to consider how best to govern an unruly province such as Ireland, you might read Livy, pen in hand, in order to draw constructive advice from Roman forms of colonisation.[5] The classics served present occasions.

Responses to classical texts were every bit as various in the sixteenth century as they are today. Early modern editions of Virgil often presented humdrum glosses for schoolchildren side by side with fragments of mora-lised allegorical commentary. Spenser might have read an anonymous vernacular life of Virgil which presented the poet as a magician-trickster,[6] and he certainly did read Donatus' life of Virgil which presents the poet as a Platonic lover of boys ('With regard to pleasure, he was partial to boys', reads Donatus; an anxious later writer inserted the rider: 'But good men have thought that he loved boys as Socrates loved Alcibiades, and Plato his sweetheart').[7] This detail works its way into E. K.'s anxious note on pederastic love in *The Shepheardes Calender* ('In thys place seemeth to be some sauour of disorderly loue, which the learned call paederastice: but it is gathered beside his meaning. For who that hath red Plato his dialogue called Alcibiades, Xenophon and Maximus Tyrius of Socrates opinions, may easily perceiue, that such loue is muche to be alowed and liked of').[8] Spenser's Virgil was more sportive than the Virgil who has been portrayed since the nineteenth century as the poet who sings the melancholy costs of empire. He also used the first person far more than his twentieth-century incarnation. The text of the *Aeneid* which Spenser read began by summarising Virgil's literary career to date (in Thomas Phaer's translation):

> I that my slender Oten Pipe in verse was wont to sounde
> Of woods, and next to that I taught for husbandmen the ground,
> How fruite vnto their greedy lust they might constraine to bring,
> A worke of thankes: Lo now of Mars, and dreadfull warres I singe.[9]

Spenser used the personal voice of this pseudo-Virgilian proem to start *The Faerie Queene*. He also attempted to make *The Shepheardes Calender* look as much like a sixteenth-century Virgilian text as he could manage by including woodcuts which are strikingly similar to those included in editions of Virgil such as that edited by Pietro Bembo and Andreaus Naugerius (Venice, 1552), in which Virgil's shepherds are depicted as sixteenth-century rustics.[10]

These features of Spenser's printed works have often led critics to claim that Spenser sought to follow Virgil's literary career, from the low form of pastoral, through the middle level of georgic (which depicts labour and sweaty toil) to epic (which tells of fierce wars and heroic actions). This is far too simple a picture.[11] Quite apart from the fact that Spenser wrote no georgics (although he does occasionally compare the labour of his muse to teams of oxen in *The Faerie Queene*), the Virgilian career pattern cannot accommodate the *Fowre Hymnes*, the *Amoretti*, the *Prothalamion* or the *Complaints*.[12] Appearing in 1591, between the two instalments of *The Faerie Queene*, the *Complaints* volume in particular looks like a highly unclassical intrusion of the peculiarly sixteenth-century-cum-Chaucerian genre of complaint into the midst of Spenser's career. In fact it shows Spenser actively responding to the whole range of the canon of Virgil's poems as it was presented in sixteenth-century editions. *Complaints* contains 'Virgils Gnat', a close translation of the pseudo-Virgilian 'Culex' 'long since dedicated to the most noble and excellent Lord, the Earle of Leicester, late deceased'. The Latin original of this poem was often presented in early modern editions as one of Virgil's 'opuscula', or minor works from the poet's youth. As Donatus put it, 'After this – though he was only 26 – he composed the *Catalecton*, as well as pieces about Priapus, as well as epigrams, as well as curses, along with poems about ciris and the gnat. The argument of this last runs as follows: just as a shepherd, wearied by the heat, had fallen asleep under a tree and a serpent from the marsh was rushing up to him, a gnat flew out and stung the shepherd between the temples. At once the shepherd crushed the gnat and slew the serpent, erecting also a tomb for the gnat.'[13] Spenser's translation is close (although he cannot resist adding a reflection on the mutability of fortune to his original), and its presence among the *Complaints* suggests that he found in it a Virgilian precedent for complaining poems written early in a poet's career.

Spenser's belief that the youthful Virgil wrote the 'Culex' and the *Ciris*, an epyllion (or mini-epic) on the desperate passion of Scylla, had a profound effect on how he responded to Virgil, and indeed to the classical tradition more widely. These highly learned epyllia were written well after Virgil's death, although no one knows exactly when.[14] They are the products of elaborately learned 'neoteric' poets (that is, poets who sought to pack sophisticated literary allusions into a short narrative form). They allude repeatedly to Virgil's mature works, as well as showing the influence of Virgil's epic successors Ovid and Statius. These poems gave to Spenser a topsy-turvy view of Virgil's career and literary influence: he would have thought that these highly allusive poems were actually the point from which Virgil's art began, and that in Virgil's early works lay the seeds of subsequent epic poetry. Spenser's tendency to allude to multiple sources at once, and to make what appear to be deliberately incongruous juxtapositions between earlier and later treatments of a classical topos, is not the product of uncritical eclecticism. When Guyon undergoes his brief allegorical cameo Odyssey to Acrasia's bower in II, xii of *The Faerie Queene* critics often casually remark that this shows that Spenser had only a dim knowledge of Homer. Spenser is in fact almost certain to have read some Homer at school. In that mini-Odyssey he is allusively miniaturising a familiar classical model in order to say to his readers, 'you know all about the *Odyssey*: look, I can pack it all in to forty stanzas'. It displays the same literary knowingness as the 'Culex', in which the gnat packs the full horrors of the Virgilian underworld into a few lines. Spenser is the central figure in the Elizabethan neoteric movement. His love of impacted allusions, tales within tales, ecphrastic descriptions of pictures and places, does not set him in a dream-world apart from other classically inspired Elizabethan writers: it shows that he is the inspiring central presence in late sixteenth-century English classicism.

The pseudo-Virgilian poems meant a lot to Spenser. He associated them with moments of personal and generic transition, when poets and people are growing up. His clearest borrowing from the pseudo-Virgilian *Ciris* occurs when he describes the youth of the heroine Britomart in Book III of *The Faerie Queene*. The *Ciris* is about a girl who falls in love with her father's enemy and decides to cut off a magic lock from his hair, a lock which protects his city from defeat. At the end of the tale she is, like one of the heroines of Ovid's *Metamorphoses*, transformed into a seabird for her treachery. This poem gave Spenser reason to suppose that Virgil and Ovid were much more similar than they appear to many readers today. His use of it in his epic also allowed him to give a sense that Britomart's future as an epic heroine was not pre-scripted for her, but could veer drastically off course and lock her into a metamorphic minor epic. After Britomart has seen Artegall in her father's magic mirror she seems to be teetering on the brink of inchastity and metamorphosis. As she herself admits, as someone in love with a man in a mirror, she is even worse off than Ovid's Narcissus:

> I fonder, then *Cephisus* foolish child,
> Who hauing vewed in a fountaine shere
> His face, was with the loue thereof beguild;
> I fonder loue a shade, the bodie farre exild.   (III, ii, 44)

Britomart's nurse Glauce does all the spitting and magical chanting of her pseudo-Virgilian original, with a bit of impious and decidedly un-Protestant praying added for good measure, and then instructs her charge to go and see the magician Merlin. From Merlin Britomart receives a prophecy of future greatness for her line, which persuades her to cease being a Scylla and turn into a dynastic heroine.

The vision of the future which Merlin gives Britomart is the first real burst of Virgilian prophecy in *The Faerie Queene*. In order to appreciate the influence of this aspect of Virgil on Spenser it helps to have some sense of the political aims of Virgil's epic in relation to Spenser's. The fifth-century commentator Servius (whose notes on the *Aeneid* were printed in almost all early modern editions) said that the intention of Virgil in writing the *Aeneid* was 'to imitate Homer and to praise Augustus through his ancestors'.[15] Virgil's *Aeneid* is about the foundation and pre-history of Rome, but it is also a highly topical poem which reflects on and seeks to direct the present life of Rome under Augustus through frequent anticipations of the city's future destiny. It gives a vision of 'empire without end' (I, 279), but also does not flinch from recognising the continuing effort, and particularly the battles against instinct, which are required to bring an empire into being and to sustain it. The *Aeneid* concentrates on these struggles to such an extent that some critics have seen it as encoding voices of counter-imperial regret, or even 'anti-Augustan' voices into its structure.[16] In Book VI Aeneas goes to the underworld and receives a prophecy from his dead father of the future of Rome. This prophetic vision ends with Augustus' nephew and heir Marcellus. He had died in 23 BC, only a handful of years before the poem's composition, and Virgil both draws attention to his early death and laments it. After this vision of a broken lineage Aeneas departs from the underworld through the gate of horn, which is the portal by which false dreams enter the world. The episode raises questions which are never fully laid to rest: are imperial visions delusive? Is there a future for Rome after Augustus?

The poem as we read it today (Virgil wished it to be burnt because it was unfinished, but this probably means that its style was less polished than he wished rather than that he had more narrative to write) ends with a perplexing reaffirmation of those questions, as the poem's hero, overcome with *furor* (a kind of wild rage from which almost all of what is painful in the poem derives), kills his adversary Turnus. By implication Aeneas thereby establishes the Roman line in Italy, and wins Turnus' fiancée Lavinia. Virgil, however, leaves us mid-way to the future at the end of the poem, as Turnus' soul flees resentfully to the underworld. Some of the uneasy emotions which this final episode leaves in the minds of its readers (Christian commentators frequently condemned Aeneas' killing of Turnus as merciless) were laid to rest in the version of the poem which most sixteenth-century readers knew, which included the 'thirteenth book' written by Maphaeus Veggius in the fifteenth century. This rounds the plot off into a dynastic tale. Aeneas and Lavinia marry and offer a potent symbol of dynastic continuity. Veggius' 'completion' of Virgil's poem had a great influence on the sixteenth-century epic tradition: heroes and heroines ultimately form dynastic partnerships and marry (at the end of Ariosto's *Orlando furioso*, for instance, Ruggiero marries Bradamante, and then reenacts Aeneas' killing of Turnus by defeating Rodomonte in single combat). This revised ending of the *Aeneid* had a profound though un-consummated influence on *The Faerie Queene*, since the ultimate, though unachieved, goal of its dynastic pair Britomart and Arthegall is to marry.

This takes us back to Britomart in Merlin's cave. When Britomart descends to the cave of Merlin there are clear signs that Spenser heard the echoes of political unease in the *Aeneid*. Britomart, like Aeneas in the underworld, receives an incomplete prophecy which breaks off abruptly:

> Then shall a royall virgin raine, which shall
> Stretch her white rod ouer the *Belgicke* shore,
> And the great Castle smite so sore with all,
> That it shall make him shake, and shortly learne to fall.

> But yet the end is not. There *Merlin* stayd,
> As ouercomen of the spirites powre,
> Or other ghastly spectacle dismayd,
> That secretly he saw, yet note discoure . . .   (III, iii, 49–50)

The whole story of Britomart's early life shows the extent to which classical influences interfuse with Spenser's efforts to think through the future of his nation and the nature of his epic. On one reading the early life of Britomart would show her growing up, not just emotionally but generically, as she moves from early Virgilian erotic epyllion into the world of epic, from young, metamorphic Virgil to imperial Virgil, and from a world of potential metamorphosis to one of dynastic generation. She goes through a career pattern not unlike Spenser's own, from Virgilian juvenilia to heroic narrative. This reading of the episode as a very self-conscious piece of literary imitation, however, is not the whole story. That Merlin's Virgilian prophecy breaks off as it does, pointing into the void beyond the age of Elizabeth, makes the episode more than a simple piece of literary Virgilianism. The anxiety about the future after the death of Augustus which is fleetingly registered at the end of *Aeneid* VI coincides with and nourishes Spenser's own Protestant fears about the succession of the dynasty after the death of his 'royall virgin', his queen who had so signally failed to resolve the issue of succession either by having children herself (which virgins rarely do) or by clearly indicating who her successor would be. That fear is both augmented and partially contained by linking the post-Elizabethan future with apocalyptic enthusiasm: will the realm disintegrate? Will the Antichrist finally be overthrown? In the tale of Britomart Spenser is not coldly juxtaposing Virgilian juvenilia with the mature voice of Virgilian prophecy, nor is he simply using Virgilian epic to praise his Queen: he is actively reworking the energies and the anxieties of his Virgilian pre-texts to suit the need of his immediate occasion. He is re-reading Virgilian imperial prophecy, responding to its doubts and uncertainties, and nervily checking to see if it fits his times. Britomart, of course, never does marry Artegall in the part of the poem which Spenser lived to write, for he, like Virgil, left behind him an incomplete poem, sprinkled, like the *Aeneid*, with half-lines to testify to its unfinished state. Spenser's attempt to make a dynastic epic for an unmarried, childless queen was bound to produce stress between the idealising world of the poem and political realities.

As well as creatively responding to the multiplicity of voices in the *Aeneid*, *The Faerie Queene* also engages with some major sixteenth-century debates about how the poem was to be interpreted and imitated. Ariosto's *Orlando furioso* presented one model: it frequently imitates the marvellous and magical moments in the *Aeneid*, and weaves them into an episodic and highly digressive structure derived from fifteenth-century romances. Ariosto's heroes systematically rewrite the ethical priorities of the *Aeneid*: where Virgil's hero is motivated by *pietas* (dutiful affection towards the gods, family and country), Ariosto's are driven by *pietá*, or pity. This quality contributes to the digressive structure of Ariosto's poem: if one of his pitying heroes sees a virgin in trouble he drops everything in order to help (or pursue) her, thus delaying any imperial task he may have in hand. In the aftermath of the publication of the final version of *Orlando furioso* in 1532, there were extensive critical arguments about the appropriateness of such digressive plot structures to the epic. These formal debates were often linked with ethical arguments about whether heroes, especially Christian heroes, should be motivated primarily by love or by martial rage, pity, piety, or political loyalty. These arguments are increasingly enacted within the structure of classicising epics in the romance tradition (they are the driving force behind Torquato Tasso's *Gerusalemme liberata*), as authors and heroes alike battle to separate themselves from deceptive women in order at once to obey their rulers, and to replicate the structural unity and animating virtues of Virgilian epic. This conflict within the sixteenth-century epic tradition had a direct influence on Spenser. It means that Virgil often acts as a form of superego within *The Faerie Queene*, pulling the heroes away from pity and passionate self-absorption, away from women, and away too from the digressions which had characterised sixteenth-century Italian epic romance.[17] Spenser's wish to reconstruct the moral rigour and the perceived structural purity of Virgil generates some of the moments in *The Faerie Queene* with which readers have felt most uneasy: as Guyon sails past pitiful siren voices to destroy the Bower of Bliss, most readers rebel against the 'rigour pittilesse' (II, xii, 83) with which he destroys the pleasant bowers and palace brave of Acrasia. The moment is acutely awkward: it shows Spenser attempting to exorcise from his hero and his poem a digressive form of romance, in which knights abandon their course to pursue pitiful ladies. And it shows him doing so with a punitive violence which exceeds anything in Virgil. Particularly disturbing for contemporary readers is the way issues of gender and questions of genre are interfolded: resisting a woman becomes a means of moving closer to Virgilian heroism.

Similar moments of pitiless destruction later in the poem have another aspect to them as well. Spenser is well aware that his queen is female; he is also well aware that she cultivated a reputation for pity. Throughout *The Faerie Queene*, and especially in the second instalment printed in 1596, Spenser uses the violence of Virgilian epic to persuade his reluctant queen to a more active 'male' policy towards Catholic Spain and towards the Catholic population of Ireland. In Books IV–VI the level of direct Virgilian allusion diminishes significantly, but Spenser's desire to turn both his genre and his queen towards Virgilian austerity comes to have a shaping effect on the structure of the poem. Political need intersects with the imitation of classical models to create this shift towards just violence. This is most apparent in v, ix, when Mercilla (an allegorical representation of Elizabeth I) is finally urged to condemn Duessa (a version of the Catholic rival for the throne Mary, Queen of Scots) to death. The reluctant decision of the pityful Mercilla to condemn Duessa is underwritten by Aeneas' pained effort in Book vi of the *Aeneid* to override his emotional attachment to Dido, Queen of Carthage in order to found his future empire in Italy.[18] Spenser's imitation of that moment of heroic *pietas* is designed to give an epic precedent for the much-publicised reluctance of Elizabeth to rid the realm of the Catholic threat posed by Mary, Queen of Scots. And it is designed to urge her to do more. The killing of the Amazon Radigund (v, vii, 33) and of Malengin (v, ix, 19) reiterate the point that England needs repeatedly to reenact the disturbing execution of Turnus with which the *Aeneid* had ended, in order to sustain its empire: it needs not a romance of unending pity, but a reiterated epic of infinitely repeated killings. These episodes urge Spenser's Queen to reenact, and then to enact again, epic violence. Virgil serves present occasions.

Spenser's other great classical model was Ovid. Born almost thirty years after Virgil, he is often regarded as a more playful, less politically orthodox poet than his predecessor. His early love elegies (the *Amores*) and erotic poems on how to get a girl (the *Ars Amatoria*) seem calculated to clash with the efforts of his Emperor Augustus to renovate the mores of Rome by tightening laws on marriage and sexual conduct. It was partly because of these works that Ovid was exiled in 8 AD to Tomi on the Black Sea, from where he wrote poetry of exile. In the *Tristia* Ovid represents his career in retrospect as one in which political authority thwarted his works: his exile broke off his composition of the *Fasti*, and made him want to burn the *Metamorphoses* as Virgil had wanted to burn the *Aeneid* (although Ovid mischievously notes that there were far too many manuscripts of his poem for him to be able to burn them all). Ovid had an incalculable influence on Spenser, and his influence mingles inextricably with that of Virgil: Ovid's unfinished calendrical poem on the feasts of the Roman year (the *Fasti*) is fused with Virgil's Eclogues (as well as the popular vernacular handbook *The Kalendar of Shepherds*) in Spenser's triumphantly completed *Shepheardes Calendar*. In *The Faerie Queene* too the linking of Ovid and Virgil is instinctive. When Spenser imitates the meeting of Aeneas with his mother Venus in Carthage, he blurs the grandeur of Virgil with a layer of Ovid: his goddess is Belphoebe, who is met by the scarcely heroic Bragadocchio in an Ovidian forest.[19] The rapes which so often occur in Ovidian woodland landscape seem to threaten, but are averted in an almost burlesquing blend of Virgilian epiphany and Ovidian salaciousness.

Ovid's great work was the *Metamorphoses*, an epic collection of tales about changes of shape, which is organised with self-consciously audacious looseness to form a chronological series from the creation of the world to Ovid's own time. It provided Spenser with stories, ecphrases (rhetorical descriptions of pictures) and imaginary locales throughout *The Faerie Queene*. It shapes the poetics, politics and metaphysics of the poem, and that influence is registered from its very first cantos. Throughout Book I Ovid is a continual underpresence: his shadow is immediately cast over the wood of Error (I, i, 8–9), which is introduced by a catalogue of trees based on the wood which gathers around the singer Orpheus in *Metamorphoses* 10. It is from Ovid that Spenser then generates the dreamy and potentially delusive underworld of the Cave of Sleep in I, i, 39–44,[20] before he springs his own underworld on us, in which Night begs Aesculapius to cure Sans Foy (I, v, 31–44). Spenser's underworld, sifted from Virgil and fused with Ovid's sophisticated rewritings of the Virgilian underworld, is more Ovidian than anything in Ovid. It artfully impacts all the elements of the classical nether world into even fewer lines than Virgil's gnat had done. The relationship between Spenser and Ovid is not an easy one, however: hovering over these Ovidian *loci* are ghosts which embody the shadowy double of Spenser's literary effort to revive pagan texts. The Ovidian Cave of Sleep is not just an eclectic Spenserian fusion of Ovid and Chaucer and Ariosto:[21] it is also the source of the phantasm who impersonates Una, and whose coupling with a squire first leads the Red Cross Knight to abandon his lady and begin his career of error. Spenser's imitations of Ovid are at every stage conscious of the potential duplicity of classical sources, and register Spenser's awareness that in imitating pagan literature he might be invoking deceitful ghosts who might take over his heroes and his poem. The underworld in which Night seeks Aesculapius shows the same self-consciousness about Spenser's literary project: in it a pagan character attempts to revive a wounded and explicitly faithless hero, Sans Foy ('Faithless').[22] These Ovidian *loci* are some of the high points of Spenser's art because they actively respond to the fear that classical literature may be a dream factory which seductively beguiles a poet into a world of faithless delusions.

It is conventional in Spenser criticism to oppose the influences of Ovid and Virgil: Virgil is often supposed to have given Spenser an imperial prophetic impulse, and to have represented for him a structural ideal of the forward-looking, politically orthodox, single-threaded narrative to which *The Faerie Queene* continually aspires. Ovid is usually said to have given him a counterpoising set of concerns. He is the source of enrapturing visual tableaux (such as the tapestries in Malecasta's castle, *FQ*, III, i, 34–8) which delay the poem and allure their fictional viewers and literal readers alike.

And it is from Ovid that Spenser derives a 'matrix' of concerns with change and narrative multiplicity which implies scepticism about the political claims of rulers to be able to shape time to their own ends.[23] Like many conventional beliefs these are part truths. The two Roman poets are in some ways adversaries: at the end of the *Metamorphoses* Ovid rehearses the early history of Rome and produces an audacious rewriting of the story of Aeneas, in which what were subordinate episodes in Virgil's poem become pretexts for extended tales of passion and change: as the Trojans reach Scylla and Charybdis Ovid embarks on the shaggy dog story of Glaucus and Scylla, which leads him to abandon the Trojan forces mid-way in their passage to Italy (*Met.* XII, 728–XIV, 74). Ovid forcibly imprints his metamorphic concerns on his predecessor's subject matter, almost to the extent of making Virgil appear to be trying to be an Ovidian poet. Neither of these two writers are either simply for or against the austere and potentially dictatorial regime which the Emperor Augustus sought to establish. Underlying Augustan ideals was a belief that political life depended on fostering a set of multi-threaded virtues, such as piety and justice. The 'auctoritas' of the Emperor (the moral foundation of his rule) depended on his continually displaying and continually renewing these virtues, which exist more as a process than as a finally realised state. As Karl Galinsky writes: 'Life is a process, characterized by steady toil and struggle, rather than restful repose at a fixed point. It is more meaningful to work toward a goal than to enjoy the fruits of reaching it.'[24] That sounds like a comment on Spenser: in fact it is about the Augustan ethos as it is presented by Virgil. Ovid too shows a taste for change and multiplicity which is not simply 'anti-Augustan': many of the architectural features in Augustus' own villa show a taste for strange hybrid creatures of a kind that people Ovid's poem, and many moments in Virgil, such as the account of the metempsychosis of souls in Book VI, or the transformation of Polydorus into a tree in Book II, show a similar taste for the changeable and the ontologically transitional.[25] Augustan poetry contributed to the complex political culture of its period rather than passively reflecting it.

This more complex view of the relations between Virgil and Ovid, and of their relations to Augustan orthodoxies, provides an extremely suggestive set of cues for interpreting Spenser's treatment of their works. Virgil and Ovid are routinely imitated side by side in *The Faerie Queene*, and their relationship modulates between counterpoint and coalescence. *The Faerie Queene* is a poem which, like Virgil's *Aeneid*, aims to refashion its monarch under the pretext of praise rather than engaging in simple adulation or flattery. Spenser's modulations from Virgilian to Ovidian matter can contribute to this form of exhortatory praise, and the counterpoint of these two authorities can have a decidedly critical edge to it. It can also have the effect of continuing Ovid's project of making Virgil appear to be trying to be a metamorphic poet. When, in III, ix, Britomart hears the story of Troy from Paridell, she enthusiastically continues it with the story of the foundation of her own nation: 'There there (said *Britomart*) a fresh appeard / The glory of the later world to spring, / And *Troy* againe out of her dust was reard' (III, ix, 44). She plays Virgil, adding a British coda to the matter of Troy as Virgil had given it a Roman one. However, Britomart, the heroine with a Virgilian destiny, is not in charge of Spenser's narrative, in which other forces play a major role. Hellenore and Paridell, downmarket, belated versions of the Paris and Helen who initiated the Trojan war, play Ovidian games of love across the table while Britomart speaks with starry eyes about her destiny.[26] As the story of Paridell and Hellenore unfolds, another thread in Spenser's Ovidianism comes to the fore. Ovid seems to run away with the plot, turning it from a ceaselessly self-perpetuating dynastic narrative into a closed tale of obsession. Hellenore's miserly and jealous husband Malbecco pursues and spies on the eloping couple, and finally is so consumed with jealousy that he metamorphoses into the abstraction itself:

> Yet can he neuer dye, but dying liues,
> And doth himselfe with sorrow new sustaine,
> That death and life attonce vnto him giues,
> And painefull pleasure turnes to pleasing paine.
> There dwels he euer, miserable swaine,
> Hatefull both to him selfe, and euery wight;
> Where he through priuy griefe, and horrour vaine,
> Is woxen so deform'd, that he has quight
> Forgot he was a man, and *Gealosie* is hight.   (III, x, 60)

This is super-Ovidianism. In the *Metamorphoses* people are frequently changed into forms which reflect their previous nature (the stony-hearted Propoetides are turned to stones, the endlessly weaving Arachne is turned into a spider). Ovid also played a major role in introducing personifications into the epic tradition. But no one in the *Metamorphoses* is ever turned into an abstraction. The effect of Spenser's metamorphosis of Malbecco is to divert readers' attention from the Virgilian plot which Britomart wishes to inhabit towards a tale of erotic passion, a tale which finally is end-stopped in the unchanging isolation of Malbecco. Ovid lures us away from the unfolding of Virgilian imperial plans into a world in which time is forgotten until the very end of time.

The metamorphosis of Malbecco might seem to affirm the cliché that Spenser read the sportive Ovid with an incongruous sense of high moral seriousness: here is a character who makes himself into a moral exemplum by turning into the vice which his conduct manifests. It is often claimed that where writers fractionally younger than Spenser such as Marlowe and Shakespeare appreciated the irony and pathos of Ovid's treatment of love, Spenser himself still read Ovid via the tradition of moralising and allegorising commentary.[27] This tradition, which originated in the *Ovide Moralisé* of Pierre Bersuire, was indeed alive and well in the sixteenth century. Arthur Golding's translation of the *Metamorphoses* (1565-7) is prefixed by a lengthy allegorical interpretation of many of the stories in the poem. He takes the tale of Actaeon (who saw the chaste goddess Diana naked and was turned to a stag and torn apart by his own hounds) as showing that it never pays to be too fond of hunting or dice-playing. But although Golding directs his readers towards moralised readings in his preface, his lively translations of Ovid's tales themselves show no signs of moral interpretation. The metamorphosis of Malbecco is not simply a sign that Spenser read Ovid through the tradition of allegorical commentary: it is part of a larger Ovidian nexus in *The Faerie Queene*. Metamorphosis is often associated with failure, but failure not of an explicitly moral kind: it frequently signifies a reluctance to participate in the processes of striving and moving and living and breeding which represent the central principles of Spenser's poem. Take, for instance, the nymph who turns into the sluggish well in Book 1, beside which the Red Cross Knight lolls poured out in looseness with Duessa:

> one day when *Phœbe* fayre
> With all her band was following the chace,
> This Nymph, quite tyr'd with heat of scorching ayre
> Sat downe to rest in middest of the race:
> The goddesse wroth gan fowly her disgrace,
> And bad the waters, which from her did flow,
> Be such as she her selfe was then in place.
> Thenceforth her waters waxed dull and slow,
> And all that drunke thereof, did faint and feeble grow.   (I, vii, 5)

The nymph has not exactly committed a sin. She has just stopped moving forward. Her metamorphosis marks a reluctance to engage in the dynamics of plot. Like Fradubio in I, ii, who is turned into a tree, her inset tale highlights the failure of the Red Cross Knight to keep moving forward. Metamorphosis stops you dead.

Why did Spenser tend to align metamorphoses with a failure to move forwards, and what does that fact tell us about how he responded to Ovid? To answer this question it is necessary to tackle a major interpretive problem in the *Metamorphoses*: its treatment of change. This takes two very different and indeed apparently contradictory forms in Ovid. The majority of the stories he relates end with an irreversible change of state from human to inhuman form. These tales are then abandoned. So Daphne flees Apollo and is a tree. End of story. Then Ovid frisks off after Io, who gets changed into a heifer. The other form of change, however, is a grand metaphysical principle: in the account of the creation in Book I, and in the discourse uttered by the philosopher Pythagoras in Book xv, change becomes the foundational drive of the cosmos. As Golding translated Pythagoras:

> In all the world there is not that that standeth at a stay.
> Things eb and flow and euery shape is made too passe away.
> The tyme itself continually is fleeting like a brooke.
> For neyther brooke nor lyghtsomme tyme can tarrye still. But looke
> As euery waue dryues other foorth, and that that commes behynd
> Bothe thrusteth and is thrust itself: Euen so the tymes by kynd
> Doo fly and follow bothe at once, and euermore renew.
> For that that was before is left, and streyght there dooth ensew
> Anoother that was neuer erst. Eche twincling of an eye
> Dooth chaunge. Wee see that after day commes nyght and darks the sky,
> And after nyght the lyghtsum Sunne succeedeth orderly.
>
> (xv, 197–207)[28]

Matter shifts form, allowing new things to grow from old, or, for Pythagoras, souls to be reincarnated in new forms. There was a period in the criticism of the *Metamorphoses* when the discourse of Pythagoras was seen as an Ovidian joke (Pythagoras does indeed go on and on about the importance of only eating vegetables, and about how in a former life he was an eye-witness to the Trojan war, in a way that may be designed to make him seem a little cracked). More recently, however, it has been reassessed as marking a claim on Ovid's part to be writing an epic in the philosophical tradition.[29] Whether or not Ovid was being serious in this section of the poem, the majority of early modern readers thought he was. And this belief raises to an acute level the internal tension within the *Metamorphoses* between the poem's closed metamorphic tales about human beings on the one hand, and on the other the unclosed, unending, changeful universe in which they take place: people endure their passions and then turn into stones or trees or spiders, but the universe embodies another form of surging change which perpetually continues, as Ovid's 'carmen perpetuum' (continual song) goes on. In Ovid these two types of change do sometimes merge: when people are metamorphosed into flowers he often reminds us that they are renewed each year, and occasionally links such metamorphoses with annually recurrent festivals.[30] Spenser's vision is harder: he takes the fixed metamorphic side of Ovid and associates it with people like Malbecco who deliberately exclude themselves from the processes of dynastic history by their actions, who are stuck until the apocalypse in the forms they have made for themselves. He is not above seizing on the metamorphic side of Virgil too, as part of his Ovidian project to metamorphose Virgil into Ovid: Fradubio, the tree that yelps with pain when the Red Cross Knight plucks a branch from him and then tells about his subservience to Duessa, has his roots in Virgil's Polydorus. He too remains fixedly metamorphosed until he is 'bathed in a liuing well'.[31]

The changeful and unstoppable cosmos of Ovid's more philosophical moments, however, is reserved for the central visionary moments of the poem. Central among these central moments is the Garden of Adonis, in which Adonis is presented as being 'eterne in mutabilitie', endlessly dying and reviving, as the souls around him, like the souls described by Ovid's Pythagoras, are endlessly metempsychosing from one form to another. The Garden of Adonis is a peculiarly pointed imitation of Ovid, and it also shows that Spenser is concerned both to follow Ovid and ethically to correct him: it is preceded by the story of the nymph Chrysogonee, a nymph who settles down to rest by a pool. In the *Metamorphoses* this woodland stasis would certainly lead to a rape or a violent pursuit by a lecherous god, and to the consequent change of form of Chrysogonee. In Spenser there is only a faint uneasy memory of these Ovidian rapes: instead of being written out of the story of life like Malbecco or the nymph of the well, Chrysogonee is gently impregnated by the sun (in an extremely sanitised allegorical representation of the conception of Elizabeth I from the union of the none too gentle sun Henry VIII and Anne Boleyn). And she breeds, with an echo of Ovid's description of the spontaneous growth of life out of the river Nile: ('So after *Nilus* invndation, / Infinite shapes of creatures men do fynd, / Informed in the mud, on which the Sunne hath shynd' (*FQ*, III, vi, 8); compare *Met.* I, 422–9). Then, after a highly Ovidian squabble between Venus and Diana, Chrysogonee's child Amoret is taken to the Garden of Adonis. Change, beneficent change, dynastic growth, is deliberately put in the place of the terminal metamorphosis which the Ovidian allusions surrounding the tale of Chrysogonee lead one to expect. A Christian poet makes a living tale about endless life out of a setting from which his classical predecessor might have generated a rape. In transforming Ovid Spenser is not simply rebuking him: he is fusing the two incompatible forms of change which had run through his predecessor's text by producing a cosmogony at the moment in his narrative where Ovid would have presented a rape and an irreversible metamorphosis. He is imitating not so as to force the superiority of a Christian vision over its pagan past, but so as to resemble his original 'as a child resembles its father' (as Seneca put it in his 84th Epistle):

he is benefiting from him, making him live, and forcing him to participate in the reproduction both of new life and of new texts.

The Garden of Adonis is not quite so cosy as this account of it would suggest, however. Adonis is 'by succession made perpetuall'. Spenser's queen was not. If, as I have suggested, Spenser made Ovid's preoccupation with endless change and Virgil's preoccupation with dynastic growth the principal positive values in his poem, then he was left with a work of which the central premises were calculated to rebuke its principal dedicatee, Queen Elizabeth I. Chaste women, like the nymph of the spring in Book I, or the nymph who becomes the stream which refuses to wash the hands of the baby Ruddymane in Book II, do not contribute the central drives of the poem: they sit rigidly apart. In this respect too Spenser may be seen as an Ovidian artist. For, apart from its irreconcilable representations of different kinds of change, the other major critical debate about the *Metamorphoses* concerns its politics. As we have seen, metamorphic art was not necessarily anti-Augustan art. But there is clearly something politically unsettling about a picture of a universe dominated by flux. In Book XV Pythagoras becomes more and more enraptured by his vision of change and becomes a prophet who foretells the rise of Rome under Augustus: 'A Citie by the ofspring of the Troians buylt shall bee, / So great as neuer in the world the lyke was seene before' (Golding, XV, 4891–2). The juxtaposition of a metaphysic of flux and a voice of prophetic permanence is clearly ironic: if change is universal, will it not it affect Rome, its Emperor, its dominion, its brass monuments, its triumphal arches, as well as people and rocks and stones and trees?[32] When Ovid claims in the final lines of the *Metamorphoses* that he will be on people's lips wherever Rome's power extends ('quaque patet domitis Romana potentia terris', *Met.* XV, 877), is his apparent optimism qualified by his earlier affirmation of the universality of change? The aesthetics of the *Metamorphoses* may not be out of step with Augustan principles, but its metaphysics quietly erode the monuments of Roman rule. Spenser learnt from Ovid how to create a work of art which does not seem explicitly critical of its times or its ruler, but which is founded upon metaphysical principles which are evidently at odds with them.

Nowhere is this more apparent than at the end of *The Faerie Queene* as we have it. The 'Two Cantos of Mutabilitie', which first appeared in the 1609 edition of *The Faerie Queene*, represent the most complex fusion of Spenser's political attitudes and his imitative practices. The mysterious posthumous publication of this work will never be fully explained, but it has clear precedents in the classical and post-classical epic tradition: Virgil was supposed to have wished to burn the imperfectly finished *Aeneid*; Ovid broke off the *Fasti* after only six of the total of twelve months; and in the more recent past Ariosto's *Cinque Canti*, a dark fragment of an incomplete and politically pessimistic revision to *Orlando furioso*, had appeared post-humously in 1545.[33] The precedent of the *Fasti* is perhaps the most thought-provoking, for Ovid claimed this poem on the Roman religious calendar was left incomplete as a result of his exile. Ovid uses its disrupted poetic form to mark a potential antagonism between power and poetry.[34] Spenser's 'Cantos of Mutabilitie', a coda to a half-completed poem written from a state analogous to exile in Ireland, are an extended meditation on both Ovid and the politics of his adoptive homeland Ireland.[35] In the long digression which describes Arlo Hill in Ireland, the scene of the judgement of Nature as to whether Jove or Mutabilitie rules the Universe, Spenser relates an Ovidian etiological tale (that is, a story about how a place or thing came to be as it is) which explains why Ireland is so overrun with wolves and robbers. The foolish Faunus spies on the Goddess Diana when she is bathing, and she wrecks the landscape in revenge. The episode has recently been shown to be deeply tangled in Spenser's political position as a 'New English' planter attempting to establish his authority in, and grow a livelihood from, Irish land.[36] It also makes extensive political use of Ovid. The tale clearly alludes to Ovid's story of Actaeon, but it metamorphoses Ovid's tale. Spenser's Faunus is not killed or metamorphosed; he is simply clad in a deer's skin and chased through the Irish landscape, because to execute him would destroy the race of woodgods 'which must for euer liue'. Diana, the goddess of chastity, then punishes the landscape by making wolves and robbers teem in the land, a result, as Spenser ruefully notes, 'Which too-too true that lands in-dwellers since haue found' (VII, vi, 55). The episode is richly overdetermined with significances. The ostentatious classical allusion may be designed partly to deflect attention from barely suppressed political allegory: that a Virgin Queen is responsible by her actions for ruining Ireland for its 'in-dwellers'. That political meaning is worked out through, and partially muted by, allusions to Ovid. The two principles of Ovidian change are set side by side: on the one hand is the endless changefulness of the Ovidian world of Nature 'which must for euer liue', and in which Faunus simply cannot be metamorphosed because life depends on him; on the other hand is the ruthless permanence of the change wrought by Diana on the landscape. Underlying Spenser's version of the Actaeon story may well be a meditation on the coda to the tale as it appears in Ovid: 'Common talk wavered this way and that: to some the goddess appeared more cruel than just; others called her act worthy of her austere virginity; both sides found good reason for their judgement' (*Met.* III, 253–5). The 'Cantos of Mutabilitie' invite their readers to debate royal policy in Ireland, as Spenser himself did in *A View of the Present State of*

Ireland. Is the Virgin Queen 'more cruel than just'? Spenser uses his Ovidianism to raise questions about his queen, her lack of an heir and her policy in Ireland. Underlying his poem is an alignment of the most highly prized virtues of his queen with chilly nymphs and vengeful goddesses, the static, the deadly, the potentially unjust. The classical tradition was a vitally topical literary resource for him. It lived, and it enabled him to argue over the nature of the state which he inhabited.

NOTES

1 Thomas M. Greene, *The Light in Troy: Imitation and Discovery in Renaissance Poetry* (Yale University Press: New Haven and London, 1982), p. 270.
2 'Unto their uryne the schollers shall goe to the places appointed them in the lane or streete without the court', quoted in H. B. Wilson, *The History of Merchant-Taylors' School*, 2 vols. (London: Marchant and Gallabin, 1812), I, 17.
3 T. W. Baldwin, *William Shakespere's Small Latine and Lesse Greeke*, 2 vols. (Urbana, IL: University of Illinois Press, 1944), I, 134–63, 285–320.
4 Baldwin, *Shakespere's Small Latine*, I, 421.
5 Antony Grafton and Lisa Jardine, ' "Studied for Action": How Gabriel Harvey Read his Livy', *P&P*, 129 (1990), 3–50.
6 *This boke treath of the lyfe of Virgilius and of his deth and many maruayles that he dyd by whychcraft* (Antwerp, ?1518), STC 24828.
7 Aelius Donatus, *Life of Virgil*, trans. David Wilson-Okamura, 1996 (at www.virgil.org/vitae/a-donatus.htm).
8 Yale, pp. 33–4.
9 Thomas Phaer, *The Thirteene Books of Aeneidos* (London, 1596), p. 1.
10 On this aspect, see Ruth Samson Luborsky, 'The Allusive Presentation of *The Shepheardes Calender*', *Sp. St.* 1 (1980), 29–67.
11 Patrick Cheney, *Spenser's Famous Flight: A Renaissance Idea of a Literary Career* (Toronto and London: University of Toronto Press, 1993).
12 Even Cheney's revisionary view of Spenser's career explicitly excludes the *Complaints*: Cheney, *Spenser's Famous Flight*, p. 3.
13 Donatus, *Life of Virgil*, trans. Wilson-Okamura.
14 For a full discussion see R. O. A. M. Lyne, ed., *Ciris: A Poem Attributed to Virgil* (Cambridge: Cambridge University Press, 1978), p. 49; *The Cambridge History of Classical Literature II: Latin Literature*, ed. E. J. Kenney and W. V. Clausen (Cambridge: Cambridge University Press, 1982), pp. 467–74.
15 *Servii Gramatici qui Feruntur in Vergilii Aeneidos Commentarii*, ed. G. Thilo and H. Hagen, 3 vols. (Leipzig: Teubner, 1881–1902), I, p. 5.
16 A. Parry, 'The Two Voices of Virgil's Aeneid', *Arion* 2 (1963), 66–80; R. O. A. M. Lyne, *Further Voices in Virgil's Aeneid* (Oxford: Oxford University Press, 1987). For a judicious general survey, see R. J. Tarrant, 'Poetry and Power: Virgil's Poetry in Contemporary Context', in Charles Martindale, ed., *The Cambridge Companion to Virgil* (Cambridge: Cambridge University Press, 1997), pp. 169–87.
17 There is a large literature on these areas. Patricia Parker, *Inescapable Romance: Studies in the Poetics of a Mode* (Princeton: Princeton University Press, 1979)

explores the role of deferral of narrative fulfilment in the romance tradition. Colin Burrow, *Epic Romance: Homer to Milton* (Oxford: Oxford University Press, 1993) considers the role of pity and its evolution from Virgil's *pietas*. John Watkins, *The Specter of Dido: Spenser and Virgilian Epic* (New Haven and London: Yale University Press, 1995) considers the ways in which departures from women mark generic battles between epic and romance. On the tendency of sixteenth-century epic to present monstrous hybrid bodies of women which represent the hybrid origins of the poems themselves, see Mihoko Suzuki, *Metamorphoses of Helen: Authority, Difference, and the Epic* (Ithaca and London: Cornell University Press, 1989).

18 Burrow, *Epic Romance*, pp. 132–4.

19 See Theresa M. Krier, *Gazing on Secret Sights: Spenser, Classical Imitation, and the Decorums of Vision* (Cornell University Press: Ithaca and London, 1990), pp. 66–79.

20 For a more detailed discussion of this episode, which draws attention to its metapoetic elements, see my 'Ovid on Imitating and on the Imitation of Ovid', in *Essays on Ovid*, ed. Philip Hardie, *Cambridge Philological Society Supplements* 23 (1999), 271–87.

21 For the earlier treatments of the topos see A. S. Cook, 'The House of Sleep: – A Study in Comparative Literature', *Modern Language Notes* 5 (1890), 10–21.

22 On the association between Aesculapius and the revival of pagan learning, see Bartlett Giamatti, 'Hippolytus among the Exiles', in Maynard Mack and George deForest Lord, eds., *Poetic Traditions of the English Renaissance* (New Haven and London: Yale University Press, 1982), pp. 1–24.

23 Angus Fletcher, *The Prophetic Moment: An Essay on Spenser* (Chicago and London: University of Chicago Press, 1971), pp. 88–98. See the excellent entry on Ovid by Michael Holahan in *Spenser Encyclopedia*, pp. 520–2.

24 Karl Galinsky, *Augustan Culture: An Interpretive Introduction* (Princeton, NJ: Princeton University Press, 1996), p. 125

25 Ibid., p. 189.

26 The writing of messages in spilt wine in *FQ* III, ix, 30 recalls *Amores* 1.4.20 and 2.5.17–18, and *Heroides* 17.75–90.

27 Notably in William Keach, *Elizabethan Erotic Narratives* (New Brunswick: Rutgers University Press, 1977).

28 *Shakespeare's Ovid, Being Arthur Golding's Translation of the Metamorphoses*, ed. W. H. D. Rouse (London: Centaur, 1961), pp. 298–9.

29 For the view that the discourse is a spoof, see Charles Segal, 'Myth and Philosophy in the *Metamorphoses*: Ovid's Augustanism and the Augustan Conclusion of Book XV', *American Journal of Philology* 90 (1969), 257–92; for the seriousness of it, see Philip Hardie, 'The Speech of Pythagoras in Ovid *Metamorphoses* 15: Empedoclean Epos', *Classical Quarterly* NS 45 (1995), 204–14.

30 E.g. the metamorphosis of Hyacinthus, *Met.*, X, 164–6 and 218–9.

31 *FQ* I, ii, 30–44; *Aeneid* III, 22–48. Spenser makes extensive use of other imitations of the episode; but unlike Ariosto's Astolfo, his most immediate post-Virgilian source, his Fradubio stubbornly remains a tree. For perceptive accounts of this episode and its debts to other versions of the topos, see Shirley Clay Scott, 'From Polydorus to Fradubio: the History of a *Topos*', *Sp. St.* 7

(1986), 27–57; and Elizabeth Jane Bellamy, 'The Broken Branch and the "Liuing Well": Spenser's Fradubio and Romance Error in *The Faerie Queene*', *RP* (1985), 1–12.

32 See Philip Hardie, 'Augustan Poets and the Mutability of Rome', in Anton Powell, ed., *Roman Poetry and Propaganda in the Age of Augustus* (London: Bristol Classical Press, 1992), pp. 59–82.

33 For a full discussion of the date, see Ludovico Ariosto, *Cinque Canti*, trans. Alexander Sheers and David Quint (Berkeley and London: University of California Press, 1996), pp. 2–5.

34 Alessandro Barchiesi, *The Poet and the Prince: Ovid and Augustan Discourse* (University of California Press: Berkeley, 1997), pp. 259–62.

35 Michael Holahan, '*Iamque opus exegi*: Ovid's Changes and Spenser's Brief Epic of Mutability', *ELR* 6 (1976), 244–70.

36 Andrew Hadfield, *Spenser's Irish Experience: Wilde Fruit and Salvage Soyle* (Oxford: Clarendon Press, 1997).

FURTHER READING

Colin Burrow, *Epic Romance: Homer to Milton* (Oxford: Clarendon Press, 1993).

Michael Holahan, '*Iamque opus exegi*: Ovid's Changes and Spenser's Brief Epic of Mutability', *English Literary Renaissance* 6 (1976), 244–70.

Theresa M. Krier, *Gazing on Secret Sights: Spenser, Classical Imitation, and the Decorums of Vision* (Cornell University Press: Ithaca and London, 1990).

Mihoko Suzuki, *Metamorphoses of Helen: Authority, Difference, and the Epic* (Ithaca and London: Cornell University Press, 1989).

John Watkins, *The Specter of Dido: Spenser and Virgilian Epic* (New Haven and London: Yale University Press, 1995).

12

ROLAND GREENE

Spenser and contemporary vernacular poetry

The scholar or student who wishes to elucidate Spenser's relations with the vernacular poetry of his time finds a curious unevenness in the received views. Spenser's career began with his participation in *A Theatre for Worldlings* (1569), an English version of the visionary anthology *Het theatre oft Toon-neel* by the Dutch poet Jan van der Noot. His debut as 'our new Poete' came in *The Shepheardes Calender* (1579), where two late medieval or early Renaissance figures, the English poet John Skelton and the French poet Clément Marot, are prominent influences, fused in the figure of Colin Clout.[1] The *Complaints*, a loose collection of nine pieces 'containing sundrie small Poemes of the Worlds Vanitie' formerly 'disperst abroad in sundrie hands', are closely modelled on the work of Joachim Du Bellay, while Spenser's sonnet sequence, the *Amoretti*, depends on that of Philippe Desportes.[2] For the epic purposes of *The Faerie Queene* Spenser is assumed to participate in a continuum that reaches back first to Lodovico Ariosto and then to Matteo Maria Boiardo, with the Portuguese Luis de Camões as a latter-day precursor. Each phase of his career, then, has its own track of established influences, but these are seldom argued to extend past their immediate sphere – Spenser's Camões, for instance, is always an epic, and never a lyric, poet. Nor are the implications of such a staggered set of models followed to obvious conclusions. Why, we might ask, is an Englishman who can read Italian, French and Portuguese with a poet's penetration not assumed to read Spanish as well? While the immediate result of this uneven pattern of what is called influence is a certain lack of flexibility in literary history's presentation of his career, the more serious consequence is that a Spenser so remorselessly divided can scarcely be thought of as a European poet. And so, as it happens, Spenser is not. Instead he comes to us constructed as perhaps the most English of early modern poets.

This essay proposes to describe the main lines of critical thought about Spenser's engagements with his continental contemporaries, and to explain what those lines are still able to tell us about the poet's achievement. At the same time, the essay will suggest that much can be gained from thinking of Spenser in a wider setting than usual – as a European poet, undoubtedly obsessed with the origins and fate of his own language (as was nearly every major vernacular poet of the time), but also writing within a larger, more diffuse area of influence than received literary history has allowed. As an opening gesture, it seems sensible to propose that what Spenser knew in one phase of his career, he must have known in the other phases: the fact that we have grown comfortable thinking of the early poems as largely based on particular French models, and the epic as grounded in the Italian models, should not preclude a more fluid conception of his engagements.[3]

The first thing to say about Spenser's European vernacular identity – in fact, almost the first thing to say about his career – is that he belongs to a class we might call the vernacular neoteric poets. Originally applied by Cicero pejoratively to a generation of Roman *poetae novi* centered on Catullus, and then extended to two further generations including Gallus, Propertius, Tibullus, Ovid and Virgil, the term 'neoteric' has some relevance to Spenser's ambitions. In its original usage the term designates a school that uses the shorter, less weighty genres (elegy, lyric, epyllion) as a lever with which to renovate epic; insists on the mutual invigorations of poetry and doctrine or theory; rethinks the relations between poetry and language, including the recuperative effects of archaism; and finally, positions its poetry against a horizon of presentness – in history, in politics, in social thought – even as that poetry may reach back with discrimination into the past for models.[4] Even among classicists, the term 'neoteric' is a flexible one that designates an attitude and a set of potential values more than it defines a specific style. Accordingly, the term allows us to locate Spenser among the European poets of his generation, such as Camões, as well as those continental poets a generation or two older who correspond better to him than to their English contemporaries, for instance through the highly visible debuts into publication of Juan Boscán and Garcilaso de la Vega in 1542. Newness is a property very much under construction in Spenser's century, and by collating him with the European poets of his extended era we can measure the different sorts of neotericism, or strategic newness, he demonstrates.

Spenser first wrote for publication in a volume that was an unusual literary franchise with a multinational character, Jan van der Noot's *Theatre for Worldlings* (1569).[5] Van der Noot, a major Dutch poet and a Calvinist exile from his homeland, seems to have designed his *Theatre* as a collection of contemporaneous short poems, from Italian and French originals, leading to a prose sermon or meditation that draws heavily on the Book of Revelation and other favourite Calvinist scriptural sources. The poems and prose together sustain a remarkable visionary quality, which is all the more intriguing when one considers the *Theatre* as a factitious production out of several voices, utterances and languages; it is as though van der Noot sets out to recover a mystic, vatic, apocalyptic undercurrent that runs through the unruly garden of mid-century European poetry. Poets who would scarcely have produced such a volume in their own oeuvres, such as Petrarch and Marot, are made subject to van der Noot's prophetic mission. But perhaps the most fascinating aspect of van der Noot's *Theatre* is that it appeared in three languages, addressed to three national readerships, within a single year – in Dutch in 1568, in French the same year, and in English in 1569. Though little discussed by scholarship, this ambitious display of internationalism in a single title encourages us to put a comparative frame around Spenser's career. It suggests that from his first published poems, Spenser sees himself as part of a circuit that extends across the vernaculars, making each poem of the *Theatre* – and perhaps each poem after that – an intervention in a cross-cultural dialogue among reformed Christians, committed humanists, and adventuresome poets.

At perhaps sixteen years old, then, Spenser became the principal English voice of van der Noot's project – an office that no other English poet shared, and one that put him in the company of such European masters as Marot and Du Bellay. What might he have learned from the *Theatre for Worldlings*? What might we learn about his production from this early venture?

Critics have largely agreed that the successive visions of the *Theatre*, where an awestruck voice describes a loosely connected series of apocalyptic scenes which appear alongside woodcuts, make a template for Spenser's mature work, especially *The Faerie Queene*. For instance, consider the experience of these two sonnets, which are adapted from Du Bellay's 'Songe' and appear one after the other in the *Theatre*:

> I saw a fresh spring rise out of a rocke,
> Clere as Christall against the Sunny beames,
> The bottome yellow like the shining land,
> That golden Pactol driues vpon the plaine.
> It seemed that arte and nature striued to ioyne
> There in one place all pleasures of the eye.
> There was to heare a noise alluring slepe
> Of many accordes more swete than Mermaids song,
> The seates and benches shone as Iuorie,
> An hundred Nymphes sate side by side about,
> When from nie hilles a naked rout of Faunes
> With hideous cry assembled on the place,
> Which with their feete vncleane the water fouled,
> Threw down the seats, and droue the Nimphs to flight.

At length, euen at the time when Morpheus
Most truely doth appeare vnto our eyes,
Wearie to see th'inconstance of the heauens:
I saw the great Typhaeus sister come,
Hir head full brauely with a morian armed,
In maiestie she seemde to match the Gods.
And on the shore, harde by a violent streame,
She raisde a Trophee ouer all the worlde.
An hundred vanquisht kings gronde at hir feete,
Their armes in shamefull wise bounde at their backes.
While I was with so dreadfull sight afrayde,
I saw the heauens warre against hir tho,
And seing hir striken fall with clap of thunder,
With so great noyse I start in sodaine wonder.[6]

Together these sonnets suggest a model for the narrative poetics of Spenser's epic: a closely observed scene comes into view, described from a vantage that suggests both sensual attraction and moral revulsion, only to be superseded by a second scene that is somehow both a continuation of the first and entirely different. The narrative unfolds in syncopation with the stanza form, working with the rhythms and contours of the sonnet but not predictably or mechanically so. John Bender has explained this dimension of Spenser's poetics as a neo-Gothic treatment of space, a 'discontinuous and fragmented anatomizing which is characteristic of the Gothic in art – and of *The Faerie Queene*'.[7] Carol V. Kaske further historicises this practice by means of what she calls a 'concordantial' reading, in which she – standing in for a putative ideal reader – traces the repetition of 'images' *in bono* and *in malo*, and emphasises those that relate to one another through *correctio*, the revision of an earlier image by a later one.[8] Oblique to both Bender and Kaske, I have suggested that this poetics might be conceived in terms of worldmaking, through which agreed-upon versions of reality are first organised and then disintegrated: in *The Faerie Queene*, where a unitary world is continually coming into sight, multiplying into alternatives and being recovered again as unitary, I call this process narrative subduction.[9]

Perhaps the most acute sense of how the *Theatre* prepares for the poetry to come is that of Ernest Gilman, who argues:

[the] pictorial Spenser seems especially congenial to the modern reader, for the core of [*The Faerie Queene*] no longer lies in the complexities of its 'dark conceit' or even in the 'good discipline' which might otherwise justify the enormous enterprise. *The Faerie Queene* may be, as Spenser goes on to concede in the prefatory 'Letter' to Raleigh, a work 'cloudily enwrapped in allegorical devices.' But behind the conceptual difficulty of [*The Faerie*

Queene], and shining through it, is a bright world of form and color registered by the eye before it is 'enwrapped' by the mind.

For this Spenser, the tutelage of the eye began with his earliest published verses, the translations from Petrarch, Du Bellay, and Van der Noot that appeared in the English version of *A Theatre for Voluptuous Worldlings* (London, 1569) . . . In at least one instance – the Coliseum in the illustration to Sonnet 7 from Du Bellay – a motif evidently remembered from the *Theatre* will surface ten years later in the woodcuts for *The Shepheardes Calendar*, appearing at the end of a decade during which Spenser also produced *The Visions of Petrarch*, *The Visions of Bellay*, and, probably, the *Visions of the World Vanitie* . . .

Even so quick a glance back over Spenser's career reveals how strongly visual his developing poetic is, and how much of Van der Noot's 'plesure of the eye' flows into *The Faerie Queene*.[10]

For Gilman and most other critics whose professed interest is to portray Spenser as going beyond his sources to produce a body of work that can be assimilated chiefly to English traditions – as where Gilman looks at the *Theatre* and sees in it 'arguably the first English emblem book' – these explanatory models represent alternate ways of describing the teeming, often contradictory character of Spenser's repertory of spaces, images, and worlds. But there is another way to consider Spenser's poetics in this light. As in the *Theatre*, these episodes, in which (as Gilman has it) a 'world' is '"enwrapped" by the mind', often represent Spenser's absorptions of his international sources. In the *Theatre*, Spenser learns not only a pictorial, corrective poetics but a way of transmuting continental models into his own English voice; he learns to narrate and domesticate 'the world' as it comes to him in contemporaneous poetry. Moreover, these adaptations demonstrate that for Spenser, international influences arrive in the form of vivid episodes that may be only loosely 'French' or 'Italian' in origin, the common property of a fairly continuous European literary culture. When we say that Spenser imitates Du Bellay, Desportes, or Camões, then, we might better say that he draws on this stock of episodes both to tie his work to a extant tradition and to distinguish himself from it. The 'pictorial space', 'images', and 'world of form and color' noted by his critics are all euphemisms for the concrete investments of Spenser's poetry in this tradition; this nomenclature tends to obscure the cross-cultural nature of the process at hand, encouraging us to absorb a poet of multifarious and international influences into a national – often nationalist – English literary history. But Spenser sees what his critics often do not, that 'the worlde' is established and maintained as a totality only by reconnaissance, conquest and subjugation (his 'naked rout of Faunes' and 'hundred vanquisht kings').

His poetry extracts and subdues not abstract 'images' nor a 'world of form and color', but a real world of concrete examples that are the living body of European poetry. When he practices moving among these examples and writing across them, as he does when he revises and adapts the *Theatre* sonnets in his *Complaints* (1591), he shows what we might see elsewhere in *Tottel's Miscellany* or Thomas Watson's *Hekatompathia*: how the substance of English poetry in this era is made out of international materials.[11]

The Shepheardes Calender is probably the outstanding example of a neoteric production in sixteenth-century English literature. By this I mean, first, that Spenser deploys the conceits of newness in ways that tie his production to other debuts of the century – a loose array of poets and volumes, not strictly contemporaneous, that are similarly positioned along a horizon of the new. The most prominent analogues are the debut volumes of Garcilaso de la Vega and Juan Boscán in 1542, Joachim Du Bellay in 1549, and Pierre de Ronsard in 1550. Moreover, Spenser gathers in as models particular poems as well as nonliterary texts that suggest innovation and contemporaneity in various ways. One such text is *Le Compost et kalendrier des bergiers* (Paris, 1493), a 'secular bible for daily reference' – combining agricultural, astrological, practical and religious lore – that had adaptations and imitations in several European capitals; the English version, which Spenser consulted for his work, is the *Kalender of Shee-pherds* (Paris, 1503, reprinted and revised many times).[12] While nothing could be more traditional than this farmer's almanac, Spenser shrewdly saw in it the outlines of a procedure for making the old new again, in the manner of a compendium that continually refreshes content within an established framework, that is often reprinted and updated and yet always somehow the same. In a much more literary vein, this is what the pastoral mode itself does: always bringing back what is familiar, including the recurrent names of the characters, and yet often announcing something new – a topical angle, a thematic innovation, a literary debut.

The second element of Spenser's neoteric stance in *The Shepheardes Calender* is the reformative claim of the poem: like neoterics from Catullus to Du Bellay, Spenser proposes to reorient contemporary poetry with the leverage of his own example. His method is, to characterise it broadly, what Leo Spitzer calls 'perspectivism', or the continual exercise of one vantage against another, until no outlook goes uncriticised and no statement uninflected by irony.[13] As critics have often observed, these perspectives occur at every level of the *Calender*. The confrontations between traditional pastoral motifs and topical references; between nativism and European (especially Italianate) influences; between the classical examples of Virgil and Marot and the demotic models of the almanacs – all of these contribute to the sense of the *Calender* as a layered, self-consciously innovative work. This description of the *Calender* is widely accepted. Less noticed, however, is that we have a ground-level awareness of Spenser's perspectivistic method but no well-defined concept of how it works as a large-scale project, how it relates to its multifarious sources in the other European vernaculars, and how the *Calender* belongs to the various categories – generational, generic, neoteric – to which it can be assimilated. In the following discussion of *The Shepheardes Calender* I will suggest some general ways of thinking about Spenser's original lyric production in an international context.

In the first place, Spenser seems to position himself in a significantly wider context than most of his critics assume for him – and to define his work inclusively, by comparison rather than contrast to others. E. K.'s notes to the *Calender* refer approvingly to poets of past and present from a wide range of literatures and cultures. One of the few notes to mention another poet in a negative light is the first (and the first quoted here), while the others quoted are more typical:

> [Colin Cloute] is a name not greatly vsed, and yet haue I sene a Poesie of M. Skeltons vnder that title. But indeede the word Colin is Frenche, and vsed of the Frenche poete Marot (if he be worthy of the name of a Poete) in a certein Æglogue.

> That by Tityrus is meant Chaucer, hath bene already sufficiently sayde, and by thys more playne appeareth, that he sayth, he tolde merye tales. Such as be hys Canterburie tales. whom he calleth the God of Poetes for hys excellencie, so as Tullie calleth Lentulus, Deum vitæ suæ .s. the God of hys lyfe.

> Such pretie descriptions euery where vseth Theocritus, to bring in his Idyllia.

> The Nightingale . . . whose complaintes be very well set forth of Ma. George Gaskin a wittie gentleman, and the very chefe of our late rymers, who and if some partes of learning wanted not (albee it is well knowen he altogyther wanted not learning) no doubt would haue attayned to the excellencye of those famous Poetes. For gifts of wit and naturall promptnesse appeare in hym aboundantly.[14]

The disrespect to Marot ('if he be worthy of the name of a Poete') is probably a gesture of neoteric solidarity with Du Bellay, whose *Deffence et illustration de la langue françoyse* (1549) includes several dismissals of the elder poet as not entirely worthy of emulation.[15] For the most part, Spenser's readings of other poets in the *Calender* are generous and ecumenical. Even Gascoigne, a journeyman of the past decade who might be expected to provoke his disdain, is treated with deference. What is Spenser's strategy? Most neoterics define their projects through manifestos that take issue with predecessors and contemporaries, defining who they are not as much as who they are. Moreover, they tend to propose interpretive protocols – insights, assumptions, purposes – that allow their own work to be more readily interpreted. In other words, they enforce a certain distance from their counterparts while drawing the reader closer to their own work. But the *Calender* does nearly the opposite: while situating the eclogues in a diverse historical and contemporary context and embracing nearly everything as an influence, E. K.'s notes widen the distance between the reader and the poems at hand. His observations about the *Calender* are as measured, elliptical and ironic as those about his sources are inclusive:

> I suppose he meane Chaucer, whose prayse for pleasaunt tales cannot dye, so long as the memorie of hys name shal liue, and the name of Poetrie shal endure.
>
> A straunge manner of speaking .s. what maner of Ladde is he?
>
> By Perigot who is meant, I can not vprightly say.
>
> This tale of Roffy seemeth to coloure some particular Action of his. But what, I certeinlye know not.
>
> I doubt whether by Cuddie be specified the authour selfe, or some other.[16]

Even his explanations seem to produce further questions, as in this gloss on 'Julye': 'the word ['ouerture'] is borrowed of the French, and vsed in good writers'.[17] The effect is to render *The Shepheardes Calender* a palimpsest in which one can find a perspectivised version of nearly everything that matters in recent European poetry – and in which the verses at hand come across as especially challenging and 'forenne', old and new at the same time.

The 'November' eclogue affords an opportunity to examine how Spenser measures perspectives against one another, because its source is the most explicit in the series: as the headnote explains, 'this Æglogue is made in imitation of Marot his song, which he made vpon the death of Loys the frenche queene. But farre passing his reache, and in myne opinion all other the Eclogues of this booke.'[18] The characteristic note of the *Calender* is here again: indebted but fresh, derivative but original, old and new at the same time. Spenser chooses a model that is the first pastoral elegy in French and an example of both Virgilian homage and Italianate innovation. Marot's 'Eglogue sur le Trespas de ma Dame Loyse de Savoye' is a neoclassical lament for the mother of Francis I that celebrates her virtues, finds consolation in her arrival at the Elysian Fields, and brings traditional pastoral elements together around the *here* of her gravesite. While maintaining some of the elements – including the proper names of Marot's shepherds, Thenot and Colin – Spenser further updates the poem with characteristic boldness. Marot's refrain runs throughout with variations that mark the progress of the elegy:

> Sus donc, mes Vers, chantez chants doloreux,
>
> Chantez, mes Vers! Chantez douleur amere!
>
> Chantez, mes Vers, chantez dueil ordonné!
>
> Chantez, mes Vers, chantez: Adieu liesse!
>
> Chantez, mes Vers, chantez douleur encore!
>
> Chantez, mes vers, fresche douleur conceue.
>
> Cessez, mes Vers, cessez de vous douleur!
>
> Cessez, mes Vers, cessez icy voz plaindz![19]

Spenser transforms the refrain into a much more substantial feature that unlike Marot's is framed by pauses, stands out metrically from the body of the poem, and becomes the culmination of each stanza:

> For dead shee is, that myrth thee made of yore.
>   Dido my deare alas is dead,
>   Dead and lyeth wrapt in lead:
>   O heauie herse,
>   Let streaming teares be poured out in store:
>   O carefull verse.[20]

For Spenser the *here* of the poem is the poem itself, playing on the two senses of 'herse' as a literal bier and (E. K. reminds us) 'the solemne obsequie in funeralles'.[21] Accordingly, the figure of the poet – both the returned Colin and Spenser himself – claims a more central role in 'November' than in Marot's elegy, and the poem strikes a new level of self-consciousness, of concern for representing its own making. Moreover, Spenser replaces Louise of Savoy with the factitious Dido, of whom 'the personage is secrete, and to me altogether vnknowne, albe of him selfe I often required the same'.[22] Instead of an elegy for a recognisable object such as Louise, Spenser's eclogue becomes its own object, a monument to its reinvention of Marot's elegy. This is the literary debut not as an event recollected after the fact, but as chronicle of itself, and it joins Spenser to the debuts of Garcilaso and Boscán, Du Bellay, and others of the sixteenth century who measure the distance from their forerunners while they renovate their national poetries. *The Shepheardes Calender* ought to be read alongside these self-introductions; together they evoke a horizon of newness around a set of debut productions that define the period in European poetry.

The next phase of Spenser's career is represented by the *Amoretti*, a sonnet sequence that – perhaps more than any other in English – renders continental models, sometimes decisively adapted and sometimes lightly paraphrased, into a conspectus of the possibilities of the sequence form.

From one point of view, Spenser's sequence is less original than the other major productions with which it is loosely contemporaneous, from Sidney's *Astrophil and Stella* (written early 1580s, published 1591) to Shakespeare's *Sonnets* (written mid-1590s, published 1609): the list of proposed sources and analogues for the particular poems in these major sequences is considerably longer in Spenser's case, including the works of Ronsard, Desportes, Pietro Bembo, Torquato Tasso and Serafino dell'Aquila as well as Petrarch.[23] The most visible, influential sequences in English tend to have fewer direct models, while the minor ones often come trailing evidence of many borrowings. The *Amoretti* is unusual among English sequences – although of a piece with the rest of Spenser's aesthetic practice – in relinquishing invention in favour of something perhaps more radical, a revisiting of convention that both honours and updates traditional models. Accordingly, the *Amoretti* is satisfying in a different way than most of the contemporaneous products of the English sonnet boom. It is a set of homages drawn from the previous fifty years of sonnets in the European vernaculars, and from the sources of those sonnets in scriptural, classical and late medieval amatory writing.[24] When scholars propose particular models for the sonnets, they tend to foreground those poems and poets they recognise best, rather than the more complex and historically nuanced motifs, often visible in many mid-century lyrics, that Spenser engages and transforms.

Consider *Amoretti* 15, a sonnet that is undeniably derivative but nonetheless striking for how it positions itself among an array of influences:

> Ye tradefull Merchants that with weary toyle,
> do seeke most pretious things to make your gain:
> and both the Indias of their treasures spoile,
> what needeth you to seeke so farre in vaine?
> For loe my loue doth in her selfe containe
> all this worldes riches that may farre be found,
> if Saphyres, loe her eies be Saphyres plaine,
> if Rubies, loe her lips be Rubies sound:
> If Pearles, hir teeth be pearles both pure and round;
> if Yuorie, her forhead yuory weene;
> if Gold, her locks are finest gold on ground;
> if siluer, her faire hands are siluer sheene:
> But that which fairest is, but few behold,
> her mind adornd with vertues manifold.[25]

The scholarship on sonnet 15 proposes a number of particular influences. Besides the Song of Songs, perhaps the most compelling of these is Desportes' *Amours de Diane* 32:

Marchands, qui recherchez tout le rivage More
Du froid Septentrion et qui, sans reposer,
A cent mille dangers vous allez exposer
Pour un gain incertain, qui vos esprits devore.
Venez seulement voir la beauté que j'adore,
Et par quelle richesse elle a sceu m'attiser:
Et je suis seur qu'apres, vous ne pourrez priser
Le plus rare thresor dont l'Afrique se dore.
Voyez les filets d'or de ce chef blondissant,
L'eclat de ces rubis, ce coral rougissant,
Ce crystal, cet ebene, et ces graces divines,
Cet argent, cet ivoyre; et ne vous contentez
Qu'on ne vous monstre encor mille autres raritez,
Mille beaux diamans et milles perles fines.[26]

Certainly Desportes' sonnet is a source, although there are several potential
French sources: the same critic who adduces this one also notices parallels
to Ronsard's 'D'un Ocëan qui nostre jour limite' (*Amours* 162), and others
remark the second of Du Bellay's *Sonnetz de l'Honneste Amour* ('Ce ne sont
pas ces beaux cheveux dorez') and Pontus de Tyard's 'Chant a son leut'.
Likewise, critics whose interest is Italian tend to cite a multifarious array of
models including Tasso and Petrarch.[27] More to the point, however, is to
ask: what is a source here? What are we looking for? Similar comparisons
marshalled in a similar way? Dozens of blazons will qualify. Blazons with
topical references to the East and West Indies or other imperial venues?
Many poems of the mid-sixteenth century and later combine these elements.
A physical blazon that turns Neo-Platonic with an emphasis on the lady's
moral qualities? French and Italian sonnets often carry out this move, and
Spenser's celebration of 'her mind' seems directly adapted from those
poems, such as Tasso's, that emphasise the lady's 'mente'. *Amoretti* 15, like
the rest of the sequence, is a tribute to a set of interlocking motifs as much
as to particular instances. In fashioning the poem, Spenser joins the blazon
to imperial trade and to the rise of the merchant class, three elements that
together become increasingly common after the mid-sixteenth century.
Moreover, and what is likely to be overlooked in traditional source study,
Spenser situates the *Amoretti* and their continuation, the *Epithalamion*, in
the late-century outlook that sees trade not as an idealised event but as
'weary toyle' and complexity. As in the work of the major Spanish and
Portuguese poets, and unlike many of the French and Italian sonneteers,
Spenser manages to give Neo-Platonic idealism something concrete to play
against, namely the covetousness of commerce and the disillusions of
empire: the realism of the first three lines of *Amoretti* 15 resonates with the

similar note in many of Camões' sonnets, where 'desenganos' (disillusions), 'interesse cobiçoso' (covetous interest), and 'esquivanças' (avoidances) are commonplace.[28] When Spenser reiterates *Amoretti* 15 as the tenth stanza of the *Epithalamion*, a sense of international complexity – in which the bride is compared to a foreign queen and to the east itself – is apprehensible behind the decorum of the occasion, leading the speaker to ask delicately: 'ye merchants daughters did ye see / So fayre a creature in your towne before?'[29] We usually call this the public dimension of the *Amoretti* and the *Epithalamion*, but it is in part the economic and geopolitical dimension too, and it prepares for the encounters with conquest, trade and difference that are indispensable to *The Faerie Queene*.[30]

All of the preceding responses and adaptations clear the ground for Spenser's work in *The Faerie Queene*, in which he draws freely on Romance models such as Ariosto's *Orlando Furioso*, Tasso's *Gerusalemme Liberata*, and Camões' *Os Lusíadas*. The eclogues of *The Shepheardes Calender* and the sonnets of the *Amoretti* prove to be anticipations of the cantos of *The Faerie Queene*, in which for the first time an English poet divides an epic in the manner of the Italians. Moreover, Spenser adapts the octave of Ariosto, Tasso and Camões to produce a unique stanza of nine lines and three interwoven rhymes (ABABBCBCC), where the initial C rhyme functions like the volta in the sonnet, providing a formal climax and preparing for the resolution of the remaining tercet.[31] Several generations of scholars have traced the impact on Spenser's epic of these Romance models in more than formal terms, such as the narrative strategies he recovers from the Italian poets, the allusions to political and social realities he observes in Camões, and the attention to surfaces and sensations he adapts from all the Romance poets, lyric and epic alike. Spenser himself announces that he intends to follow the example of Ariosto and Tasso among vernacular poets.[32] In describing the terms of that example, A. Bartlett Giamatti will have the penultimate word here:

[Spenser] took the mood of the dream vision and the method of allegory from the French and English poets of the Middle Ages and mingled them with motifs, scenes, characters, and structure from the Renaissance poems of Boiardo, Ariosto, to some extent Trissino, and Tasso. In doing so, he created *The Faerie Queene* – that is, something very similar to its predecessors, and yet completely different . . . From the Italians, Spenser inherited not only motifs and structure, but also what we can term the materials of a point of view. He took, in general, the grand romance-image of questing, wandering heroic action in a hostile world. From Ariosto he appropriated the theme of illusion and reality as the result of magic, and he used it through the figures of Archimago, Duessa, and the witch who creates the false Florimell . . . From

Tasso, Spenser directly inherited the tradition of heroic duty opposed to personal pleasure – the ethical categories which preoccupied the Italian so much. And through the Italians (and ultimately all the 'Platonic' philosophy in the air), Spenser learned to equate the good with the real, the evil with the illusory; and he finally saw how a landscape could be the symbol of evil masquerading as the good.

In those earlier poems, [however,] the conflicts, like their precise geography, were primarily of this world. And from the urgency of the conflict between what seemed and what was in Ariosto, or what one wanted to do and what one ought to do, in Tasso, came the energy, the immediacy, indeed the relevancy to our own feelings and situations. However, in *The Faerie Queene* the essential conflict is not of this world, and as a result there is no corrosive irony dissolving all into a masterful illusion of futile reality; there is no deadly opposition between pleasure and honor, delight and duty. The conflict in *The Faerie Queene* is between this world and the next; and all the mundane conflicts found in the Italians are absorbed or reconciled into this greater, cosmic tension between flux and permanence, mutability and eternity.[33]

'Something very similar and yet completely different' – that rubric, in all its ambiguity, seems to govern Spenser's imaginative relations with his vernacular contemporaries. At every stage of his career, he exerts his powers on the example of Romance poetries, and builds his most ambitious works as responses to them. Accordingly, Spenser is the most Latin of English poets in this era, embracing the precedents of the French, the Italians and the Portuguese together and turning them into something that has always been seen as a monument to the possibilities of English. The Romance dimension of his work is often apparent, however – in the affinity of Romance-language poets for *The Faerie Queene*, in the esteem of another Italianate English poet, Milton, and in the Spenser revival of the Romantics, who championed Romance–English relations in their time. As the borders between the national literatures become more permeable, perhaps it will become possible to see Spenser's work as a nexus of international models and an instance of how – from Petrarchism to pastoral and to epic – those elements that seem most characteristic of Elizabethan literature are often most indebted to the contemporary vernaculars.

NOTES

1 Variorum, VII, p. 7.
2 Variorum, VIII, pp. 29, 33.
3 The classic studies of Spenser's debts to the vernaculars are W. L. Renwick, *Edmund Spenser: An Essay on Renaissance Poetry* (London: Edward Arnold, 1925); Alfred W. Satterthwaite, *Spenser, Ronsard, and Du Bellay: A Renaissance Comparison* (Princeton: Princeton University Press, 1960); and Anne

Lake Prescott, *French Poets and the English Renaissance* (New Haven: Yale University Press, 1978), esp. pp. 43–52 on Du Bellay. See also Anne Lake Prescott, 'Spenser (Re)Reading Du Bellay: Chronology and Literary Response', in Judith H. Anderson et al., eds., *Spenser's Life and the Subject of Biography* (Amherst: University of Massachusetts Press, 1996), pp. 131–45.

4 Cicero, *Letters to Atticus*, trans. E. O. Winstedt, 3 vols. (London: Heinemann, 1912–18), II, p. 12. On neoteric poetry, see Brooks Otis, *Virgil: A Study in Civilized Poetry* (Oxford: Clarendon Press, 1963), pp. 26–35.

5 Jan van der Noot, *A Theatre for Worldlings*, introduced by Louis S. Friedland (New York: Scholars' Facsimiles and Reprints, 1939).

6 Variorum, VIII, pp. 20–1.

7 John B. Bender, *Spenser and Literary Pictorialism* (Princeton: Princeton University Press, 1972), p. 146.

8 Carol V. Kaske, *Spenser and Biblical Poetics* (Ithaca: Cornell University Press, 1999), esp. pp. 65–97.

9 Roland Greene, 'A Primer of Spenser's Worldmaking: Alterity in the Bower of Bliss', in Patrick Cheney and Lauren Silberman, eds., *Worldmaking Spenser: Explorations in the Early Modern Age* (Lexington: University Press of Kentucky, 1999), pp. 9–31.

10 Ernest B. Gilman, *Iconoclasm and Poetry in the English Reformation: Down Went Dagon* (Chicago: University of Chicago Press, 1986), pp. 63–4.

11 Cf. Prescott, *French Poets*, pp. 43–51.

12 *The Kalender of Sheepehards*, ed. S. K. Heninger, Jr. (Delmar, NY: Scholars' Facsimiles and Reprints, 1979).

13 Leo Spitzer, 'Linguistic Perspectivism in the "Don Quijote"', in *Linguistics and Literary History: Essays in Stylistics* (Princeton: Princeton University Press, 1948), pp. 41–85, repr. in *Representative Essays*, ed. Alban K. Forcione et al. (Stanford: Stanford University Press, 1988), pp. 225–71. I develop a perspectivistic approach to the *Calender* in 'The Shepheardes Calender, Dialogue, and Periphrasis', *Sp. St.* 8 (1987), 1–33.

14 Variorum, VII, pp. 17–18, 64–5, 83, 111.

15 Joachim Du Bellay, *La Deffence et illustration de la langue françoyse* (Versailles: Cerf, 1878); *The Defence and Illustration of the French Language*, trans. Gladys M. Turquet (London: J. M. Dent, 1939).

16 Variorum, VII, pp. 27, 41, 83, 94, 99.

17 Variorum, VII, 7:73.

18 Variorum, VII, p. 104.

19 Clément Marot, *Oeuvres lyriques*, ed. C. A. Mayer (London: Athlone Press, 1964), 325, 326, 327, 330, 331, 334, 335, 337.

20 Variorum, VII, p. 106.

21 Variorum, VII, p. 111.

22 Variorum, VII, p. 104.

23 Variorum, VIII, pp. 417–54.

24 Israel Baroway, 'The Imagery of Spenser and the *Song of Songs*', *JEGP* 33 (1934), 23–45.

25 Variorum, VIII, p. 201.

26 Philippe Desportes, *Les amours de Diane*, ed. Victor E. Graham, 2 vols. (Geneva and Paris: Droz and Minard, 1959), I, p. 73.

27 Variorum, VIII, pp. 424–5.
28 Luís de Camões, *Lírica*, ed. Aires da Mata Machado Filho (São Paulo: Editora Itatiaia, 1982), pp. 153–236.
29 Variorum, VIII, p. 245.
30 On the public dimension of the *Epithalamion*, see Thomas M. Greene, 'Spenser and the Epithalamic Convention', *CL* 9 (1957), 215–28.
31 On these formal aspects, see A. Bartlett Giamatti, *Play of Double Senses: Spenser's* Faerie Queene (Englewood Cliffs, NJ: Prentice-Hall, 1975), p. 33.
32 Variorum, I, p. 167.
33 A. Bartlett Giamatti, *The Earthly Paradise and the Renaissance Epic* (Princeton: Princeton University Press, 1966), pp. 236, 238–39.

FURTHER READING

Anne Lake Prescott, *French Poets and the English Renaissance* (New Haven: Yale University Press, 1978).
'Spenser (Re)Reading Du Bellay: Chronology and Literary Response', in Judith H. Anderson, Donald Cheney and David A. Richardson, eds., *Spenser's Life and the Subject of Biography* (Amherst: University of Massachusetts Press, 1996), pp. 131–45.
W. L. Renwick, *Edmund Spenser; An Essay on Renaissance Poetry* (London: Edward Arnold, 1925).
Alfred W. Satterthwaite, *Spenser, Ronsard, and Du Bellay: A Renaissance Comparison* (Princeton: Princeton University Press, 1960).

13

PAUL ALPERS

Spenser's influence

The title of this chapter presumably does not puzzle its readers, but its complications should be spelled out. In its earliest English uses, 'influence' (from Latin *influere*, to flow in) is an astrological term, referring to the way emanations from heavenly bodies affect human affairs. Human beings can be metaphorically represented as having such powers. As a term of literary study, 'influence' also draws on the image of flowing water, which is central to its Latin meaning. Spenser's best-known references to Chaucer use this image. In *The Faerie Queene* (IV, ii, 32) he calls him 'well [i.e. spring, source] of English vndefyled'; Spenser's pastoral alter ego, Colin Clout, conscious of his distance from his dead predecessor, imagines that he could be eloquent 'if on me some little drops would flowe / Of that the spring was in his learned hedde' (*SC*, 'June', 93–4). Traditional studies of a poet's influence engage both these metaphors. Nineteenth-century philology emphasised 'source study', tracking down to their origins specific details of phrasing, plotting, or representation, as if following a stream to its head. At the same time, major poets could be viewed as having broad, as if more than earthly, powers in relation to their successors. Responding to this double understanding of influence, the articles on later poets in *The Spenser Encyclopedia* record specific imitations, borrowings and allusions, but also seek to identify broad and fundamental ways in which the later poet's work shows that s/he has felt the power of Spenser's.

In the past twenty-five years, views of literary influence have changed markedly, as part of a widespread effort to demystify literary tradition and authority. The most important single work has been Harold Bloom's *The Anxiety of Influence* (1973), which argues against a benign construction of literary indebtedness. In Bloom's view all writers – or at least, in English, all since Milton – are necessarily 'belated', that is, dependent on what powerful predecessors have established as literary or poetic for a given culture. 'Strong' writers resist this dependency. To use the word with which

Spenser's friend Gabriel Harvey described the relation between *The Faerie Queene* and Ariosto's *Orlando Furioso*, they seek to 'overgo' their predecessors; in appropriating their work for their own purposes, they distort and 'misread' them.[1] 'Weak' writers, on the other hand, merely follow or go along with their poetic masters. Bloom construes the relation between poets as oedipal rivalry, and this essay will not adhere to his psychoanalytic model. But his account of poetic influence encourages us to distinguish, in our own terms, between 'strong' and 'weak' responses to Spenser and imitations of his poems.

Spenser burst on the Elizabethan literary scene with considerable éclat, and he was immediately influential. His first poem, *The Shepheardes Calender* (1579), the first book of English eclogues modelled on Virgil's, held out the promise that its author would write an English epic. In the decade before the publication of Books I–III of *The Faerie Queene*, *The Shepheardes Calender* was reprinted twice and was repeatedly commended and imitated. Sidney's *Defence of Poesy* calls it one of the few English works with 'poetical sinews', and another critic hailed it as the equivalent of Theocritus and Virgil.[2] *The Faerie Queene* itself was cited and imitated before 1590 – most famously by Marlowe in *Tamburlaine* (Part II, IV, iii. 119–24) – and its publication prompted a torrent of praise and imitation. Spenser was regularly hailed as the English Homer or Virgil. Throughout the 1590s there are frequent imitations and citations of Spenserian episodes and characters. Passages from *The Faerie Queene* fill the pages of *England's Parnassus* (1600), an anthology of quotations organised under various moral, phenomenological and descriptive headings.

The 'strongest' response to Spenser in the 1590s is Marlowe's *Hero and Leander*. This witty, consciously extravagant poem handles various Spenserian specialities – blazons of god-like beauty, descriptions of artworks and mythological narrations – with so different a pace and tone that one commentator concludes that Marlowe was not influenced by *The Faerie Queene*; rather both poets were working from a stock of common materials.[3] It is true that the elements common to both poems go back to Ovid's *Metamorphoses*, but it was *The Faerie Queene* that brought Ovidian description and eroticism definitively into English poetry. What is distinctive in the description of Busyrane's tapestries (*FQ*, III, xi, 28–46, an imitation of Arachne's tapestries, *Met.*, vi, 103–28) has an essential relation to what is distinctive in *Hero and Leander*. Spenser's rendering of these scenes of the gods in love combines, for the reader, aesthetic bedazzlement and erotic allure, and for the represented lovers the energies, glamour, confusions and humiliations of desire. In giving a cooler, more humorous, consciously naughtier tone to such aesthetic and experiential phenomena,

Marlowe is not simply different from Spenser, but is developing (even when he mocks by exposing) potentialities and implications of the latter's verse.

Were we to judge by citations and imitations, we would say that Spenser's pre-eminence lasted some decades beyond his death. A group of poets who invoked him as their master has traditionally been identified as 'Spenserians', of whom the most accomplished are Michael Drayton, Giles Fletcher, Phineas Fletcher, George Wither and William Browne. Interestingly, none of these writers undertook to complete the epic scheme that Spenser left unfinished. When they emulate the *Faerie Queene*, it is by developing one aspect of it. Giles Fletcher's short biblical epic, *Christ's Victory and Triumph* (1610), adapts the allegorical houses of Books I and II, while his brother Phineas' *The Purple Island* (1633) develops to the point of gigantism the allegory of the body in II, ix. Drayton's *Poly-Olbion* (1613, 1622), a topographical and historical survey of Britain, resembles *The Faerie Queene* in scale, patriotic fervour and antiquarian interest. But as a poem its Spenserian roots are in a single canto, the marriage of the Thames and the Medway (IV, xi), with its procession of English rivers. To look at it from another angle, the Spenser who matters to these followers is as much the pastoral poet as the writer of allegorical epic. Drayton, Browne, Wither and Phineas Fletcher wrote eclogues that emulate *The Shepheardes Calender*, while other poems – most notably Browne's *Britannia's Pastorals* (1613, 1616) – single-mindedly develop the pastoral vein of *The Faerie Queene*, as it is found in various characters, landscapes and erotic situations.

None of these Spenserians is among the poets who make the first half of the seventeenth century memorable in English poetry. In those poets – Donne, for example, or George Herbert or Herrick – we do not find allusions to Spenser or his poems. We can understand this state of affairs by considering Ben Jonson's remark that 'Spenser, in affecting the ancients, writ no language'. Jonson's animus is against Spenser's programmatic use of archaic words. This practice had attracted criticism from the beginning (e.g. in Sidney's *Defence*), and it became something of a critical red herring, in that it distracted attention from other aspects of Spenser's poetry. Jonson puts his critique in a large context, namely the proper nurturing of the young writer:

> As it is fit to read the best authors to youth first, so let them be of the openest and clearest, as Livy before Sallust, Sidney before Donne. And beware of letting them taste Gower or Chaucer at first, lest falling too much in love with antiquity, and not apprehending the weight, they grow rough and barren in language only . . . Spenser, in affecting the ancients, writ no language; yet I would have him read for his matter; but as Virgil read Ennius.[4]

Unlike the Spenserians, Jonson will not take Spenser as a model for contemporary poetry; but at the same time, he clearly regards him as an 'ancient' who is to be honoured. When he invokes Spenser in the masque *The Golden Age Restored* (1615, lines 112–19), he associates him with Chaucer, Gower and Lydgate, England's greatest medieval poets.

The one major poet profoundly influenced by Spenser was Milton, who invoked him as 'our sage and serious poet' in *Areopagitica*. Spenser's impress is to be found throughout Milton's poetry, and a summary account is therefore difficult. The perceived likeness between the two poets prompted twentieth-century critics to oppose the Romantic idea of Spenser as a poetic sensualist, and to emphasise his power as a moral, political and visionary poet. These critics tended to see imaginative continuities between *The Faerie Queene* and *Paradise Lost*, whereas more recent studies have been attentive to the differences between the two poems. Since much of this work makes holistic arguments, it may be useful to observe that Spenser appears in many different ways in Milton's poetry. St Peter's speech in *Lycidas* (lines 113–31) derives its pastoral authority from one of the styles of *The Shepheardes Calender* – the harsh vehemence with which some of the eclogues treat ecclesiastical affairs. *Paradise Lost* is severe about the materials of Spenser's epic (I, 579–81, IX, 28–41), but the poet of *Il Penseroso* is entranced by the powers of Spenserian fictions, 'where more is meant than meets the ear' (line 120). In *Comus*, Spenser is a less important stylistic influence than Shakespeare, but the masque's central situation – the chaste heroine tempted and confined by Circe's enchanting son – draws on more than one Spenserian fiction, both *FQ*, II, xii, the realm of the Circean Acrasia, and III, xi–xii, Busyrane's castle, a prison of chastity. Its resolution too – both the presence of certain pastoral figures and the final glimpse of a heavenly realm modelled on the Gardens of Adonis (III, vi) – is deeply indebted to Spenser, who may be seen as providing a poetic example strong enough to be an alternative to the secular, sensual blandishments of Comus/Shakespeare.[5] By the time he wrote *Paradise Lost*, Milton was a different poet. *The Faerie Queene* remained his vernacular example of a Christian epic. But given the prominence of Homer, Virgil and Italian epic-romance in the way *Paradise Lost* represents heroic poetry and its traditions, we may ask what *The Faerie Queene* specifically contributed. There are surprisingly few Spenserian phrases or other specific citations; but Spenser clearly influenced the representation of both evil and good places in the opening books. From the point at which the fallen angels begin to build Pandemonium, their infernal habitation, 'Spenser's Cave of Mammon is Milton's Hell'.[6] The portrayal of the dragon Error (*FQ*, I, i) informs the representation of Sin (*PL*, II,

650–9), and various details of Satan's physical movements in Books I and II draw on Orgoglio (*FQ*, I, vii–viii) and the dragon, himself a figure of Satan, whom the Red Cross Knight defeats in his final battle (I, xi). Most important of all, the Garden of Eden (*PL*, IV) draws on both the good and evil earthly paradises of *The Faerie Queene* – the Gardens of Adonis (III, vi) and the Bower of Bliss (II, xii) – as well as other numinous *loci amoeni* in Spenser's epic.

There has been considerable discussion of how to assess Spenser's influence on Milton. A traditional account would say that Spenser's earthly paradises were enabling to Milton, in that their rhetoric and modes of representation – and the issues of human nature they encode – were essential to the representation of Eden in human, i.e., fallen, language. A more Bloomian account would emphasise what is implied by Milton's claim that if 'Hesperian fables' are true, they are 'true, here only' (*PL*, IV, 250–1) – i.e., that his Garden of Eden is the original of and 'transumes' his predecessor's ideal landscapes. Without necessarily choosing between these views, let us take, as a representative example, Milton's last significant use of *The Faerie Queene*. In *Paradise Regained*, Satan first comes to Christ in the following guise:

> But now an aged man in rural weeds,
> Following, as seemed, the quest of some stray ewe,
> Or withered sticks to gather; which might serve
> Against a winter's day when winds blow keen,
> To warm him wet returned from field at eve,
> He saw approach. (I, 314–19)

The biblical accounts of Christ's temptation in the wilderness say nothing about the form in which Satan appeared; the sources of Milton's lines, it is generally agreed, are Archimago's appearance to the Red Cross Knight as a hermit, and Giles Fletcher's representation of the biblical scene in *Christ's Victory and Triumph*. Now what is interesting is that Fletcher's description of the disguised Satan is itself based on Spenser's of Archimago. Here is Spenser:

> *At length* they chaunst to meet vpon the way
> *An aged Sire*, in long blacke weedes yclad,
> His feete all bare, his beard *all hoarie gray*,
> And by his belt his booke he hanging had;
> *Sober he seemde*, and very sagely sad,
> . . .
> *And all the way he prayed, as he went*,
> And often knockt his brest, as one that did repent.
> (*FQ*, I, i, 29, emphasis added)

The details I have emphasised are those which we meet again in Fletcher:

> *At length an aged Syre* farre off he sawe
> Come slowly footing . . .
> *And all the way he went, he ever blest*
> With benedicities, and *prayers store*,
> But the bad ground was blessed ne'r the more,
> And all his head with snowe of *Age* was waxen *hore*.
> A good old Hermit he *might seeme to be*,
> That for devotion had the world forsaken,
> And now was travailing some Saint to see,
> Since to his beads he had himselfe betaken.[7]

The beads of Fletcher's hermit and his retreat from the world come from the next stanza in *The Faerie Queene*, and his 'benedicities' were surely suggested by the Ave Maria's strewn by Archimago, now called a hermit (I, i, 34, 35). Fletcher specifies in the margin that this is 'some devout Essene', but the description is, almost laughably, of a Christian hermit, such as could not have existed at the time of the narrated event. Whether or not Fletcher courts this absurdity specifically to make evident his use of Spenser, we can agree that his piggybacking on Spenser's fictional device and his reiteration of Spenserian details is imitation in the weak sense. How, on the other hand, shall we describe the relation of Milton's lines to their Spenserian original? The only common verbal details are 'an aged man' and 'weeds'. We can say too that both descriptions are of a humble, apparently virtuous old man, a guise meant to deceive. But the important connection is a deeper one. Archimago's disguise is the antithesis of the Red Cross Knight's holiness – not simply in its falsity or in its superstitious devotion, but also in its withdrawal from the world of action, the sphere, as Milton put it when he paid tribute to Spenser in *Areopagitica*, of 'the true warfaring Christian'. By the same token, Satan's disguise mimics Christ's holiness, as the metaphorical Good Shepherd and as the actual man who endures the deprivations of the wilderness. Unlike some allusions in *Paradise Lost*, this does not seem to claim to represent the true original of its Spenserian source. But it is certainly a strong appropriation.

Though Milton was the poet to whom Spenser mattered most, I think it can be shown that Spenser's poetry made a difference to poets who did not explicitly cite him. Let us begin with a final Miltonic example, from the description of Eden:

> Another side, umbrageous grots and caves
> Of cool recess, o'er which the mantling vine
> Lays forth her purple grape, and gently creeps
> Luxuriant.   (*PL*, IV, 257–60)

This is never cited as a Spenserian allusion. But the way the enjambment springs upon us the suspect word 'luxuriant' (whose 'fallen' meanings we must undo, as with 'error' and 'wanton' elsewhere in this passage) is a rhetorical trick learned from the Bower of Bliss.[8] Given the way both poets are concerned with the language of paradisal imaginings, I would say that Milton's use of Spenser is quite conscious here. But what of these lines from Andrew Marvell's 'The Garden'?

> What wondrous life in this I lead!
> Ripe apples drop about my head;
> The luscious clusters of the vine
> Upon my mouth do crush their wine.   (33–6)

Whether or not this is a Spenserian allusion,[9] it exploits a trait of style that in Spenser's hands acquired unusual vividness and complexity – descriptive language that both conveys sensory experience and opens up its moral or spiritual implications. In Marvell's lines, 'crush' picks up the sounds of 'luscious clusters', so that mouthing the line brings us close to the represented experience; but the lines also foreground the artfulness of this effect, and thus enter into the poem's witty exploration of the way desire and passivity, body and spirit, may be conceived as compatible with each other. Language that is similarly rich in effect and complex in implication appears in a very different situation, the literary renunciation of Herbert's 'The Forerunners':

> Lovely enchanting language, sugar-cane,
> Honey of roses, whither wilt thou fly?
> Hath some fond lover ticed thee to thy bane?[10]

No poem could be more different from this than Herrick's 'The Lily in a Chrystal', which plays out the erotics of transparent veils, but it too could not have been written without Spenser's example (cf. especially *FQ*, II, xii, 64–7). The 'line of wit', as F. R. Leavis called it, pays its full tribute to Spenserian eroticism in Thomas Carew's 'A Rapture', which invokes the Bower of Bliss on the way to its goal. These seventeenth-century lyrics may ironise the endeavour of *The Faerie Queene*, but they were informed and enabled by resources Spenser brought to English poetry.

Milton's poetry brings to an end the first chapter in the story of Spenser's influence. After the Restoration, Spenser and his contemporaries appeared to belong to an earlier age, discontinuous with the cultural present. Thus Dryden begins a tribute to the young Congreve:

> Well then, the promised hour is come at last;
> The present age of wit obscures the past:

> Strong were our sires; and as they fought they writ,
> Conqu'ring with force of arms, and dint of Wit;
> Theirs was the giant race, before the Flood.[11]

In the same year as Dryden's poem (1694), Joseph Addison published an 'Account of the Greatest English Poets':

> Old Spenser next, warmed with poetic rage,
> In ancient tales amused a barb'rous age . . .
> But now the mystic tale, that pleased of yore,
> Can charm an understanding age no more.   (17–18, 23–4)

The idea that *The Faerie Queene* belongs to a remote past explains why the eighteenth century was an age of notable editions and commentaries. John Hughes' edition of Spenser's *Works* (1715) was prefaced by a long essay on allegory that identifies a major question about *The Faerie Queene*: in the face of its swarming multiplicity, how can one grasp it as a single poem? This was perhaps the central question about the poem for Augustan poetics, and Hughes addresses it with the clarity and recognition of issues that are always attractive in eighteenth-century criticism. These qualities are especially evident in two later commentaries – John Upton's, in his edition of *The Faerie Queene* (1758), and Thomas Warton's *Observations on the Faerie Queene* (1754; 2nd edn, 1762). Upton's notes, with their precise interpretive questions and their resourceful answers remain valuable to this day.[12]

There are several reasons for this activity around Spenser's poetry, beyond its perceived remoteness and obscurity. For one thing, *The Faerie Queene* still stood, with *Paradise Lost*, as the greatest English epic, the form of poetry that was the benchmark for all other kinds. In addition, it seemed evident that Spenser was a formidable poet, and not only in *The Faerie Queene*. Different aspects of *The Shepheardes Calender* influenced two very different sets of pastorals – Pope's art pastorals on the seasons (1704), a scheme adapted from Spenser's calendar device, and John Gay's *The Shepherd's Week* (1714), an exercise in comic rusticity. More broadly, critical commentary on Spenser has a part in two major endeavours of literary culture in the eighteenth century. The general satisfaction with what made this culture different from that of preceding ages – rationality, refinement, aesthetic correctness – was counteracted by an anxiety that 'the giant race before the Flood' was more in touch with essential springs of poetic power. Spenser stood to benefit from this attitude, as he did also from the institutionalisation of English literature and its canon that occurred in the course of the century.[13] But his eminence was interestingly compromised. Though certainly considered one of the three greatest English poets, he was not perceived to be the equal of Shakespeare and Milton. Spenser's situation as the 'third wheel' on the chariot of Apollo is made clear in William Collins' 'Ode on the Poetical Character' (1746). This poem begins by recalling Florimell's cestus (*FQ*, IV, v, 2–6), a girdle which can only be worn by a chaste woman; Collins updates this as an allegory of poetry, the 'cest of amplest power' with which few can 'gird their blest prophetic loins'. Spenser the allegorist would seem to give the poem's youthful speaker access to this power; but at the end of the poem it is Milton alone whose intimidating presence is invoked. Similarly, though Collins' editor calls the diction of 'Ode to Fear' 'consciously Spenserian', this lyric attempt to regain the central power of ancient tragedy invokes only Shakespeare as its modern inspiration.[14]

Everywhere one turns in eighteenth-century verse, one encounters the fictions and rhetoric of Milton's poems. Spenser's influence is more limited and specialised. One of its first manifestations is Pope's 'The Alley', a coarse representation of an urban scene (like Hogarth's 'Gin Lane'), in six Spenserian stanzas. This poem certainly contains some adolescent mischief, but it is also a skilful performance in a common Augustan mode – the urban mock-heroic (as in Dryden's 'MacFlecknoe') and mock-idyllic, as in countless self-styled 'town eclogues'. *The Faerie Queene* is eligible for such use, because it is full of epic scenes and personifications. But what seems especially to have engaged Pope was the idea of inverting the music of Spenser's verse. The scenes of 'The Alley' are full of harsh sounds and abusive language (the mock personifications are of Obloquy, Slander, etc.), and the central stanza wittily inverts Spenserian harmonies of winds, voices, and waters (*FQ*, II, xii, 33, 71) in a chorus of dogs, hogs, children and whores. This is mockery, of course, but it may also have been a way of turning to account the harshness, as it must have seemed to Pope, of Spenserian diction. One of the most famous Spenserian imitations of the eighteenth century, William Shenstone's 'The Schoolmistress', began in a similar vein. Its first version (1737) includes a mock-allegorical scene of a schoolboy being birched and a good deal of archaism and coarse diction – including a stanza in which the boys go outside to 'p-ss' and 'cack' (a word taken from Pope's opening stanza, for it is not in Spenser).[15] When Shenstone decided to publish the poem separately, he doubled (1742), then tripled its length (1748), and he cleaned up its act. The portrait of the schoolmistress is expanded, both by further comedy and mock-heroics and by a quite different touch of Spenser, praise of her staunch Protestantism. The new poem's emphasis on the potentialities of young spirits and the pathos of childhood responds to what Shenstone's headnote calls 'a peculiar tenderness of sentiment remarkable throughout [Spenser's] works'.

'The Schoolmistress' is part of a surge of Spenserian activity in the mid-eighteenth century. To these decades belong an edition of *The Faerie Queene* by Thomas Birch (1751) and the first annotated editions of the poem, by Upton and Ralph Church (1758–9); Warton's *Observations* and Richard Hurd's *Letters on Chivalry and Romance* (1762), which developed the idea, already advanced by Hughes, that *The Faerie Queene* 'is to be read and criticized' as 'a Gothic, not a classical poem';[16] and the poems of Collins and Thomas Gray, which responded with particular sensitivity to Spenser's fictions and rhetoric and expressed a new sense of belatedness in the face of his imaginative power. There were also a very large number of imitations of Spenser, of which the most interesting is James Thomson's *The Castle of Indolence* (1748).[17]

Where most eighteenth-century writers identify allegory with personified abstractions, Thomson understands the centrality of Spenser's allegorical locales and turns them to significant contemporary uses. His castle is modelled on the Bower of Bliss (with elements, inter alia, of the House of Pride and Busyrane's castle), but it engages quite different issues. Spenser's false paradise is a threat to human (figured as masculine) integrity. Its mistress Acrasia personifies intemperance; the episode contrasts Sir Guyon, controlling his impulses with the help of the Palmer as superego, and the young knight Verdant, who is 'molten into lust and pleasure lewd' (*FQ*, II, xii, 73). There is none of this interest in Thomson and therefore none of the disturbing eroticism, directly represented or pervading the landscape, that is the hallmark of Spenser's Bower. What engages Thomson is the attraction of a life free from toil and from the false values and pursuits of the city. Hence the 'tempting verses' of the wizard Indolence, even though they are called a 'syren melody' (I, 8), are not an Acrasian seduction, but lead to stanzas praising the retired life. The castle is a realm of the aesthetic, where 'amid the groves you may indulge the muse' (I, 18) and where, it turns out, the narrator of the poem is himself a denizen. So too, we learn, are a number of his friends, and we may ask what is wrong with the place. Officially it is said to be decadent, a realm of luxury; its inhabitants are therefore in need of rescue by the Knight of Arts and Industry, whose story is told in the second canto. But where it can plausibly be argued of the Bower of Bliss that something is 'subtly wrong throughout',[18] that is not the case with Thomson's realm of indolence. Its unambiguous attractiveness is the sign of a cultural dilemma which has been acutely analysed by John Barrell.[19] On the one hand, Thomson admires the retired life of the country gentleman, contemplating nature and conceiving the world as orderly; on the other hand, he espouses values which show the world to be corrupt, in need of the aristocrat's moral intervention. Hence when he turns to the career of the Knight of Industry, he first shows him endowing primitive Britain with the arts of government and culture, making it an ideal society. But when the knight has fulfilled this mission and withdrawn to the countryside – the Spenserian quest-epic becoming an eighteenth-century retirement poem – he realises that Britain, now represented by the Castle of Indolence, must be released from spiritual decay. This seems to be the work of the poet, since the knight's mission is accomplished with the help of a druid bard; at the same time, the poem's narrator is one of those in need of rescue. In thus exposing its dilemmas, the poem suggests both its own interest and its understanding of *The Faerie Queene*. Beyond his debt to Spenser's rhetoric of alluring ease and to his moral and patriotic fictions, Thomson recognised the potential openness of Spenserian allegory in presenting the phenomena of cultural life and their relation to human desires and values.

The formal means of Thomson's achievement is the Spenserian stanza, which he understands better than any of his contemporaries. He is not subject to Samuel Johnson's dismissive remark that 'the imitators of Spenser . . . seem to conclude, that when they have disfigured their lines with a few obsolete syllables, they have accomplished their design'.[20] *The Castle of Indolence* exploits the fact that the length of the stanza and its line-by-line progression permit representational fullness, while at the same time each stanza is sealed off and made a separate unit by the concluding Alexandrine. Hence each stanza can be a set piece in itself (eighteenth-century poets often imitate Spenser's heroic similes) or can be a building block in a larger set piece. Alternatively, any stanza can be a fresh start in a new direction. Combining fullness and segmentation, the Spenserian stanza allows Thomson to lay out various cultural myths and claims. If we feel that the price is fragmentation, this makes all the more impressive the continuities achieved in the episodes and cantos of *The Faerie Queene* itself.

The formal capacity of the Spenserian stanza proved to be more important than the patina of archaisms, about which many eighteenth-century poets felt ambivalent. 'Antique expressions' are explicitly disavowed in James Beattie's *The Minstrel* (1771), the most important Spenserian imitation between Thomson and the Romantics. This poem narrates the hero's 'progress of genius' from primitive beginnings – a childhood in rural Scotland, amid powerful scenes of nature – to full, cultured maturity. The minstrel's life history recalls that of Thomson's Knight of Arts and Industry, who is born in the woods to Poverty (an adaptation, in a typically transparent neoclassical allegory, of the story of Satyrane, *FQ*, I, vi) and is then educated by Minerva so that he can 'civilize' the 'barbarous world' (II, 14). Spenser, epic poet and accomplished rhetorician, whose work is nevertheless rooted in the extravagant mores and imaginings of an earlier time, must have seemed to Thomson and Beattie a model for accommodating the powerful 'false themes' of earlier poetry to the 'gentle minds' of the Enlightenment.[21] Beattie's failure in this project is less interesting than Thomson's: when the minstrel, in canto ii, is freed from superstition and fancy by a relentlessly didactic sage, the poem loses its poetry. But the first canto has much that would have been compelling for the young Wordsworth, who always admired it, and it is the Spenserian stanza that enables its poetic force. In his preface, Beattie speaks of the stanza's flexibility, the way it permits 'the sententiousness of the couplet, as well as the more complex modulations of blank verse'. This stylistic openness and the stanza's inherent segmentation allow Beattie to include everything in this myth and manifesto of poetic genius – sublime mountain scenery, the minstrel's mooning about the graveyard, his dream vision of chivalric spirits, a catalogue of rural sounds, lofty invectives against the world. No poem better shows what Shelley meant in the introduction to *The Revolt of Islam*: 'I have adopted the stanza of Spenser . . . not because I consider it a finer model of poetical harmony than the blank verse of Shakespeare and Milton, but because in the latter there is no shelter for mediocrity; you must either succeed or fail'.

Except for Milton, no English poets felt Spenser's influence more deeply or pervasively than the Romantics. But it is not easy to speak in general terms of that influence. In the eighteenth century, a common idea of Spenser is shared by most poets and critics (even his champions frequently criticise him for failing to satisfy neoclassical criteria). In each of the great Romantic poets, on the other hand, we find a distinct and individual idea of him and his works. Blake, surprisingly, scarcely mentions him; his main Spenserian work is a painting that represents the characters of *The Faerie Queene*.[22] In the absence of explicit commentary, we must leave as an open question whether or not there is a fundamental sympathy – as Northrop Frye, a profound critic of both poets, thought – between *The Faerie Queene* and Blake's prophetic writings.

In Wordsworth, on the other hand, Spenser is a continual point of reference. His fullest imitations are the various 'Salisbury Plain' poems. The first, *Salisbury Plain* (1793), tells of an anonymous traveller, struggling in a fearsome night across the desolate waste of the plain, and of a wretched woman whom he encounters in a ruined shelter; her story of her loss of father, husband and children, to both economic hardship and wars overseas, leads to a vehement attack on the way ordinary people are victimised by governmental policies and actions. Wordsworth kept working at the poem, but did not succeed in publishing its next version, *Adventures on Salisbury Plain* (1795); only the woman's narration of her story appeared, as 'The

Female Vagrant', in *Lyrical Ballads* (1798).[23] These poems have received a good deal of attention, because they are important expressions of Words-worth's early political radicalism. But why did he cast them as Spenserian poems? Many elements are suggested by his eighteenth-century models – the idea of Spenser as an English patriot (therefore providing a voice in which to attack the betrayal of national ideals), landscapes which reflect spiritual states (not only the traveller's and woman's suffering, but also the pastoral scenes which relieve them at the end), and the primitive past from which the present emerges (the ruins of Stonehenge and the druid rites thought to occur there). In its diction and its use of the Spenserian stanza, indeed, the poem seems more like *The Castle of Indolence* and *The Minstrel* than like *The Faerie Queene* itself.

But there are important innovations in *Salisbury Plain*. Wordsworth reconceives the figure of the narrator-poet, as he appears in Thomson and Beattie, to make him a fellow of the victimised woman. Without indulging in any pseudo-Spenserian fictions, like Thomson's Knight of Arts and Industry, he gives a current form to the knight-errant – the ordinary human being wandering through the wilderness of the world. There is thus a sense that the woman and her story are genuinely discovered and encountered, in the manner of various episodes in *The Faerie Queene*. At the same time, there is a greater sense of the historical remoteness of Stonehenge and the druids, and hence a greater tension in their relation to the present. For all their traces of eighteenth-century Spenserianism, the 'Salisbury Plain' poems are 'strong' revisions – not only of Thomson and Beattie, but also of Spenser. Hence there is a limit to what we can explain in them by reference to *The Faerie Queene*. The conception of the narrator as a fellow of the victimised woman is further developed in *Adventures on Salisbury Plain*, in which the vaguely fictionalised traveller becomes a discharged sailor who is guilty of murder. With this change, the 'questing' figure is taken over by Wordsworthian conceptions and interests. Similarly, the discovery of the suffering woman and her narration of her story is a Spenserian plot, like Arthur's meeting with Una (*FQ*, I, viii), Guyon's coming upon the dying Amavia (II, i, 35–55), or (with genders reversed) Britomart's discovery of the wretched Scudamour (III, xi). But the woman and her story are fully Wordsworthian: female vagrants had already appeared in his earlier long poems, *An Evening Walk* and *Descriptive Sketches*, and the story in *Salis-bury Plain* foreshadows that of Margaret in *The Ruined Cottage*.

Wordsworth soon distanced himself from political radicalism, and his Spenserianism takes different forms after 1800. In the 1815 preface to *Lyrical Ballads*, he says that Spenser's genius was 'to give the universality and permanence of abstractions to his human beings, by means of attributes and emblems that belong to the highest moral truths and the purest sensations, – of which his character of Una is a glorious example'. Una so conceived is the model, as the prefatory verses make explicit, for the heroine of *The White Doe of Rylstone* (1815). We might use the suffering females in Wordsworth's two most Spenserian narratives to allegorise the change in his politics – 'heavenly Una with her milk-white Lamb', as she is called in another poem ('Personal Talk'), replacing the more painfully actual female vagrant. But this would give too neat an account of Wordsworth's response to Spenser. The Spenserianism of his poetry is impressively various – from the pastoralism of 'A Farewell' to 'Artegal and Elidure', a retelling of a tale from Milton's *History of Britain*. The 1805 *Prelude* contains both a famous tribute to Spenser (III, 279–83) and a recollection of 'May' in *The Shepheardes Calender* (VIII, 191–203), in a context which shows how well Wordsworth understood the debate in that eclogue between 'soft' and 'hard' versions of pastoral. The glance at Spenser in the opening account of the young poet's search for a theme (I, 181–4) is expanded, in the 1850 *Prelude*, in lines that wonderfully express the energies of allegorical epic – 'Where spear encountered spear, and sword with sword / Fought, as if conscious of the blazonry / That the shield bore' (I, 177–9).

The most remarkable instance of Spenser's influence on Wordsworth is in 'Resolution and Independence'. The freshness and vernal beauty of the initial landscape – amid which the speaker is overcome by thoughts of the troubled fate of 'poets in our youth' – owes much to *Prothalamion*, which William and Dorothy had been reading at the time he composed the poem.[24] In one of its aspects, then, 'Resolution and Independence' traces the same change in English poetics as *The Prelude* when it invokes the 'May' eclogue – from a pastoral of innocence to a sterner representation of humans in the natural world. Though the old leech-gatherer may seem purely Wordsworthian, the poem's action distils that of *Salisbury Plain*: it tells how the speaker, who 'was a Traveller then upon the moor', comes upon a disturbing, emblematic figure. Finally, the poem uses a condensed Spenserian stanza, to such powerful effect that one critic explains the leech-gatherer's imaginative presence by the stanzas' autonomy and their 'halting but inexorable' pace.[25] Nor is this all. While working on 'Resolution and Independence', Wordsworth composed 'Stanzas Written in my Pocket-Copy of Thomson's "Castle of Indolence"', in which he takes on the manner of Thomson's narrator to represent himself and Coleridge as different inhabitants of the same locale of the imagination. In these few weeks of 1802, when Wordsworth reconceived Spenser to write one of his most enduring poems, he also paid tribute to eighteenth-century Spenserianism with a milder imitation.

In its range and intimacy, Wordsworth's use of Spenser bears witness to a fresh and productive understanding that is equally evident when we turn to Byron, Keats and Shelley, each of whom wrote notable Spenserian poems. *Childe Harold's Pilgrimage*, 'The Eve of St. Agnes' and 'Adonais' are utterly distinctive, but they share (apart from the Spenserian stanza itself) a revisionist attitude towards the older poet. Like Blake, they reject his moralism, theology and politics – both Keats and Shelley made a point of siding with the egalitarian Giant of *FQ*, v, ii[26] – and instead looked, as they would have put it, to what makes him truly a poet. 'Imitation' does not capture the relation of these poems to Spenser's, for their revisionism is too strong; at the same time, it is more conscious and less conflicted than Bloom's model suggests. It seems right to argue, as Greg Kucich does, that 'gentle' Spenser, as he was constantly called (e.g. 1805 *Prelude*, iii, 279), was an importantly benign predecessor, whose works, because of their character and imperfections, made him a more possible companion in the poetic enterprise than Shakespeare and Milton, the most daunting of England's literary giants.

Within the confines of this essay, it is impossible to treat each of these poets, much less the flood of quasi-Spenserian work by their contemporaries.[27] For one thing, Byron, Keats and Shelley each have a different idea of what makes Spenser 'truly a poet'. I will concentrate on Keats, because it is his idea of Spenser and his poetry that most decisively influenced later poetry and criticism. Reading *The Faerie Queene* made Keats decide to be a poet; his first poem, accordingly, was an 'Imitation of Spenser', and Spenserian figures and fictions pervade his early poetry; the title page of his first volume of poems bore a quotation from 'Muiopotmos'. The idea of Spenser found in this early work is largely attributable to Leigh Hunt, who was important to Keats when he was finding himself as a writer. Its most memorable contemporary expression is in William Hazlitt's *Lectures on the English Poets* (1818):

> [Spenser's poetry] is inspired by the love of ease, and relaxation from all the cares and business of life. Of all the poets, he is the most poetical . . . Spenser's poetry is all fairy-land . . . We wander in another world, among ideal beings. The poet takes and lays us in the lap of a lovelier nature, by the sound of softer streams, among greener hills and fairer valleys. He paints nature, not as we find it, but as we expected to find it . . . He waves his wand of enchantment – and at once embodies airy beings, and throws a delicious veil over all actual objects.

This Spenser, the dreamer and escapist, was a powerful cultural idea which inspired the greatest post-Romantic imitation of his poetry, Tennyson's 'The Lotus-Eaters', and prompted Yeats, the last major poet to be influenced by him, to say: 'he is a poet of the delighted senses, and his song becomes most beautiful when he writes of those islands of Phaedria and Acrasia, which . . . gave to Keats his *Belle Dame sans merci* and his "perilous seas in faery lands forlorn".'[28] It is this Spenser against whom academic critics of our time reacted, insisting that the poet's theology, morality and monarchism were not alien impositions on his imagination, as Yeats said, but were at the heart of his poetic powers. The key text is the Bower of Bliss (*FQ*, II, xii). The nineteenth-century tradition regarded the alluring visions and music of this canto as at odds with the moral judgement represented by Guyon's destruction of the Bower. In an essay that inaugurated modern attention to Spenser, C. S. Lewis argued that the moral awareness is of the essence of the Bower's poetry: it is a place of debased sexuality, a fantasy of displaced and unfulfillable desire.

There is no doubt that this modern correction of the nineteenth-century tradition was called for (and no doubt, either, that it in turn called for the counter-correction, more recently, of new historicist and feminist critics, who are attentive to the impasses and contradictions of Spenser's most powerful imaginings). It is also clear that there was plenty of evidence for the Romantic view that twentieth-century Spenserians attacked: it was a whipping boy, but not a straw man. The question to ask here, however, is whether this view adequately represents what Romantic poets and critics wrote and thought. Despite Hazlitt's calling him quintessentially 'poetical', he had a strong sense of the moral dimensions of Spenser's representations. In a searching comparison, he says: 'Milton's voluptuousness is not lascivious or sensual. He describes beautiful objects for their own sakes. Spenser has an eye to the consequences, and steeps everything in pleasure, often not of the purest kind.'[29] By the same token, his list of 'the finest things in Spenser' includes the House of Pride (I, iv–v), Mammon's abode (II, vii) and the Cave of Despair (I, ix), and he singles out 'the truth of passion' in Malbecco's transformation into Jealousy (III, x). Though he shares his contemporaries' resistance to what they considered outmoded in *The Faerie Queene*, his idea of the poem includes the moral psychology that informs its central episodes. The Romantic Spenser is thus far more than an aesthetic voluptuary. Coleridge encourages us to 'take especial note of the marvellous independence and true imaginative absence of all particular space or time in *The Faerie Queene* . . . It is truly in land of Fairy, that is, of mental space.' Similarly, Charles Lamb, objecting to the notion that the poet is a dreamer, cites the Cave of Mammon episode as the clinching example in his essay, 'The Sanity of True Genius': 'The things and persons of *The Faerie Queene* prate not of their "whereabout". But in their inner nature, and the law of their speech and actions, we are at home and upon acquainted ground.'

Spenser the elfin voluptuary, the poet of bowers and idyllic landscapes, aroused the imagination of the young Keats, but was a figure to overcome when he turned to 'the poetry of earth' and the realities of the human heart. Spenser himself, understood more adequately, was an ally in this endeavour. In what seems a scenario scripted by Bloom, Keats turned from the ardours of blank verse in *Hyperion*, his first, uncompleted attempt at a Miltonic epic, to write 'The Eve of St. Agnes', perhaps the finest Spenserian poem in English. Like Guyon's voyage to the Bower of Bliss and Britomart's penetration of Busyrane's castle, the poem narrates a hero's entering a richly symbolic inner sanctum and achieves, with unique success, the kind of continuity found in Spenser's great narrations. But the poem is not an imitation like *The Castle of Indolence*. In reading Thomson's poem one is aware of the various Spenserian models for his settings and episodes and of his deploying the rhetoric of Spenser's stanza. From the intimate sense perceptions of its beginning to its ambiguous end, everything in 'The Eve of St. Agnes' is Keatsian, even elements that clearly derive from *The Faerie Queene* – eroticised descriptions, the ambiguous world of dreams, and the sensory contrasts that adapt Spenserian dichotomies to a less clearly moralised world. Kucich calls the poem 'both quintessentially Spenserian and utterly modern'.[30] The same praise can be given to 'The Lotus-Eaters'. In turning an episode in the *Odyssey* into a narrativised lyric, Tennyson makes double use of Spenser. The entrancing landscape with which the poem begins has the steadiness and fullness of detail that Spenserian stanzas invite; the danger, however, is not the moral dissipation of Acrasia's victims, but the Victorian anxiety about surrendering purposive action to the lure of the aesthetic. Hence the descriptions do not appeal, as Hazlitt put it, to impure pleasures, suggestive of troubling consequences, but are laden with Tennysonian mixtures of the vivid and the evanescent. The mariners' 'Choric Song' brilliantly puts Spenserian expressions of desire for *luxe, calme, et volupté* – which in *The Faerie Queene* are explicitly temptations (by Despair, Phaedria, the mermaids of II, xii, 30–3, and Acrasia's rose song) – into the mouths of the mariners, far from home and eager to have their toil and their memories cease.

The generation of Keats, Byron and Shelley was the last in which Spenser was a presence for contemporary poets. Tennyson's Spenser is so mediated by the Romantics, especially Keats, that he eludes one's grasp even in poems where one expects to find him, such as 'The Lady of Shallot', 'The Palace of Art', and 'Tithonus'. For English and American modernism, Spenser was neither a challenging master, like Shakespeare, nor a significant roadblock, like Milton. In the twentieth century, his poems have been kept current in the curricula of schools and universities. But if we do not today read

Spenser 'as we read the living' (Leavis' tribute to Donne), our awareness of those who did in the past may have a salutary influence on the way we teach and discuss him.

NOTES

1 Letter of Harvey to Spenser, in *Three Proper and Witty Familiar Letters* (1580); *Poetical Works*, p. 628. This and unless otherwise stated, all of the other allusions to Spenser and his works quoted in this chapter can be found in one of the following: Paul Alpers, ed., *Edmund Spenser: A Critical Anthology* (Harmondsworth: Penguin, 1969); R. M. Cummings, ed., *Spenser: The Critical Heritage* (London: Routledge, 1971); William Wells, 'Spenser Allusions in the Sixteenth and Seventeenth Centuries', *SP* 68 (1971), part 5, and 69 (1972), part 5.

2 *Sir Philip Sidney*, ed. Katherine Duncan-Jones (Oxford: Oxford University Press, 1989), pp. 242–3; William Webbe, *A Discourse of English Poetrie* (1586). SC was also praised by George Puttenham, *The Arte of English Poesie* (1589), ch. 131.

3 Roma Gill, 'Marlowe, Christopher', *Spenser Encyclopaedia*, pp. 453–4.

4 'Timber, or Discoveries' in *Ben Jonson*, ed. Ian Donaldson (Oxford: Oxford University Press, 1985), pp. 568–9.

5 See John Guillory, *Poetic Authority: Spenser, Milton and Literary History* (New York: Columbia University Press, 1983), ch. 4 and Guillory's excellent, rather Bloomian article, 'Milton, John', in *Spenser Encyclopaedia*, pp. 473–5. See also Maureen Quilligan, *Milton's Spenser* (Ithaca: Cornell University Press, 1983).

6 Harold Bloom, *A Map of Misreading* (Oxford: Oxford University Press, 1975), p. 128. The whole chapter, on 'Milton and His Precursors', is full of interest.

7 *Christ's Victory*, II, 15–16, in William B. Hunter, Jr., *The English Spenserians: The Poetry of Giles Fletcher, George Wither, Michael Drayton, Phineas Fletcher, and Henry More* (Salt Lake City: University of Utah Press, 1977), emphasis added.

8 Cf. especially II, xii, 61, the description of the fountain with its trompe-l'oeil ivy. After we are told that 'wight, who did not well auis'd it vew, / Would surely deeme it to be yvie trew', the stanza structure – a resource as central to Spenser's verse as enjambment to Milton's – springs the trap: 'Low his lasciuious armes adown did creepe'. 'Creep' is common to both passages, but note especially, as Milton must have, the way the length of 'lascivious' suggests a physical spreading that sustains its troubling moral sense.

9 As suggested by Donald M. Friedman, 'Marvell, Andrew', in *Spenser Encyclopedia*, pp. 455–7.

10 Lines 19–21. Cf. *FQ*, II, v, 33 – surely not a source of Herbert's lines, but an example of the way Spenser realised for English poetry language that is sensual and morally evocative.

11 'To my Dear Friend Mr. Congreve, on his Comedy called The Double-Dealer', lines 1–5.

12 For a discriminating appreciation of Upton, see Herbert F. Tucker, Jr., 'Spenser's Eighteenth-Century Readers and the Question of Unity in *The Faerie Queene*', *UTQ* 46 (1977), 322–41.

13 See John Guillory, *Cultural Capital* (Chicago: University of Chicago Press, 1993), ch. 2: 'Mute Inglorious Miltons: Gray, Wordsworth, and the Vernacular Canon'.

14 Roger Lonsdale, ed., *The Poems of Thomas Gray, William Collins, Oliver Goldsmith* (London: Longman, 1969), p. 418.

15 This first version of 'The Schoolmistress' can be found in Roger Lonsdale, ed., *The New Oxford Book of Eighteenth Century Verse* (Oxford: Oxford University Press, 1984). On the three versions of the poem, see Virginia F. Prettyman, 'Shenstone's Reading of Spenser', in Frederick W. Hilles, ed., *The Age of Johnson: Essays Presented to Chauncy Brewster Tinker* (New Haven: Yale University Press, 1949), pp. 227–37.

16 Richard Hurd, *Letters on Chivalry and Romance*, ed. Edith J. Morley (London: Henry Frowde, 1911), p. 115 (Letter 7; see also Letter 8).

17 See Richard Frushell's article, 'Imitations and adaptations, 1660–1800', in *Spenser Encyclopedia*, pp. 396–403, and his even more exhaustive book, *Edmund Spenser in the Early Eighteenth Century* (Pittsburgh: Duquesne University Press, 1999). Greg Kucich, *Keats, Shelley, and Romantic Spenserianism* (University Park, PA: Pennsylvania State University Press, 1991) gives an informative and interesting account of eighteenth-century Spenserianism.

18 C. S. Lewis, *The Allegory of Love* (Oxford: Oxford University Press, 1936), p. 333.

19 *English Literature in History, 1730–80: An Equal, Wide Survey* (London: Hutchinson, 1983), pp. 79–90.

20 Samuel Johnson, *The Rambler* 121 (14 May 1751), in *The Yale Edition of the Works of Samuel Johnson*, ed. Walter Jackson Bate and Albrecht B. Strauss (New Haven: Yale University Press, 1969), pp. 285–6.

21 See Geoffrey Hartman, *Beyond Formalism* (New Haven: Yale University Press, 1970), pp. 283–97.

22 According to its most authoritative analyst, this painting is 'a searing criticism of Spenser as well as an heroic attempt to redeem the "true" imaginative Spenser from his "spectrous" self labouring benightedly under the burden' of conventional moral and religious ideas. Robert F. Gleckner, 'Blake, William', in *Spenser Encyclopedia*, pp. 94–6; see also Gleckner's *Blake and Spenser* (Baltimore: Johns Hopkins University Press, 1985).

23 He finally published a late revision under the title *Guilt and Sorrow* (1742); almost all the changes are for the worse. This poem absorbed 'The Female Vagrant', which therefore disappeared from Wordsworth's collected poems; readers can find it in separate editions of *Lyrical Ballads*. *Salisbury Plain* is reprinted in Stephen Gill, ed., *William Wordsworth* (Oxford: Oxford University Press, 1984). All three versions of the poem are in Stephen Gill, ed., *The Salisbury Plain Poems of William Wordsworth* (Ithaca: Cornell University Press, 1975).

24 Entry for April 25, 1802, *The Journals of Dorothy Wordsworth*, ed. E. de Selincourt, 2 vols. (London: Macmillan, 1941), I, p. 138.

25 Steven Knapp, *Personification and the Sublime* (Cambridge, MA: Harvard University Press, 1985), p. 119.

26 Shelley told Thomas Love Peacock, 'I am of the Giant's faction' (Stuart Curran, 'Shelley, Percy Bysshe', in *Spenser Encyclopedia*, pp. 644–5). Keats wrote (in

what are probably his last verses) a Spenserian stanza narrating the Giant's resuscitation by the sage Typographus and his vengeance on Artegall and Talus.

27 See Kucich, *Keats, Shelley, and Romantic Spenserianism*.
28 *Essays and Introductions* (London: Macmillan, 1961), p. 370.
29 'On the Character of Milton's Eve', in Alpers, ed., *Edmund Spenser*, pp. 126–7.
30 Kucich, *Keats, Shelley and Romantic Spenserianism*, p. 209.

FURTHER READING

Paul Alpers, ed., *Edmund Spenser: A Critical Anthology* (Harmondsworth: Penguin, 1969).

R. M. Cummings, ed., *Spenser: The Critical Heritage* (London: Routledge, 1971).

Richard C. Frushell, *Edmund Spenser in the Early Eighteenth Century* (Pittsburgh: Duquesne University Press, 1999).

John Guillory, *Poetic Authority; Spenser, Milton, and Literary History* (New York: Columbia University Press, 1983).

William B. Hunter, Jr. ed., *The English Spenserians: The Poetry of Giles Fletcher, George Wither, Michael Drayton, Phineas Fletcher, and Henry More* (Salt Lake City: University of Utah Press, 1977).

Greg Kucich, *Keats, Shelley, and Romantic Spenserianism* (University Park, PA: Pennsylvania State University Press, 1991).

Maureen Quilligan, *Milton's Spenser* (Ithaca: Cornell University Press, 1983).

William Wells, 'Spenser Allusions in the Sixteenth and Seventeenth Centuries', *SP* 68 (1971), part 5, and 69 (1972), part 5.

INDEX

Index